Second Edition

The Messerschmitt
Bf 109

Early Series (V1 to E-9 including the T-Series)

A Complete Guide To The Luftwaffe's Famous Fighter

by Richard A. Franks

Airframe & Miniature No.5 Second Edition
The Messerschmitt Bf 109 Early Series (V1 to E-9 including the T-series)
A Complete Guide to the Luftwaffe's Famous Fighter
by Richard A. Franks

First published 2013 & 2022 by Valiant Wings Publishing Ltd
Unit 3 Glenmore Business Park, Stanley Road,
Bedford, MK42 0XY, UK
+44 (0)1234 413843
enquiries.vwp@gmail.com
www.valiant-wings.co.uk

ISBN 978-1-912932-25-2

Acknowledgments

The author would like to give a special word of thanks to Josef
Andal, Jim Grant, George Papadimitriou, Michael Payne &
Przemyslaw Skulski for their invaluable help with photographs.
Special thanks must go to Steve A. Evans and Libor Jekl for
their excellent model builds and Jerry Boucher, Richard J,
Caruana, Jacek Jackiewicz and and Juraj Jankovic for their
superb artwork.

We would also like to thank the following companies for their
support of this title.

• Airfix, Hornby Hobbies Ltd, Westwood Industrial Estate,
Margate, Kent, CT9 4JX
Tel: +44 (0)1843 233500 Fax: +44 (0)1843 233513
www.airfix.com

• A2Zee Models, 48 Ambrose Rise, Dedridge, Livingstone,
West Lothian, EH54 6JT
Tel: +44 (0)1506 461 790
Email: a2zeemodels@aol.com

• Eduard M.A., 170 Obrnice, 435 21, Czech Republic.
Tel: +420 35 6 11 81 86 Fax: +420 35 6 11 81 71
Email: info@eduard.com

• CMK & MPM Production s.r.o, Mezilesí 718, 193 00 Horni
Pocernice, Praha 9, Czech Republic
Tel: +420 2 8192 3907 Fax: +420 2 8192 3892
www.cmkkits.com

Author's Note

There are many contradictions in documentation about the
early Bf 109 series, both genuine German as well as all written
accounts since the end of WWII. As a result of this throughout
the title you will find details of contradicting information that
was discovered by myself during the compilation of this book.
I have done this to give you as much data as possible, so that
you can make your own decision as to the most likely scenario.

Cover

The cover artwork depicts Bf 109E-7 (W/Nr.1326) flown by
Oblt Erbo Graf von Kageneck of 9./JG27. He claimed an SB-2
shot down west of Vitebsk early in the morning of the 8th July
1941, it was his 22nd victory. This artwork was specially com-
missioned for this title ©Jerry Boucher 2022

Contents

Airframe Chapters

Miniature Chapters

Appendices

Glossary

BFW ....*Bayerische Flugzeugwerke*
(Bavarian Aircraft Factory)

BMW ....*Bayerische Motorenwerke*
(Bavarian Motor Works)

DB ....Daimler-Benz

Feldwebel (Fw.)....................Sergeant (RAF) or
Airman 1st Class (USAAF)

Funkgerät (FuG) ....Radio or Radar Set

General.................................Air Marshall (RAF)
or Lieutenant General (USAAF)

Generalleutnant...................Air Vice-Marshall (RAF)
or Major General (USAAF)

Generalmajor.......................Air Commodore (RAF)
or Brigadier General (USAAF)

Geschwader ....Fighter Wing comprising three
Gruppen and one *Stab*

GM-1....................................Nitrous Oxide injection system

Gruppe ....Group

Hauptmann (Hptm.).............Flight Lieutenant (RAF)
or Captain (USAAF)

IFF ....Identification Friend or Foe

Jäger ....Fighter

Jagdeschwader (JG)..............Fighter Wing

JUMO ....Junkers *Motorenbau*

Kommandeur........................Commanding Officer

Kommodore ....Commander of a *Geschwader*

Maj. (Major) ....Squadron Leader (RAF)
or Major (USAAF)

MG.......................................Machine Gun

MK (*Machine Kanone*) ....Cannon

Oberfeldwebel (Ofw.) ....Flight Sergeant (RAF)
or Master Sergeant (USAAF)

Oberleutnant (Oblt).............Flying Officer (RAF)
or Lieutenant (USAAF)

Oberst.................................Group Captain (RAF)
or Colonel (USAAF)

Oberstleutnant (Obstlt) ......Wing Commander (RAF)
or Lieutenant Colonel (USAAF)

OKL (*Oberkommando der Luftwaffe*) ..Luftwaffe High Command

Revi (*Reflexvisier*) ....Reflector Gunsight

RLM (*Reichsluftfahrtministerium*) ......Third Reich Air Ministry

Rüstsätze.............................Auxiliary Apparatus

Staffel ....Equal to Squadron in RAF

Staffelkapitän ....Commander of a squadron

Stammkenzeichen ....Primary identification (code letters)

Technisches Amt...................Technical Department of the RLM

Unteroffizier ....Corporal (RAF & USAAF)

Versuchs or *Versuchsmuster* ....Research or test aircraft (V-series)

Werknummer (W/Nr.).........Works (construction) number

ZFR (*Zielfernrohr*) ....Riflescope (Telescopic Sight)

Preface

The story of the Bf 109 starts in 1933 with the combination of two events, the first was the signing by Willy Messerschmitt and Rakan Kokothaki, directors of BFW (*Bayerische Flugzeugwerke*), a contract with a Romanian company for the construction of M 36 transport aircraft. This annoyed Obsltl. Wilhelm Wimmer at the RLM, who accused BFW of producing aircraft for foreign countries. To this Messerschmitt countered that the RLM had placed no production orders with BFW, so they had to solicit orders from foreign countries to survive. The other event that influenced the development of the Bf 109 started when the technical department (*Technisches Amt C-Amt*) of the RLM (*Reichsluftfahrtministerium*) undertook research into the future requirements of air combat and the aircraft types that would be required to meet them. The studies resulted in the creation of four broad outlines for future aircraft types:

- *Rüstungsflugzeug* I – Medium bomber (multi-seat)
- *Rüstungsflugzeug* II – Tactical bomber
- *Rüstungsflugzeug* III – Fighter (single-seat)
- *Rüstungsflugzeug* IV – Heavy fighter (two-seat)

Thus *Rüstungsflugzeug* III envisaged a short-range fighter/interceptor to replace the Arado Ar 64 and Heinkel He 51 biplanes that were in service at the time and in March 1933 the RLM released the requirements for this new single-seat fighter (L.A.1432/33). This called for a top speed of 400km/h (250mph) at 6,000m (19,690ft), which was to be maintained for 20 minutes and with total flight duration of 90 minutes. The required 6,000m had to be obtained in no more than 17 minutes, while its operational ceiling was to be 10,000m. Power was initially envisaged as the new Junkers Jumo 210 engine that was to offer 522kW (700hp) and armament was to be either a single 20mm MG C/30 engine-mounted cannon that fired through the propeller hub (*Motorkanone*) or either two upper cowl-mounted 7.92mm (0.312in) MG 17 machine guns, or one lightweight, engine-mounted 20mm MG FF cannon with two 7.92mm MG 17 above. The MG C/30 cannon was adapted from the Flak 30 anti-aircraft gun, with its 'Long Solothurn' ammo, but it was heavy and had a very slow rate of fire. Wing loading was seen to be an important aspect of a new fighter, so this was required to be below 100kg/m2 and performance was considered as level flight speed, rate of climb, and manoeuvrability, in that order of importance. For many years it was thought that BFW was not invited to create a new design to meet the new requirement, but recent research in Germany seems to confirm that all three firms, Arado, Heinkel and BFW, all received the development contract for the requirement in February 1934,

A very atmospheric image of the spinner and propeller on a Bf 109D
(*©Real Photogaphs*)

while Focke-Wulf only received a copy of the contract in September 1934. The initial requirement stipulating the Jumo 210 was revised with the addition of a proviso that the design must also be able to accept the more powerful, but (at that time) less developed Daimler-Benz DB 600 engine. All four firms were asked to deliver three prototype airframes for head-to-head evaluation.

The first three prototypes

The first prototype was designed by Willy Messerschmitt and Robert Lusser under Messerschmitt Project Number P.1034 and work began in March 1934, just a few weeks after they received the development contract. A basic mock-up was completed by May 1934 with a much more detailed mock-up ready by January 1935. The new type was designated as the 'Bf 109', this being the next available number from a batch allocated to BFW by the RLM. The V1 (*Versuchsflugzeug 1*) prototype was given the civil registration D-IABI and completed by May 1935, however neither of the new engines were ready, so in order to get the aircraft flying the RLM acquired four Rolls-Royce Kestrel VI engines by trading a Heinkel He 70 Blitz with Rolls-Royce for them to use as an engine testbed. BFW were given two of these engines and set about adapting the engine mounts of the V1 to take this upright V-12 engine unit (the Jumo and DB 600 were both inverted V-12 units). The V1 made its maiden flight, powered by the Kestrel, from Haunstetten in May 1935 with Hans-Dietrich 'Bubi' Knoetzsch at the controls. Four months later, after completing its flight testing with BFW the V1 was delivered to the Luftwaffe test centre at Rechlin for acceptance trails. The second prototype, the V2 (D-IUDE), was nearing completion in the summer of 1935 when the first Jumo engines became available, so it was completed with the 449kW (600hp) Jumo 210A in October 1935. The V3 (D-IHNY) was next to be completed and it was the first to carry armament, although it did not fly until May 1936 due to the delay in the supply of another Jumo 210 engine.

A Bf 109E being flown by Rudi Rothenfelder at some stage prior to August 1940
(© via M Payne)

Once the Luftwaffe acceptance trials were completed at Rechlin, all the prototypes were moved to Travemünde for the head-to-head evaluation. These trials involved the Arado Ar 80 V3, Focke-Wulf Fw 159 V3, Heinkel He 112 V4 and the Bf 109 V2, with the He 112 arriving first during early February 1936 and the rest arriving by the end of the month. Initial thoughts by service pilots, who were used to biplanes with their open cockpits, low wing loading, light G-forces and easy handling were very critical of the Bf 109, as it showed none of these characteristics. The wing loading was quite an issue for Messerschmitt because although the *Rüstungsflug-*

zeug III called for this to be less than 100kg/m2 Messerschmitt felt that this was unreasonable. When applying a low wing loading to a fighter using the (then) available engine types, it would end up being slower than the bombers it was tasked with intercepting. Also a fighter is designed mainly for high-speed flight and so a small wing area is optimal in achieving high speed, however the downside to this is that low-speed flight suffers as a result (a smaller wing needs more airflow to generate enough lift to maintain flight). To get around these problems the Bf 109 had a series of advanced high-lift devices including automatic leading-edge slats and large flaps on the trailing edge. The slats increased wing lift considerably when deployed and greatly enhanced horizontal manoeuvrability. The type also included ailerons that were linked to the flaps, so 'drooped' when the latter were lowered, thus increasing the flap surface area. All of these factors, when deployed, effectively increased the wing's co-efficient of lift but the small overall dimensions of the wings led to a higher wing loading. As the trials progressed, though, the Bf 109 soon became one of the frontrunners, as the Arado and Focke-Wulf designs had only ever been intended as 'back-ups' to safeguard against failure of the He 112 and Bf 109, and both proved to be completely outclassed. The Arado Ar 80 initially had a gull wing, although that was replaced with a straight, tapered wing on the V3, and its fixed undercarriage meant it was overweight and underpowered so it was abandoned after just three prototypes were built. The Fw 159 with its parasol wing was considered by the Travemünde staff to be a compromise between a biplane and monoplane and although it had some advanced design features, it had a very unusual undercarriage system that proved to be very unreliable. The Bf 109 was also not liked by the E-Stelle test pilots because of its steep nose-up angle on the ground, which gave very poor forward visibility when taxiing. They also did not like the sideways-hinged cockpit canopy that could not

The Bf 109E-4 of Hptm Wick from I./JG2 with its speckled camouflage and armoured windscreen
(© via M. Payne)

be opened in flight, nor the automatic leading-edge slats on the wings because it was thought they would inadvertently open during aerobatics and this might lead to crashes. This latter comment would prove to be correct, as found out during air combat and aerobatics, when the leading-edge slats and ailerons would flutter rapidly in fast tight turns, making it very difficult to track a target and eventually putting the aircraft into a stall. There were also grave concerns about the high wing loading in comparison to biplanes. The Heinkel He 112 was the main contender, as it was favoured by the Luftwaffe hierarchy and in comparison with the Bf 109 it was also cheaper to produce. The He 112 had a wide-track and robust undercarriage that opened outwards from the mid wing, while the 109 had narrow track undercarriage mounted on the lower fuselage sides (to allow the wings to be removed without the need to trestle the fuselage) making it prone to failure, while the He 112 also gave its pilot considerably better visibility from the cockpit and its lower wing loading made it a lot easier to land. The He 112 V4 was fitted with a single-piece, clear-view, sliding cockpit canopy and had the more powerful Jumo 210Da engine with a special (modified) exhaust system, but the main downfall of the type was that it was complicated from a structural point of view and was 18% heavier than the Bf 109. On top of this it became apparent that the thick 12.6m (41ft 4in) wing was a great disadvantage for a light fighter as it decreased the type's manoeuvrability and rate of roll. Knowing this Heinkel revised the V4, which was used for the trials, with new wings of 11.5m (37ft 8.75in) span, but these improvements had not been fully tested so it could not be demonstrated in accordance with the rules laid down by the Acceptance Commission, thus putting it at a distinct disadvantage. The Bf 109 was much smaller and thus lighter than the He 112 and was therefore 30km/h (20mph) faster than it in level flight, and superior in both the dive and climb. The Acceptance Commission ruled in favour of the Bf 109 mainly because of the Messerschmitt's test pilot's demonstration of the type's capabilities during dives, flick rolls, spins and tight turns, throughout which the pilot was always in complete control. By this stage the RLM had received news that the Supermarine Spitfire had been ordered into full-scale production by the RAF, so it was felt that a quick decision was needed in order to get the new design into production as quickly as possible. As a result on the 12th March the RLM announced the results of the competition in a document entitled 'Bf 109 Priority Procurement', that placed the new Bf 109 into series production. The Bf 109 made its first public appearance during the 1936 Berlin Olympics, when the V1 was flown.

Record-breaking flights

The Bf 109 was to gain quite a few awards and records before war came and the first of these were in July 1937 when three Bf 109Bs took part

Mechanics of JG 53 take a break during the summer of 1939

in the *Flugmeeting Airshow* in Zürich. The aircraft won in several categories:
- First Prize in a speed race over a 202 km course
- First Prize in the Class A category in the international Alpenrundflug for military aircraft
- First place in the international *Patrouillenflug* category

On the 11th November 1937, the V13 flown by Messerschmitt's chief pilot Dr. Hermann Wurster and fitted with a special 1,230kW (1,650hp) DB 601R racing engine set a new world air speed record for landplanes with piston engines at 610.55km/h (379.38mph), thus giving Germany the record for the first time.

Having had the He 112 rejected Heinkel designed and built the He 100 and on the

6th June 1938, the V3, flown by Ernst Udet, took the world air speed record at 634.7km/h (394.4mph). Then on the 30th March 1939, the He 100 V8 being flown by Hans Dieterle, surpassed that record with a speed of 746.61km/h (463.92mph). The record was soon recaptured by Messerschmitt, though, when on the 26th April 1939 the Me 209 V1 flown by *Flugkapitän* Fritz Wendel set a new record of 755.14km/h (469.22mph). For propaganda purposes, this pure prototype was called the 'Bf 109R', thus claiming it to be another version of the standard Bf 109 fighter, but it had little in common with the type. This world air speed record for a piston-engined aircraft was to stand for 30 years, before in 1969 Darryl Greenamyer in a modified Grumman F8F Bearcat called 'Conquest I', set a new speed of 777km/h (483mph).

The Bf 109 V13 modified for an attempt at the World Air Speed record; revision to the canopy, cowl shape change, a much bigger spinner and no bulge to the chin radiator housing

Production

For many years it was always held that no A-series machines were built, however there were three machines that are best considered as A-series. These were W/Nrs.808, 809 and 810, which were registered as D-IIBA, D-IUDE and D-IHNY. It should be noted that D-IUDE is often mis-identified as the V2 and D-IHNY as the V3. By this stage the RLM had decided that heavier armament would be needed in a modern fighter, so changed their plans to have the type armed with three guns, one of which would be of 20mm calibre (they intended to use a licence-built Oerlikon, once they could go into production as the MG FF) and it would fire through the propeller boss. This armament would be used in the new B-series and the Bf 109 V4 (D-IALY) acted as the first series prototype (the B-01). It only actually carried the two MG17s over the engine, and although many claim it had another firing through the propeller boss, it was never installed. The wing was revised in relation to the previous prototypes, as was the undercarriage,

A very useful shot of AE479 from underneath, talk about oil leaks!

and the type first flew on the 23rd September 1936. This was followed by the V5 through to the V12, as B-02 to B-09 prototypes testing various equipment and armament for the proposed B series. A series of five pre-production B-0 airframes followed, all basically similar to the V4 with the addition of a luggage compartment aft of the cockpit.

The production B-series started with the B-1, which was similar to the B-0 except it was fitted with FuG VII radio equipment. The B-2 series came next and this was the first version to be built under contract by other firms, with the

type being made by Fieseler and Erla as well as BFW. These machines differed from the B-1 in having short wing leading-edge slots and a VDM-Hamilton two-blade, variable-pitch propeller.

The C-series was intended to have great firepower and the prototypes for the series were W/Nrs.1720 (V19) and 1731 (V18). Although heavier calibre weapons were envisaged for the C-series, these two prototypes had just one MG 17 added to each wing, mid-span, in addition to the two firing over the engine. The production C-1 series was similar to the late-production B02s made by Fieseler but with the addition of the MG 17s in the wings. All C-1s were built by BFW at Augsburg and in all fewer than 60 are thought to have been made. Five of these were sent for operational evaluation with J/88 in Spain (marked as 6•46 to 6•50). The C-2 series was intended to be the first with the MG 17 firing through the propeller boss, but this series never went into production. The C-3 series were all conversions from C-1s and they had the wing-mounted MG 17s replaced with 20mm MF FF/A cannon. The C-4 was another one that never reached production, and it was intended to have the MG FF/A cannon replacing the MG 17 firing through the propeller boss.

Many state that the D-series was intended to be powered by the new DB 600 engine, but this is not the case, as the series retained the Jumo

E-Series Production

The E-series was produced in the following variants.

- E-1 – 2x 7.92mm MG 17s above the engine and two more in the wings. Later, many were modified to the E-3 armament standard.
- E-1/B – small batch of E-1s modified as fighter-bombers (*Jagdbomber* – usually abbreviated to *Jabo*). These were fitted with either an ETC 250 bomb rack, carrying one 250 kg (550 lb) bomb, or two ETC 50 bomb racks, each carrying a 50 kg (110 lb) bomb under both wings. A total of 1,183 E-1 were built, 110 of them were E-1/B.
- E-2 – Intended to have two wing-mounted MG FFs, and one engine-mounted MG FF cannon, and although some claim that II./JG 27 operated the type, it was never put into production.
- E-3 – This version had some structural improvements and more powerful armament. The new armament comprised two MG 17s above the engine and one MG FF cannon in each wing. The type was also produced in E-3/B *Jabo* form with an ETC 50/VIII or ETC 500 bomb rack under the fuselage. A total of 1,276 E-3 were built, including 83 export versions.
- E-4 – Basically a modified E-3 this version had 20 mm MG-FF/M cannon in the wings and improved head armour for the pilot. The new cannon took an improved type of explosive shell, called *Minengeschoß* (or 'mine-shell'), which was drawn instead of cast. This allowed a much larger explosive charge to be used and the resulting higher recoil required modification to the MG FF's mechanism, hence the MG FF/M designation. The E-4 was offered in the following sub-variants:
  - E-4/B – Fighter-bomber version, 1x 250kg, usually with DB 601Aa engine
  - E-4 Trop – For operations in tropical regions (rifle and survival equipment in rear fuselage) and sand filter on supercharger intake
  - E-4/N Trop – Same as E-4 Trop but with DB601N engine
  - E-4/N – E-4 with DB 601N engine
  A total of 561 of all E-4 versions were built.
- E-5 – Reconnaissance variant of the E-3, twenty-nine were built. Also offered with desert equipment as the E-5 Trop.
- E-6 – Reconnaissance variant of the E-4/N, nine were ordered.
- E-7 – First version to be able to carry a drop tank, usually a 300lt unit mounted on a rack under the fuselage, which increased the range to 1,325km. Alternatively, a bomb could be fitted, when the type was designated E-7/B. Early E-7s were fitted with the DB 601A or DB 601Aa engine, while late-production ones received the DB 601N – this latter was thus designated the E-7/N. The Bf 109E-7Z was fitted with the GM-1 nitrous oxide injection system. A total of 438 E-7s of all variants were built.
- E-8 – Long-range version of E-1 with the drop tank installation of the E-7.
- E-9 – Reconnaissance version of E-7, also offered with DB 601N engine as the E-9/N and with tropical equipment as the E-9 Trop or E-9/N Trop. All versions had an Rb 50/30 camera installed in the rear fuselage.

210. The V16 had many of the attributes of the D-1 series, although no surviving official documents list it as a D-series prototype? Production of the D-1 was undertaken by Erla at Leipzig and although it is not known how many were built, W/Nrs.0417 through to 0539 are known to relate to the type. The series was powered by the Jumo 210D. had the new 'universal' wing that allowed light (MG 17) or heavy (MG FF) armament to be fitted, although it retained the two MG 17s in the wings. The D-1 had the Jumo 210Da engine and ejector style exhaust stacks and this version was later used in the early nightfighter role with the *Abshußrohr* telescopic gunsight and anti-glare shields fitted over the exhausts. By this stage the new DB 601-powered E-series was on the horizon, so the D was considered outdated and was therefore offered for export. Ten were supplied to Switzerland, where they became J-301 to J-310 and were used in the border protection role. These machines were supplied without armament, so the MG 29 machine-guns were fitted in the wings instead.

Initially the E-series was to use the DB 600 engine and the first prototype was converted from the unfinished B-010 (V13). Considerable modification was required to the airframe, mainly to deal with the additional coolant required for this engine, so two radiators were added under the wings and the oil cooler was enlarged and repositioned from under the wing to under the nose. The prototype first flew on the 10th July 1937 and it won the climb and dive competition at the Zürich air races later that year. This machine was later heavy modified for an attempt on the World Air Speed Record and fitted with a special DB 601/III engine, it took the record in November 1937. The V14 was converted from a B-1 and it used the DB 601. This engine was developed from the DB 600 and only really differed in having direct injection in place of a carburettor. The V14 is notorious as it is the all-red machine flown and crashed so publicly by Ernst Udet at the Fourth International Flight Meeting in Zürich during July/August 1937. The V15 and V15a can be considered the first true E-series prototype, not just one-offs for publicity. These used the DB 601A engine and a VDM three-bladed, variable-pitch propeller. They were both armed with two

Notes on designation & nicknames

The original RLM aircraft designation for the type was 'Bf 109', since the design was created and submitted by *Bayerische Flugzeugwerke* (Bavarian Aircraft Factory or BFW). The company was renamed Messerschmitt AG after the 11th July 1938 when Willy Messerschmitt finally acquire the company and so all Messerschmitt aircraft that originated after that date carry the 'Me' designation.

Despite the regulations, wartime documents from the RLM, Messerschmitt AG and the Luftwaffe use both designations, sometimes even on the same page. All surviving airframes bear the official 'Bf 109' designation on their identification plates, right up to the final K-4 variant. The only exceptions are those initially built or refitted by Erla Flugzeugwerke, which sometimes bear the 'Me 109' designation on their identification plates.

The 109 was given several nick names by its operators and by those that met it in battle, which were usually derived from the name of the manufacturer (e.g. Messer, Mersu [originally the Finnish nickname for the prestigious Mercedes-Benz cars], Messzer etc.), or due to its appearance (e.g. *Badewanne* (Bath Tub), *Kahn* (Canoe) or *Kiste* (Box)), plus it was also known to Luftwaffe crews as the Molle, the name given to a large size glass in a Berlin restaurant! The official names for each series were A = Anton, B = Berta, C = Caesar, D = Dora and E= Emil and are based on the German phonetic alphabet of World War II, a practice that was also used for other German aircraft designs (e.g. the Fw 190D 'Dora' or Ju 87D 'Dora') – only the Fw 190 seems to have got away from this system, with it generally being known, regardless of sub-variant, as the *Würger* (Shrike) or 'Butcher Bird'.

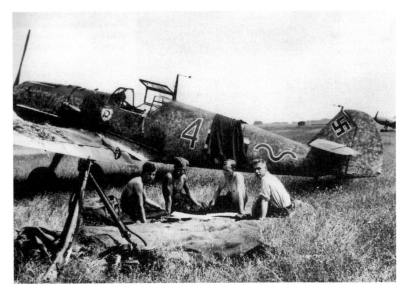

MG 17s firing over the engine and had the Revi gunsight fitted. A number of E-0 pre-production prototypes were built, although most of these were then used for development of other series such as the T and two were used in various pre-war propaganda images claiming to be 'in service' Bf 109Es.

Bf 109Es of III./JG2 including 'Red 4' seen in mid-August 1940
(© via M. Payne)

Aircraft Photographed for Chapter 10
This title includes extensive photographic coverage of a number of preserved Bf 109 airframes around the world; those featured are as follows:

• Bf 109E-3 Technical Museum, Berlin, Germany by Josef Andal, George Papadimitriou & Przemyslaw Skulski

• Bf 109E-3 Swiss AF Museum, Dubendirf, Switzerland by Josef Andal, George Papadimitriou & Przemyslaw Skulski

• Bf 109E-4 Technical Museum, Munich, Germany by Josef Andal, George Papadimitriou & Przemyslaw Skulski

• Bf 109E-4/b Battle of Britain Museum, RAF Museum, Hendon, London, UK by the author

Chapter 1:   **Evolution**

The Versuch (V) Series

The road to the production Bf 109 was not that involved, with only a couple of machines as listed here being built as prototypes. These were in fact pre-production machines for the B-series (See Chapter 2).

* A literal translation of Versuch is 'attempt', so in technical terms that is a prototype.

Note – Due to the large number of airframes we have to cover we will not be duplicating data between variants, instead we will only identify those changes in relation to a previous version, identifying that version in the text e.g. 'Same as Bf 109 V3 except:'.

Bf 109 V1 (Bf 109A)

W/Nr. 758
Registration: D-IABI

- First flew in September 1935
- Rolls-Royce Kestrel V engine (some state IIS)
- Air intake, both sides at wing root
- External oil cooler system built into the in-board leading edge of each wing
- Original undercarriage legs that featured doors of a different shape to those of later machines – more rounded due to the round profile of the wheel well
- 650x150 wheels and hubs that either have disc covers or are solid
- There are bulges from the wing leading edge to 3/4 span above the main wheel well areas, a bit like those seen later on the G/K series
- Long leading-edge slots fitted, although later

in its test life the shorter-style ones were fitted

- Five inspection panels on upper surfaces of each wing
- No aerial behind cockpit or mast on vertical fin tip
- Fuel filler cap below cockpit on port fuselage side
- No armament or gunsight fitted
- Venturi on both sides of fuselage, forward and below windscreen
- Some form of probe can be seen fitted to each wing tip in early photos, this is probably a pitot of some type, but is fitted directly into

A nice close-up image of the tail of the V1 during final assembly
(© via NASM)

Now a world-famous image, this shot of the Bf 109 V1 ground running has been reproduced many times, and modified, cleaned-up and even flipped round, so here we thought we would bring you the image in an untouched form, direct from the original print
(© via NASM)

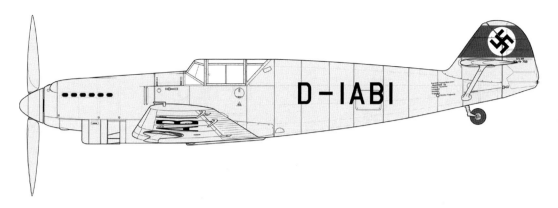

Bf 109 V1 (Bf 109A)
W/Nr. 758

the end of the wing projecting outwards by about 18in, then turning through 90° at the extreme tip to face forward – probably associated with stall and spin testing that it undertook
- Fitted with a Schwarz two-blade, wooden propeller
- First flew on the 28th May 1935, pilot Hans-Dietrich Knoetzsch

Camouflage & Markings

One of the earliest photographs of this machine shows it ground-running. The sheen on the wings etc., combined with the contrast to the unpainted oil coolers in the wing leading edges, confirm that it was painted. The most likely colour is RLM 01 *Silber* overall, but with a high gloss finish (although some state RLM 02 or 63?). The propeller blades look to be in a darker shade, so could be RLM 70 or a dark grey, and the spinner seems to be unpainted metal. This machine does not seem to have the radiator unit in the chin intake unpainted, although later images that may be this machine certainly do show this unpainted so you get a wide metal band under the chin intake.

No markings were initially applied, but once the aircraft undertook flight trials the swastika was applied across the vertical fin/rudder hinge line mounted on a white disc that itself was on a red band that went across the entire fin and rudder, from a point just about from the tailplane fillet to 10cm from the top of the fin. The civil registration, D-IABI, was applied in black characters on each side of the fuselage and a large 87 Octane fuel symbol can be seen directly below the filler point on the port fuselage side. The registration was repeated on the wings, but in much larger characters, with 'D-I' on the port and 'ABI' on the starboard, both read from the trailing edge looking forward. This was also repeated under the wings, although reversed, with 'D-I' under the starboard and 'ABI' under the port, both outboard of the wheel wells and read from the leading edge looking aft. Apart from the weight and lifting stencils applied in black on either side of the rear fuselage, by the jacking point, the only other marking seems to be the type and W/Nr. stencil on the rudder, below the red tail band, which reads 'Bfw 109' on one line with 'WrNr 758' below it, in black characters of two sizes (5-7.5cm top line, 10cm lower?).

The Bf 109 V1 seen assembled and painted at the company airfield at Haustetten
(© via J. Grant)

Lovely head-on shot of the Bf 109 V1 at Haustetten, showing the ring radiator that was only used on this Kestrel-powered prototype

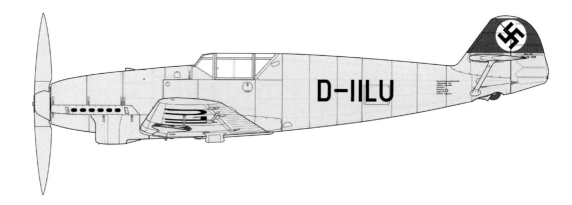

Bf 109 V2
W/Nr. 759

No images exist of the entire Bf 109 V2, although many claim this one shows it when in fact this is a Bf 109A (see Chapter 2 p15 for more details)

Bf 109 V2

W/Nr. 759

Registration: D-IILU (often mis-identified as D-IUDE)

- Intended as the prototype for the production A-series
- Jumo 210a engine
- Schwarz two-blade, wooden propeller
- No spinner cap
- Ventilation holes exposed just behind the propeller due to smaller diameter spinner – this applied for many prototypes and the early production B-series machines
- TZ-3 coolant radiator under the chin
- Small oil cooler under the port wing
- Only three inspection panels on the upper surfaces of each wing
- Unarmed, although it is claimed that it had

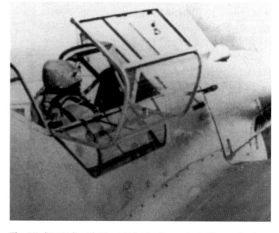

The V2 (D-IILU) with Ernst Udet in the cockpit, Travemünde, January 1936
(© via J. Grant)

the facility to have the two MG 17s above the engine, but they were never installed
- Retractable tailwheel
- No aerial or mast
- Angular windscreen and canopy
- Triangular clear panel deleted in the windscreen
- Air intake on starboard side of nose
- Type 1A engine cowling (See details elsewhere)
- First flew 12th December 1935, pilot Joachim von Koppen
- Crashed at Ivendorf, south of Travemünde on the 1st April 1936 (Pilot Mr Trillhase) due to windscreen glazing disintegrating. Airframe dismantled and later scrapped (photo exists showing the fuselage and the odd 'pointed' nature of the windscreen framework is evident?)

A useful shot showing the cowls off the V2 and the first installation of the Jumo engine into the Bf 109 airframe

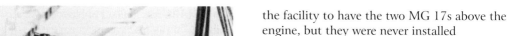

Camouflage & Markings

Few, if any, images of the complete V2 exist, the only one we found showed the wrecked fuselage and it carried its registration on the fuselage side in the same manner as the V1, so we presume when complete it also had the other markings applied as per the V1?

Bf 109 V3

W/Nr. 760

Registration: D-IOQY (sometimes mis-identified as D-IHNY)
- Two MG 17 machine-guns above engine
- Intended to have the C/30 L cannon between the engine cylinder blocks, firing through the propeller hub, but problems with this weapon resulted in it not being installed
- Ventilation holes in top of cowling
- Revi C/12B gunsight
- It is claimed that this machine was equipped to test the SC10 bomb dispenser
- FuG VII radio and antenna
- Non-retractable tailwheel
- Windscreen shape revised
- Type 1A engine cowling (See details elsewhere)
- Sent to Spain by sea in October 1936 for use in semi-operational evaluation with J/88

Camouflage & Markings

Initially this machine carried the same style of markings as seen on the V1 and V2, with the only difference being the codes (D-IOQY) on the fuselage and above and below the wings. There is a photo showing the tail swastika and white disc overpainted in red on the fin/rudder, but this may just be censorship? The type certainly had the radiator element unpainted within the chin intake and the area around the exhaust stacks was painted black, with a sharp point at the (aft) trailing edge. Photos also confirm that the wing walkway markings were applied on the inner area of each upper wing surface and these are presumed to have been in black. When in Spain this machine remained in the same overall scheme, but the Spanish black disc was applied to either side of the fuselage, rather high up in comparison with later machines, aft of which was the code '6-2' in black characters that also displayed a different style and size to those of

other J/88 machines. A large stylised skull and crossbones was applied below the cockpit on the port side and it is not known if it was repeated on the starboard as no photos survive. Photos at this time confirm that the backs of each propeller blade were painted black, although not right to the root (squared-off at point where the blade starts to twist). Period photos are not sufficient to confirm or deny the application of the white rudder with black 'X', nor of the black roundels above and below the wings on this machine.

After its accident, the V2 was used to test various items, including the angular canopy shown in this well-known image of the remains

There is a series of publicity images of the V3, all taken whilst flying over the Lech River north of Augsburg on the 29th June 1936. Hermann Würster was at the controls
(© via J. Grant)

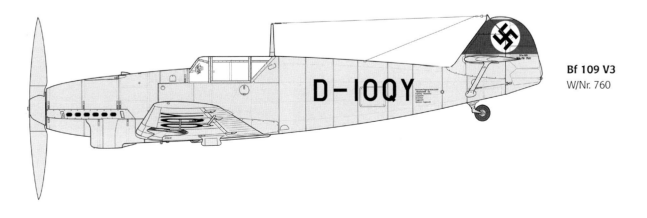

Bf 109 V3
W/Nr. 760

Chapter 2: **Bf 109B Series**

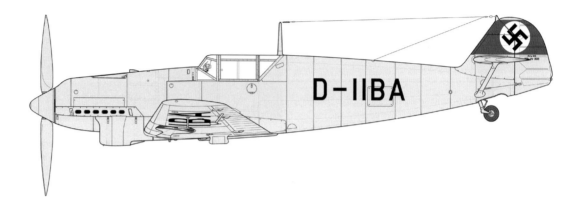

Bf 109A
W/Nr. 808

W/Nr.808 after its crash-landing, the odd thing being that this machine is listed as having a wooden propeller, yet this machine definitely has a metal propeller and other images of the same incident confirm it is D-IIBA?

Production started with the B series because evolution of the type was so fast that the proposed A-series was superseded once it was realised that its intended armament was too light for modern warfare and the series thus never reached full production.

Bf 109B Pre-production

Bf 109A

W/Nr. 808
Registration: D-IIBA
Same as the Bf 109 V4 except:
- Schwarz two-blade, wooden propeller
- Type 2 engine cowling (See details elsewhere)

Camouflage & Markings
This machine may have been in the standard prototype scheme of RLM 01 *Silber* (glossy) overall, but photos seem to show a darker shade, so we suspect it is RLM 62 (grey) overall with the registration in black on the fuselage sides and above and below the wings. The red band with

white disc and swastika was applied across the fin/rudder and the 'BFW 109' and 'W/Nr.808' stencils were on either side of the rudder below the red band. No other markings are apparent, although the spinner looks a lighter shade (polished metal?).

Bf 109A W/Nr.808, D-IIBA seen here after a belly landing

above: This shot of the nose of W/Nr.808 gives some idea of the damage caused by a wheels-up landing – the big chin intake of the Jumo was disliked because it often dug in and caused the aircraft to flip over

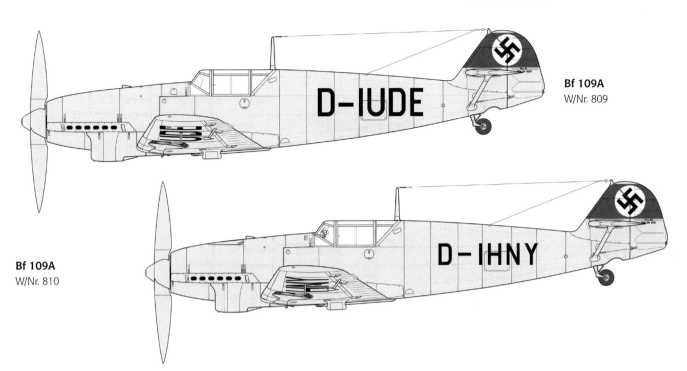

Bf 109A
W/Nr. 809

Bf 109A
W/Nr. 810

Bf 109A

W/Nr. 809
Registration: D-IUDE (Often mis-identified as the V2)
Same as the Bf 109 V4 except:
- No machine-guns fitted above engine
- No gunsight
- Type 1b engine cowling (See details elsewhere)

Camouflage & Markings
No photographs exist of this machine, but it is likely that it had the same overall scheme as D-IIBA.

Bf 109A

W/Nr. 810
Registration: D-IHNY (Often mis-identified as the V3)
Same as the Bf 109A D-IUDE except:
- MG 17 machine-guns fitted above engine
- Revi C/12B gunsight
- Type 1b engine cowling (See details elsewhere)

Camouflage & Markings
No photographs exist of this machine, but it is likely that it had the same overall scheme as D-IIBA.

Bf 109 V4 (Bf 109B-01)

W/Nr. 878
Registration: D-IALY
Same as the Bf 109 V2 except:
- Intended as prototype for B-series
- Junkers 210B engine
- MG17 machine-guns above engine (some claim this machine had the engine-mounted MG 17, but this was not the case)
- Ventilation holes in the top of the cowling aft of the gun troughs
- Windscreen was heated
- Revi C/12B gunsight
- The bulges above the wheel bays in the upper wing surfaces were deleted

The V4 (W/Nr. 878) marked as D-IALY and seen at Sevilla-Tablada, Spain on the 9th December 1936
(© via J Grant)

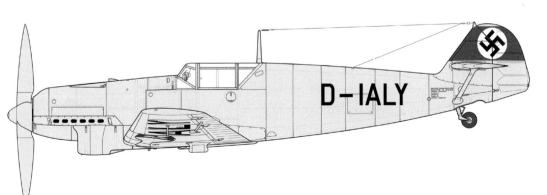

Bf 109 V4
(Bf 109B-01)
W/Nr. 878
Registration: D-IALY

Nice head-on shot of the Bf 109 V4 (D-IALY), showing many details of the early series

- 650x150 wheels with six-spoke hubs fitted
- Revised undercarriage legs and doors
- Type 2 engine cowling (See details elsewhere)
- First flight 23rd September 1936, piloted by Dr.-Ing Hermann Wurster
- Sent by sea to Spain on the 30th November 1936 for two months of semi-operational evaluation with J/88. Flown there by *Lt* Hannes Trautloft

Camouflage & Markings

The initial scheme applied to this machine was identical to the V1 to V3, the only changes being in the registration (D-IALY) applied to the fuselage and wings, although in one published source it was shown with the W/Nr. under the tailplane,

The Bf 109 V4 was sent to Spain from the 14th December 1936 to the 14th January 1937, where it was flown by Hannes Trautloft. It is seen here at Sevilla-Tablada in December 1936

(© via M Payne & Jim Grant)

on the fuselage side just above where the rudder linkage wire was (displayed as 'wn 878', with the numbers in larger-sized characters than the 'wn'). Once in Spain this machine was initially only to receive new markings with the black roundels applied to each fuselage side, and above and below the wings, these latter markings having the white 'X' on them as well (although some sources claim the airframe was repainted RLM 63).. The rudder was painted white with the black 'X' at this

stage and Trautloft's 'Green Heart of Germany' marking was applied below the cockpit on the port side. The code '6-1' was applied in black characters, aft of the fuselage roundel on both sides and again the style/size of the font used is unusual. Photos at this time seem to suggest that the propeller blades were painted (grey?) on the outer faces and black on the back, with the leading edges left with their bare brass sheathing. It is difficult to tell, but we suspect the spinner cap is unpainted, while the bulk of the propeller hub is in the same colour as the front of the blades. Later, when the other Bf 109s arrived in Spain this machine may have been repainted in the RLM 63/65 scheme. The tips of the wings were certainly done in white at this stage and all other national insignia remained as before. The only changes were that the green heart motif was overpainted, resulting in a lighter panel in this area and aft of it the large top hat marking was applied in black. Also at this time the area around the exhaust stacks was painted black, with another area above the mid-section of the exhausts also painted black (the radiator unit was unpainted at this stage so also looks dark in photos). From the contrasts in the photos at this stage, our guess is that actually the aircraft was not repainted, and remained it its original scheme with just the panel for the green heart being repainted RLM 63 and, so it seems, the entire set of engine and gun access cowlings?

Bf 109 V5 (Bf 109B-02)

W/Nr. 879
Registration: D-IIGO (often mid-identified as D-IEKS)
Same as the Bf 109 V4 except:
- Jumo 201D engine (some state 210B)
- Two-blade variable-pitch VDM metal propeller
- No radio or aerial mast/leads
- Type 2 (adjusted) engine cowling (See details elsewhere)
- First flew on the 5th November with Dr. Ing. Hermann Wurster at the controls
- Sent to Spain with V3 in December 1936 for two months of semi-operational evaluation with J/88
- Later undertook trials at E site, Travemünde, ultimate fate unknown

Bf 109 V5 (Bf 109B-02)
W/Nr. 879

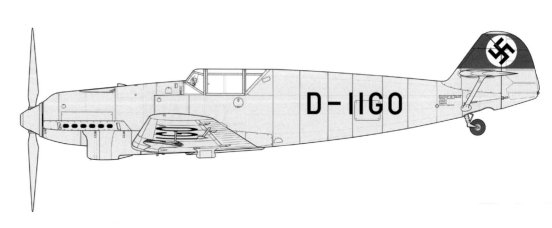

Camouflage & Markings

There is only one image we could find of this machine, and that shows just the front with the engine cowls off, so any commentary on C&M is pure speculation until better images surface. It is most likely that this machine carried the same overall scheme as the V1 to V4, with just the registration (D-IIGO) being different. Whilst in Spain this machine seems to have carried the standard overall colours (RLM 63/65?) and markings and the code '6-3'. See the image at right for more details.

Bf 109 V6 (Bf 109B-03)

W/Nr. 880
Registration: D-IHHB
Same as the Bf 109 V4 except:
- No MG 17s above engine
- No gunsight
- Pitot mounted on framework above canopy
- Ciné camera mounted on fin top
- Type 2 (adjusted) engine cowling (See details elsewhere)
- Used to study accelerated stalls

Camouflage & Markings
Period photos show this machine to be in a 'dark' scheme, which is presumed to be RLM 70/71 over 65. The coverage is very patchy, though, with what looks like the panel at mid wing root in bare metal on the port side and the flaps, ailerons and wing tips in a very dark shade (or just very glossy in comparison with the rest of the wing?) The red band was applied across the fin/rudder, with the swastika mounted on a white disc on that – the cross-over of the arms of the swastika is exactly

on the point where the vertical hinge line goes at 45° forward. The registration, D-IHHB, was applied in black characters on either fuselage side, but much larger then seen previously. It is not known if this was also applied above and below the wings, but it seems most likely. The large 87 Octane fuel triangle was once again applied below the filler point on the port fuselage side. No W/Nr. can be seen on the rudder and the entire nose area looks to be a different colour, or a lot dirtier, as is the spinner. The propeller blades once again seem to be bare metal(?) on the front of the blade and black on the rear. The big ciné camera housing on the vertical fin is probably RLM 02, as it is a distinctly different shade.

This is the Bf 109 V5 (D-IIGO) seen during two months semi-operational evaluation as 6-3 with with 2.J/88 in Spain in late 1936, early 1937. This photo was taken at Herrera de Pisuerga
(© via J. Grant)

This is the Bf 109 V6 (D-IHHB) with the ciné camera mounted on the fin top in relation to the study of accelerated stalls

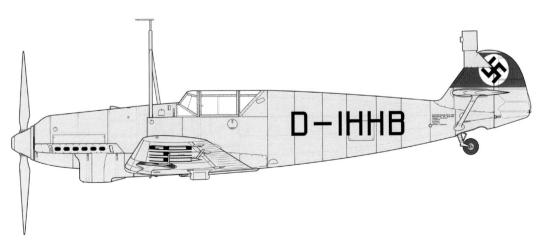

above and above left: The Bf 109 V6 (D-IHHB) was used to study accelerated stalls, but it had a camera on the vertical fin for this, so we suspect this image shows it at an earlier stage prior to the fitment of the camera on the vertical fin

Bf 109 V6 (Bf 109B-03)
W/Nr. 880

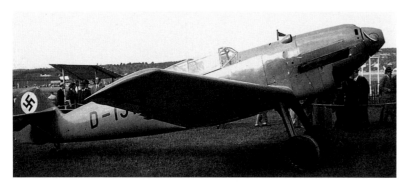

The Bf 109 V7 (D-IJHA) seen at the event at Zurich in 1937

Bf 109 V7 (Bf 109B-04)

W/Nr. 881
Registration: D-IJHA
Same as the Bf 109 V5 except:

- Jumo 210G
- No MG 17s above engine
- No gunsight
- Luggage space added aft of cockpit
- Additional ventilation outlets on the side of the nose, aft and above the exhaust outlets
- Additional air intake can be seen under the nose, forward of the radiator

Camouflage & Markings

This machine had the same overall scheme as the V1 through V6 and only differed in its registration (D-IJHA) applied to the fuselage sides and upper and lower wings. Period photos of this machine at Zürich show it to be quite dark, but we suspect it was RLM 02 overall, albeit very glossy and this included the propeller spinner, whilst the blades were bare metal(?) on the front and black on the back. At the event this machine along with the V8 and V10 had entry number '1' (and for later events '4') applied on a white box forward of the fuselage registration number on each side, and this box was approximately twice the height of the registration characters and was positioned on a point central to that of the fuselage, resulting in the lower flat on the '1' being below that of the bottom of the registration characters. The only other marking was that the panel immediately around the exhaust outlets was painted black – this was not the same as seen on the prototypes sent to Spain, it only covered the single small oblong panel that contained the exhaust outlets.

Bf 109 V8 (Bf 109B-05)

W/Nr. 882
Registration: D-IMQE (Often mis-identified as D-IPLU)
Same as the Bf 109 V7.

- Sent to Zürich in 1937 to take part in the Fourth International Flight Meeting from the 23rd July to 1st August 1937.
- Later fitted with Jumo 210Ga and used for C-series development programme

The Bf 109 V7 (D-IJHA) seen at Zürich-Dubendorf in July 1937
(© via Jim Grant)

- Cut-out ventilation holes with square edges can be seen at the front of the engine cowling, both above and below the centreline
- First flown on the 5th November 1936 (pilot, Dr.-Ing. Hermann Wurster)
- Sent to Zürich in 1937 to take part in the Fourth International Flight Meeting from the 23rd July to 1st August 1937.
- Won the race on the 25th July at Zürich flown by Dipl.Ing. Carl Francke of E-Stelle, Rechlin
- Also won races on the 29th July with *Capt.* Werner Meier at the controls
- Returned to Augsburg and used by Messerschmitt for various trials, ultimate fate unknown

A useful close-up of the nose of the Bf 109 V7 (D-IJHA) showing the little 'V7' applied in this area

**Bf 109 V7
(Bf 109B-04)**
W/Nr. 881

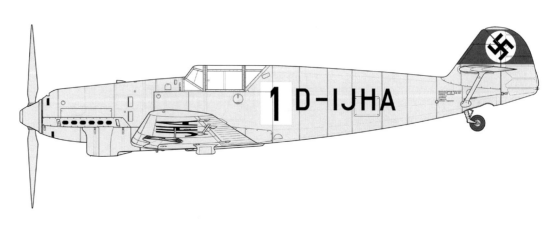

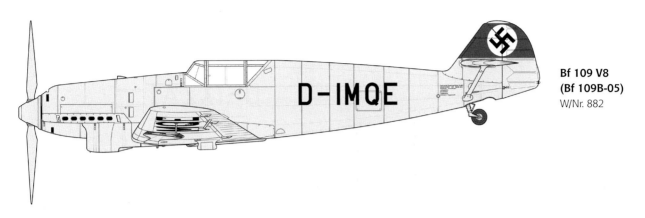

Bf 109 V8
(Bf 109B-05)
W/Nr. 882

Camouflage & Markings

This machine carried the same markings as the V7 and this includes those at the Zürich event, including the entry number '4' on the fuselage sides and the small black panel around the exhausts. The W/Nr. was applied forward of the bottom mount for the tailplane strut, on either side of the rear fuselage as 'W 882'. The black characters used were probably only about 5cm high.

Bf 109 V9 (Bf 109B-06)

W/Nr. 883
Registration: D-IPLU
Same as the Bf 109 V8 except:

- No additional air intakes under chin
- Small mast on top of vertical fin
- First flown by Fritz Wendel on the 23rd July 1937
- Sent to Zürich in 1937 to take part in the Fourth International Flight Meeting from the 23rd July to 1st August 1937
- Won Class A of the 'Alpine flight for military aircraft' at Zürich on the 27th July 1937 with Maj. Hans Seidemann at the controls and Class C with *Oblt*. Hannes Trautloft flying
- Flown to Rechlin on the 28th October 1937 for further trials and development work, where it is claimed it was fitted with armament?
- Later fitted with Jumo 210Ga and used for C-series development programme

Camouflage & Markings

This machine carried the same markings as the

V7 & V8 and this includes those at the Zürich event, with the entry number '4' on the fuselage sides. The only difference seems to be with the panel around the exhaust outlets, which in this instance seems to be black but takes the area right forward to the very front of the cowl edge, instead of stopping just past the front exhaust opening where the panel ends.

The Bf 109 V7 (D-IJHA) and V9 (D-IPLU) in the company of a Bf 109B at Bellinzona getting ready for the Zürich event in 1937

The Bf 109 V9 (D-IPLU) at Zürich

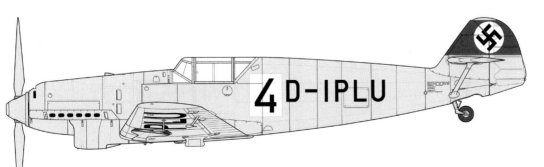

Bf 109 V9
(Bf 109B-06)
W/Nr. 883

**Bf 109 V10
(Bf 109B-07)**
W/Nr. 884

Bf 109 V10 (Bf 109B-07)

W/Nr. 884
Registration: D-IXZA
Same as the Bf 109 V9 except:
- Jumo 201D
- No ventilation holes in the front engine cowls (upper or lower)
- No ventilation outlets in the side cowls
- Short leading-edge slots fitted to wings
- First flew on the 30th December 1936 with Dr.-Ing. Hermann Wurster at the controls
- Sent to Zürich in 1937 to take part in the Fourth International Flight Meeting from the 23rd July to 1st August 1937.
- Later used for C-series development programme

Camouflage & Markings
The only photo of this to come to light shows just the tail unit of this machine at Zürich, but it can be assumed that it carried the same markings as the V7, V8 & V9 and this includes those at

the Zürich event, with the entry number '4' on the fuselage sides.

Bf 109 V10a

W/Nr. 1010
Registration: D-IAKO
Same as the Bf 109B-2 Fieseler-built.
- The first flight of this machine probably took place in the Autumn of 1937, although some state it was the 1st November 1937.
- It was used by the Bavarian Aircraft Works (BFW) for various trials, including testing the MeP 6 propeller unit
- The remains (about 70%) of this machine were dug up at Oberpfaffenhofen in December 1989 and its restoration continues

Camouflage & Markings
This machine had the full operational scheme of RLM 70/71 in a splinter pattern applied to the upper surfaces and fuselage sides, plus

This image claims to show the Bf 109 V10a (D-IAKO), although there are no identifying marks to confirm this

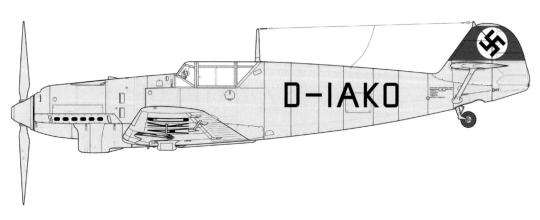

Bf 109 V10a
W/Nr. 1010

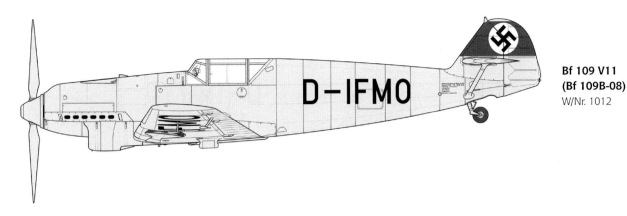

Bf 109 V11
(Bf 109B-08)
W/Nr. 1012

RLM 65 on all the undersides, with the demarcation between the upper and lower colours low on the fuselage sides. The swastika was applied on a white disc over the red band put across the fin/rudder units and the registration (D-AIKO) was applied in black on either fuselage side (facing forward on the starboard side and aft on the port) and above and below the wings. No other markings were applied and the spinner and propeller blades seem to be in RLM 70. When the remains were dug up, however, that airframe was devoid of any traces of paint, so it seems in later life when used for instructional purposes all colour and markings were removed.

Bf 109 V11 (Bf 109B-08)

W/Nr. 1012
Registration: D-IFMO
Same as the Bf 109 V10 except:
- MG 17 machine-guns above engine
- Revi C/12 B gunsight
- Access panels for wing armament added
- One MG 17 machine-gun in each wing, mid-span
- Short wing leading-edge slots installed
- Some state that later this machine was used to test DB 600 installation for the D-series (unconfirmed)
- First flew on the 1st March 1937

Camouflage & Markings
No photos of this machine exist (the one that claims to be this machine in fact shows the V13 or V14 heavily retouched), but it is safe to as-

sume that at this stage it too would have received the same C&M as all the previous V-series (e.g. RLM 02 [glossy] overall).

Claimed by many in the past to show the V11, this image is in fact a heavily retouched image of the V13 or V14

Bf 109 V12 (Bf 109B-09)

W/Nr. 1016
Registration: D-IVRU
Same as the Bf 109 V11 except:
- MG FF/A cannon in place of MG 17 in each wing (some state in the port wing only, with the MG 17 remaining in the starboard?). Later these were replaced with MG 17s
- First flown by Fritz Wendel on the 13th March 1937

Camouflage & Markings
No photos of this machine exist, but it can be assume that at this stage it would have received the same C&M as noted for the V11.

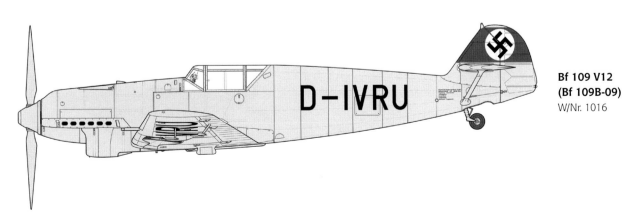

Bf 109 V12
(Bf 109B-09)
W/Nr. 1016

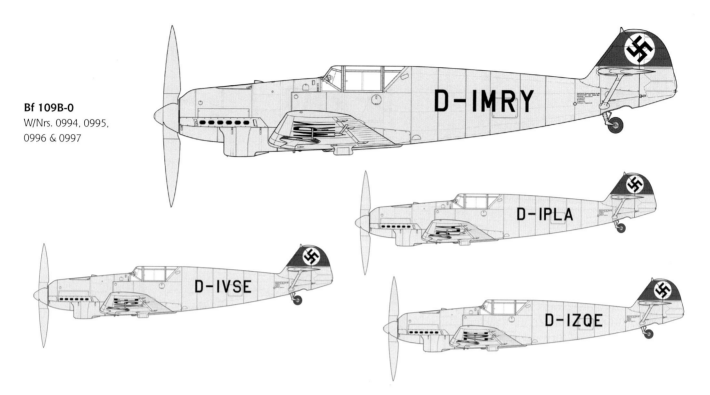

Bf 109B-0
W/Nrs. 0994, 0995,
0996 & 0997

A very atmospheric shot of the nose and propeller of a Bf 109B

Bf 109B-0 Pre-production

Note – For camouflage and markings details of this pre-production series please see Chapter 7.

Bf 109B-0

W/Nrs. 0994, 0995, 0996 & 0997
Registrations: D-IMRY, D-IPLA, D-IVSE and D-IZQE
Same as the Bf 109 V4 except:
- Luggage space aft of cockpit, with access through hatch in upper/rear decking in cockpit
- No radio or aerial mast/leads

Bf 109B Production

Note – For camouflage and markings details of these production series machines please see Chapter 7.

Bf 109B-1

Known W/Nr. 1000, 1001, 1002, 1003, 1004, 1005, 1006, 1007, 1008, 1009 and 1013 (in the range 0998 to 1064 allocated to the B-1 and prototypes built/converted from B-1s)
Registrations: D-IMTY, D-IPSA, D-IQMU, D-IVTO, D-ILZY, D-IJFY, D-IBLE, D-IHDU, D-IYTY, D-IOMY & D-IMSY
Note – There is no photographic evidence to prove if armament was or was not fitted to any of the above listed machines.
Same as the Bf 109B-0 except:
- No windscreen/gundsight heating
- FuG VII radio with triple wire to top of fin and tailplane edges – note machines used in Spain dispensed with radio equipment, so no mast or wires fitted

Period publicity shot of a Bf 109B in flight

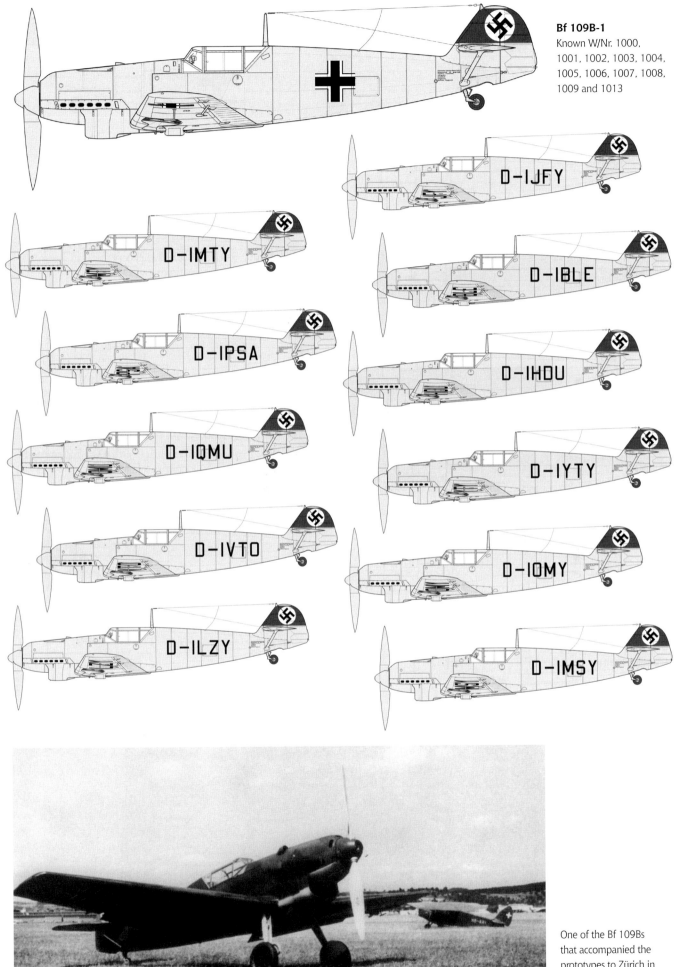

Bf 109B-1
Known W/Nr. 1000,
1001, 1002, 1003, 1004,
1005, 1006, 1007, 1008,
1009 and 1013

D-IJFY

D-IMTY

D-IBLE

D-IPSA

D-IHDU

D-IQMU

D-IYTY

D-IVTO

D-IOMY

D-ILZY

D-IMSY

One of the Bf 109Bs
that accompanied the
prototypes to Zürich in
1937

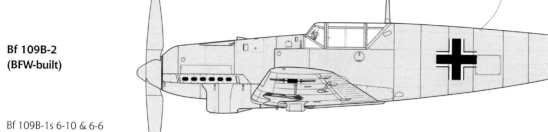

**Bf 109B-2
(BFW-built)**

Bf 109B-1s 6-10 & 6-6
of 1.J/88 at Escraton in
1937
(© via J. Grant)

Bf 109B-2 (BFW-built)

Same as the Bf 109B-0 except:
- No windscreen/gunsight heating
- FuG VIIa radio with single wire to top of fin
- Short wing leading-edge slots
- Single ventilation outlet aft of the main
  engine cowl, on each fuselage side

Bf 109 B-2 (Fieseler-built)

Same as the Bf 109B-2 (BFW-built) except:
- Stamped-out ventilation holes (created a
  depression, not a hole in the cowling)
- Two ventilation outlets aft of the main engine
  cowling on either fuselage side
- VDM two-blade, variable-pitch metal
  propeller

Bf 109B-2s 6•26 & 6•27,
1.J/88 in 1937, displaying
what must be RLM 70/71,
as the contrast is not high
enough for an RLM 02/71
scheme?
(© via J. Grant)

**Bf 109 B-2
(Fieseler-built)**

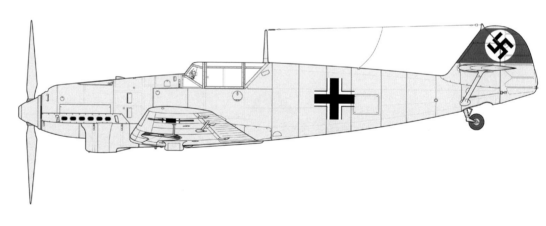

A Bf 109B called 'Luchs'
from J/88 that was flown
by Fw Werner Mölders

**Bf 109 B-2
(Fieseler-built)**
Late production

**Bf 109 B-2
(Erla-built)**

The first Bf 109 to fall
into enemy hands was
6-15, seen here just after
capture by Republication
Forces in Spain
(© via J. Grant)

Bf 109 B-2 (Fieseler-built) – Late production

Same as the Bf 109B-2 (Fieseler-built) except:
• The upper ventilation outlet of the pair on the fuselage side, aft of the main engine cowling, was moved up and, in some instances, also moved forward

Bf 109 B-2 (Erla-built)

Same as the Bf 109B-2 (Fieseler-built, late production) except:
• Ventilation holes cut out (oblong) in top/front of engine cowling

This Bf 109B-2 (D-IEKS,
W/Nr.0320) is often
misquoted as being a
prototype

Bf 109B-1 Specifications	
Span	9.87m
Length	8.55m
Height	2.45m
Weight	(Empty) 1,505kg, (Loaded) 2,150kg
Range	690km
Maximum Speed	465km/h at 4,000m
Cruising Speed	350km/h at 2,500m
Service Ceiling	8,200m

Chapter 3: Bf 109C & D Series

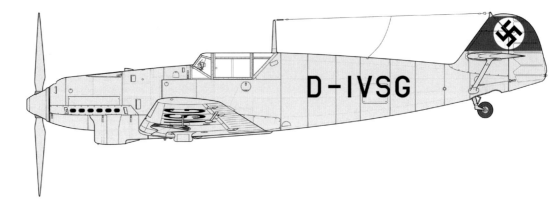

**Bf 109 V19
(Bf 109C-0)**
W/Nr. 1720

A Bf 109C with the Stammkennzeichen VE+LL applied is seen here in Germany in the late 1930s

As production of these two series was extremely limited we will cover both together in this chapter.

Bf 109C Pre-production

Note – The Bf 109 V8 (W/Nr. 882, D-IMQE), V9 (W/Nr. 883, D-IPLU) and V10 (W/Nr. 884, D-IXZA) were all used in conjunction with what became the C-series when they were fitted with the Jumo 210Ga engine, but they really always remained B-series airframes so see the entries in the previous chapter for these three machines.

Bf 109 V19 (Bf 109C-0)

W/Nr. 1720
Registration: D-IVSG
Same as the Bf 109B-2 Fieseler-built, late production except:
• Jumo 201G
• Gun access panels on upper wings

• MG 17 machine-gun, one each wing, mid-span

Camouflage & Markings
It is presumed that this machine was in the same scheme seen on the V18

Bf 109 V18 (Bf 109C-0)

W/Nr. 1731
Registration: D-ISDH
Same as the Bf 109B-2 Fieseler-built, late production except:
• Jumo 201G
• Access panels on upper wings
• MG 17 machine-gun, one each wing, mid-span

Camouflage & Markings
This machine was in the standard scheme of RLM 70/71 over 65 with the demarcation of these colours low on the fuselage sides. The swastika was applied on a white disc within the red band that went across the vertical fin and rudder and the registration was applied in black on the fuselage sides and under the wings, with it read as D-I under the starboard and SDH under the port. No crosses were applied to the fuselage or under the wings, and we have not found an image that shows the upper surface of the wings, so cannot confirm if a Type B1 cross was applied?

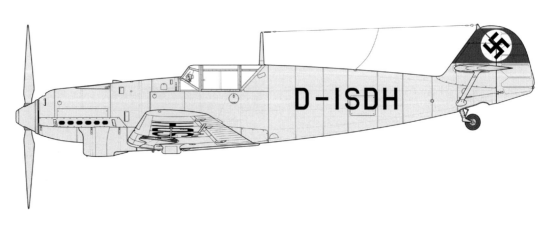

**Bf 109 V18
(Bf 109C-0)**
W/Nr. 1731

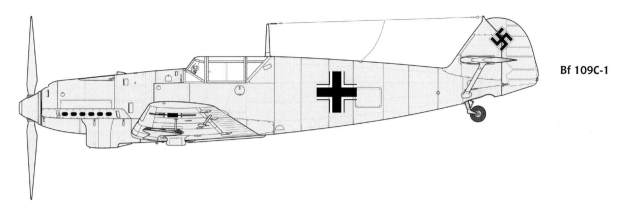

Bf 109C-1

Bf 109C Production

Note – For camouflage and markings details of this production series please see Chapter 7.

Bf 109C-1

Same as the Bf 109B-2 Fieseler-built, late production except:
- Jumo 201G
- Gun access panels on upper wings
- MG 17 machine-gun, one each wing, mid-span
- Production undertaken entirely at Messerschmitt's Augsburg factory
- Production total not known, but thought to be fewer than 60
- First five sent to Spain for operational evaluation with *Jagdgruppe* 88 (marked 6•46 to 6•50)

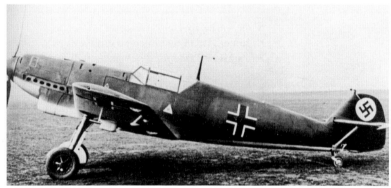

above right: This Bf 109C-1 was operated by 1.J/88 Legion Condor in Spain and carried the codes 6•49 – note 'Jaguar' painted on the nose
(© via J. Grant)

This side shot of a C may well actually show the V18 or V19, with the image modified to remove any codes etc. in an attempt to pass it off as a 'production' machine
(© via J. Grant)

Here armourers are seen at work re-arming a Bf 109C. The wing-gun access panel is up and you can see how the access panel for the engine spark plugs was used to rest the mid-upper cowling on

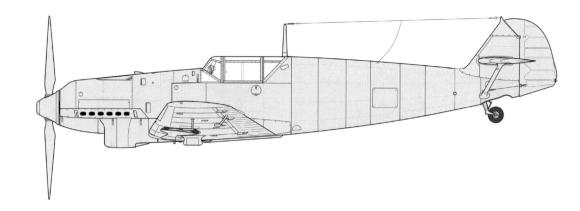

Bf 109C-2

A Bf 109C-2 taking off,
circa 1937
(© via J. Grant)

- wing at mid-span
- It is not known if any C-3s were used operationally by the Luftwaffe

Bf 109C-4

Same as the Bf 109C-1 except:
- MG FF/A fitted between engine cylinder blocks, firing through propeller hub
- Never placed into series production

Bf 109C-2

Same as the Bf 109C-1 except:
- Jumo 210Ga fuel-injected engine
- 1x MG 17 mounted between engine cylinder blocks firing through propeller hub
- Never placed into series production

Bf 109C-3 (Converted from C-1)

Same as the Bf 109C-1 except:
- 2x MG FF/A replaced MG 17s, one in each

A Bf 109C or D seen in the company of Luftwaffe high-ranking officers with He 51s and Ar 95s in the background

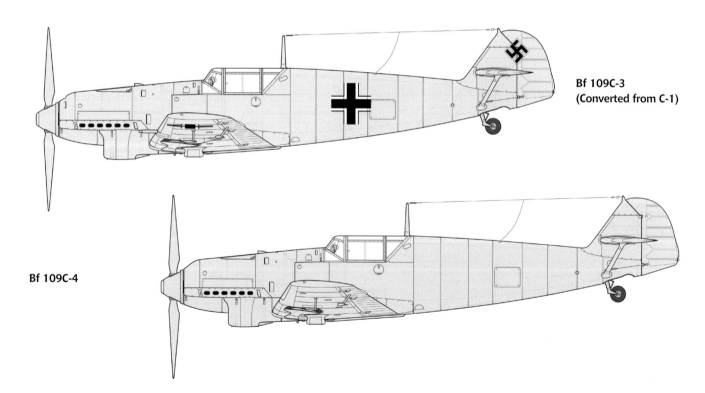

**Bf 109C-3
(Converted from C-1)**

Bf 109C-4

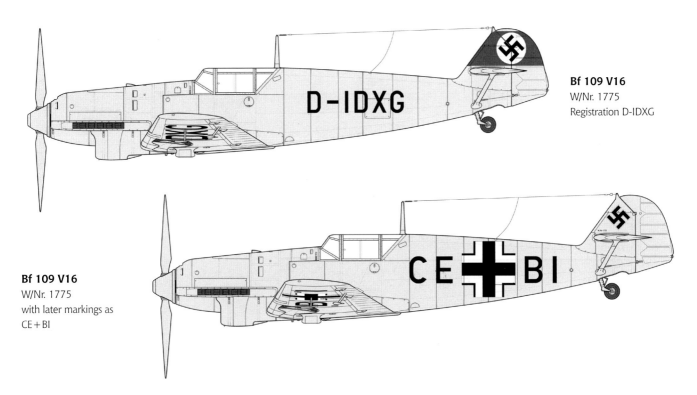

Bf 109 V16
W/Nr. 1775
Registration D-IDXG

Bf 109 V16
W/Nr. 1775
with later markings as
CE + BI

Bf 109D Production

Note – For camouflage and markings details of this production series please see Chapter 7.

Bf 109 V16

W/Nr. 1775
Registration D-IDXG (later became CE + BI)
Same as the Bf 109D-1 except:
- Jumo 210Da engine
- Machine-gun troughs blanked over
- No gunsight
- Lower ventilation outlet moved up and forward
- Unarmed wings
- Exhaust stacks similar to DB 601 system and fitted with anti-glare shields

Note – Although we list the V16 here in relation to the D-series, it was never officially listed as a prototype for that series, even though it had many of the attributes of the type.

Hptm. Werner Mölders'
Bf 109D-1, 6•79, 'Luchs',
3.J/88, July 1938
(© via J. Grant)

This Bf 109D has the name 'Cissy' applied as well as a cockerel emblem – location/unit unknown

We found this photo on the Internet and it is included because it may well be an image of the Bf 109 V16 in its later markings of CE + BI. The 'L' by the cockpit may indicate this is CE + BL, but that was an E-series prototype and this machine is definitely Jumo-powered

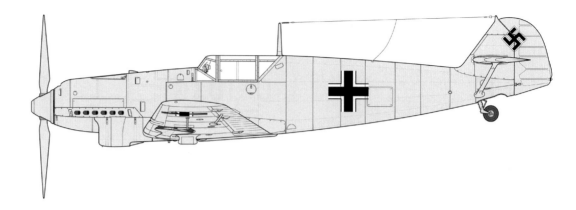

Bf 109D-1
W/Nr. 0417 to 0539
range

The '51' painted on
this machine probably
identifies this as a D-1
built by Erla (W/Nr.0451).
The scheme and markings
are factory-fresh and
typical of the era

Bf 109D-1, J-310
(W/Nr.2305) of
Fliegerkompanie 15,
Swiss Air Force, circa
1939
(© via J. Grant)

Bf 109D-1

W/Nr. 0417 to 0539 range
Same as the Bf 109C-1 except:
- Jumo 210D engine
- External exhaust stacks
- 2x MG 17, one in each wing at mid-span

- 'Universal' wing allowing light (MG 17) or heavy (MG FF) armament
- Production undertaken by Erla at Leipzig
- Total production unknown
- Six sent to Spain for operational evaluation with *Jagdgruppe* 88 (marked 6•51 to 6•56)
- Type superseded by E-series so offered for export – 10 supplied to Switzerland in January 1939 (J-301 to J-310)

Bf 109D-1 (Last production series)

Same as the Bf 109D-1 except:
- Jumo 210Da engine
- Exhaust stacks similar to DB 601 exhaust system
- Lower ventilation outlet moved up and forward

**Bf 109D-1
(Last production
series)**

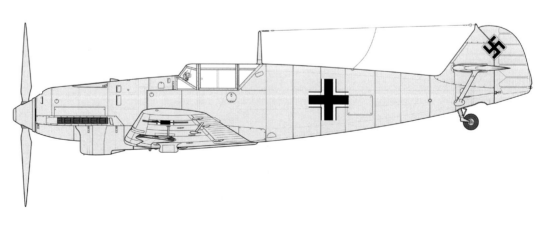

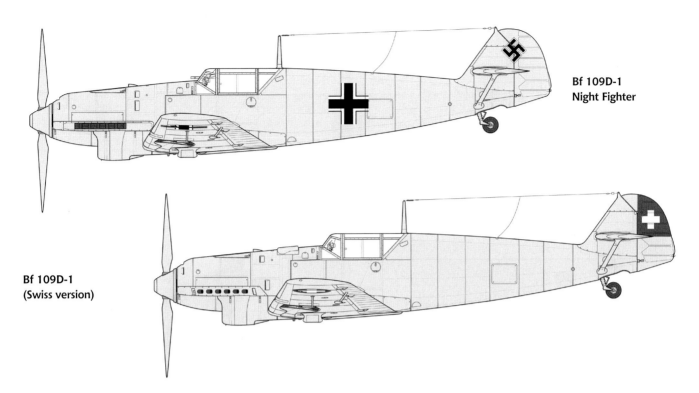

**Bf 109D-1
Night Fighter**

**Bf 109D-1
(Swiss version)**

Bf 109D-1 Night Fighter

Same as the Bf 109D-1 (Last production series)
except:
- *Abshußrohr* telescopic gunsight
- Anti-glare exhaust shield

Bf 109D-1 (Swiss version)

Same as the Bf 109D-1 except:
- MG 29 machine-guns above engine
- Bulged MG cowling

A factory-fresh line-up,
including Bf 109D-1
FO + QU seen here
outside the Fieseler plant
where they were built

- Wild R-VI gunsight
- Lorenz FGVII radio and mast
- MG29 machine-gun, one in each wing,
  mid-span

This Bf 109D-1 is seen
here in use by a training
unit once withdrawn
from frontline service.
The aircraft carries a fleet
number '16' on the aft
fuselage band (yellow),
and this blots out part
of the radio call-sign,
however the way these
were handed means
that another shot of this
machine from the other
side tells us it was VA + ER

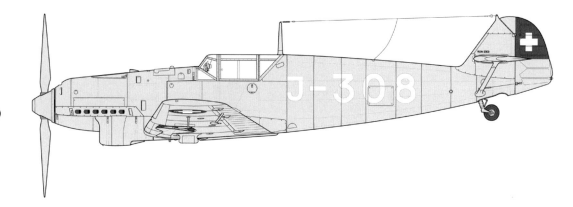

Bf 109D-1
(Swiss version J-308)
W/Nr. 2303

Bf 109D-1, 6-86 of 1.J/88 in 1938, this was the last D
delivered to the Condor Legion
(© via J. Grant)

Found on the Internet,
this image is included
because it shows how
these early machines
moved to training units
and were repainted in
accordance with the then-
new regulations.
This Bf 109D-1 (W/Nr.
2576) came from
Jagdfliegerschule 3 and
crash-landed in Norway
on the 29th January 1942

Bf 109D-1 (Swiss version J-308)

W/Nr. 2303
Same as the Bf 109D-1 (Swiss version) except:
* Bulged MG cowling differed from those seen
  on other Swiss Doras

*Note – It has been mentioned over the years since the
end of WWII that other D-series machines existed,
with the D-0, D-2 and D-3 often being quoted. No
evidence can be found to support this, although some
may assume that the D-2 and D-3 were just C-2 and
C-3s with a return to the Jumo 210Da engine?*

Bf 109C and Bf 109D Specifications	
Span	9.87m [C-1 & D-1]
Length	8.55m [C-1 & D-1]
Height	2.45m [C-1 & D-1]
Weight	(Empty) 1,597kg [C-1], 1,630kg [D-1]
	(Loaded) 2,296kg [C-1], 2,106kg [D-1]
Range	652km [C-1], 690km [D-1]
Maximum Speed	420km/h at 4,500m [C-1],
	499km/h at 5,100m [D-1]
Cruising Speed	344km/h at 3,100m [C-1],
	350km/h at 2,500m [D-1]
Service Ceiling	8,400m [C-1], 8,100m [D-1]

Always a favourite, this
image has been seen
many times, both in
colour and mono. It
seems to be an unarmed
D, probably in use as a
hack or with a training
unit in the mid-war
period, as it has the grey
scheme introduced in
late 1941
(© via M. Payne)

Chapter 4: **Bf 109E Prototypes**

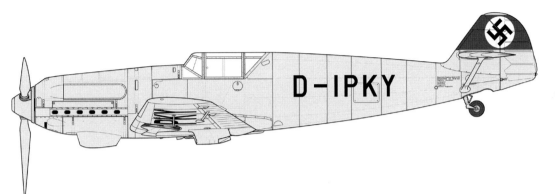

**Bf 109 V13
(Bf 109E-01)**
W/Nr. 1050

Bf 109E Prototypes

Note – Production machines are covered in chapter 5.

Bf 109 V13 (Bf 109E-01)

W/Nr. 1050
Registration: D-IPKY
- Previously Bf 109B-010 (*see Note below*)
- VDM three-blade variable-pitch metal propeller
- Long air intake fitted to port side of nose
- Two ventilation cut-outs can be seen on the dorsal cowling, aft of the main engine cowling and forward of the windscreen, with another further down on each side of this access panel
- DB 600A engine
- No armament was installed
- No gunsight
- Luggage space aft of the cockpit, with access via a door in the aft bulkhead within the cockpit
- No radio mast or lead
- Fuel filler cap below cockpit on port fuselage side
- Modified wings featuring SKF F456C coolant

radiator units under each
- Deeper oil cooler radiator under chin
- First flew on the 10th July 1937
- Won the Climb and Dive competition at the 1937 Zürich event

Note – This machine is often quoted as the B-010, and although initially it may have been intended as a

This close-up of the nose of the V13 shows how different they were from the eventual E-series production machines. The size and depth of the chin radiator is probably the most prominent element

The V13 seen here at the Zürich event taxiing out

Seen at the Zürich air races, the V13 shows off details such as the long supercharger intake on the port side of the nose, the revised undercarriage doors and, with the mid-cowl off, the lack of guns and mounts in this area are evident

B-series airframe it is unlikely it was ever completed as such, taking the role of an E-series prototype instead

Camouflage & Markings

This machine carried the same overall RLM 02 (glossy) scheme as seen on all previous prototypes. The swastika was applied to the white disc on the red tail, although in this instance the band was much wider, going from just above the tailplane to almost the top of the fin/rudder. The codes were applied in the smaller-sized characters to either side of the fuselage in black, with them under each wing in the larger size. No W/Nr. seems to have been applied to the rudder, and the spinner was RLM 02, with the blade front probably bare metal, with black rears. The panel directly around the exhaust outlets was painted black.

Bf 109 V13 (Record Attempt)

W/Nr. 1050
Registration: D-IPKY (unmarked for record)
- VDM three-blade variable-pitch metal propeller
- One-piece pointed spinner
- Two air scoops aft of the spinner on the upper engine cowling
- Fitted with special DB 601A (DB 601/III) engine
- Ventilation slots seen aft of the main engine cowling, on the dorsal spine to allow hot air to exit the engine bay
- No armament was fitted
- No gunsight
- Modified windscreen and canopy for better aerodynamics
- Luggage space retained aft of cockpit

Once the event at Zürich was over, the V13 was rebuilt into this form for an attempt on the World Air Speed record

Bf 109 V13 (Record Attempt)
W/Nr. 1050

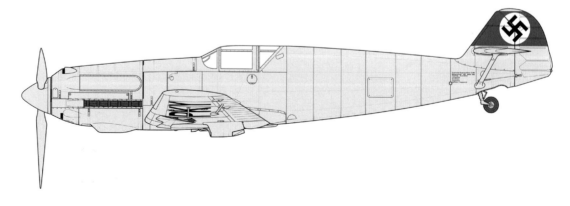

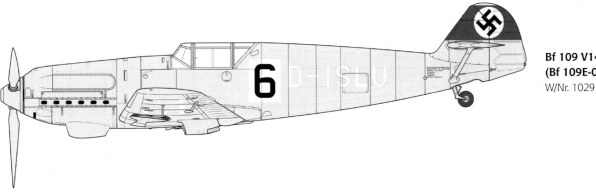

**Bf 109 V14
(Bf 109E-02)**
W/Nr. 1029

- No radio mast (behind cockpit or on fin top) or lead
- Fuel filler cap remained below cockpit on port side
- Retained the modified wings with the SKF F456C coolant radiators under each
- Long air intake on port side of cowling
- Revised longer, but more aerodynamic, oil cooler radiator under chin
- DB 601 ejector exhaust stacks
- Two ventilation hole cut-outs under the chin
- Took the World Air Speed Record in November 1937

Camouflage & Markings
This machine retained the glossy RLM 02 scheme for the record attempt, along with the red band, white disc and swastika on the tail, all the registration markings however were removed.

Bf 109 V14 (Bf 109E-02)

W/Nr. 1029
Registration: D-ISLU
Same as Bf 109 V13 (D-IPKY)
- First flight probably took place on the 28th April 1937

- Sent to Zürich in 1937 to take part in the Fourth International Flight Meeting from the 23rd July to 1st August 1937.
- This aircraft was crash-landed by *Generalmajor* Ernst Udet during the Zürich event

Camouflage & Markings
This machine is the well-known red example (for years thought to be dark blue), with a deep scarlet colour being applied overall in lieu of the RLM 02, including the spinner. A red band was applied across the fin/rudder with the edge thinly outlined in white and all the codes (fuselage and wings) were also done in white. A black race number '6' was applied on a white block forward of the fuselage registration, in the same manner as seen on the V7, V8 & V10.

This head-on view of the modified V13 shows how low and smooth its profile had been made – the wings seem to have the slats removed as well

The V14 seen at Zürich being prepared for flight – the overall glossy (red) scheme is evident even in this B&W image

An embarrassment we are sure, when Udet crash-landed the V14 the press took no mercy, as this excellent cartoon from a period newspaper shows!

- Modified wings with SKF F456C radiator under each (with horizontal bar across the middle of the front intake in these units)
- Armament access panel in upper wing
- Square air intake on port side of nose
- Deeper oil cooler
- Ejector exhaust stacks

Camouflage & Markings

This was one of the first true E-series prototypes and as such had the full operational scheme of RLM 70/71 in a splinter pattern on the upper surfaces and fuselage sides and RLM 65 underneath. The demarcation of the upper and lower colours was low down on the fuselage sides. The red band across the fin rudder with white disc and swastika had a thin outline of white and crosses were applied to the fuselage sides and upper and lower wings. These were B1 style with the narrow white/black edging and those on the wings were out towards the tips, running from the centre of the leading edge right back to, but not overlapping, the aileron hinge line. No registration was applied to fuselage or wings and there is no sign of the W/Nr. on the fin or rudder. The spinner is RLM 70 with the propeller blades bare metal on the front face and probably RLM 70 on the back. The entire nose is another solid colour, which initially looks like the yellow of the wartime Es, but in fact is supposed to be RLM 02. The wheel hubs are gloss black for the main wheels and RLM 02 for the tail wheel.

Bf 109 V15 (Bf 109E-03)

W/Nr. 1773
Registration: D-IPHR

- DB 601A engine
- VDM three-blade, variable-pitch metal propeller
- Armed with 2x MG 17 machine-guns over the engine, with small blisters at the rear of the engine cowling
- Revi C/12 C gunsight
- FuG VIIa radio mast and single wire to top of vertical fin
- Fuel filler cap moved to dorsal spine

**Bf 109 V15
(Bf 109E-03)**
W/Nr. 1773

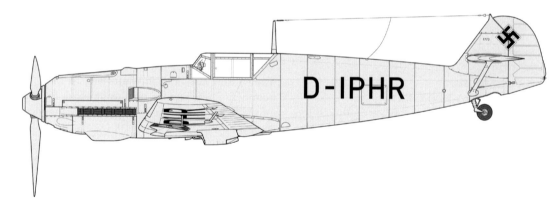

Having hit the wires of the tram-line, Udet crashed the V14 in a field near Thum and it obviously slewed round as it slid to a halt, twisting the rear fuselage round on itself

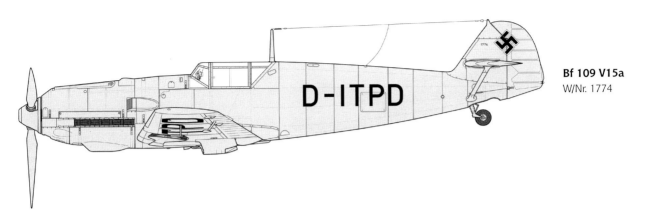

Bf 109 V15a
W/Nr. 1774

Bf 109 V15a

W/Nr. 1774
Registration: D-ITPD
Served as E-1 prototype
Same as Bf 109 V15 except:
- MG 17 machine-gun, one in each wing, mid-span

Camouflage & Markings
This machine carried the same colour and markings as the V15.

Bf 109 V17

There is much confusion about this machine, as over the years it has been listed as D-IYMS and/or D-IWKU. The former (D-IYMS) was a prototype for the T-series (see Chapter 6), it later carried the markings TK+HK and was a C-series airframe in most respects. D-IWKU was an E-3a (export) intended for the Yugoslavian Air Force. This aircraft crashed during its ferry flight in March 1940 near Regensburg and was totally written off. The registration had only been applied temporarily for the ferry flight and confirmation of all this data can be found in the excellent *'Les Messerschmitt Yougoslaves'* in the *Avions Hors* series published by Lela Presse in 2009. We can find no evidence to support the existence of the V17 at this time.

Bf 109 V19

W/Nr. 1797
Registration: D-IRTT (Later CE+BL)
- Prototype E-3 (probably converted from a

partially-built E-1 airframe)
- DB 601A engine
- Armed with 2x MG 17 machine-guns over the engine
- Two MG FF cannon, one in each wing
- Radio mast and single wire to top of vertical fin

Camouflage & Markings
This machine seems to have displayed a very unique scheme, in so far as it is believed to have been deep scarlet overall, except for the wings, which were cream with scalloped demarcation between themselves and the fuselage both on the upper and lower surfaces. The registration was applied in cream on the

The Bf 109 V19 ((D-IRTT) carried the outlandish cream and red scheme, it is no wonder it was dubbed the 'cockatoo'

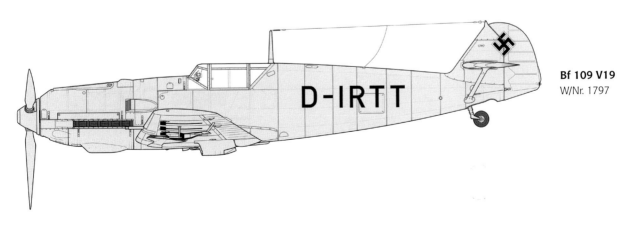

Bf 109 V19
W/Nr. 1797

Often quoted as the V17, this machine (D-IWKU) was in fact an E-3a (export) intended for the Yugoslavian Air Force, but it was lost in a crash-landing during a ferry flight in March 1940

fuselage sides and in scarlet above and below the wings. The undersides of the tailplanes were entirely in cream. It is not known if any other markings were applied, but it is assumed that the tail band (outlined in white or cream?) was there along with the white disc and swastika. Its brights colours led to this one being dubbed the 'cockatoo'.

- 2x MG FF, one in each wing
- Type did not have the engine-mounted MG FF as some claim (see Note)
- Radio mast and single wire to top of vertical fin

Note – Many claim this to be a prototype for the E-2 series, whilst others say it was an E-4, the W/Nr. puts it in the E-0 production batch, so it is most likely it is an E-0 and it was used for various trials, including towing – hence the claim it was an E-2 with the engine-mounted cannon, but the item projecting from the centre of the propeller hub is the towing pick-up!

Camouflage & Markings

A fine in-flight photograph of this machine proves that it wore the standard military scheme of RLM 70/71 in a splinter pattern over RLM 65, with the demarcation low on the fuselage sides. Type B1 crosses were applied to the wings, with the B2 version used on the fuselage sides. The *Stammkenzeichen* codes were applied in black characters either side of the fuselage cross, with CE forward on the port side and aft on the starboard. These codes were also applied under the wings, in larger black characters with CE under the starboard and BM under the port, read from the trailing edge looking forward. The swastika on the tail is probably H2, although it could be without the thin black edging making it a type H2a? With the fuel filler point now moved to the port dorsal spine, the accompanying fuel triangle can now be seen just below it. It is not possible to discern if the W/Nr. is applied either on the fin or rudder. What most of the in-flight images prove is that this machine had the troughs for the guns above the engine in bare metal, if not permanently, at least at the time the photos were taken! There are no photographs showing this machine marked as D-ICZH, so it is likely that if this marking was ever applied, it was only for an initial test flight.

The Bf 109 V20 (CE + BM) is often quoted as the prototype for the E-2 series, due to the tube projecting from the spinner, but this test machine was just involved in towing trials, and that tube is a cable pick-up

Bf 109 V20

W/Nr. 1779 (often mis-identified as W/Nr. 5601)
Registration: D-ICZH
Stammkenzeichen: CE+BM
- DB 601A engine
- Armed with 2x MG 17 machine-guns over the engine

Note – The V22 (W/Nr. 1800, D-IRRQ), V23 (W/Nr.1801, D-ISHN), V24 (W/Nr.1929, D-ITDH) and V25 (W/Nr.1930, D-IVKC) although all E-series prototypes, were in fact used for development of the F-series and as such are outside the scope of this book.

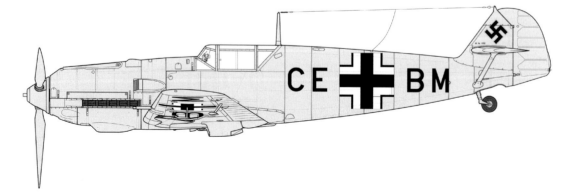

Bf 109 V20
W/Nr. 1779

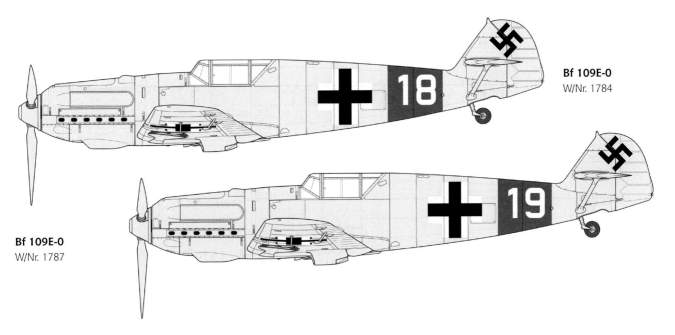

Bf 109E-0
W/Nr. 1784

Bf 109E-0
W/Nr. 1787

Bf 109E Pre-production

Bf 109E-0

W/Nr. 1784 & 1787
Registration None
- Machine-gun ports covered over
- No gunsight
- Fuel filler point moved to dorsal spine, aft of cockpit
- Small mast on top of vertical fin
- 'Universal' wing for light (MG 17) or heavy (MG FF) armament
- SFK F456C coolant radiator under each wing
- Production-style of oil cooler under chin

Camouflage & Markings
These are the two machines shown in the propaganda images claiming to be operational Bf 109s that were circulated before WWII. Both machines can be seen to be in a dark scheme that we assume is RLM 70/71 over 65, with large crosses as just white elements like the late-war B5 style applied to the fuselage and the standard B2 versions on the wings – neither are really this version, as their dimensions are all wrong, this was just for propaganda. The swastika on the tail is huge, covering all available space and it is of the H2 style. In one image the tail bands have been censored, but another in colour shows them to have a contrasting red band around the rear fuselage, on one (W/Nr.1787) the number '19' is applied in large white letters, with 18 on the other (W/Nr.1784). The spurious scheme is completed with a small crescent moon motif forward of the fuselage cross, this is only on the starboard side. The colour photos show that there are bands of what look to be shiny paint across the upper surfaces of the wings. We assume the outer ones are where the original crosses were over-painted, while the inner ones are restricted to the perimeter of the inner crosses, so we wonder if they are because the rest of the paint is water-based, whilst that under the markings had

to be permanent, leading to a different 'sheen'? Close examination of the colour images proves the identity of these machines, not just because of the intakes on the port side of the nose, but because on the very top of the vertical fin in very small white characters is '1784' and '1787' respectively! The spinners are red, the backplates remain RLM 70, as do the blades, and the only stencils we can confirm are the fuel filler triangle on the port fuselage dorsal spine, and the red wing walkway markings. It is interesting to note that in the colour photos the canopy framework and cockpit interior are all very dark, so they must be RLM 66. We are not sure if these aircraft ever carried (or had reapplied) a standard set of markings with their registrations etc., because to date no photographs have been found.

The two 'Phantom 109s', V-series machines masquerading as production 'in service' Bf 109Ds

This shot of one of the early E-0s, probably W/Nr. 1784 or 1787, does show how the cowling and radiator unit differed from this area seen on the V13 image shown earlier

Bf 109E-0
W/Nr. 1781

Bf 109E-0
W/Nr. 1783

Bf 109E-0

W/Nr. 1781 & 1783
Registration D-IECY and D-IBFD
Same as Bf 109E-0 W/Nrs.1784 and 1787
except:
• MG 17 machine-guns over the engine
• Revi C/12 C gunsight
• FuG VIIa radio with single lead to top of fin
*Note – Later both used for T-series development (see
Chapter 6).*

Camouflage & Markings
The only confirmed images of these machines
that do exist, both show them as prototypes
for the T-series, so we cannot assume that the
scheme applied by that stage was the one they
worn initially. There is a series of well-known
photos that show an, as yet unknown E-0,
and it is in a full operational scheme of RLM
70/71 in a splinter pattern applied to the upper
surfaces and fuselage sides, plus RLM 65 on all
the undersides, with the demarcation between
the upper and lower colours low on the fuselage sides. A swastika is applied on a white disc
over a red band across the fin/rudder unit. The

early style B1 crosses are applied to the fuselage
and above and below the wings, the position
of those on the wings being 3/4 span and they
do not look as if they overlap either aileron of
slats. No other markings are applied, but the
entire nose section is in yellow, while the spinner and propeller blades are RLM 70.

Bf 109E-0

W/Nr. N/K (See Note)
Same as Bf 109E-0 W/Nrs.1784 and 1787
except:
• MG 17 machine-guns over the engine
• Revi C/12 C gunsight
• FuG VIIa radio with single lead to top of fin
*Note – E-0 production ran from W/Nr.1781 to
1790, but photographic evidence only exists for the four
W/Nr. listed previously, so the above comments should
cover all the remaining pre-production airframes.*

Camouflage & Markings
These would all probably be in the same scheme
seen on the E-0s W/Nrs.1781 and 1783.

Bf 109E-0
W/Nr. N/K

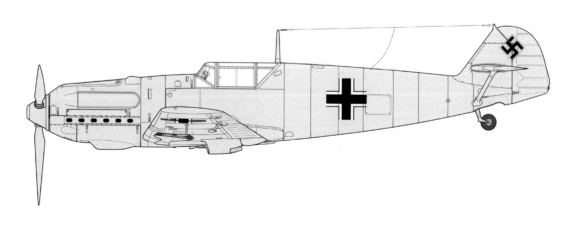

Chapter 5: **Bf 109E Production**

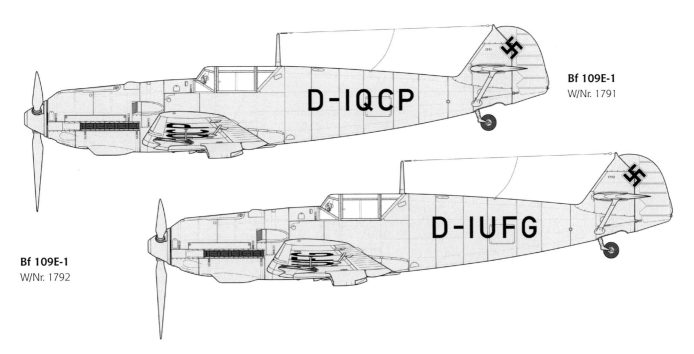

Bf 109E-1
W/Nr. 1791

Bf 109E-1
W/Nr. 1792

Bf 109E-1

W/Nr. 1791 & 1792
Registration D-IQCP and D-IUFG
Same as the Bf 109 V15a D-ITPD except:
- 2x MG 17, one in each wing
- Modified 'Universal' wing for light (MG 17) or heavy (MG FF) armament
- SKF F456C radiator under each wing

Bf 109E-1

W/Nr. In the range of 0666 to 0757 allocated to the E-1 series as a whole
Same as the Bf 109E-1 W/Nr.1791 & 1792

Bf 109E-1/B

W/Nr. In the range of 0666 to 0757 allocated to the E-1 series as a whole
- DB 601 engine with direct fuel-injection

- Modification from E-1
- 2x MG 17 above engine
- 2x MG 17, one in each wing
- Fighter-bomber modification fitted with ETC50 or ETC250 racks under fuselage centreline *(illustrated next page)*

A pilot of III./JG53 stands by his Bf 109E-1, of note is the very large white tactical number

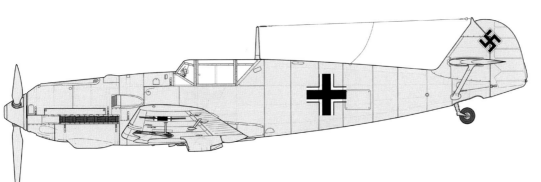

Bf 109E-1
W/Nr. In the range of 0666 to 0757

Bf 109E-1/B
W/Nr. In the range 0666 to 0757 (see previous page)

Bf 109E-1/U3
W/Nr. In the range 0666 to 0757

Bf 109E-1/U3

W/Nr. In the range of 0666 to 0757 allocated to the E-1 series as a whole

Same as the Bf 109E-1 except:
- Able to carry a 300lt drop tank on the centre-line rack
- Two Rb12.5/30 cameras in rear fuselage

Bf 109E-2

W/Nr. N/A
Same as the Bf 109E-1 except:
- 1x MG C/3 cannon mounted between cylinder blocks firing through propeller hub
- 2x MG FF/B cannon, one in each wing
- Never put into production

This shot possibly shows Bf 109E-3s during the Battle of France at Ferschweiler bei Trier landing ground
(©via M. Payne)

Bf 109E-2
W/Nr. N/A

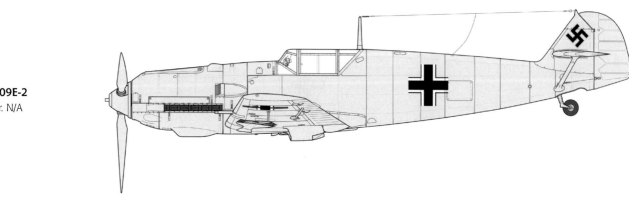

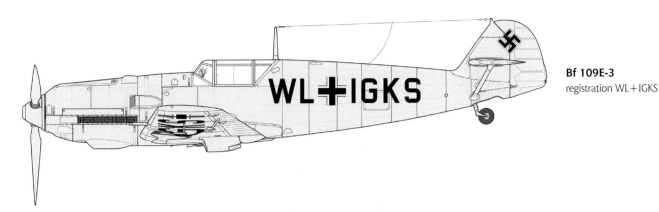

Bf 109E-3
registration WL+IGKS

Bf 109E-3

W/Nr. Unknown
Registration D-IGKS (later WL+IGKS)
Same as the Bf 109E-1 except:
- 2x MG FF/B cannon, one in each wing
- Little is known about this machine, it seems to be a production E-3 that was allocated to trials, hence the WL-prefixed codes. It is seen with the tail up in what looks like a firing butt and may be seen in the wind tunnel at Chalais Meudon? There seems to be a projection from the spinner that some think is a cannon (e.g. E-2 series), but we feel that this is just a pick-up for the tethers used to keep the aircraft steady.

Bf 109E-3

Same as the Bf 109E-1 except:
- 2x MG FF/B cannon, one in each wing.

WL+IGKS suspended in the wind tunnel, probably at Chalais Meudon

WL+IGKS, an E-3 made from an E-1 is seen here trestled and in front of what looks like a firing butt? The location looks high in the mountains in Germany (or Austria?) somewhere

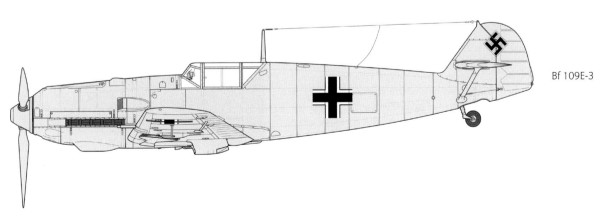

Bf 109E-3

The Bf 109 V26 carried the codes CA+NK and was used for the fighter-bomber modification trials. Here you can see a 500kg SC500 bomb under the fuselage and the rejection of this size of weapon is understandable when you look at how little ground clearance it had!

Bf 109 V26
W/Nr.1361

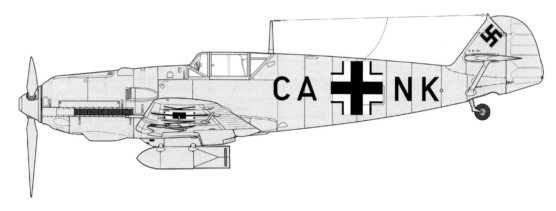

Bf 109E-3

W/Nr.1952
Stammkenzeichen: CE+BM
See Bf 109 V20 in Chapter 4 (*not illustrated*)

A Bf 109E-3 (W/Nr.3190) being rearmed by ground crew from 8./JG51

Bf 109 V26

W/Nr.1361
Stammkenzeichen: CA+NK
Same as the Bf 109E-1 except:
- Prototype for bomb-carry versions
- Centreline ETC500 bomb rack
- Tested SC500 and SC250 bombs as well as the SD250 fragmentation bomb

Camouflage & Markings
This machine was in a standard scheme of RLM 02/71/65 with the demarcation high on the fuselage side, from a point parallel with the bottom sill of the canopy. Type B2 crosses were applied above and below the wings and on either side of the fuselage. The codes were applied in black characters either side of the fuselage cross and under the wings. These latter markings were positioned to be read from the trailing edge looking forward with C+A under the starboard and N+K under the port. The underwing crosses did not overlap the aileron or flaps, but the 'A'

and 'N' went over the cannon bulges. A small Type H2 swastika was applied on the top of the vertical fin, with 'W/Nr.1361' in black characters below it, just above the leading edge of the tailplane. The spinner looks to be red and the propeller blades are RLM 70.

The Bf 109 V26 again, this time with the SC250 250kg bomb, a type that was accepted for use by the Bf 109E-series

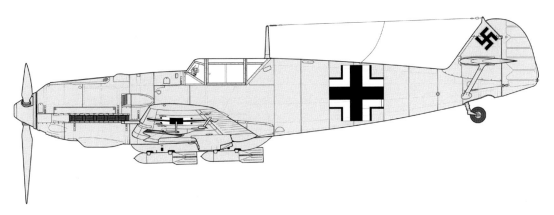

Bf 109E-3/B

The other type of bomb tested by the Bf 109 V26, as seen here, was the SD250 250kg fragmentation bomb

Bf 109E-3/B

Same as the Bf 109E-1 except:
- Centreline ETC50/VIII or ETC500 bomb rack

Bf 109E-3 (Swiss Version)

Same as the Bf 109E-1 except:
- DB 601Aa engine
- MG29 machine-guns over the engine
- The blisters seen at the rear of the upper engine cowling were deleted
- Small (long) blisters for MG29s added to upper cowling, forward of windscreen
- Revi 3C gunsight
- Lorenz FGVII radio with single lead to fin top
- Oerlikon MG FF/K cannon, one in each wing at mid-span

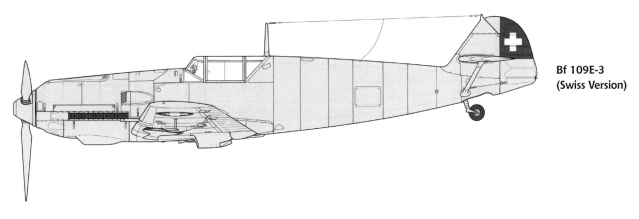

Bf 109E-3 (Swiss Version)

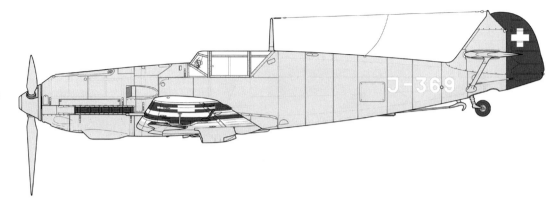

**Bf 109E-3
(Swiss Version – J-369)**
W/Nr.2442

Bf 109E-3 (Swiss Version – J-369)

W/Nr.2442
Same as the Bf 109E-3 (Swiss Version) except:
• Arrestor hook fitted under rear fuselage, forward of the tailwheel

Bf 109E-3 (Swiss Version – J-340)

J-340 'Super S.F.R' and J-378 'U-boot'
W/Nr.2198 and 2359
Same as the Bf 109E-3 (Swiss Version) except:
• Used for trials of long-range radio equipment
• Large mast added to starboard nose, forward of cockpit

The Swiss modified a couple of their Bf 109E-3s, where you can see J-340 the 'Super S.F.R' used for long-range radio equipment trials. The masts on the fuselage and extended one on the fin took the wires of the Lorenz FG IX

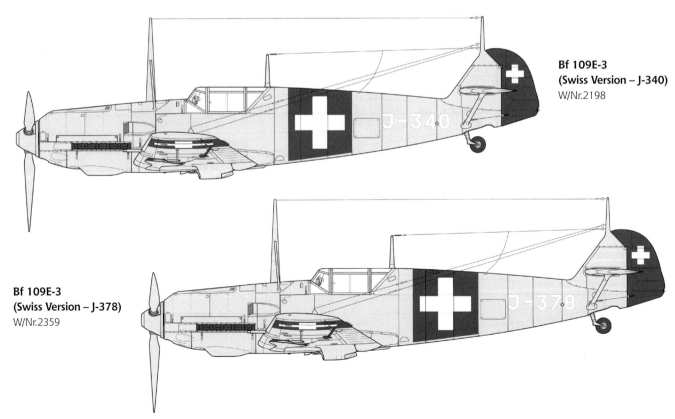

**Bf 109E-3
(Swiss Version – J-340)**
W/Nr.2198

**Bf 109E-3
(Swiss Version – J-378)**
W/Nr.2359

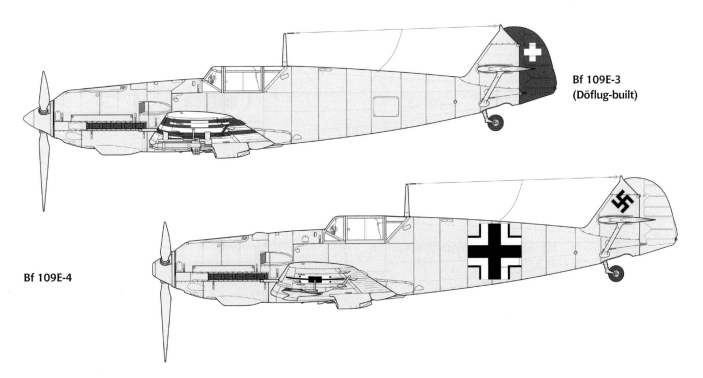

Bf 109E-3
(Döflug-built)

Bf 109E-4

- Extended mast on top of vertical fin
- Lorenz FG IX long-range radio wires from extended masts and from two points above each wing
- Type retained Lorenz FG VII radio mast and single lead to top of fin

Bf 109E-3 (Döflug-built)

Same as the Bf 109E-3 except:
- One-piece spinner
- DB 601A engine
- MG29 machine-guns above engine
- The blisters seen at the rear of the upper engine cowling were deleted
- Revised machine-gun access panel with small (long) blisters for MG29s, forward of windscreen

- EZ 42 gunsight
- Canopy-mounted head armour
- SIF 450 radio with single lead to fin top
- 50kg bomb racks under outer wing panels, could also be used for unguided rockets
- Oerlikon MG FF/K cannon, one in each wing at mid-span
- Escher Wyss EW.V6 three-blade, variable-pitch metal propeller

Bf 109E-4

Same as the Bf 109E-3 except:
- DB 601Aa engine
- Revi C/12 D gunsight
- 2x MG FF/M cannon, one in each wing
- Main canopy squared off and fitted with armoured headrest

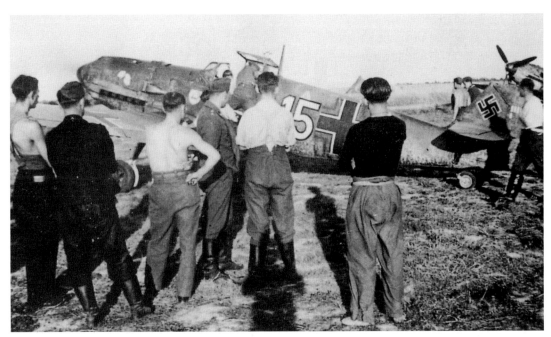

A Bf 109E-4 probably flown by Fw Werner Machold of 1./JG2 based at Beaumont-le-Roger early in the Battle of Britain. The speckled camouflage and the slight-overpainted cross was common on JG2 machines
(© via M. Payne)

**Bf 109E-4
Doppelreiter**
W/Nr. 2574

Bf 109E-4 Doppelreiter

W/Nr. 2574
Stammkenzeichen: CI + EJ
Same as the Bf 109E-4 except:
- Fitted with DB 601N engine with its 96 to 100 octane C3 fuel
- Experimentally fitted with overwing fuel tanks (*Doppelreiter*)

Bf 109E-4 Trop

Same as the Bf 109E-4 except:
- Blunt spinner cap

- Air intake with tropical dust filter
- Tropical equipment in aft fuselage comprising First Aid kit, water, food and Mauser 98K rifle
- Could carry a 300lt drop tank on the centre-line rack

Bf 109E-4/B

Same as the Bf 109E-4 except:
- Fighter-bomber modification fitted with ETC50/VIII or ETC500 racks under fuselage centreline

A Bf 109E-4 Trop of 1./JG27 seen flying over the North African desert in 1942. The white band around the rear fuselage was a theatre marking for the North African campaign
(*© via M. Payne*)

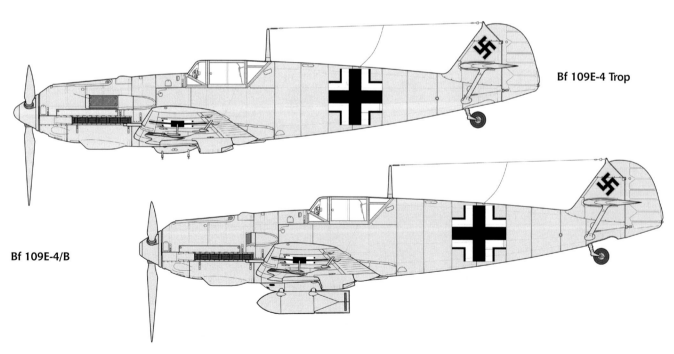

Bf 109E-4 Trop

Bf 109E-4/B

Either a Bf 109E-4B or E-7B of 5./LG2 is seen with an ETC 50 rack under the fuselage containing four 50kg bombs
(© via M. Payne)

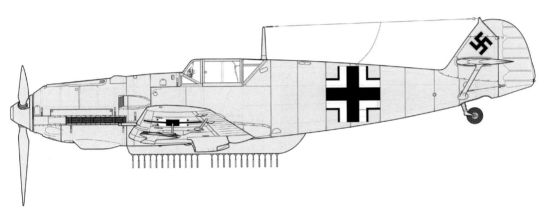

Bf 109E-4/B with SD2

A Bf 109E-4b with the standard 250kg SC250 bomb on the centreline rack. This machine was operated by 4./LG2
(© via M. Payne)

Bf 109E-4/B with SD2

Same as the Bf 109E-4/B except:
- Centreline rack for 96x SD2 'butterfly' fragmentation anti-personnel mines

Bf 109E-4/N

Same as the Bf 109E-3 except:
- Fitted with DB 601N engine with its 96 to 100 octane C3 fuel
- Revi C/12 D gunsight
- 2x MG FF/M cannon, one in each wing
- Main canopy squared-off and fitted with armoured headrest

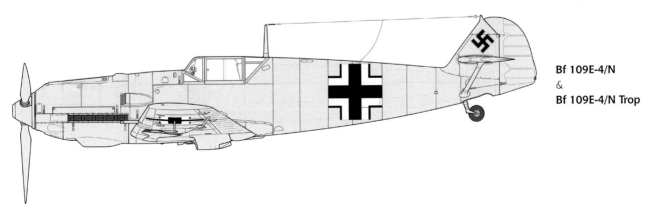

Bf 109E-4/N
&
Bf 109E-4/N Trop

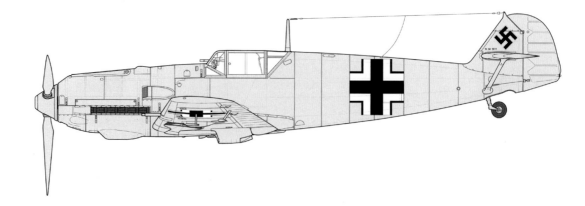

Bf 109E-4/N
(ZFR-4 tests)

Bf 109E-4, W/Nr.1480
flown by Oblt Franz von
Werra, II./JG3 that was
shot down and crash-
landed near Marden on
the 5th September 1940
(© via M. Payne)

Bf 109E-4/N (ZFR-4 tests)

W/Nr. 5819
Same as the Bf 109E-3 except:
• Fitted with DB 601N engine with its 96 to
  100 octane C3 fuel
• Tested the ZFR-4 telescopic gunsight

Bf 109E-4/N Trop

Same as the Bf 109E-4 except:
• Fitted with DB 601N engine with its 96 to
  100 octane C3 fuel
• Blunt spinner cap
• Air intake with tropical dust filter
• Tropical equipment in aft fuselage comprising
  First Aid kit, water, food and Mauser 98K rifle
• Could carry a 300lt drop tank on the centre-
  line rack *(illustrated previous page)*

Bf 109E-5

Type – Reconnaissance Fighter
Same as the Bf 109E-1 except:
• DB 601A-1 engine
• Blunt spinner cap
• Revi C/12D gunsight
• Main canopy squared-off and fitted with
  head-armour plate
• Could carry a 300lt drop tank on the centre-
  line rack

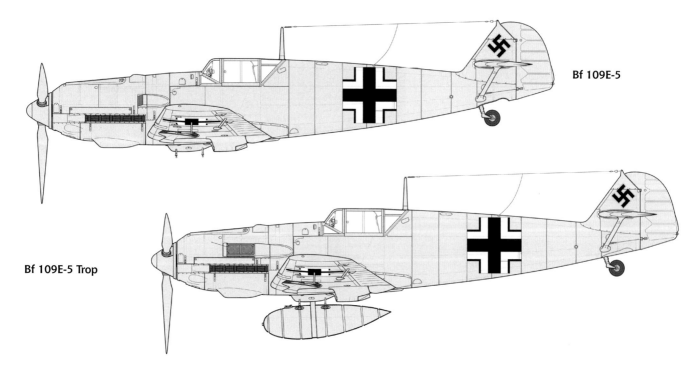

Bf 109E-5

Bf 109E-5 Trop

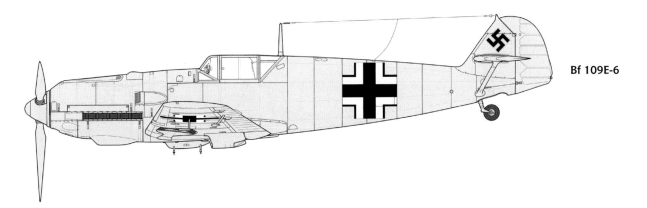

Bf 109E-6

Bf 109E-5 Trop

Type – Reconnaissance Fighter
Same as the Bf 109E-1 except:
- DB 601A-1 engine with direct fuel-injection
- 2x MG 17 above engine
- 2x MG 17, one in each wing
- Rb 21/18 camera mounted in rear fuselage
- Main canopy squared off
- Fitted with equipment for operation in a desert environment, such as supercharger air intake dust filter and survival equipment in the rear fuselage

Note – There is some doubt that the E-5 Trop ever existed, but we cannot prove one way or the other, so have included it?

Bf 109E-6

Type – Reconnaissance Fighter
Same as the Bf 109E-5:
- Fitted with DB 601N engine with its 96 to 100 octane C3 fuel
- Blunt spinner cap
- Revi C/12D gunsight

- Main canopy squared off and fitted with head-armour plate
- Could carry a 300lt drop tank on the centre-line rack
- Hand-held camera in cockpit

Bf 109E-7

Type – Long-range Fighter or Fighter-bomber
Same as the Bf 109E-4 except:
- Blunt spinner cap
- Able to carry 1x 300lt drop tank under fuselage centreline
- Could be fitted with either ETC50/VIII or ETC500 racks under fuselage centreline

Bf 109E-7/B

Type – Long-range Fighter-bomber
Same as the Bf 109E-7 except:
- Could be fitted with either ETC50/VIII or ETC500 racks under fuselage centreline

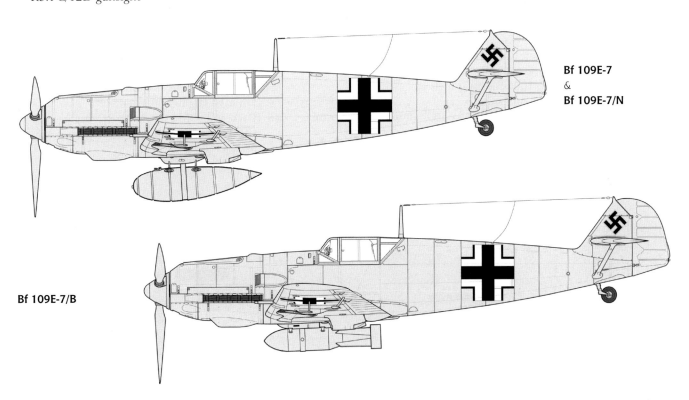

Bf 109E-7
&
Bf 109E-7/N

Bf 109E-7/B

A Bf 109E-7 of 8./JG27
seen in Romania in April
1941. This machine
has the yellow bands
and wing tips that were
applied in the Balkans
campaign
(© via M. Payne)

Bf 109E-7 Trop
&
Bf 109E-7/N Trop

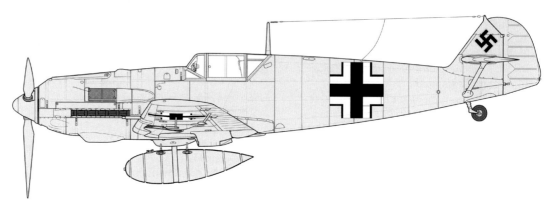

Bf 109E-7 Trop

Type – Long-range Fighter or Fighter-bomber
Same as the Bf 109E-4 Trop except:
• Able to carry 1x 300lt drop tank under
  fuselage centreline

Bf 109E-7/N

Type – Long-range Fighter or Fighter-bomber
Same as the Bf 109E-4 except:
• Fitted with DB 601N engine with its 96 to
  100 octane C3 fuel
• Blunt spinner cap
• Able to carry 1x 300lt drop tank under fuse-
  lage centreline
• Could be fitted with either ETC50/VIII or
  ETC500 racks under fuselage centreline
  (illustrated previous page)

Bf 109E-7/N Trop

Type – Long-range Fighter or Fighter-bomber
Same as the Bf 109E-4 Trop except:
• Fitted with DB 601N engine with its 96 to
  100 octane C3 fuel
• Able to carry 1x 300lt drop tank under
  fuselage centreline

Bf 109E-7Z

Type – Long-range Fighter or Fighter-bomber
Same as the Bf 109E-7 except:
• DB 601A engine
• Fitted with GM1 power boost system,
  resulting in two oval access panels in port
  fuselage side

Bf 109E-7Z

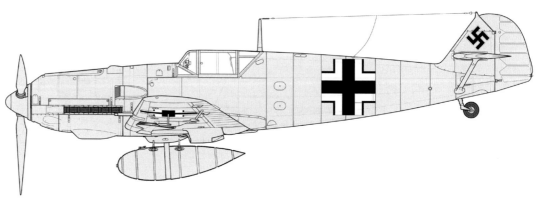

Bf 109E-7Z Trop

Bf 109E-8

Bf 109E-7Z Trop

Type – Long-range Fighter or Fighter-bomber
Same as the Bf 109E-4 Trop except:
- DB 601A engine
- Fitted with GM1 power boost system, resulting in two oval access panels in port fuselage side
- Able to carry 1x 300lt drop tank under fuselage centreline

Bf 109E-8

Type – Long-range Fighter
Same as the Bf 109E-5 & E-6 except:
- Fitted with DB 601N engine with its 96 to 100 octane C3 fuel
- Able to carry 1x 300lt drop tank under fuselage centreline

Bf 109E-8 with skis

W/Nr.: Unknown
Same as the Bf 109E-8 except

- Fitted with the older style propeller spinner within the cap installed
- External armoured glass fitted to windscreen
- Tail wheel replaced with ski
- Undercarriage replaced with non-retractable Schneekufen skis – wheel wells temporarily covered over

This Bf 109E-8 was delivered to the Heine Company and experimentally fitted with skis

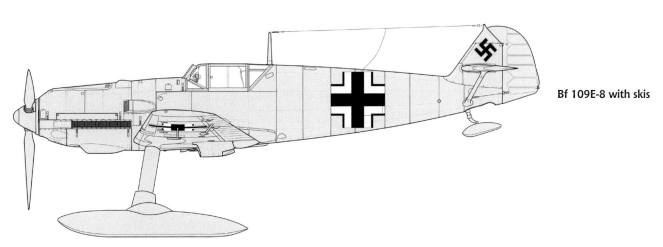

Bf 109E-8 with skis

A nice line-up of new Bf 109E-9s prior to delivery to JG2

Bf 109E-9
&
Bf 109E-9/N
&
Bf 109E-9/N Trop

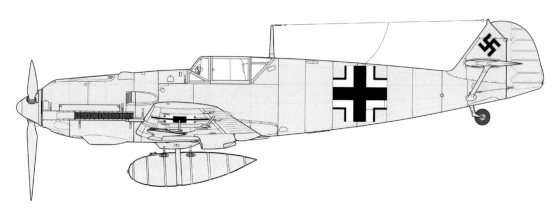

Bf 109E-9

Type – Long-range Reconnaissance Fighter
Same as the Bf 109E-7 except:
• Rb 50/30 camera in rear fuselage

Bf 109E-9/N

Type – Long-range Reconnaissance Fighter
Same as the Bf 109E-7 except:
• Fitted with DB 601N engine with its 96 to 100 octane C3 fuel
• Rb 50/30 camera in rear fuselage

Bf 109E-9 Trop

Type – Long-range Reconnaissance Fighter
Same as the Bf 109E-7 except:
• Rb 50/30 camera in rear fuselage

Bf 109E-9/N Trop

Type – Long-range Reconnaissance Fighter
Same as the Bf 109E-7 except:
• Fitted with DB 601N engine with its 96 to 100 octane C3 fuel
• Rb 50/30 camera in rear fuselage

Bf 109E-3 Specifications	
Span	9.90m [E-3]
Length	8.80m [E-3]
Height	2.50m [E-3]
Weight	(Empty) 2,037kg [E-3], (Loaded) 2,586kg [E-3]
Range	660km [E-3]
Maximum Speed	555km/h at 5,960m [E-3]
Cruising Speed	480km/h at 4,000m [E-3]
Service Ceiling	10,500m [E-3]

Bf 109E-9 Trop

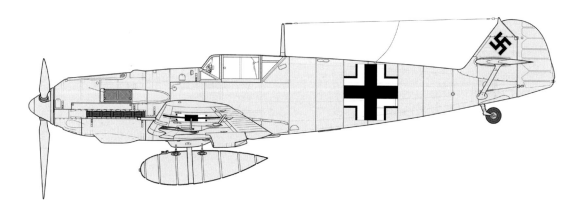

Chapter 6: Bf 109 T-series, Projects and One-off Conversions

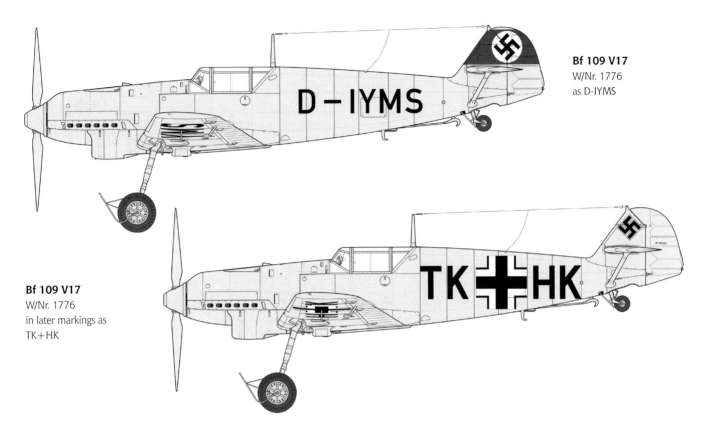

Bf 109 V17
W/Nr. 1776
as D-IYMS

Bf 109 V17
W/Nr. 1776
in later markings as
TK+HK

T-Series

Bf 109 V17

W/Nr. 1776
Registration D-IYMS (later TK+HK)
Same as the Bf 109 C-1 except:
- No ventilation holes in to top/front of cowling
- Jumo 210Da engine
- External ejector exhaust stacks
- Undercarriage locked in down position, doors removed, tubing protectors to main wheels
- Catapult spigots
- Arrestor hook
- Tubular protector ahead of tailwheel unit

Camouflage & Markings
This machine had the then standard scheme of RLM 70 *Schwarzgrün* (black-green) and RLM 71 *Dunkelgrün* (dark green) in a splinter camouflage pattern on the upper surfaces, and RLM 65 *Hellblau* (light blue) underneath. The swastika was applied to a white disc on the red band that ran across the vertical fin and rudder, with the swastika positioned across the rudder hinge line. The

The V17 (D-IYMS) as a prototype for the T-series. The basic C-series airframe has been modified with the undercarriage locked down, doors removed and tubular protectors added to the main wheels. Catapult spigots, an arrestor hook and tubular protectors ahead of the tailwheel can also be seen

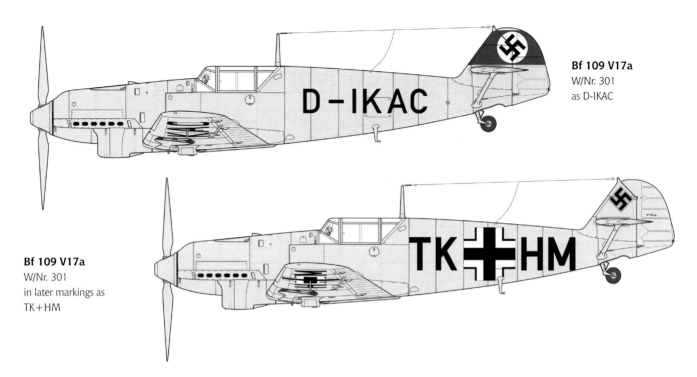

Bf 109 V17a
W/Nr. 301
as D-IKAC

Bf 109 V17a
W/Nr. 301
in later markings as
TK+HM

codes (D-IYMS) were applied in black on either side of the fuselage and under the wings, with D-I under the starboard and YMS under the port (read from the trailing edge looking forward). There are no crosses under the wings or on the fuselage and there are no images to confirm if they were applied above the wings. Once again, the gun troughs seem to be unpainted or in a much lighter colour (RLM 65?).

Few images seem to exist of this machine marked as TK+HK, but it is presumed by this stage it had the later RLM 02/71 over 65 scheme with a high fuselage demarcation. The codes would be applied either side of the crosses on the fuselage and under the wings (T+K under the starboard and H+K under the port). Crosses would be Type B2 and the tail swastika probably Type H2, with the latter at the top of the vertical fin not on a white disc/red band. The W/Nr. was applied in an odd fashion on the rudder, between the 3rd and 4th rib from the top. It was written as 'BF-109/1776', with a stagger at the point of the '/'.

Bf 109 V17a

W/Nr. 301
Registration D-IKAC (later TK+HM)
Same as the Bf 109 C-1 except:
- No ventilation holes in to top/front of cowling
- Jumo 210D engine
- Catapult spigots on aft/lower fuselage – different location in relation to those on W/Nr.1886

Camouflage & Markings
This machine had the same latter style of camouflage and markings as seen on the V17, right down to the odd application of the W/Nr. on the rudder in its latter scheme. The only photos that exist of this machine show it in the later (high demarcation) scheme so we are not 100% sure if it ever carried the earlier scheme?

The V17a (TK+HM) differed from the V17 as it seems to have been used predominately for catapult launch trials. Here is it seen just after one such launch, the lack of arrestor hook etc. being very evident

Two Bf 109E-0s were used for T-series trials, this is WL-IECY (W/Nr.1781, later TK+HL). The early style of supercharger intake and the arrestor hook under the rear fuselage are very prominent

Bf 109E-0

W/Nrs.1781 & 1783
Registration WL+IECY (later TK+HL) and GH+NT
Same as the Bf 109E-0 W/Nr.1784 except:
- Square-framed style canopy and windscreen with armoured glass
- Arrestor hook

Camouflage & Markings
This machine carried the early and late style of camouflage and markings as seen on the V17, right down to the odd application of the W/Nr. on the rudder in its latter scheme, albeit for this machine the stagger did not seem so pronounced. The crosses for the early scheme are confirmed as Type B1, revised to Type B2 for the later scheme. The swastika looks to be Type 2 in both schemes, albeit the contrast of the photo of the early scheme makes it look more like a Type 2a without a border?

This is the second Bf 109E-0 used for T-series trials, W/Nr.1783 (GH+NT), being shown to high-ranking Luftwaffe officers visiting the test centre. The high demarcation of the camouflage on the fuselage and the way in which the W/Nr. was applied to the rudder are confirmed in this shot

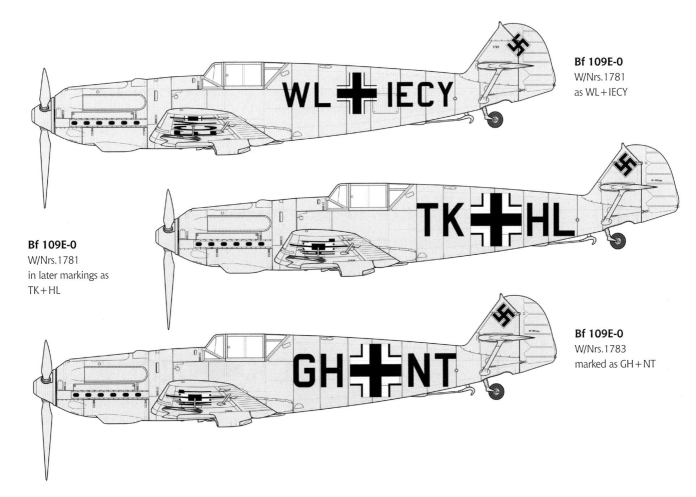

Bf 109E-0
W/Nrs.1781
as WL+IECY

Bf 109E-0
W/Nrs.1781
in later markings as
TK+HL

Bf 109E-0
W/Nrs.1783
marked as GH+NT

Bf 109E-3
W/Nr.1946

Bf 109 V15
W/Nr. 1773

Bf 109E-3

W/Nr.1946
Registration GH+NU
Same as the Bf 109E-3 except:
- Me P.6 three-blade metal propeller
- Square-framed style canopy and windscreen with armoured glass

Camouflage & Markings
This machine was in the later high demarcation RLM 02/71/65 scheme. Type B2 crosses and a Type H2 swastika were applied and the W/Nr. was in the more usual size and location, just above the leading edge of the tailplane, on either side of the fin. The codes were applied either side of the fuselage and under the wings in the usual manner

Bf 109 V15

W/Nr.1773
Stammkenzeichen: CE+BF
Same as Bf 109 V15 W/Nr.1773 D-IPHR except:
- New wing of 11.08m span
- Airbrakes on upper surface of wing
- Extended ailerons

Camouflage & Markings
This aircraft would be in the same overall scheme as GN+HU. This machine has been depicted in kits as being in an RLM 70/71/65 scheme with the codes (D-IPHR) applied on the fuselage and under the wings and the swastika in the white disc on the red band across the fin/rudder, however we have found no photographic evidence to support this scheme.

Bf 109T-0

W/Nr. 6153
Stammkenzeichen: CK+NC
Same as the Bf 109 V15 W/Nr.1773 CE+BF except:
- Square-framed style canopy and windscreen with armoured glass
- No airbrakes on upper surface of wing
- Arrestor hook under aft fuselage
- FuG 25 IFF antenna under fuselage

Camouflage & Markings
Again, it is presumed that this aircraft would be in the same overall scheme as GN+HU.

Bf 109T-0
W/Nr. 6153

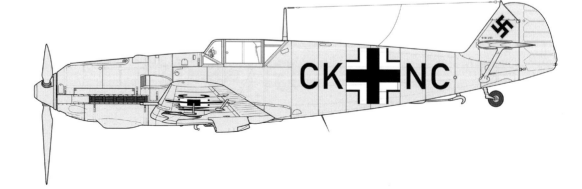

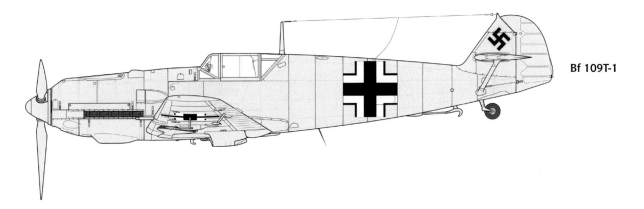

Bf 109T-1

Bf 109T-1

Same as Bf 109T-0 W/Nr.6153 CE+NC except:
- Blunt spinner
- DB 601N engine
- The supercharger air intake front was of a different (squarer) shape

Camouflage & Markings

The production T-series was in the standard RLM 02/71/65 scheme with a high demarcation on the fuselage sides. Type B2 crosses and a Type H2 swastika were applied with the W/Nr. in the more usual size and location on either side of the fin.

Bf 109T-2 converted from T-1

Same as the Bf 109T-1 except:
- DB 601N engine with GM-1 boost system
- 300lt drop tank and rack
- External armoured glass on windscreen
- Two filler points for the GM-1 system on port fuselage side
- Arrestor hook deleted

Camouflage & Markings

By the time most of these machines were converted they had the later grey scheme of RLM 74 *Dunkelgrau* (Dark Grey) and RLM 75 *Grauviolett* (Grey-Violet) over RLM 76 *Lichtblau* (Light Blue). The demarcation of the upper and lower colours was usually high on the fuselage sides and the straight edges of the camouflage pattern on the wings and fuselage was broken up by applying 'worms' of RLM 76 all over them (this type of marking was not the same as the 'mirror wave' application of RLM 76

seen on other maritime aircraft). A Type B5 simplified cross was applied on either side of the fuselage and under the wings, plus a Type B5a on the upper surface of the wings. The well-known machine of *Oblt.* Herbert Christmann of 11./JG11 has a large red flame down either side of the nose/fuselage, plus a black tactical number ('6') on the fuselage and aft band of RLM 04. The swastika remained a Type H2. The scheme applied to machines of 2./JG77 in Norway used a speckled application of the RLM 74 over the base RLM 75 on the fuselage, with this more akin in style and application to that seen on the machines of JG27 in the North African desert in 1942. The wings remained in a standard splinter scheme of RLM 74/75. The fuselage and wing underside crosses were all type B2, whilst the ones on the upper surface of the wings was the earlier Type B1. A tactical number was applied on the fuselage side, forward of the cross, and this was black outlined in red with a Type H2 swastika applied to the top of the vertical fin.

Projects and One-off Conversions

Bf 109S

Same as the Bf 109E-3 except:
- Revi C/12C gunsight
- Curved top (early) style canopy and windscreen without armoured glass
- Student's cockpit at front
- Instructor's cockpit added aft of existing one
- Unarmed wing (retained nose armament)
- Fuel tank in fuselage must have been repositioned aft – Not shown
- Project only, never built *(illustrated next page)*

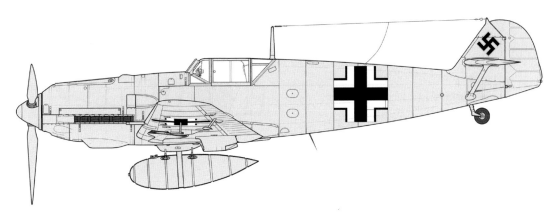

Bf 109T-2 converted from T-1

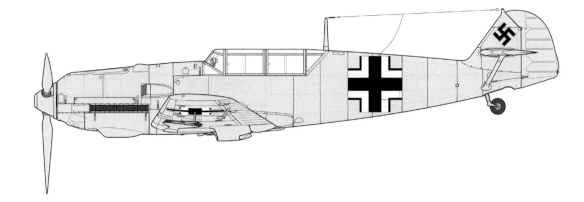

Bf 109S
(see previous page)

Bf 109 V21

W/Nr.1770
Registration: D-IFKQ
- Initially built as a C-1
- Front fuselage modified and fitted with a P&W Twin Wasp SC-G radial engine
- First flown in this configuration on the 17th August 1939

Note – Many people say that this was the 'Bf 109X', but that designation relates to the fitment of the BMW 801A to an F-series airframe, this was a one-off trial fitment of the engine type to the Bf 109 airframe, and no development resulted from it, nor was it ever given a designation beyond V21.

Camouflage & Markings

No photographs of this machine exist, all the well-known images show KB+II, which was fitted with the BMW 801 engine in relation to the Bf 109X project and because it is based on a modified F-series airframe it is outside the scope of this title. We would therefore assume it is the same overall scheme as other such prototypes and was probably thus RLM 02 overall with the registration applied to the fuselage and under

the wings as usual. A swastika may have been applied to the fin, on a white disc/red band and upper wing crosses would most likely have been Type B1.

Bf 109E-1 Spanish conversion

Same as the Bf 109E-1 except:
- Hispano-Suiza HS 12Z-89 engine
- No gunsight
- Unarmed
- Oil cooler set back under fuselage
- Air intake with tropical filter in place usually occupied by the radiator on the DB-powered versions
- Hamilton-Standard three-blade metal propeller

Camouflage & Markings

This machine was coded 6•119 originally and we presume it remained in the original scheme of RLM 63 over 65. All other markings should be the same as that seen on other Spanish Bf 109Es of the era, so see Chapter 7 for more details.

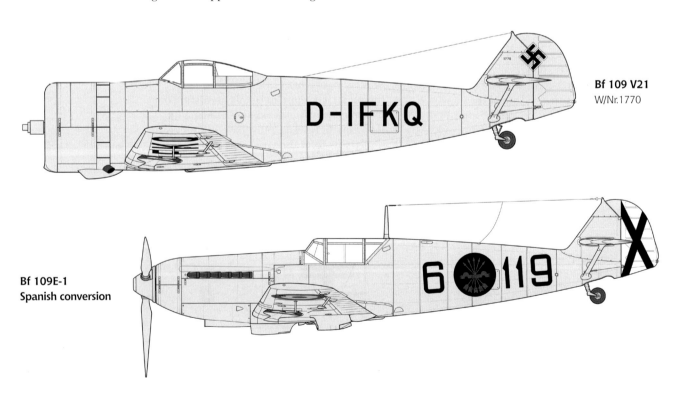

Bf 109 V21
W/Nr.1770

Bf 109E-1
Spanish conversion

Chapter 7:   Camouflage & Markings

Let us first start by saying that nothing is certain when trying to deduce colours from old black and white photographs. The best you can make is an educated, and with luck, intelligent guess using both photographic and documentary evidence. The regulations with regard to the camouflage and markings of Luftwaffe aircraft during the war period are well known and most survive, the problem is that at the front line when the regulations changed it was highly unlikely that the ground crew rushed out to paint every aircraft in their charge, it was simply not practical. This whole subject is massive, you can write volumes on the subject, with some publishers having done just that, but we will try and keep it concise. Just remember, nothing is an absolute when it comes to camouflage and markings, and nothing illustrates that more graphically than Luftwaffe C&M!

For the C&M applied to the various prototypes, please see their individual entries in the previous chapters. Although we all use the term 'RLM' to prefix Luftwaffe colours it should be noted that in period documents the only colour designated in this manner was RLM 02, the rest were simply prefixed 'Farbton' (shade/tone/hue of a colour). The confusion lies in the fact that the main paint manufacturer (Warnecke und Böhm) issued paint charts that prefixed all colours with 'RLM', followed by Farbton 65, 70, 71 etc. However for consistency throughout this book we will prefix all colours with 'RLM'

The Bf 109 in Spain

For many years it was thought that the initial batch of machines to reach Spain, designated by most as Bf 109A, but in fact all pre-production machines, were in an overall RLM 01 *Silber* (silver) scheme. This has been challenged over the years, with some claiming the machines were bare metal with a clear lacquer protective coating that had a slight greenish hue to it, or that they were part painted (rear fuselage) and bare metal (vertical fin and forward fuselage) with all control surfaces also in silver. The one thing that seems to be consistent is that these machines had the panel lines on the fuselage filled with putty, as none can be seen in photographs, even really clear close-up shots. If that is the case, then the airframe must have been painted, as the filled panel lines would show up as darker lines, which they don't, and as there is no contrast with the rest of the airframe, that too must also be treated in the same manner, e.g. painted. Certainly these early machines have contrast in certain areas that may well be unpainted metal, these being on the square panel directly aft of

Bf 109B-1 of 1 Jagdgruppe J88, circa 1937. Note the RLM 70/71 camouflage, the white wing tips and the white 'x' in the centre of the fuselage roundel
(© via J. Grant)

the cowl behind the engine that allows access to the upper guns, all of the forward (engine) cowls and the vertical fin, along with sometimes the wing root fillets. We have also seen images of very early machines in Spain where the cowling over the nose gun area is also of high contrast in comparison with the rest of the airframe and thus you would assume, in bare metal. Usually all these machines also had the wings painted as well, as they are uniform in tonal quality and show signs of wear at the roots where the groundcrew and pilot tread. More recent research seems to point to these machines having been supplied in a uniform scheme, either using DKH L40/52 light grey lacquer or Avionorm Nitro-paint 7375 matt light grey (Note – both colours are, due to the lack of documentation at the time, often officially designated as 'Farbton 63' or 'RLM 63'!). The former seems to have had little tonal depth, resulting in the various shades of the metal panels underneath affecting the overall tone and this is why these early machines look so patchy. Two styles of markings were also applied to these machines and we feel these reflect the 'early' and 'late' style, probably down to experience gained in operations. The early scheme saw just the wing tips in white, along with the rudder, onto which was also applied a black X – note that this X is not applied parallel to the ground with the aircraft in an in-flight position (e.g. tail up), but parallel to the ground with the aircraft on the ground, which results in it 'leaning' forward slightly in relation to the rudder hinge line (the width and exact location of this cross was not universal, and we

Bf 109B-1, 6-7, of 2.J/88 displaying the early scheme of grey over bare metal. The contrast in certain panels shows that this machine is not painted in one shade that has good density, as the underlying material is affecting the colour
(© via J. Grant)

This shot of Bf 109B-2, 6•29 of 1.J/88 in 1937 clearly shows the RLM 70/71 splinter camouflage pattern on the upper surfaces, as well as the white wing tips

(© via J. Grant)

have seen images of a line-up of early machines, none of which have the marking applied in the same manner). Identification markings consisted of large black circles above and below the wings and on either side of the fuselage. The diameter of these on the early machines was larger than that seen later on the Bs, with those on the wings overlapping onto the ailerons and those on the fuselage being positioned slightly farther forward than later machines, with the arc just crossing over the radio hatch. The wing roundels also carried a cross in white, positioned centrally within the black circle and with bars of the same width as seen on the tail cross, so these could vary but were thinner than that see in the later scheme. Exact dimensions of all the markings

A nice shot of Hptm. Wolfgang Schellmann in his Bf 109D-1 (6•51) in flight in 1938. The consistent tone of the colour seems to indicate that this machine is RLM 02/65, as it is too dark in comparison with the lower shade to be RLM 63

(© via J. Grant)

are unknown, as no records survive, but going by existing regulations in Germany at the time, the black roundels were probably 4/5th the height of the fuselage or depth of the wing. Each aircraft carried a code, applied in black characters 2/5th the depth of the fuselage, and applied aft of the roundel in a set format. These codes were all pre-fixed '6', then a dash, then a number, so you get 6-1 through 6-12. The access panel for the spark plugs, the surround of the exhausts and the chin radiator area were all painted in black, mainly we suspect because these would otherwise suffer deterioration due to heat and exhaust staining. The propellers were wooden, so the hubs were treated in the same way as the rest of the airframe, but the blades were painted a glossy grey on the front and a matt black on the back, whilst the extreme tips were probably in bare metal, as they are far lighter than the rest of the airframe. There are many exceptions to the rules, with personal insignia etc., but the best-known exception to markings is the machine of Ofw. Otto Polenz (6-15), captured by the Republicans, as this carries all the markings already discussed, but the fuselage black discs have small (1/3rd diameter)

crosses, that are not white and are orientated as an 'X' in the centre. These markings seem to be in the same shade as the rest of the airframe, so are probably grey.

The later scheme just saw a change in the dimensions of the black roundels, which were reduced, probably to around 3/5th the fuselage/ wing depth, and the application of the codes. The white crosses in the black roundels also changed, as these became thicker than seen previously, again probably moving up to a percentage of the roundel diameter? The codes were now applied in a different format, with the '6' one side of the black roundel (aft on the starboard and forward on the port side) and the rest of the serial number the other side of the roundel. Although the style of the characters did not change, retaining the characteristic shape of the '6', the brush stroke increased, so the letters were more prominent. The height of these characters also increased, probably to be in line with other marking regulations at the time, so these were now 4/5th the height of the fuselage, but no larger than 2.5m. The reduction in the diameter of the wing roundels also seems to coincide with an increase in the area of wing tip that was painted white, probably to increase visibility in combat, so that now the white extended to a point 1/5th the length of the aileron.

When the second batch of Bs started to arrive in 1937 they had a new scheme which saw the application of a light grey to the upper surfaces and light blue underneath. Official designations for these colours were RLM 63 *Lichtgrau* and RLM 65 *Hellblau*. It should be noted that many people state that RLM 02 *Grau* was used, but there is confusion as both RLM 02 and RLM 63 have similar qualities. The Paint Companies Handbook of 1944 lists RLM 02 as RAL7003 and RLM 63 as RAL 7004, so as you can see they are both basically the same colour, it is just that RLM 63 is a lighter shade (if you want to match RLM 63 today, it is almost identical to the modern RAL 7033). Demarcation for these colours was low down on the fuselage side, then projected on a straight line from the wing leading edge centreline forward onto the chin cowling, before following a line up the front of the cowl to retain the same split of the colours in this area (probably 4/5th RLM 63 and 1/5th RLM 65). The small cross in the centre of the fuselage roundel seen on 6-15 was often applied in white on these machines, but not all of them as 6•38 and 6•42 certainly had it, but 6•47 did not. Propellers were metal, so you can see them with the front of the blades in bare metal or light grey (gloss) and the backs in black (matt) or RLM 70. The hub gear is visible at the root of each blade and that was bare metal, but the spinner could be in a number of colours. The most common seems to be white, although there are various combinations of bands using red, yellow and green. Major Gotthard Hendrick's machine is well known, as it is the one with the Olympic rings on the spinner, because he won the pentathlon in the 1936 Olympics, and this also carried thin bands of red, yellow, red at the extreme spinner tip (the Spanish national colours). This machine also had a heraldic 'h' in a gothic font applied in white to the centre of the fuselage black roundel. Werner Mölders had his D (6•79) with the spinner in red, but there are others that appear to be yellow, red or combinations of these colours (and maybe others?). The later machines also often carried names in various places and to varying sizes. Mölders' machine was called 'Luchs' (Lynx), with this applied in quite large white characters directly below the lower edge of the gun cowl access panel on each side of the fuselage, while 6•10 had the name 'Altertum' (Antiquity) on either side of the cowling, directly above the spark plug access panel and again in white. Other known named machines include C-1, 6•49 'Jaguar', E-4, 6•107 'Mors-Mors!' (Mutter-Mutter!) and E-3, 6•111 'Bärchen' (Bear). A number of the second batch of aircraft came to Spain in the then current Luftwaffe scheme of RLM 70/71 over RLM 65 combined with the white rudder and wing tip and black roundels of the Legion Condor. We have not determined the exact extent of the aircraft this affected, but various airframes in the 6•26 through to 6•42 range are certainly seen in the RLM 70/71 scheme. The later C and D-series machines seem to have had (on the whole) the overall RLM 63/65 scheme with the later style of markings.

When the E-series reached Spain it too carried the same RLM 63/65 scheme used by the B, C and D, along with the later style of markings. The only real deviations were in the application of a large area of black around the exhaust stacks and sweeping back along the fuselage and wing root. This was probably to just cover up where the exhaust staining would be anyway, and was a carry-over from the black areas seen on the previous marks. These machines had various colours used for the propeller blades, as we have seen images that clearly show them as polished metal fronts with black (or RLM 70) at the back of each blade, or a dark shade overall that we assume to be RLM 70. The spinners usually remained in RLM 63, although again there are instances of it being white, or with various

coloured bands.

When the Condor Legion pulled out of Spain, the remaining machines, comprising mainly Es but also a number of the old C and D versions, were handed over to *Grupo* 5-G-5 of the Nationalist Air Force in March 1939. The overall scheme remained unchanged, but the black roundel on the fuselage was modified to carry the Falangist (Fascist movement in Spain under Franco, 1935-1940) insignia in the centre in white. Some machines also carried the unit insignia of *Grupo* 5-G-5 (three diving birds on a white disc with a black rim) on the vertical fin, although we have only found one such image, showing 6•56 and with the marking only visible on the port side of the fin.

Bf 109B-2, 6•34 of 1.J/88 flown by Oblt Erich Woitke Alfamen in Feb 1938. The RLM 70/71/65 scheme is evident, as is the small white 'x' in the centre of the fuselage roundel
(© via J. Grant)

Bf 109E, coded 6-111 of 2.J/88 flown by Lt Werner Ursinus, it had the name Bärchen (Bear) on the fuselage side
(© via M. Payne)

Unit Markings

- **'Wooden Eye' (1.J/88)** – Usually this marking was applied on the port fuselage side directly under the cockpit area although it is also noted further back on some machines. This marking consisted of a white disc with black details and apparently was done with a stencil so remained constant in size and detail. The official insignia for this unit was a diving raven, and this too can be seen on some machines

- **The Hat (2.J/88)** – This marking was applied in the same style, but in various locations. Applied in black, with the underlying colour used to create highlights and detail, it was

usually the same overall height as the fuselage roundel. It was applied forward of the roundel and is known to have been applied just on the port side. The early scheme, due to the location of the code aft of the roundel and the larger size of that roundel, usually saw the marking applied higher up the fuselage and below the aft section of the cockpit canopy. In the later scheme, with the smaller roundel, but larger codes that went ahead of it, the hat was usually slightly smaller and applied further down the fuselage side and forward, so that the middle of the top edge lined up with the rear edge of the opening section of the canopy. Not all

machines carried this marking, and if you look at something like 6•47 you will see that it is applied in the same location as the early scheme, but with later style markings so that the rim of the hat almost touches the bottom arc of the '6'.

- **'Mickey Mouse' (3.J/88)** – Due to its large size, this marking was applied on the port fuselage side below the aft canopy section as per the hat insignia. Its location usually means that it overlaps the first fuselage frame, with the topmost ear directly below the middle of the hand-hold behind the aft canopy section and the lower ear in line with the bottom sill of the canopy.

A good example of the initial splinter pattern applied to the early series machines
(© via J. Grant)

The well known scared cat emblem of 8./JG51 seen here on the side of a Bf 109C in 1938

Bf 109B-2 of 6 (Jagd) Trager Gruppe 186 'Graf Zeppelin' based at Keil-Holtenau in December 1938. The airframe carries the standard scheme of RLM 70/71 over 65, but again shows yet another style of demarcation on the nose area
(© via J. Grant)

Bf 109 in Luftwaffe Service

Bf 109B, C, D and E

The Bf 109B came into service with the Luftwaffe with II./JG132 in February 1937 at Jüterbog-Damm and it would not be until November 1937 that the second unit formed with the type, that of II./JG234. Each of the *Geschwadern* was made up of three *Gruppen* and each *Gruppe* had three *Staffeln*. A *Stab* (staff) flight of four aircraft was assigned to the *Geschwader* itself and each *Gruppe* had a staff flight of three aircraft. The numbering system used for these machines was as follows:

- White numbers, often with black edges = 1st, 4th, 7th & 10th *Staffel*
- Red numbers, often with a white border on the RLM 70/71 scheme = 2nd, 5th, 8th and 11th *Staffel*
- Yellow numbers, often with black borders = 3rd, 6th, 9th and 12th *Staffel*

On top of this, machines of the 2nd *Gruppe* had a horizontal bar (often outlined in black or white) in the *Staffel* colour aft of the fuselage cross, those of the 3rd *Gruppe* had a horizontal wavy line ('welle') aft of the fuselage cross and those of the 4th *Gruppe* had a black circle with a white outline or a small cross.

The 1938 edition of L.Dv. 521/1, the painting regulations for German military aircraft,

standardised the colours into the RLM coded system we all refer to today, even though the paint handbook from the main manufacturer still referred to them as 'Farbton' (shade or colour). The original technical designations used prior to 1938 were numerical, so you had 7115.02, 7136.70 etc., but when the new regulations came into effect the system only used the last two numeric, which identified the shade, thus you got 02 *Grau* and 70 *Schwarzgrün*, which we all refer to nowadays as 'RLM 02', 'RLM 70' etc. The three-tone (RLM 61/62/63) scheme seen prior to 1938 was never applied to the Bf 109 because by this time the doctrine of the Luftwaffe was set, as support to the infantry and this combined probably with the expense and time needed to apply a three-tone camouflage scheme resulted in a new simplified scheme. This was RLM 70 *Schwarzgrün* (black-green) and RLM 71 *Dunkelgrün* (dark green) in a splinter camouflage pattern on the upper surfaces, and RLM 65 *Hellblau* (light blue) underneath. The splinter scheme was less complex in its shapes to that seen in the previous three-tone scheme, but was

still different from that which was seen once the regulations changed in 1939. All new-built aircraft after 1938 were finished in the new scheme and all in service had to be revised to the new scheme as and when the units could manage it. Demarcation of the upper and lower colours was low down on the fuselage sides, with this carried forward under the chin, although some aircraft show various ways of determining the demarcation in this area on the Jumo-powered machines – these included straight line forward from the wing lending-edge centreline, with the same area done in the curve under the forward section; or a curve up from the centreline of the wing leading edge to the top of the intake rim, then a straight line forward following the edge of the exhaust surround panel; or a low demarcation on the aft section, the whole of the forward lip of the intake done in RLM 65 (resulting in a wide vertical band), then carrying forward following the line of the exhaust surround panel. It has been claimed for many years that some Bf 109Ds of certain units adopted a single-colour upper scheme, using just RLM 71, but there are no surviving official documents that support this. National insignia at this time comprised Type B1 *Hakenkreuz* crosses of 660mm high by 440mm wide (with arms of 110mm) on the upper and lower wings and fuselage sides, plus a Type H1 swastika on a white disc, surmounted on a red band on the vertical fin – the position and size of this marking was determined by a complex system of measurements, but basically the band height was the main measurement, the white disc was in the centre of it, and had to be inside the band at its top and bottom by 1/8th the height of the band. The arms of the swastika were 3/10th the height, while the thickness of the stroke was 2/10th and the swastika was set at 45°. This resulted in the swastika being in the middle of the fin, across the rudder hinge line. As of the 1st January 1939 in accordance with Luftwaffe Regulation Notice No.5 dated the 30th January 1939, the way in which national markings were to be applied changed as follows.

The red background to the swastika was to be removed and a white edge was to be created (probably by overpainting the white disc) that was 1/6th the breadth of the arms and a black edge was then applied to no more than 1/4 of the width of the white – all other dimensions of the swastika remained the same, but this change resulted in the swastika becoming what we now all call Type H2. This results in images of Ds in late 1939 with the band and disc overpainted but with the swastika remaining in the middle of the fin/rudder and this is also still to be seen in later Bf 109Es with the RLM 02/70/65 scheme, that for some reason have the swastika across the hinge line? All the other national insignia remained unchanged, although any aircraft not bearing military markings, would have the

This Bf 109C-1 without wing armament was used by Jagdfliegerschule 4, Fürth in 1941
(© via J. Grant)

registration changed from the D-prefix to 'WL' (*WehrmachtLuft*), hence why some test Bf 109s show this type of code. This type of code remained in use through to about March 1940. It should be noted that any Bf 109 used in the night fighter role received an 'N' as a code letter, applied forward of the fuselage cross, with the individual aircraft number moved aft of the cross. These could be in a variety of colours but usually if the machine was in the day-fighter scheme of 71/02/65 then the characters were red, maybe with a thin black outline, while later the overall

A good example of the very first style of camouflage applied to the Bf 109C and D-series, with RLM 70/71 over 65 – although little contrast can be seen, close inspection reveals that there are two distinct shades on the wings. Unusually the red band on the rudder goes right to the top and the white disc is positioned in a relation to it, resulting in the swastika being bigger and higher up than you would usually expect
(© via J. Grant)

This Bf 109D-1 of I JG1 has a very unusual style of identifying marking on the fuselage, unlike the official ones for specific ranks

Many earlier series airframes ended up with training schools, this Bf 109D-1 (VA+ER) carries the tail band and individual fleet number (16) that clearly identifies it as a trainer
(© via J. Grant)

Either a C or D-series machine, the 'N' code seems to indicate that this machine was used by one of the early night fighter units
(© via J. Grant)

A clear example of the later scheme, with RLM 02/71 over 65, but with a high demarcation on the fuselage sides. The fuselage and (we suspect) lower wing crosses are Type B2, while those on top of the wing remain Type B1. Note the two kill markings on the vertical fin
(© via J. Grant)

black machines had the codes in light grey.

The regulations changed again on the 18th October 1939, with the issuing of Luftwaffe Directive No.3500/39. This saw revised dimensions for the national insignia, so that the one on the fuselage had to be the whole height and in the case of those with a round fuselage, it had to be 25% of the circumference of the fuselage to a maximum of 2m in length. The crosses on the wings were to be the whole width of the wing and were positioned at a point mid-way between root and tip (both upper and lower surfaces) – maximum 2m length underneath and 1m on top. The style of cross also changed, with the dimensions now determined by the height, the centre cross is 1/4th the height in its thickness, the white surround is 1/8th the height and the black edge was 1/32nd the height. In this form the marking became what we all now call Type B2 and usually it was applied on the fuselage and below the wings, with those on the upper wings remaining Type B1. Those aircraft not used on the front line were to have codes applied on the fuselage sides and under the wings, these codes (*Stammkennzeichen* – factory identification code) were four letters, the first could not be a vowel or a Y. These were applied in black characters 1/2 the height of the cross, with those on the fuselage orientated with the first two one side of the cross and the other two on the other side (e.g CA+NK), this code was also applied under the wings, again in black, with them read from the trailing edge looking forward. The code was split so that the first two went either side of the cross under the starboard wing (e.g. C+A) and the other two did the same under the port (e.g. N+K). Only a few test and development Bf 109s carried these markings, our example (CA+NK) being the E-4 (W/Nr.1361) used to test bomb carrying for the E-4b and E-7b variants.

On top of the *Staffel* and *Gruppe* markings, there were a number of others applied to aid quick recognition of unit leaders whilst in

This shot of a Bf 109E on its nose does clearly show the later (simplified) splinter camouflage pattern, but check out the leading edges, the lower camouflage colour has been sprayed up around the edges to conceal the hard edge created by the existing demarcation on the centreline

In this shot of the victory tally being updated on the rudder of Oblt Heinz Ebeling's (9./JG 26) machine, the wing camouflage pattern is fine, but what is going on with the tail? Proof that battle damage was often just sprayed over with the most convenient colour – the top/front of the rudder also looks to be in a different colour

A nice PR colour photo of an E-series airframe, showing the underwing Type B1 crosses and the RLM 70 spinner and propeller – we doubt many production machines had the VDM stamps on the blades, this is a PR photo after all!

flight. These included the *Geschwaderkommodore* (Squadron commander), whose machine wore <-+- on the fuselage sides. The < (*Winkel*) had arms at 60° and 110mm thick, while the forward and aft bars were of the same thickness and placed 200mm away from the cross (the extreme tip of the < being 1,500mm from the centre of the cross). The aft bar was 1,150mm long, whilst the < and forward bar were 970mm each long. The *Geschwaderadjutant* carried the marking <|+, with the '<' and '|' 110mm wide and 200mm forward of the cross. The *Geschwader Techniker Offizier's* machine was marked as <|0+, the *Gruppenkommander* as <<+, the *Gruppenadjutant* as <+ and the *Gruppen Techniker Offizier* as <0+. The positioning of these markings is pretty constant, with the stroke of the characters being 110mm and the distance from the cross usually 200mm, although the use of the '0' does result in it looking closer due to optical distortion.

One other change that can be seen to Bf 109s after the Polish campaign is the use of extremely large underwing crosses. These are so large as to cover the entire width of the wing, including the ailerons, although the style still remains as Type B1 with the narrow white bands, not the thicker ones of the later Type B2. This type of marking was also sometime seen on the upper surface of the wing as well. It should be noted that upper wing crosses are probably the most varied thing about the E-series, as these are seen small and positioned towards the tip at 3/4 the span, as the later B2 but also positioned towards the tip and there are even instances of the upper wing cross being in the later B5 (white outline) style, again very large and crossing over the ailerons.

A lovely photo of Bf 109E-3, W/Nr.3576 flown by Uffz Arno Zimmermann of 7./JG54 that crashed near Lydd on the 27th October 1940. This clearly shows the application of RLM 02 and 71 on the fuselage sides, plus a nose cowling painted with water-soluble paint

As the battle moved from Europe to across the Channel and into the UK the bright sides of RLM 02/71/65 led to the application of various intensities of green to break up the hard lines. Here you can see Werner Machold's Bf 109E 'Yellow 5' of 9./JG2 at Cherbourg-Querqueville with a dense application of green that has modified the fuselage cross to reduce the size of the white areas
(© via M. Payne)

Moving the tactical numbers from the fuselage to the nose seemed to occur during the Battle of Britain period and here you can see Bf 109E-4 'White 8' of 7./JG27 on the beach in Northern France in 1940 with the white '8' applied onto the yellow nose
(© via M. Payne)

An example of a Bf 109 with two sets of insignia, this is the Bf 109E-3 of Oblt Hermann Staege from 2.(J) LG2, probably seen crash-landed in France in May 1940. The aircraft has a personal emblem on the cowl as well as a unit one on the aft fuselage
(© via M.Payne)

The Change from 70 to 02

Initial operations in Poland during the first stages of WWII had highlighted that the dark shades of RLM 70 and 71, although suited to conceal an aircraft on the ground, were less than ideal for air combat. As a result trials were undertaken during late 1939, early 1940 with combinations of RLM 70 and 71 with RLM 02 and in the end it was decided that RLM 02 and 71 were the best option for a new upper surface scheme. The splinter pattern was also revised from that previously used, being now of a simplified style to ease application. At almost the same time the demarcation of upper and lower colours changed, with it moving right up the fuselage sides, so that the RLM 65 covered 3/4 of the surface area and the entire vertical fin and rudder. Application of the new schemes resulted in some unusual interpretations, with photos showing machines with the upper surface colours running under the tailplanes, or with the demarcation line taken parallel along the whole of the fuselage from the lower sill of the canopy (this was quite common on C and D versions that were repainted). There are also examples of the rules not being followed and the RLM 71 being replaced with RLM 02 instead of the RLM 70, while others just repainted the vertical fin and a portion of the fuselage sides in RLM 65. Most E-versions prior to the E-4 had the new scheme applied over the older one, and

Bf 109E-3, 'Yellow 3' of III./JG3 on the beach at Ambleteuse in September 1940. Of note here is the aft demarcation of the yellow nose cowling
(© via M. Payne)

it was only in early 1940 as the E-4 started to roll off the production lines that these had the scheme applied in the factory.

Although the new RLM 70/02/65 scheme worked well in the campaign over France, when the Luftwaffe started operations over the Channel and South of England, they found the bright blue on the fuselage sides stood out against the sea and English countryside. The first change saw the application in a mottle of RLM 02 on the fuselage sides, sometimes on its own or with RLM 70 or 71, or all three. This type of mottling was never uniform and there are huge variations in how it was applied and how intensely it was done. There are also those units that applied the greens (RLM 70/71) in this manner to such an intense level that it almost became a solid colour and in these instances the fuselage crosses usually had the width of the white segments reduced by half by applying the green over them – this was done with an airbrush, brush or sponge, all three methods must have been employed going by the variety. If you look at something like *Lt* Wübke's Bf 109E 'Yellow 11' of 9./JG54, you will see that this machine displays the toning down on the fuselage side, but it is done as vertical wavy stripes, obviously applied with an airbrush. Then *Hptm.* Hans-Karl Meyer's Bf 109E 'White 8' of I./JG53 had the vertical fin and fuselage sides covered in a solid area of what is thought to be RLM 02, with a soft-edge demarcation swooping down from the fin, then running along the fuselage at half-way down, before swooping down to meet the wing root. There are also instances of the centres of the fuselage and upper wing crosses being toned down by spray application of light grey or RLM 02. As no documents survive to support this, it is not known if this was general practice or just done at squadron level by certain units? The other toning down of the camouflage that appeared at the same time was that of lightly overspraying the RLM 65 along the length of the wing leading edge, to break up the clear line between the upper and lower colours, which is presumed to have made this less obvious when viewed from in front. Taking into account the above attempts to tone down markings, it is strange to consider that in the same period the Bf 109 had some very bright identification markings applied. These comprised RLM 04 *Gelb* (yellow) to the

A very odd range of shades on the fuselage sides of this Bf 109E-3 from JG 53. Is that RLM 02 applied lightly over the RLM 76 to break up its brightness, or some other colour?

An example of the tactical number being on the nose, this Bf 109E-4/b of 19(Jabo) JG27 in France in 1941 has the '2' applied on what looks like an area that has been scrubbed off the surrounding yellow

This Bf 109E-7/b flown by Lt Seidl Stab of II./JG54 in Hungary during March 1941 in preparation for the attack on Greece has the dense vertical stripes of the upper surface colours on the fuselage sides. Note also that in the original you can see that the yellow nose is also very faintly speckled, so we would assume that to be with RLM 65 to offer a lower contrast with the yellow?
(© via M. Payne)

This E-3 of 7./JG2 in France during May-June 1940 displays the dense speckling that JG2 seemed to like, plus the way that it has reduced the size of the cross. The swastika is yet to be reapplied to the new rudder
(© via M. Payne)

This Bf 109E-4 (W/Nr.1588) flown by Franz Laenisch of 1./JG2 has the camouflage intact on the upper fuselage spine and the dense speckles applied to the fuselage sides only. The patch round the swastika confirms the speckling was applied at a later date from the overall scheme
(© via M. Payne)

entire engine cowling and lower chin and/or the rudder. On top of this, the machines of III./JG27 had the aircraft number, in white, moved from the fuselage side to either side of the nose, usually in a dark green panel to give contrast against the yellow. Bf 109Es during the Battle of Britain also sometimes had white tips to the wings, at about the 1/5th aileron length as per the earlier Condor Legion machines.

Grey-scheme

By mid-August 1940 many of the Bf 109s shot down over the UK were examined and found to be in various shades of grey on the upper surfaces. Now the official use of the new grey shades RLM 74 and 75 was never sanctioned until November 1941, but it appears that experience over the Channel led many units to mix up shades of

OK, so maybe the grey scheme did exist, but probably not official prior to the take on of RLM 74/75 in 1941. This period colour image certainly seems to show an E-series in the two greys

grey to apply to their aircraft in an attempt to make them less obvious over the grey of the sea. With an abundance of white and black paint used for national markings at most units, the creation of grey was never a problem, and when you consider that RLM 65 could also be the basis of these shades, you can see why they are often referred to in reports as 'blue-grey' or 'Battleship grey'. It is not know if this experience led to the official development and adoption of the later RLM 74 and 75 shades, or if in some way the colours mixed at unit level were their basis, but it is certain that no Bf 109s flew prior to the 1941 regulations with official shades of grey.

The photo that begs the question, "is that RLM 74/75?". Taken from publicity material released in late 1940, this colour shot of Bf 109E-7 WNr.2574 (CI + EJ) seems to confirm a grey upper camouflage, or does it?

Once you change the colour photo of Bf 109E-7 WNr.2574 (CI + EJ) into black and white the contrast in colours is not unlike that of an RLM 02/71 scheme?

The exception, not the rule!
There is always an exception in Luftwaffe colours and in this instance it is all down to a colour photo taken of an E-7 on, it is presumed, a pre-delivery flight that seems to have upper camouflage in two shades of grey? The problem is that colour negatives degrade with age and in different ways depending on how the emulsion is laid down/created. As a result some images go yellow, others green, others blue and all of this affects how the print will look. Looking at the image it does not look like RLM 74/75, as the tonal contrast between each is far too great, we suspect it is therefore in RLM 02 and a mixed grey and all the greyish shade is down to degrading of the negative and/or print (we are unsure if the original negative survives, or if all images are copies off another – if the latter is the case the problem with the colours will get worse with each copy). We therefore stick with what we have said above, that no official application

of the RLM 74/75 scheme was present on frontline
Bf 109Es until 1941, but mixed-greys may have
existed from mid-1940.

Desert Scheme

Those E-versions that served in Sicily retained
the RLM 02/70/65 scheme, plus the yellow tail
and nose. They also had a white band around the
aft fuselage to denote operations in the Mediterranean, and this varied in width, with some being
larger (750mm) than others (500mm). When
the type was used in North Africa it had two
schemes applied, the first was the solid application of sand yellow (RLM 79 *Sandgelb*) over a
bright blue (RLM 78 *Hellblau*). With this scheme
the demarcation between the two colours was usually low down on the fuselage sides, just like the
early RLM 70/71/65 scheme and was soft-edged.
The white theatre band remained around the aft
fuselage, but was supplemented by white wing
tips, again to a point about 1/5th the length of the
aileron, on both upper and lower surfaces. The
spinner was also usually white, although segments
of RLM 70, red and other colours are known. The
second scheme saw the move to the high demarcation of the RLM 02/70/65 scheme, but now the
upper surfaces were covered in speckles of green
(RLM 80 *Grün*), and these extended down the
fuselage side and onto the vertical fin and rudder.
These speckles could be quite small, or larger areas of green that sometimes merged into strands,
especially along the fuselage sides. Unit markings
throughout remained constant with those used
in operations in Europe and elsewhere, although
fighter-bomber units used the four-digit codes
seen in the ground attack roles, such as S9+AS of
III./SKG210 shot down over Quatarra in 1942,
which still had the low-demarcation scheme by
this date. Most of the machines used in North
Africa were from JG27, so these carried that units
emblem in a round disc on either side of the nose,
forward of the tropical filter on the port side and
matching this location on the starboard.

The initial machines operated by JG27 in the desert all retained their European theatre
camouflage, like this E-4 Trop

The yellow nose used in the theatre was a bit obvious, so various methods of toning it
down were done, such as the mottling of green seen on the nose of this Bf 109E-4 Trop of
I./JG27

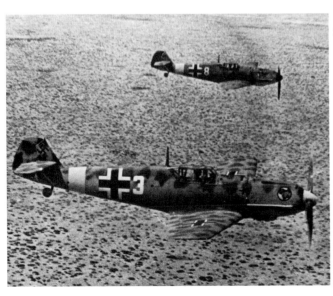

This in-flight shot of a Bf 109E-4 Trop shows just how effective the 'spotty'
camouflage was over the desert

Here is an example of the 'tiger striped' scheme on a E-4 Trop (Black 3) of
I./JG27 in North Africa. This machine is probably in the old RLM 70/71/65
scheme and has had the colours toned down with the application of stripes
created by spraying RLM 78 on the fuselage sides, plus, we suspect, the
other lighter patches are RLM 79. The nose is probably yellow, while the tail
band is white

Bf 109 in Foreign Service

Bulgaria

This nation had 19 Bf 109Es, comprising ten E-4s delivered in June 1940 and a further nine E-7s in 1941. These machines seem to have used a scheme that comprised RLM 71 (or 70) on the upper surfaces and dorsal spine, plus RLM 02 on the fuselage sides and RLM 65 underneath. The demarcation of the dark green is soft-edged and

Bf 109E-4 'Strelas' of the Bulgarian Air Force seen at Sarafovo airfield

A Croatian Bf 109E-4 'Green 15' seen in Russia in 1942. The only thing that gives away the nationality of the pilot is the Croatian shield on the fuselage side

A Rumanian Bf 109E-4 marked as 'Hai Fetito!' (Up little girl!). This machine displays the later (Michael's cross) style of national insignia

runs from the high demarcation point forward of the leading edge of the fin (the entire vertical fin is green) in a gentle slope to the canopy sill, then in a straight line forward. The few photos that exist, show what looks to be two contrasting colours on the wings, so this may mean these machines had the RLM 70/71 scheme on both wings and upper fuselage? The rudder and the nose is yellow, with this extending back along the fuselage centreline to a point below the leading edge of the fin – this results in a curved demarcation on top of the cowl, just forward of the bulges on top, but a straight demarcation under the nose, at the back of the chin radiator tub. National insignia comprised black-outlined white squares on top of which was superimposed a black 'X'. The size of the ones on the fuselage sides are much smaller than those above and below the wings. Each aircraft carried an identification number in white from 1 through to 19, and these are applied aft of the fuselage insignia. The number is also repeated we believe in black characters under each wing, outboard of the national insignia. The style and size of these characters is unlike any used in Germany, being very stylised and they are slightly shorter that the height of the fuselage national insignia. Oddly, the W/Nr. seems to have been applied in a red triangle on

either side of the vertical fin, with 'No.' in the top of the triangle, a horizontal line half-way down and the number below that. The spinner seems to be consistently in RLM 70, as are the propeller blades.

Croatia

Formed as the pro-German Independent State of Croatia on the 14th April 1941 after the German invasion of Yugoslavia on the 6th April, the area was split into two halves, with Italian forces controlling the south and German forces the north. Within the northern area the 4th Fighter Group was formed, with the 10th and 11th Fighter Squadrons within it, during July 1941 and all potential pilots were sent to *Jagdfliegerschule* (Fighter Pilot School) 4 at Fürth in Germany to learn to fly the Bf 109. By late September the pilots of the 10th Fighter Squadron and their eleven Bf 109Es were made operationally subordinate to 3./JG52 at Poltava, where they were incorporated as 15.(Kroat)/JG52 and went operational on the 10th October. They were followed by the 11th Fighter Squadron, who joined 15.(Kroat)/JG52 at Taganrog in December. The 4th Fighter Group was disbanded in January 1942, and its

place taken by the 10th Reinforcement Wing, which used seven aircraft from the 10th Fighter Squadron. The Bf 109Es remained in service until July that year, when they were replaced with new Bf 109G-2s.

All of the aircraft operated by Croatian pilots retained their standard Luftwaffe camouflage and markings, the only addition is a Croatian national crest, comprising a red and white checkered shield with a knot above that and on either side wings that can be white or silver. The aircraft all carried code numbers, and these all seem to be applied in green with a white outline, those known for the E-series include 2 and 15. Most of the surviving images show the machines with the dense application of green on the fuselage sides that was used by the Luftwaffe from mid-1940.

Rumania

This nation ordered fifty Bf 109Es in December 1939, and had eleven of them by the spring of 1940. These aircraft equipped the 57th Fighter Squadron of the 7th Fighter Group based at Pipera. The overall scheme for these machines seems to be a solid upper green, probably RLM 70

or 71, over light blue (RLM 65) with the soft-edged demarcation low down on the fuselage sides. The rudder had equal width bars of blue, yellow, red (blue forward) on it and the nose and aft fuselage bands were yellow. An identifying number was applied in yellow characters, mid-fuselage. Initially these machines received the then current national insignia comprising a red/yellow/blue roundel above and below the wings, but not on the fuselage sides. By the autumn of 1940 Rumania had joined the Axis forces and this resulted

in new national insignia. This comprised a yellow cross, with a thin blue outline, the tips of each arm bent in to form an 'M' shape, apparently in tribute to Prince Michael. The original roundel was now placed in the middle of the new cross, but at a much smaller size, being about half the width of the cross arms in its total diameter. This cross could be placed mid-way along the fuselage, or often it was seen high up and just behind the cockpit canopy. Aircraft of the 7th Fighter Group all seem to have had a Donald Duck character applied at some point on the airframe, some have it between the code number and aft fuselage band, others have it under or ahead of the cockpit; it also varies in overall size. There are also instances of aircraft carrying names and slogans, usual in a very fancy script and usually on the nose – a well-known example is *'Hai Fetito!'* ('Up Little Girl!')

Slovakia

Conversion of this nation's air force to the Bf 109E took place in February 1942, with the unit becoming operational in July as 13 Letka, which was subordinate to JG 52 as 13.(Slovak)/JG52.

All the Bf 109Es operated by Slovak pilots were

in Luftwaffe camouflage of RLM 70/71 over 65, but the demarcation was high on the fuselage sides, with the remainder of the fuselage sides covered in a very dense (almost solid) application of the upper colours – some state this was just one colour, probably RLM 71? Photographs shows that the mottle on the nose was not constant, as in some instances it is solid right down to the exhausts, whilst others have only a light covering of the mottle from about 1/3rd down, others also have mottle below the line of the exhaust stacks. Looking at the contrast in the area of the nose on some machines, it could well be that the entire nose was originally in yellow and this was then covered with the dense green mottle, as the underlying shade of the area is different to the rest of the airframe and continues round the entire lower area of the nose? A RLM 04 *Gelb* (yellow) band of 500mm was applied around the aft fuselage and the wing tip undersides were also yellow – probably again to 1/5th the length of the aileron. The national insignia comprised a cross, of similar size and proportions to the later Luftwaffe Type B3, but with that cross's black sections in blue and the arms in white. In the centre of this cross was a red dot of a diameter that meant it was only on the blue segment and did not go over the white elements. The underwing crosses had their outmost tip touching the yellow bands. A single white code number was applied aft of the fuselage cross in a position that resulted in it usually overlapping the aft fuselage yellow band. No other markings were applied except the national marking of a white cross on blue mountains against a red sun, and this was usually applied either side of the nose, above and at mid-point in the exhaust stack.

above left: This shot of the mid-fuselage of a Slovakian E does show the addition of the 'B-4' stencil under the more usual 87 Octane triangle
(© via J. Andal)

above: In this shot, you can see the insignia carried on either side of the nose of Slovakian Bf 109Es
(© via J. Andal)

A Bf 109E of 1° Gruppo Caccia, Rumanian AF is seen here with the initial style of roundels, later replaced with the cross

A lovely in-flight shot of a Bf 109E-4 of 13.(Slovak)/JG52, showing the combination of Luftwaffe and Slovakian markings
(© via J. Andal)

A Bf 109D with the marking style that was imposed in September 1944

J-333 is one of the first series of Bf 109Es in its RLM 70/71/65 with the initial style of markings, seen at Dudendorf in the summer of 1939

J-370 seen in the revised marking style introduced in April 1940 with the 'Fiz' number reduced to 25cm

Bf 109E-3, J-326, which crash-landed at Thun on the 11th April 45. The fuel triangle visible reads 'K-Kraftstoff 93'

Switzerland

Switzerland purchased ten Bf 109D-1s and fifty Bf 109E-3s, all without armament, so they fitted them with guns of Swiss manufacturer (the D-1s had MG 29s in the wings and nose, the E-3s had MG 29s in the nose and FF-K 20mm cannon in the wings). These machines wore five different schemes throughout their career. The ten Bf 109D-1s were delivered in RLM 70 over RLM 65, with the demarcation low on the fuselage sides etc., and soft-edged. The first batch of Bf 109Es were delivered in an RLM 70/71 over 65 scheme, but the splinter demarcation of the upper colours was soft-edged, not hard as applied to Luftwaffe machines – it is believed this covers J-311 to J-340. Once the Bf 109Es received their MG 29 armament, however, the nose cowls were sprayed in KW 2 (RLM 70). It is thought, as no records survive, that the rest of the fuselage was also resprayed overall in KW 2 (RLM 70) when the markings were revised in April 1940 – note that the colour was just sprayed over the existing camouflage, so the demarcation lines would have remained visible in the new paint and the camouflage on the wings, tail and tailplanes remained, albeit applied with Swiss-made paints. The second batch of Bf 109Es, J-341 to J-390, were supplied in the KW 2/KW 1 (RLM 70/65) scheme. Initially all paints were obtained in Germany, but by the summer of 1939 the colours were being made by K+W and DMP as follows:

RLM	K+W	DMP
RLM 65	KW 1	602 344
RLM 70	KW 2	602 342
RLM 71	KW 3	-

All of the Swiss-built machines, J-391 to J-399 were sprayed in KW 2 over KW 1.

The initial markings comprised a three-digit serial number (*Fiz* number) in white characters 50cm high and in 1938 the character 'J' for *Jäger* (Fighter) was applied ahead of the serial in 40cm high white characters and separated from the serial by a dash. The national insignia comprised a red disc of 820mm, with a white cross in the centre that was 470mm across and had arms 145mm thick. This roundel was positioned above and below the wings 1110mm inboard of the tip, centrally and did not overlap either ailerons or slats. The top half of the rudder was also painted red, with a small white cross on it, the red only extended vertically up from the hinge line, the forward/top of the rudder remained in the airframe colour and onto it was the Kp (*Kompanie*) number (two numeric) in small (5cm) white characters. In January 1940 a red band was applied to the underside of the wings, 1,300mm wide and positioned 460mm inboard of the tip – it went across the aileron but not the slat. On to this a cross of 920mm was applied with arms of 285mm thickness. At the same time, the entire rudder was now painted red and the cross, although the same size, moved down to a position approximately 2/3rd of the way up. At some point during 1940 white safely stripes were added to the front faces of each propeller blade, one just inboard of the

A Bf 109E with sharksmouth motif of Fl Kp 21 seen at Buochs airfield in the winter of 1943-44. Note the two white hazard bands on each propeller blade

Kompanie Insignia

Initially such badges were not tolerated, but in the summer of 1940 such emblems were officially accepted to help raise morale. Those that applied to the units that used the Bf 109 in Switzerland are as follows:

- Cp av 6 and Fl Kp 4 – Witch on a broom on a white six-pointed star (the witch was often in red)
- Fl Kp 7 – Initially they had a shark going through a yellow ring, but this was later changed with the shark's teeth removed to turn it into a happy trout!
- Fl Kp 7 – They often used artwork created by Hans Träutlien depicting a farmer wielding a three-pronged rake after a high-ranking officer called them a band of farmers during inspection (they often helped local farmers with the harvest!)
- Fl Kp 8 – This unit's emblem depicted the silver star (Edelweiss) with four flowers on a white ring – usually at the base of the stem a name was applied, such as 'Elsbeth', 'Narziss' or 'Margrit'
- Fl Kp 9 – This unit had a gold comet and tail as their emblem, but from the 25th April 1941 this was changed to be mounted

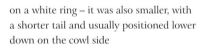

Examples of badges from Fl Kp 8 with the various names added within the ring

The badge of Fl Kp 9 in early (top) and later (bottom forms

on a white ring – it was also smaller, with a shorter tail and usually positioned lower down on the cowl side
- Fl Kp 15 – A black eagle was this unit's motif and it was initially applied directly onto the aircraft camouflage within a black ring. This was later changed to be either on a white disc, or a white disc with a ring around it of the camouflage colour, then another white ring outside of that
- Fl Kp 21 – These are the famous sharkmouth Bf 109Es. The style and number of teeth

changed over the years, but the overall shape of the mouth and its position remained constant, as did the eye above it on each side of the cowling

Note – Many publications mention the trout 'Jaqueline' emblem of Fl St. 7 in relation to the Bf 109 in Switzerland, but this emblem was created in 1952 and thus has nothing to do with the type, as the Bf 109 was retired from Swiss service on the 28th December 1949.

Examples of the styles of badge used by Fl Kp 15

The badge of Cp av 6

Badge of Fl Kp 7 – this is the initial one as a shark

J-328 in flight, showing the April 1940 marking style

J-371 in the marking style that was applied in July-August 1944. You can see how the stripes looked very much like the Allied invasion markings

tip and another about 15cm below it – both were 25mm wide bands. Due to confusion between types Switzerland flew and other nations (e.g. MS.406 and Bf 109E) a red band was applied to the fuselage with the same size white cross as introduced under the wings. The aircraft number was also moved aft and reduced in size to characters of 250mm high. This scheme remained in use until September 1944, when clashes with USAAF aircraft during the 5th to 10th of the month highlighted that the crews could not identify the aircraft as Swiss until the very last moment (something the Swiss had also discovered in co-operation trials with the army), so red and white stripes of 500mm widths were applied to the fuselage and wings. These were added aft of the existing fuselage red band/white cross and inboard of those on the upper and lower wing surfaces. Because the fuselage stripes would go over the aircraft serial number, where this happened the number remained in a block of the underlying green within the stripes. It should also be noted that the cross on the

This image of Bf 109B-1 with the codes 23•15 and Bf 109B-2, 23•3 of Banolas Grupo 27 was taken in the late 1940s, by which time the Spanish roundel had replaced the black ones of the Civil War era
(© via J. Grant)

upper wing was of the same size as the lower one (920mm with 285 wide bars), but it had the front edge directly in line with the back edge of the slat, so did not go as far over the ailerons as those did under the wings. The final change to the scheme came in the Summer of 1945, when the red and white stripes and cross were removed from the fuselage, all other markings remained though, including the stripes around the wings. There are instances during 1945 where this regulation change was not adhered too, as there are images of aircraft with the fuselage stripes removed but the red band and white cross remaining.

Spain

The famous 'Blue Squadron' (*Patrilla Azul*) fought alongside the *Wehrmacht* in WWII. After initial training at *Werneuchen* the unit received twelve Bf 109E-4s and E-7s in September 1941. The unit moved to Moschna airfield and was incorporated under the command of JG27 as 15.(Span.)/JG27. The unit returned home in January 1942 and was disbanded, but another group formed in June 1942 and was supplied with a mix of Bf 109Es and Fs to serve under JG 51 as 15.(Span.)/JG51 in the Orel area until November that year, when they went back to Bordeaux and retrained to fly the Bf 109F.

All the aircraft used by Spanish pilots were in full Luftwaffe camouflage and markings of the era. About the only thing we did note was that they all carry really large yellow bands around the aft fuselage, running from the last fuselage rib to meet the aft arm of the cross.

Bf 109Es of the Yugoslavia Air Force seen in January 1941

Yugoslavia

This nation was one of the first to order the Bf 109E and after some delay they received one hundred Bf 109E-3s and an additional twenty-five DB 601 engines from April 1939. The type was only operated by the 6th Fighter Regiment in the JKRV (Royal Yugoslav Air Force) and just 73 aircraft entered service, as the loss rate in

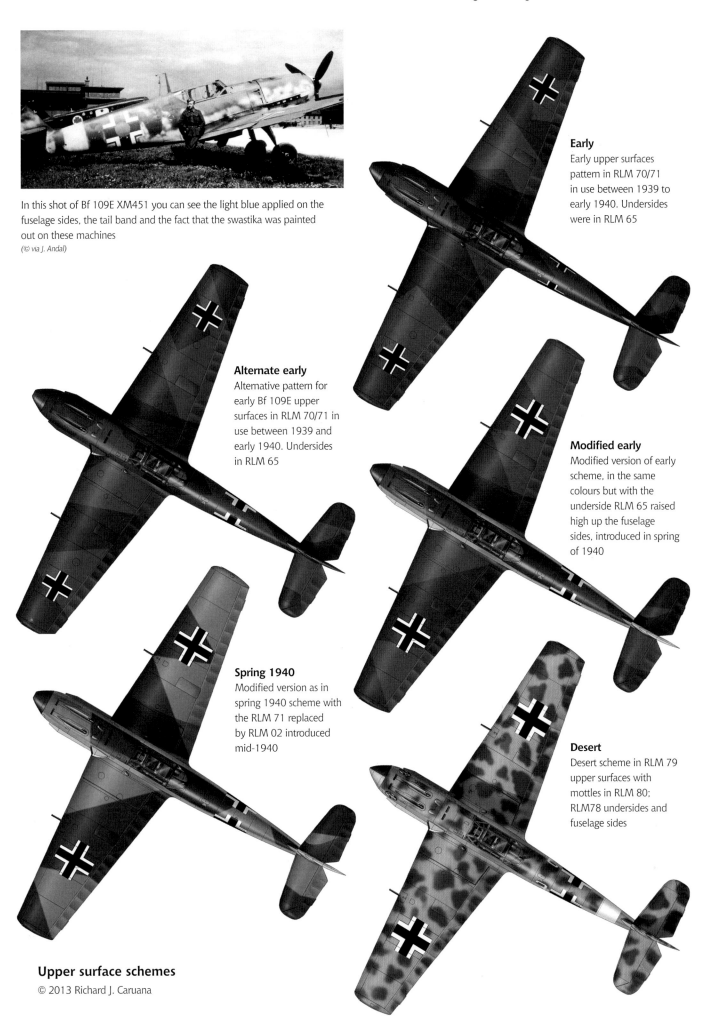

In this shot of Bf 109E XM451 you can see the light blue applied on the fuselage sides, the tail band and the fact that the swastika was painted out on these machines

(© via J. Andal)

Early
Early upper surfaces pattern in RLM 70/71 in use between 1939 to early 1940. Undersides were in RLM 65

Alternate early
Alternative pattern for early Bf 109E upper surfaces in RLM 70/71 in use between 1939 and early 1940. Undersides in RLM 65

Modified early
Modified version of early scheme, in the same colours but with the underside RLM 65 raised high up the fuselage sides, introduced in spring of 1940

Spring 1940
Modified version as in spring 1940 scheme with the RLM 71 replaced by RLM 02 introduced mid-1940

Desert
Desert scheme in RLM 79 upper surfaces with mottles in RLM 80; RLM78 undersides and fuselage sides

Upper surface schemes
© 2013 Richard J. Caruana

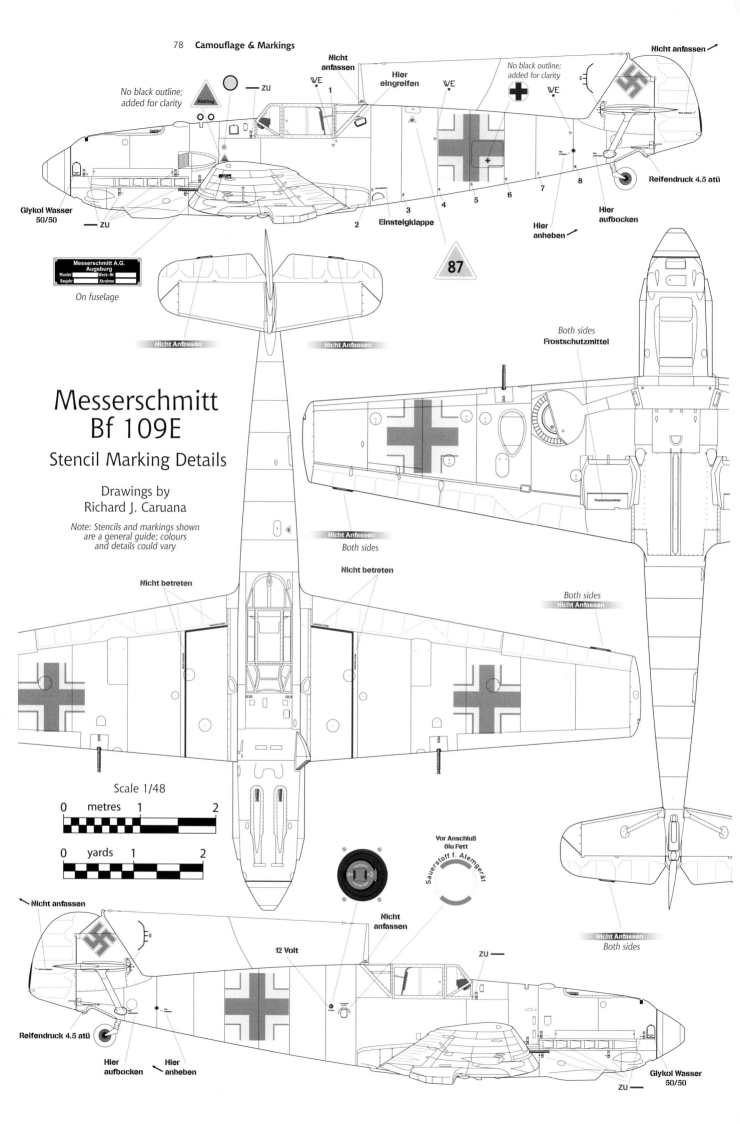

Messerschmitt Bf 109E
Stencil Marking Details

Drawings by
Richard J. Caruana

*Note: Stencils and markings shown
are a general guide; colours
and details could vary*

*No black outline;
added for clarity*

Nicht
anfassen

Hier
eingreifen

*No black outline;
added for clarity*

Nicht anfassen

Rotring

ZU

WE

WE

WE

Nicht anfassen

Reifendruck 4.5 atü

Glykol Wasser
50/50

ZU

Einsteigklappe

Hier
anheben

Hier
aufbocken

87

Messerschmitt A.G.
Augsburg
Muster   Werk-Nr
Baujahr   Abnahme

On fuselage

Both sides
Frostschutzmittel

Nicht Anfassen

Nicht Anfassen

Both sides

Frostschutzmittel

Nicht betreten

Nicht betreten

Both sides
Nicht Anfassen

Scale 1/48

| 0 | metres | 1 | 2 |

| 0 | yards | 1 | 2 |

Vor Anschluß
ölu Fett

Sauerstoff f. Atemgerät

Nicht
anfassen

Nicht anfassen

12 Volt

ZU

Nicht Anfassen
Both sides

Reifendruck 4.5 atü

Hier
aufbocken

Hier
anheben

Glykol Wasser
50/50

ZU

Captured & Evaluated

Bf 109E-4/b W/Nr.4101 after capture and during evaluation (probably from Boscombe Down) seen repainted in RAF Dark Earth/Dark Green upper surfaces with yellow underneath. Type B roundels have been applied above the wing with a Type C fin flash and Type C1 fuselage roundel, albeit the latter is very much over-size for this size of aircraft and was therefore probably applied that big to be very visible from both the ground and air

Underside view of captured Bf 109E-4/b W/Nr.4101 in RAF C&M, note the odd proportions of the roundels and the fact they are applied well inboard, probably as a result of them being applied big and needed to therefore fit between the hinge line of the aileron and the wing leading edge

The Bf 109E was evaluated in Japan. Check out the dense fuselage mottle and what are those markings on the flaps – were they supplied unpainted?

In this shot of a Royal Yugoslavian Air Force E3(a) you can see the way in which the code was applied to the fuselage

The solid colours of the Royal Yugoslavian Bf 109E(a)s is well illustrated in this shot

Bf 109E-3(a) for Yugoslavia seen lined up prior to delivery and confirming that the overall scheme was applied in Germany. The aircraft are fitted with propellers that have only two blades installed
(© via B Roberson)

pilot transition to the type was high.

All of the Yugoslavian machines were painted in Germany prior to delivery, as proved by period images, so they were in a simple two-colour scheme that is most likely RLM 70 over RLM 65 with a low demarcation on the fuselage sides and along the nose. Images showing the airframes lined up without wings prior to delivery seem to show the area around the exhausts and the areas directly below it, which we would assume to be RLM 70, to be in a shiny shade that is much darker, so was this area black? The propeller and spinner is in RLM 70 and the rudder was initially painted in bands of equal width in blue (top), white (middle) and red (bottom). Later these bands were removed then in 1941 they returned but now the bands were reduced in width so that the whole thing only covered about 1/5th of the rudder, and this marking was positioned above the rudder's centreline. The national insignia was applied above and below the wings only, and positioned mid-way along the aileron. This is not universal, however, as there are examples with no roundels under the wing, or below the starboard and above the port only. No roundel was applied to the fuselage but instead this area was taken with an identification code. These were in black characters probably to the same criteria as Luftwaffe codes (e.g. 4/5th the depth of the fuselage) and they comprised one alpha, a dash and one or two numerics (e.g. L-7, L-10, L-21, L-52 or L-80). The positioning of this marking seems quite constant, with the first number usually over the radio hatch and the L just below the fuel filler stencil. There are also examples of this code applied in white, in the same style, and

these seem to only have been applied when the full bands of colour on the rudder were used, and there is even an example of one that has half and half – L-33, where the 'L' is black and the '-33' is white. Aft of this marking in small black characters was the W/Nr., just expressed as a number (e.g. 2525). There are also images that show machines with an identification marking that is only numeric and applied in white characters (e.g. '8' or '11'), again with this letter positioned below the fuel filler stencil. What most people seem to miss is the data stencil on the vertical fin. This is applied in black characters, probably around 4-5cm high and not a lot can be made out, however thanks to the guys at Lift Here Decals we are able to confirm the data as follows:

It reads – top to bottom
Me 109
Br.2530 (the individual Yugoslav AF number {2=fighter, 5=type, 30*=aircraft number})
T. S. ("težina samog" – empty weight, 1835kg, written as 1835Kg)
T. K. ("težina korisna" – useful weight, 775kg, written as 775Kg)
T. U. ("težina ukupna" – gross weight, 2610kg, written as 2610Kg)

A note on the aircraft numbers – These were preceded by an 'L-' on fuselage sides, then the last one or two digits of the aircraft number, BUT the sequence was broken as a result of crashes and overhauls. Therefore L-7 and L-21 were Br.2507 and Br.2521 respectively, but L-33 was Br.2532.

Operational Markings

See the colour profiles on pages 81-89 for a selection of unit markings and insignia applied to the early Bf 109 series. We would also recommend the following titles for those wishing to read more on this complex subject.

• Luftwaffe 1935-1945 Camouflage and Markings Part 1 by Jaroslaw Wróbel and Janusz Ledwoch (AJ Press 1994, ISBN: 83-86208-08-2)
• Luftwaffe 1935-1945 Camouflage and Markings Part 2 by Jaroslaw Wróbel (AJ Press 1995, ISBN: 83-86208-14-7)
• Luftwaffe Colours 1935-1945 by M. Ullmann (Hikoki Publications Ltd 2002/Crécy Publishing Ltd 2008 ISBN: 9-781902-109077)
• The Official Monogram Painting Guide to German Aircraft 1935 – 1945 by Kenneth A. Merrick & Thomas H. Hitchcock (Monogram Aviation Publications 1980 ISBN: 0-914144-29-4)

Note – Some references on early machines to the use of 'RLM 63' may in fact be DKH L40/52 light grey lacquer or Avionorm Nitro-paint 7375 matt light grey as the term 'RLM 63' was used for all these colours in official documents of the period.

Messerschmitt Bf 109 V1, D-IABI
Silver overall with all lettering in black. Red band across vertical tail surfaces with black swastika over a white disk.
Spinner is polished natural metal

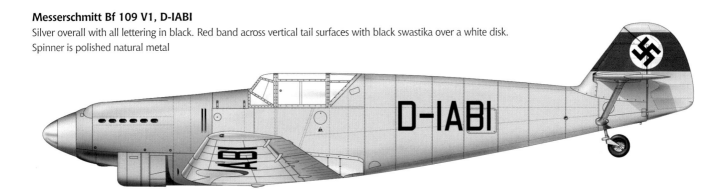

Messerschmitt Bf 109 V3, D-IOQY
Silver overall with all lettering in black. Red band across vertical tail surfaces with black swastika over a white disk.
Spinner is grey

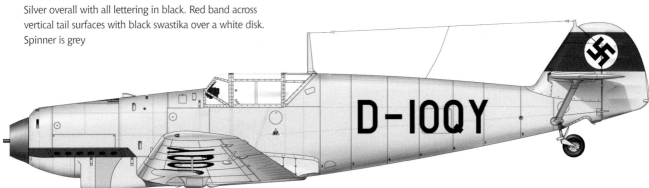

Messerschmitt Bf 109 V4, D-IALY
RLM 01 Silber overall with all lettering in black. Red band across vertical tail surfaces with black swastika over a white disk.
Spinner front is polished natural metal

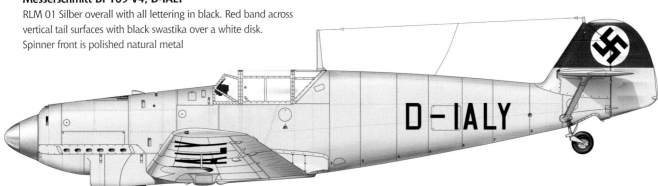

Messerschmitt Bf 109 (V4), W/Nr.878
One of the first four Bf 109s delivered to Spain and flown by Oblt Hannes Trautloft of J/88, Sivilla/Tablada, December 1936.
DKH L40/52 light grey lacquer or Avionorm Nitro-paint 7375 matt light grey overall with all markings in black;
white rudder with black 'St Andrew's Cross'. White/green front
of spinner; green 'heart' emblem below cockpit (both sides)

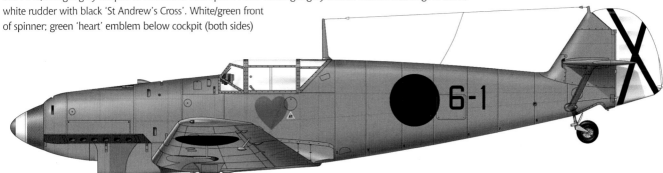

©Richard J. Caruana 2013

Messerschmitt Bf 109B-1, 6•42, 2.J/88

Spain, March 1937. RLM 62 upper surfaces with RLM 65 undersides; white wing tips and rudder, the latter having also a black 'St Andrew's Cross'. Codes in black; black discs with white crosses above and below wings. Spinner remains in the previous RLM 63

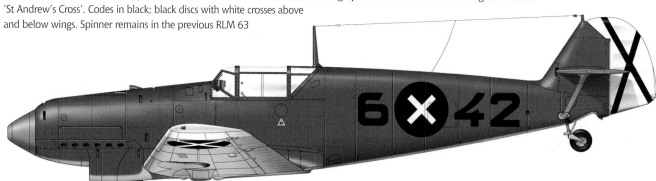

Messerschmitt Bf 109B-2, 6•56

Flown by Haupt. Gotthardt Handrick whilst Staffelkapitän of 2.J/88, Spain, 1937. RLM 63 upper surfaces with RLM 65 undersides; white wing tips and rudder, the latter having also a black 'St Andew's Cross'. Black codes, white 'H' on fuselage black disc; black discs with white crosses above and below wings. Olympic symbols on either side of spinner as shown, denoting the gold won by Handrick in the Pentathlon of the Olympics at Berlin in 1936 and a question regarding the next games (1940). Note that these markings were also carried, in modified form, on the Bf 109D-1 that he flew later

Messerschmitt Bf 109B-2, 73•79

Escuela de Caza, Morón de la Frontera, 1945. RLM 63 upper surfaces with RLM 65 undersides; white rudder with black 'St Andrew's Cross'. Roundels in red/yellow/red in six positions; black codes

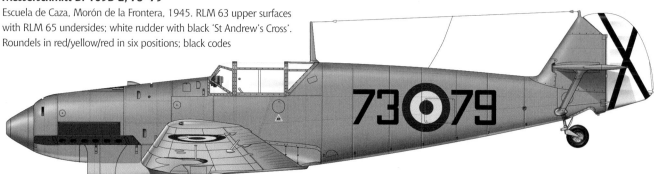

Messerschmitt Bf 109C, N+8, 10 (Nacht)/JG 77

Aalborg, July 1940. RLM 70/71 upper surfaces with RLM 65 undersides. All lettering in black. Unit badge on forward fuselage

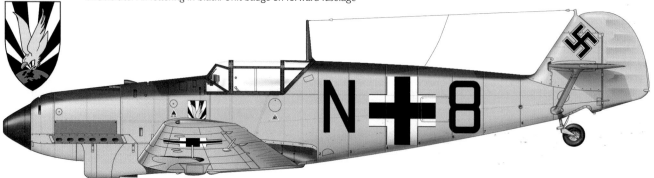

Messerschmitt Bf 109D-1, 'Red 11', 2./JG 71

September 1939. RLM 70/71/65 finish with red '11', outlined in white; white spinner backplate. Unit badge below cockpit. This unit was stationed at Fürstenfeldbruck to protect Munich in case of a Polish counter-attack

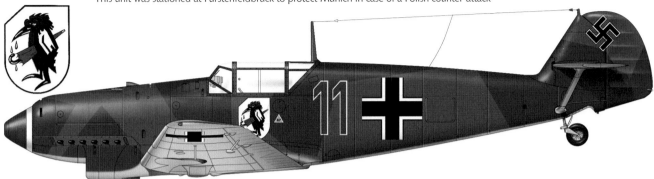

Messerschmitt Bf 109D-1, W/Nr.2302 J-307

In the full neutrality markings introduced on 16th September 1944. RLM 71 upper surfaces with RLM 65 undersides and white nose section. White codes on fuselage sides. 50cm bands in red and white around fuselage sides and around wings with a 130cm wide red panel on fuselage sides and wings carrying a white cross. Red rudder with white cross superimposed; note while the fuselage bands wrap around the whole fuselage, the red panel on the fuselage ends in line with the camouflage demarcation mark

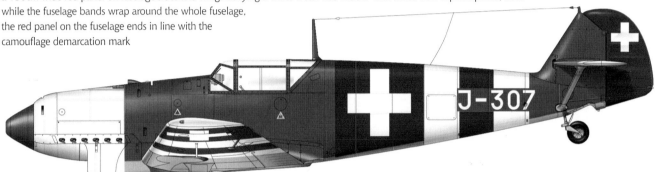

Messerschmitt Bf 109D, GA+MK

Flugzeugführerschule A/B 123 (Kroat), Agram, Zagreb, early 1943. RLM 70/02 uppersurfaces with 76 undersides. Codes in black. Yellow bands around rear fuselage and below wingtips. Unit badge on forward fuselage

Messerschmitt Bf 109E-3, 6./JG51

Flown by Staffelkapitän Josef 'Pips' Priller, Autumn 1940. RLM 71/02/65 scheme with RLM 71 and 02 mottling on fuselage sides; RLM 70 spinner. RLM 04 cowling, rudder and '1' on fuselage, the latter outlined in black. Ace of Hearts card emblem is pilot's personal insignia; 20 kills marked in white on fin

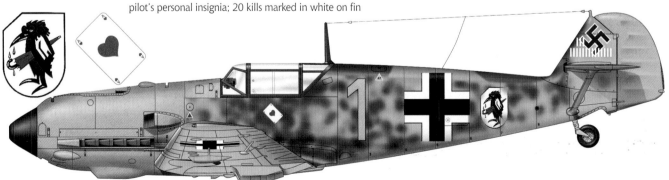

©Richard J. Caruana 2013

Messerschmitt Bf 109E-7 Trop, Black '1', 2./JG27, 1941

Top surfaces are in RLM 79 with large mottles of RLM 80, over RLM 78 undersurfaces and sides of fuselage. RLM 04 nose section and rudder and RLM 21 rear fuselage band. Numeral is black with thin red outline. Spinner is red and white

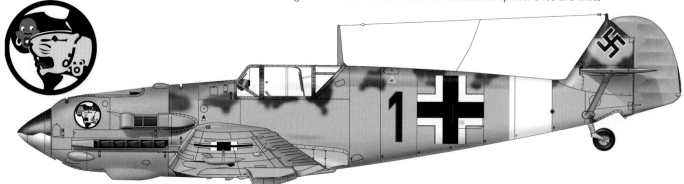

Messerschmitt Bf 109E-7 Trop, 'Black 3', 2./JG 27

Gazala, Spring 1941. RLM 74/75 on upper surfaces with RLM 76 undersides and fuselage sides; overpaint is probably in RLM 70 or RLM 71 on the fuselage and tail area. Red/white spinner, black '3' outlined in red

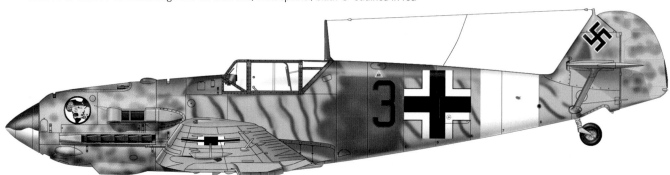

Messerschmtt Bf 109E-7 Trop

Flown by Oblt Ludwig Franzisket, Gruppen Adj. of I./JG27, El Gazala, Libya, 1941. RLM 79 upper surfaces with RLM 78 undersides; yellow nose with spinner in RLM 70 and white. White rear fuselage band. Black chevron, outlined in white, on fuselage sides

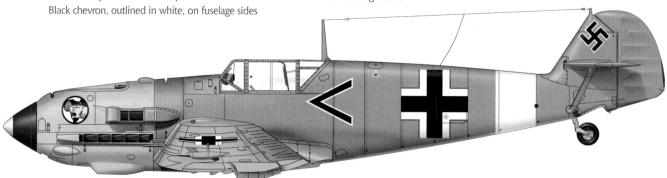

Messerschmitt Bf 109E (probably an E-7)

Flown by Staffelkapitän Max Dobislav of III./JG 27, Sicily, 1941. RLM 71/02 upper surfaces over RLM 65 undersides, with RLM 71 mottles on fuselage sides extending onto the fin. RLM 27 nose section, white rear band and rudder, which carries 14 victories. Note white metal pennant on aerial mast, and four white bars on the spinner

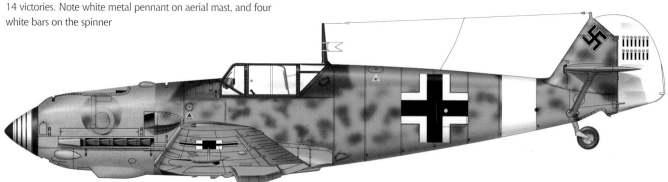

Messerschmitt Bf 109E-4, G9+JM, III./NJG 1

Black overall with RLM 77 code, except for 'J', which is RLM 23 outlined in white. Spinner tip is also RLM 23

Messerschmitt Bf 109E-1, W/Nr.4172, 'Red 1', 2./JG 77

Flown by Staffelkapitän Oblt. Hannes Trautloff, September 1939. RLM 70/71/65 finish with early style crosses on fuselage and wing upper surfaces. All markings red, outlined in white, as is the bar on spinner. Personal marking is in white without the black outline as shown on the enlarged version

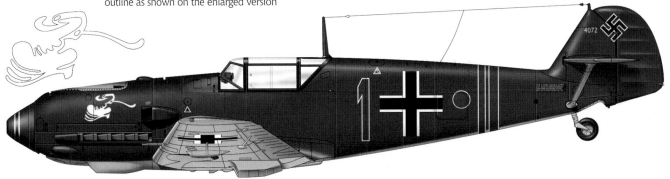

Messerschmitt Bf 109E, 2./JG 52

Laon-Couvron (France). RLM 71/02/65 scheme with RLM 70 spinner; RLM 23 '14' outlined in white on fuselage. Note 2 kill markings at base of fin, ahead of swastika. Shot down at Berwick (Sussex) on 12th August 1940

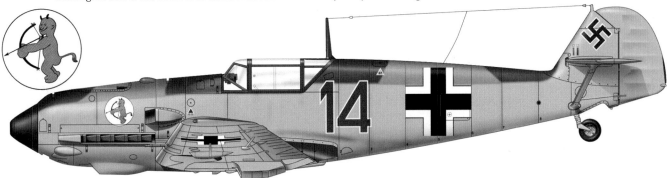

Messerschmitt Bf 109E, I./JG 53

Flown by Gruppenkommandeur Hptm Hans-Karl Meyer, September 1940. RLM 70/71 uppersurfaces with RLM 65 undersides; RLM 02 has been added to the fuselage sides. RLM 04 cowling and rudder; RLM 70 spinner. '8' in white; note white kill markings painted over the original RLM 70/71 colours of the rudder, the yellow having been painted around them

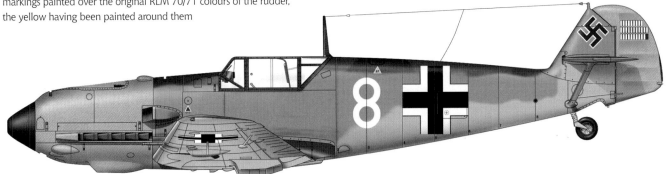

Messerschmitt Bf 109E-4

Flown by Kommander of I./JG 2 Helmut Wick, September 1940. RLM 71/02/65 scheme with heavy stippling of RLM 71 on fuselage sides; RLM 04 cowling, wing tips and rudder (the latter covered also in RLM 71). 42 kill markings on the rudder in white

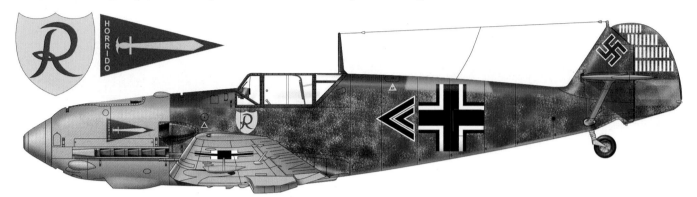

Messerschmitt Bf 109E-4 'Yellow 1'

Flown by Oberleutnant Gerhard Schöpel, Staffelkapitän of 9./JG 26 'Schlagater', based at Caffiers (France), August 1940. RLM 71/02/65 finish with RLM 04 '1' and vertical bar, outlined in black. RLM 04 wing tips, tailplane tips and top of rudder; 12 victories on rudder

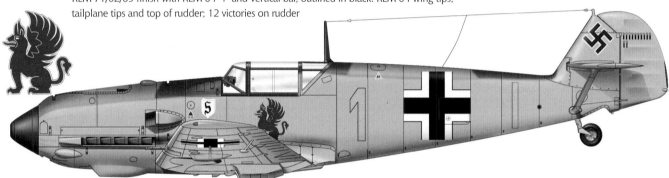

Messerschmitt Bf 109E-4

Flown by Gruppenkommandeur Hans von Hahn, I./JG 3, France, summer 1940. RLM 71/02/65 scheme, with Gelb 27 nose and rudder, 3/4 white and 1/4 black spinner tipped in RLM 02. Note 18 victories on the rudder

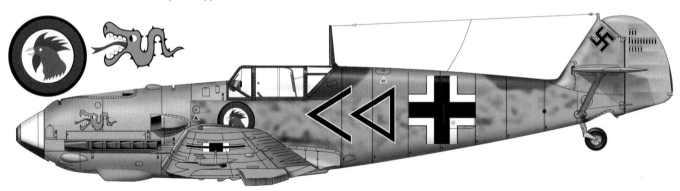

Messerschmitt Bf 109E-3, 9./JG54

RLM 71/02 upper surfaces with RLM 65 undersides. RLM 02 applied in streaks over the fuselage sides. RLM 04 '11', outlined in black. Unit badge on engine cowling

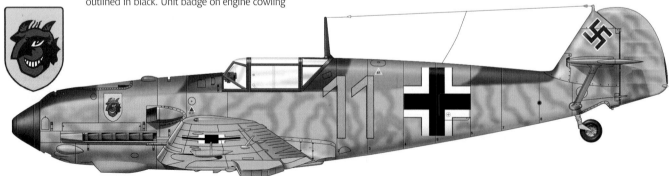

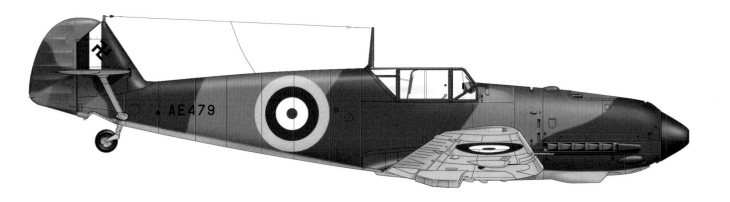

Messerschmitt Bf 109E-3, AE479, ex-W/Nr.1304

In RAF markings and additional 'swastikas' applied during the Air Cavalcade tour of US, as photographed at La Guardia airport (NYC), spring 1942. Dark Earth/Dark Green upper surfaces with yellow undersides. Standard RAF markings in all positions, except that 'swastikas' were overpainted in black. Black spinner and serial. Note (1) not known if these were also applied to the underwing roundels (2) they are applied in mirror fashion between port and starboard (3) canopy is different from the one it had when captured in France

Although not a Bf 109 in Luftwaffe or foreign service, the first intact E captured by the Allies was this machine, which became AE479 and is seen here in the USA undergoing flight testing, where it was sadly crashed. It had a standard RAF day fighter scheme of Dark Green and Dark Earth, but being a test aircraft the undersides were yellow

©Richard J. Caruana 2013

Messerschmitt Bf 109T, 'Yellow 7', NJG 101

RLM 74/75 upper surfaces with RLM 76 undersides
and fuselage sides. Spinner in RLM 70 with a
white quarter. Codes in black

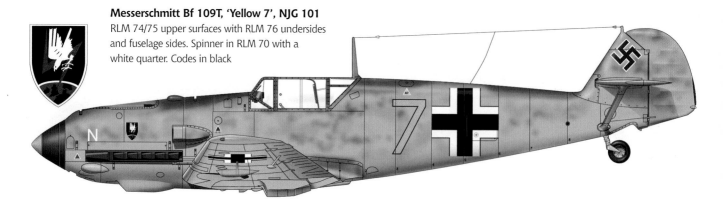

Messerschmitt Bf 109E-3, 'Green 15'

Flown by Oberfeldwebel Veca Mikovic, 15 (Kroat)./JG 52, Mariupol, summer 1942. RLM 74/75 upper surfaces
with RLM 76 undersides. Yellow front fuselage, rear fuselage band and underside of wing tips. Green '15' outlined
in white. National markings in six positions with Croatian marking below windscreen. Eight kill markings on rudder

Messerschmitt Bf 109E-3, V5+06

5/1 Fighter Group, Hungarian Air Force, 1943. RLM 02 with Dark Green and Dark Brown upper surfaces and RLM 76
undersides. Yellow rear fuselage band and underside of wing tips. National markings in six positions, codes in black.
Green/white/red bands across vertical and horizontal tail surfaces.
Unit badge on forward fuselage

Messerschmitt Bf 109E-3, 37

Flown by Lt Ion Dicezare, Escadrila 58, Grupul 7 Vanatoare, Romanian Air Force, 1941. RLM 70 upper surfaces with
RLM 65 undersides. Yellow nose, rear fuselage band and underside of wing tips. Tricolor in blue/yellow/red on rudder.
National markings in six positions. Codes on fuselage in yellow. Name 'Hai Fetito!' on nose and five kill markings in white.
Unit badge ahead of rear fuselage band

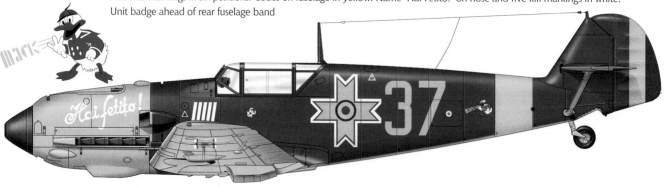

©Richard J. Caruana 2013

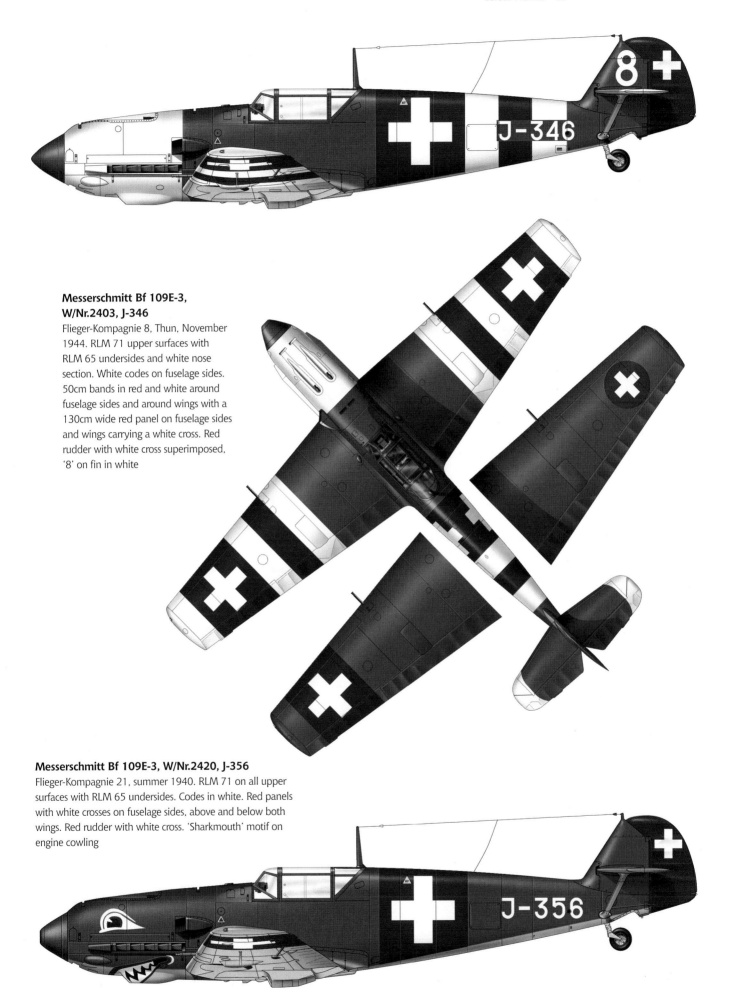

Messerschmitt Bf 109E-3, W/Nr.2403, J-346

Flieger-Kompagnie 8, Thun, November 1944. RLM 71 upper surfaces with RLM 65 undersides and white nose section. White codes on fuselage sides. 50cm bands in red and white around fuselage sides and around wings with a 130cm wide red panel on fuselage sides and wings carrying a white cross. Red rudder with white cross superimposed, '8' on fin in white

Messerschmitt Bf 109E-3, W/Nr.2420, J-356

Flieger-Kompagnie 21, summer 1940. RLM 71 on all upper surfaces with RLM 65 undersides. Codes in white. Red panels with white crosses on fuselage sides, above and below both wings. Red rudder with white cross. 'Sharkmouth' motif on engine cowling

©Richard J. Caruana 2013

Messerschmitt Bf 109E-3, W/Nr.1304

Flown by Fw. Karl Hier of 1./JG 76 , captured by the French near Würth, 22nd November 1939. RLM 70/71 upper surfaces with RLM 65 undersides. All German markings overpainted. national French markings applied in six positions. Original 'White 1' and unit badge retained. Handed over to the RAF on 2 May 1940 and received the serial AE479

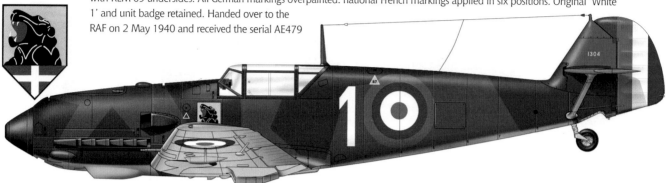

Messerschmitt Bf 109E-3, W/Nr.2945, 'White 2'

Flown by Jan Reznak, No.13 Squadron, Slovak Air Force, Piestany, October 1942. RLM 74/75 upper surfaces with RLM 76 undersides. Yellow spinner front, rear fuselage band and underside of wingtips. White '2' on rear fuselage. National markings in six positions. Marking is carried on nose, both sides

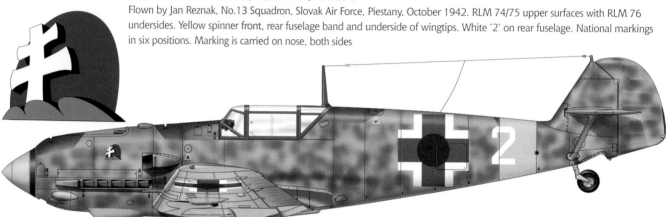

Messerschmitt Bf 109E-4, 7047/11

Flown by Mihail Grigorov, CO of 672nd Yato, 3.6 Orlyak, Royal Bulgarian Air Force, Karlovo, 1942. RLM 70/71 upper surfaces with RLM 65 undersides. Yellow front fuselage section, fuselage stripe and rudder. National markings in six positions. White '11' repeated in black below wing tips. Badge on nose based on that of Luftwaffe's IV./JG1

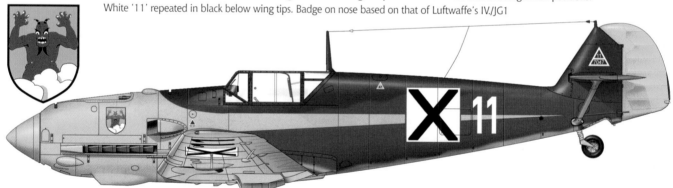

Messerschmitt Bf 109E-3, S/No.2532

L-33, Yugoslav Air Force. RLM 70 upper surfaces with RLM 65 undersides. Codes in black and white. Tail lettering in white. National markings above port wing and below both wings

©Richard J. Caruana 2013

Examples of unit badges applied to the early Bf 109 series

JG 2

JG 3

JG 3

JG 26

JG 26

JG 26

JG 27

JG 27

JG 27

JG 52

JG 52

JG 53

JG 76

JG 77

LG 2

Galland

B1

B1a

B2

B3

B5

National markings applied to the early Bf 109 series

H1

H2

H2a

H4

©Richard J. Caruana 2013

Chapter 8: **Bf 109 V1 to E-9 and T-series Kits**

The early-series Bf 109 has been a very popular subject with kit manufacturers over the years, so once again we thought we would have a look through the kits that we could find and give you our assessment of them.

As far as we are aware no one has ever attempted to do this before, and there is a reason, it is a massive undertaking. We have a large number of kits to look at and this is further complicated when you start to consider the whole issue of 'accuracy'.

Although our assessments cannot be definitive, none ever will be, they are, we feel as even-handed and accurate as they can be.

The list below is arranged by scale, then by manufacturer and variant.

With so many kits to cover, we have opted to go for a selection in each scale, mainly selecting those that are considered the most accurate or the most recent. Assessments of older kits will be made available to download as PDFs on our website (www.valiant-wings.co.uk) as soon as this title becomes available.

Revell 04916

The Bf 109 in scale

Please note, although we initially wanted to use commercially produced and published scale plans in the below assessments, we have found that many are at odds when you convert the real measurement from the official manuals to scale and then compare that with the drawings. We have therefore worked from the following scale conversions (to one decimal place) for the major dimensions based on those quoted in the General Arrangement diagram in each type's manual (please note that the dimensions listed in many published sources, online and by kit manufacturers have often been 'rounded up', the below reflect those seen in the manual).

Bf 109E	1/144th	1/72nd	1/48th	1/32nd	1/24th
Span (9.87m)	68.5mm	137.0mm	205.6mm	308.4mm	411.2mm
Length (8.64m)	60.0mm	120.0mm	180.0mm	270.0mm	360.0mm
Height (2.5m)	17.3mm	34.7mm	52.0mm	78.1mm	104.1mm

1/144th Scale

Revell, Germany

Bf 109E #04916

This kit was first released in 1973 as #H1017 and was not reissued again until 1992 as #4045. Its most recent re-emergence was in 2012 as #04916 with the new 'Micro Wings' series and it is that edition that we have to assess here.

Plastic: Light grey-coloured, with raised panel lines.

Wings: Moulded as 'solid' one-piece; span within 0.2mm; ailerons, flaps and slats defined by deep engraved lines, no other detail; panel lines do not match plans; no access panels, cannon bulges good, but odd shape; attempt to add scoop and wing bolt blisters, but former too big in comparison with latter; radiators separate, but moulded as one with bulges on flaps.

Wheel wells: Moulded within 'solid' wing, very shallow with no detail; correct position and overall shape.

Undercarriage: Leg, wheel and door moulded as one; correct length, but doors suffer from shrink marks, wheels have hubs that are raised and overall detail is poor/inaccurate; tailwheel and yoke moulded as one to one fuselage half, little detail, tyre looks small in comparison with size/thickness of yoke; no tailwheel well.

Fuselage: Correct length; rudder profile more like F-series as is the shape of the nose area; rudder has raised ribs across entire surface; exhaust stacks moulded in situ, heavy detail and six complete stacks visible (sixth [front] should only be partial); access step in port side partial relief, oversize and very heavy; supercharger intake just a blob; vents etc. in nose all too heavy/large recesses; gun troughs too wide; aerial mast moulded to fuselage half.

Tailplanes: Separate; correct span and good profile; hinge line accurate; rudder has raised ribs, inaccurate and only partial; no trim tabs.

Engine: None supplied.

Propeller: Moulded as one unit spinner/propeller; propeller diameter good; blade profile a bit too broad at base; spinner has cannon hole in centre.

Interior: None.

Detail: None.

Canopy: One-piece; good clarity; length OK but the windscreen angle is too steep; no framing in lower windscreen and upper rear section panels.

Decals: One options; 'White <<', flown by Maj. Erich Mix, III./JG2, France, May 1940; decals good but being a German firm there are no swastikas; no stencils.

Verdict: *This is very much a product of its era, as it is as basic as all the other 1/144th and smaller kits we have seen in the 1950s, 60s, 70, 80s and even 1990s. It leaves a lot to be desired, but is still probably the best in this scale to date? Hopefully before too long the likes of Eduard may consider doing one to add to their existing 1/144th scale range, but until then, this is as good as it gets.*

1/72nd Scale

Academy, Korea

1/72nd Messerschmitt Bf 109E #2133

Academy produced their first Bf 109E back in 1990 (#1668), but this had various shape errors so they retooled it and reissued it in 1993 as #2133. The basic revised tooling was used for the Bf 109E-3/4 'Heinz Bär' with Kettenkrad kit (#2214) released in 2003. We have #2133 for assessment here.

Plastic: Light grey-coloured with engraved panel lines and other details.

Wings: Correct span but slightly narrow in chord from tip to root; tips slightly too rounded at front; panel lines match published plans; couple of hatches are wrong; radiator units wrong shape & moulded with rear flap and bulge on flaps (no gap); thick bar in front of radiator intakes; cannon bulges too small; cannon barrels moulded to wing; oblong hole in semi-relief at flap mid-span, should just be hinge point, but too big/deep; ribs for fabric on control surfaces, but wrong number and v-shaped ones in flaps missing; wing bolt bulges and centreline scoop present; two further bulges forward of centreline scoop, should not be there; step in hinge line of flaps/ailerons; access hatch behind cannon port is oval, should be half-round; tip lights moulded as projecting bulges, should be recessed; wheel wells correct position and shape; oleo legs mount into roof, no fuselage side; oleo legs basic 'stepped' tubes; rear brake plate moulded to oleo + combines linkage; u/c doors inboard bottom corners cut off at 45°; wheels correct diameter; with tread pattern; hub details includes spokes; tailwheel separate moulded as yoke and wheel; tailwheel tyre slightly small and devoid of detail.

Fuselage: Correct length; overall profile good; leading edge of vertical fin slightly too steep an angle; some access panels are raised lines, others recessed; oxygen charging point on starboard fuselage side as recessed hole, should be engraved outline; ribs on rudder go all the way across/do not match plans; no fixed trim tab on rudder; rudder control linkage as raised

Academy 2133

line on fuselage; edges to exhaust stacks too thick, resulting in little detail/narrow exhaust stacks; bulges under exhausts small and wrong shape; gun troughs too far down side of cowling (should be on top), also wrong shape; no oblong vents forward of gun troughs; cowl under nose not correct profile (angular, not bulged); panel lines match published plans; tropical and standard filters included, both are accurate in size/shape and former is moulded with front shutter open.

Tailplanes: Correct span but slightly too broad; cut-back at fin wrong angle and does not have rounded edges; trim tab too far inboard; rib details across entire control surface; rib number/style does not match plans.

Engine: None supplied.

Propeller: Propeller, backplate and spinner separate; spinner slightly long, but correct diameter; capped or cannon spinners included; propeller slightly undersize (marginal), but blade shape good.

Interior: Floor, rear bulkhead, seat, control column, rudder pedals and instrument panel; seat moulded with cushion and seat belts; two styles of instrument panel (E-3 and E-4) with raised detail (no decals); separate trim wheel; sidewall detailed moulded to fuselage halves, very good.

Detail: SC250 bomb and centreline rack; rack is inaccurate in shape/details; separate supports for bomb fins, but latter over-thick; separate pitot and aileron counter-balance weights.

Canopy: Three-part in both E-3 and E-4 styles; correct length and width of each element; moulded windscreen armour; framework a little thick resulting in small windscreen panels; separate head armour (2 styles) with cushion detail.

Decals: This version has three options: Bf 109E-4, 'Black <' flown by *Capt.* Hans von Hahn, JG3, 1940; Bf 109E-4, 'Yellow 1', flown by *Maj.* Gerhard Schoepfel, 1940; Bf 109E-3, 'Yellow 11', flown by *Lt* Waldemar Wuebke, JG54, 1941; decal sheet does not include swastikas; stencils included; size/style of national insignia correct.

Verdict: *This is not a bad kit with the exception of the cowl guns, so probably the best way around it is to see if you can substitute the cowl from the Hasegawa kit instead? Not the best in the scale, but a sound basis and a cheap alternative nowadays.*

AeroPlast, Poland

1/72nd Messerschmitt Bf 109C #00264

This firm came into existence in 1999 and the series of early Bf 109s they offered were from RPM who released the B in 1998, with the E-series in 1999, although these were back-dated from the Face Bf 109T kits. The Aeroplast kits included the B (#00257), C (#00264) and D (#00271) versions and were probably released around 2003? We have the C-version here for evaluation, but all three kits contain the same basic parts.

Plastic: Medium grey-coloured plastic with engraved panel lines and other details.

Wings: The wings in this kit are identical in all their early version, B, C & D; 1-2mm too great in span; all panel lines and access hatches are from B-series; separate cannon bulges and barrels; oil cooler separate, but undersized; most of the round access hatches missing; rib detail on the flaps and ailerons uses thick raised lines/too few; no tip lights; cannon ports slightly too far outboard; wheel well inner edge straight, should be an angle; each wheel well is slightly oversize in both length and overall proportions; wheel bay shape is correct for early series; centreline detail at odds with scale plans; wing bolt bulges look too small and should be teardrop-shaped; oleo legs about 1mm too long; detail on oleo legs not accurate; no compression linkage; main wheels correct diameter and with tread pattern; hubs feature six spokes but lack other detail; tailwheel and yoke moulded as one; overall length of oleo OK, but features compression link not applicable to type (from B/C kits); tailwheel tyre diameter good, but lacks any detail.

Fuselage: Correct length but cockpit is 2mm too far aft; nose contours not bad, but aft fuselage is too thick at the mid-point, then too skinny by the tail; panel lines match plans, but round access panels omitted; radio hatch correct in port side; vents in side of nose cowling missing, whilst ones at front depicted as shapeless dimples; rudder separate, has good shape and rib detail; no trim tab on rudder; three styles of exhaust includes (open ports, short ejectors and the later square stacks); gun troughs are too short and very shallow, plus no gun barrels; chin intake is separate, but little depth; scoop intake on upper cowl separate and good shape/size.

Tailplanes: Correct span; tip shape too square; trailing edge profile wrong and cut-back at wrong angle; fabric and rib effect quite effective.

Engine: None supplied

Propeller: Kit includes both two-blade versions; B-series version is OK for diameter, but the blades are too narrow; C/D-series blades slightly too long; tips need to be rounded off more anyway; spinner diameter correct for both versions.

Interior: Floor, rear bulkhead, control column, rudder pedals, trim wheel, instrument panel and gunsight; seat depicted as correct early-style 'pan' built into floor; instrument panel has pretty good raised dials; gunsight moulded in grey-coloured plastic; also on sprue, but not mentioned is the oxygen regulator unit for the port sidewall; sidewall detail moulded inside each fuselage half, very basic and a bit heavy.

Detail: The sprues actually contain a centreline rack and drop tank, but these are not

applicable to the B, C or D; pitot and aileron counterbalance weights separate, but both suffer from poor moulding and flash.

Canopy: One-piece; correct length and width; framework accurate; suffers from flow marks in plastic.

Decals: The C-version offers two decal options, as per the illustrations on the back of the box: 73•79, Spanish Air Force in the late 1940s; 'Red 3', 1./JG20, Berlin-Döbernitz, 1939; both of these options are in fact more likely to be Ds; the instructions are generic, so they also list the following two options for which decals are included, but which are both definitely Ds: 6•60, J/88 Condor Legion; 'Yellow 11', 2./JG71. Fürstenfeldbruck. September 1939: this last option should be 'Red 11'; swastikas are included as multi-part to get round restrictions; only four stencils included, no walkways etc.

Verdict: *Looking at this kit it is more like a limited-run product than mainstream, as the parts are chunky and there is a lot of flash and ejector pin marks to contend with. The Heller kit is easier to build but not as accurate, however for this early series a better E-airframe and a good conversion set would probably be the better option.*

Airfix, UK

1/72nd Messerschmitt Bf 109E #02048-8

Released as a new tooling in 1976 this kit reappeared marked as 'New' in December 1977 with the same kit number, it was renumbered #02048 in 1983, as #902048 in 1985 and as #02048 in 1986.{actually released late 1987}. It was reissued in late 1988 in the 'Aircraft of the Aces Special Edition' series as #02086 'General Leutnant Adolf Galland', reissued again as #02048 in 2000, as a 'Starter Set' in 2001 (#92048) and as a Gift Set (#02048G) in 2005. It was renumbered in 2008 as #A02048, then issued as the new-style Gift Set in 2008 (#A50088), finally reissued in the Battle of Britain 70th Anniversary Gift Set in 2010 (#A50022). This tooling has probably now been retired, as it has been replaced with a new tooling by Hornby.

Plastic: Both versions we have come in a light blue-coloured plastic with raised panel lines and other surface detail.

Wings: Overall span and shape correct; cannon bulges not bad and cannon barrel position correct; flap/aileron hinge line correct; rib detail on flap and aileron do not match published plans; fairing behind the radiators moulded with the flap; panel lines at odds with scale plans; covered in mass of raised rivets and a series of odd dashes down the centreline; cannon access panel in leading edge too big, whilst other access

Airfix 02048

panels are omitted; wheel well correct size and location; oleos mount into fuselage half; ledge moulded to hold doors in closed position; no interior detail or sidewalls; no detail in corresponding area of upper wing halves; oleo legs correct length; oleos just generic 'stepped' tubes; rear hub moulded to oleo combining compression linkage; main wheels correct diameter; raised tread pattern wrong; hub detail heavy and inaccurate (rims too pronounced); tailwheel and yoke moulded together; tailwheel tyre and hub devoid of detail.

Fuselage: Overall length correct; diameter towards vertical fin slightly skinny; rudder profile at lower/rear corner slightly too rounded; rudder rib detail good but no trim tab; no linkage for rudder depicted; most panel lines accurate, as are most access panel; filler hatch on port, upper fuselage missing; chin radiator shape good, although a little shallow towards rear; exhaust stacks moulded in situ, little shallow in relief and slightly too long forwards; bulge below exhausts correct shape/location; vents forward of windscreen depicted as dimples; engine cowl separate, gun troughs correct position, but shape is wrong; oblong vents forward of gun troughs shown as raised detail.

Tailplanes: Span OK but too broad in chord; hinge line correct; main panel lines match plans but unit covered in raised rivets; trim tab correct size/location.

Engine: None supplied.

Propeller: Separate propeller, spinner and backplate; propeller correct diameter but blade profile slightly too thin towards root; spinner correct diameter and length; spinner only offered with cannon hole in centre.

Interior: Basic floor/bulkheads with separate seat, pilot figure and instrument panel; no control column, rudder pedals, gunsight or sidewall detail; instrument panel has raised dials, but these are inaccurate; head armour fitted to rear bulkhead, not inside canopy.

Detail: The kit includes 300lt drop tank, ETC 50 rack and bombs and ETC rack and SC250 bomb; all bombs have thick fins; SC250 does not have any support rods between the fins; both ETC racks lack detail and are not very accurate; tropical and standard filters included; separate cannon barrels and pitot; aileron counter balance weights missing.

Canopy: Single-piece; correct in overall shape/dimensions; vertical (pane) divider in the mid-section missing.

Decals: Both version we had offered the same two decal options, although the instructions do not identify them in any way: 'White F' and 'Black 8': the former shows the Mickey Mouse emblem of Adolf Galland, but is not one of his JG26 machines, while the latter is probably supposed to be the E-7/trop of Lt Werner Schroer of 2./JG27, Libya, 1941, so would need the capped spinner of that type. When reissued as #A02048 it offered two schemes: E-4, 'Black 13', flown by Oblt. Helmut Teidmann, 2 Staffel, I./JG3, Grandvillers, France, August 1940; E-7/trop, 'Black <A', flown by Oblt. Ludwig Franzisket, I./JG27, Castel Benito, Libya, April 1941.

Verdict: *Overall not bad and certainly one of the better kits of its era, this one shows many similarities with the Heller kit and the heavy rivet detail etc., all mean this it is probably only for the collector, especially as Airfix do a newer and better one now.*

Airfix, UK

1/72nd Messerschmitt Bf 109E-4

Under Hornby ownership many of the older Airfix toolings have been shelved to be replaced with nice new ones and this is one such kit. It was released in May 2012 (#A01008) and also offered as a 'Starter Set' with paint/glue/brush as #A55106, then in June 2012 it was reissued with the Spitfire Mk Ia as a 'Dogfight Double' (#A50135) and with the Spitfire Mk Ia and P-51 as a boxed set entitled 'Aircraft of the Aces' in association with the IWM (#A50143). As we write this it is due for reissue with the Spitfire Mk Ia and Hurricane Mk I as the 'Battle of Britain Experience' gift set (#A50153) to tie in with a display including a replica Spitfire/Hurricane/Bf 109E due at events throughout the year. The kit was also reissued with new decals as #A01008A in 2018 and the basic toolings were used in the E-4/E-7 (#A02048A) version released in 2010, the E-7/E-7 Trop (#A02062) of 2013 and included along with the Tomhawk Mk IIb in the 'El Alamein' (#A50148) set in 2012.

Plastic: Medium grey-coloured with engraved panel lines and details

Wings: Span correct; trailing and leading edge profiles OK; cannon bulges and ejector ports correct shape and location; panel lines match plans; access panels match plans; centre-line detail good, wing bolt bulges correct shape/size; radiators separate and correct size/shape, but no vertical bar in intake; leading edge slats moulded to upper wing halves; aileron moulded complete and correct size/rib detail; flap moulded separately and complete with bulge behind radiator; couple of access panels missing from upper wing halves; wheel wells correct squared-off outline and position/size; roof ribs moulded into underside of upper wing panels; sidewalls moulded in both wing halves to enclose the wheel wells once assembled; wheels mounted into lower wing half; oleo leg correct length; links moulded to each oleo; main wheels slightly underside (marginal); main wheel tyres 'weighted' and with tread detail; hubs have correct six-spoke style but detail heavy; tailwheel moulded with oleo leg; tailwheel tyre undersize, hub lacks depth or detail; tailwheel tyre 'weighted'.

Fuselage: Correct length and overall profile; panel lines match published plans; fuel, filler on port side missing; vertical fin slightly too narrow; aerial mast on top of rudder too big; rudder actuating wires moulded as raised lines on aft fuselage; vents in front of upper cowling slightly too big; gun troughs correct size/shape/location and gun barrels nicely moulded (al-

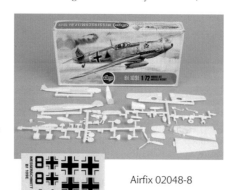

Airfix 02048-8

though oval in cross-section); supercharger intake correct size/shape/location; separate chin radiator of correct shape and with interior bulkhead and roof to stop you seeing inside fuselage.

Tailplanes: Correct size; tip profile too square; panel line missing along leading edge; rib effect on elevators matches plans; support arms separate.

Engine: Moulded 'block' with bearers, but undersize due to need to fit under (thick) cowling.

Propeller: Separate propeller, spinner and backplate; propeller blades correct length but too thin; spinner correct diameter and profile.

Interior: Floor/front/rear bulkhead, with separate seat, control column, rudder pedals and instrument panel; moulded detail in each fuselage sidewall; correct style separate seat unit; gunsight moulded in clear plastic; decals for instrument panel.

Detail: No additional items such as bombs or racks included; aileron mass balance weights separate; pitot separate; flaps can be posed up or down.

Canopy: Three-part canopy; no head armour; can pose canopy open or closed; frames match plans; aerial separate and correctly depicted fitted in aft canopy section.

Decals: Each kit comes with the following decal options:

#A01008
• 'Black <-', flown by *Oblt* Franz von Werra, I./JG3, France, August 1940

#A01008A
• 'Yellow 13', flown by *Oblt* Anton Schön, 9./KG54, Holland, January 1940

In each instant the accompanying decal sheet does not include swastikas, but along with the unique markings and Balkenkreuz, there is a good set of airframe stencils.

Verdict: *This kit is a real gem, probably in third place behind ICM and Tamiya for the 'best' Bf 109 in 1/72nd and well worth building. Don't forget Brengun do a superb etched detail set (#BRL72044) and Eduard do masks (#CX331).*

AML, Czech Republic

1/72nd Messerschmitt Bf 109 in the Legion Condor #AMLA72016

This kit was released in 2010 and because it is based on the Avis tooling, you can also consider this assessment as applicable to the kits from that firm as well.

Plastic: Light grey-coloured with

Airfix A01008

engraved panel lines and other detail.

Wings: 4mm too great in span; profile and chord is correct; main panel lines match plans; set of panel lines mid-span that should not be there; not all access panels present; wing bolt bulges accurate; centreline scoop from the later series present; oil cooler right length but 'skinny', also solid with no intake/exhaust openings (earlier versions had this cooler inboard, the location shown is only applicable to the later machines); port wing panel shows the cannon access panel of the D/E series; number of other access panels missing in upper wing halves; trim tab missing from aileron; rib detail faint and matches that of D-series; wheel wells about 1mm too far outboard due to oversize span; roof detail moulded inside upper wing halves; additional details supplied for sidewalls and roof in etched brass; overall shape of bay, if not dimensions, good; oleo legs correct length; compression links moulded to oleo; injected doors replaced with etched brass examples in two-parts; tailwheel and yoke moulded as one; tailwheel tyre correct diameter but lacks detail, as does hub; tailwheel oleo lacks compression linkage.

Fuselage: Marginally too long (between canopy and vertical fin, but <1mm); panel lines match plans (very faint); three vents aft of engine cowl, thus depicting the early (one vent) and later (2 vents) versions both together; jacking hole in aft fuselage in half relief; rudder separate, good shade, but ribs more like the E-series; exhausts depicted as raised oval rings; chin intake correct dimensions but no leading edge 'lips' to unit; two different front/lower cowl/intakes included, these depict the B-1 and B-2 types; two styles of upper engine cowling, for B-1 or B-2; both cowls show correct staggering of machine-guns; oblong vents in the front of the B-2 unit poorly defined indentations.

Tailplanes: Correct span and overall shape; rib detail faint and more like E-series; trim tab correct shape/location; separate support struts

Engine: None supplied.

Propeller: Two styles included; B-1 unit has blades 1mm too long (each), profile is good though; B-2 unit has separate propeller, spinner and backplate, blades again about 1mm each too long, but tip profile too pointed anyway; spinner diameter and profile correct.

Interior: This is the main area of change over the original Avis kit, as the limited interior is completely replaced in resin and etched, comprising floor/rear bulkhead, seat, control column, rudder pedals, sidewalls and instrument panel in resin, with trim wheel, throttle, various levers, seat belts and instrument panel facia in etched.

Detail: Aileron mass balance weights separate, as is pitot; no aerial mast.

Canopy: One-piece; two styles included, one with and one without windscreen armour; rear section lacks upper framework; both suffer from flow lines in clear plastic.

Decals: This kit includes two decal options: B-1, 6-10, flown by *Uffz.* Ernst Mratzek of VJ/88, Tablada, March 1937; B-2, 6•10, flown by *Oblt* Günther Lützow, 2.J/88, Spain, 1938; decals include all national insignia but only black crosses for rudder; no stencils.

Verdict: *There is very much a 'limited-run' feel to this kit and even with the addition of the resin and*

etched parts it is going to be a hard build. The kit parts seem to be a confusion of B, C/D and even E characteristics, so overall this is probably one only to be attempted by the real 109 fan who is also experienced with this type of low-volume product.

Eduard, CZ

1/72nd 'Adlergriff' (#2136)

This is actually a limited edition release of the newly-tooled E-series from Special Hobby, whom Eduard assisted with in producing. As a result the main kit parts remained unchanged, although this kit combines all the E-1. E-3 and E-4 parts in one box, so see the listing under Special Hobby elsewhere in this section for a detailed assessment of the base kit/s, all we will therefore only cover here those aspects that differ. Eduard also offered 'Overtrees' for the E-1 (#7031X), E-3 (#7032X) and E-4/7 (#7033X) in 2021 for a limited period directly from the Eduard website only.
Note: As a 'Dual Combo' this kit offers two complete models, one of the MG 17-armed E-1 series and another of the MG FF-armed E-3/E-4/E-7 series.

Eduard 2136

Wings: The coolant radiator matrix are depicted with photo-etched and the exhaust flaps on each fairing are also replaced with photo-etched; the brake lines on each oleo leg are depicted with photo-etched; self-adhesive paint masks are included for the main wheel hubs (not the tailwheel though)

Fuselage: The oil radiator matrix (front and rear) are depicted with photo-etched.

Interior: The rudder pedals are replaced with photo-etched versions; the seat belts are pre-painted photo-etched; the perforated cover of the oxygen bottle is depicted via etched brass; the distribution panel on the starboard sidewall is depicted via pre-painted photo-etched; the chain drive of the trim tab wheel is depicted via photo-etched.

Detail: The main wheels are replaced with highly-detailed resin versions with excellent hub detail and tread pattern; a standing pilot figure is also supplied in resin.

Canopy: The windscreen frame edge is depicted with photo-etched, as is the release toggle for the main canopy; a rearview mirror is also offered in photo-etched; the main canopy retaining strap is offered as photo-etched; self-adhesive masks are included for all elements of both styles of canopy.

Decals: This kit comes with the following decal options:
E-3, W/Nr.5102, flown by *Lt* Herbert Kunze, *Stab* I./JG77, Döberitz, Germany, June

1940; E-4, W/Nr.5274, 'White 15', flown by *Lt* Werner Machold, 1./JG2, Marigny, France, June 1940; E-1, W/Nr.3413, 'Black 5', flown by *Lt* Hans Krug, 5./JG26, Marquise, France, July 1940; E-4, W/Nr.3709, 'White 1', flown by *Oblt* Josef Fözö, 4./JG51, Desvres, France, July 1940; E-3, flown by *Maj.* Adolf Galland, III./JG26, Caffiers, France, August 1940; E-3, flown by *Maj.* Adolf Galland, III./JG26, Caffiers, France, late August 1940; E-4, W/Nr.1480, flown by *Oblt* Franz von Werra, Gruppen-adjutant of II./JG3, Wierra-au-Bois, France, September 1940; E-1, W/Nr.3771, 'Yellow 12', flown by *Fw.* Ernst Arnold, 3./JG27, Peuplingues, France, August 1940; E-1, W/Nr.3417, 'White 2', flown by *Gefr.* Erich Mummert, 4./JG52, Peuplingues, France, September 1940; E-4, W/Nr.5375, flown by *Hptm.* Wilhelm Meyerweissflog, *Stab* JG53, Etaples, France, September 1940; E-4, W/Nr.3709, 'White 1', flown by *Oblt* Josef Fözö, 4./JG51, Desvres, France, second half of September 1940; E-4, W/Nr.5153, 'Yellow 5', flown by *Oblt* Egon Troha, 9./JG3, Desvres, France, October 1940; E-4, W/Nr.4869, flown by *Lr* Bernhard Malischewski, *Stab* II./JG54, Campagne-les-guines, France, October 1940.

The decal sheets, which are printed by Eduard, are excellent and have perfect register and colour density. The swastikas are placed along the top edge of the main sheet so that they can be clipped off in those countries where the symbol is banned, with split versions on the main sheet. There are also two separate sheets containing a complete set of airframe stencils on each in both red and black.

Verdict: *As with the Special Hobby original, this E-series is now in the top slot for the scale and the additional parts offered in this special edition make it one what many will rightfully want to own.*

Hasegawa, Japan

1/72nd Messerschmitt Bf 109E #JS-107

This kit was first released in 1973 as JS-107 and remained as such until 1977 when it was renumbered as #A25 although the box also still carried the code JS-107 as well. This kit remained in production until 1992, when it was finally replaced by the new tooling released that year.

Plastic: Dark green-coloured plastic with engraved panel lines.

Wings: Span and chord correct; radiators moulded with wing, complete with vertical bar in intake and blanking plates inside; panel lines match scale plans; one access hatch missing towards tip; centreline detail good although bulges over wing bolts are very small; cannon blisters undersized; underside of flaps include bulge behind radiator moulded to upper halves; fabric/rib effect on flaps and aileron very good; trim tab correct size/location; tip lights moulded with wing as bulge; cannon barrels with wing, correct length/position; oval access panel towards wing root missing in upper panel; wheel wells correct size/shape/location; partial sidewall in lower wing halves, but none in top; no detail inside upper wing halves; undercarriage mounted into wing; oleo legs correct length; no compression linkage; rear brake plate moulded to oleo; main wheels slightly small, but have tread pattern; hub detail correct six-spoke, but lacking other detail and rims

Hasegawa JS-107

heavy; undercarriage doors correct length but main section slightly undersize; tailwheel and yoke moulded to one fuselage half; tailwheel tyre/hub undersize and lacks any detail.

Fuselage: 2-3mm short, all at vertical fin/rudder; rear fuselage 'skinny' towards tail; whole tail/rudder slightly undersize; panel lines match plans; ribs on rudder do not match plans; rudder control lines moulded as raised lines on rear fuselage; exhaust stacks correct in style/location/size; supercharger intake correct; gun troughs correct size/location; oblong vents forward of troughs only semi-relief; radio hatch in port side correct size/location; aerial mast moulded to one fuselage side; tropical filter unit correct length/profile.

Tailplanes: Correct span and chord; tips slightly too square; panel lines match plans; too few/inaccurate rib detail.

Engine: None supplied.

Propeller: Separate propeller, spinner and backplate; propeller 1.5mm short per blade; blade profile very good; cannon-style spinner too long, capped one is fine.

Interior: Basic floor/rear bulkhead unit, with wedges for rudder pedals; separate control column; moulded sidewall detail in fuselage halves, basic; instrument panel with decals for detail; no gunsight other than blob moulded with instrument panel.

Detail: Offers a 'bomb' that is more like a cluster bomb unit by its shape; thick fins; rack basic in detail; separate aileron counterbalance weights. separate pitot.

Canopy: One-piece; offers early (E-3) and later (E-4/7) styles; size and shape accurate; framework accurate, including sliding panel vertical line in side panels.

Decals: All versions of this kit came with two decal options: S9+CD of III./SKG210, Eastern Front, 1941; 'Yellow 16', flown by Adolf Galland, JG26, 1940; decal sheet includes swastikas; national insignia size/proportions good; stencils only comprise two warning triangles and first aid marking vs walkways etc.

Verdict: *When Hasegawa claimed they produced the new tooling in the 1990s most soon understood that it was heavily based on this older kit and as it is not that bad as far as accuracy goes, you can see why they did. In some areas it is superior to a lot of newer kits, but the deficiencies in the rear fuselage are difficult to put right, so we suspect most will go with newer products.*

Hasegawa, Japan

1/72nd Messerschmitt Bf 109E-4/7 #AP9

This new-tooled Bf 109E was released by Hasegawa in 1992 to replace their ageing kit from 1973. It was followed by the E-3 (#AP8) and E-4/7 Trop (#AP10) in 1993, along with a special limited edition version containing the E-7 and Fw 190A-5 in Imperial Japanese Army Air Force markings (#02014) in 2012.

Plastic: Light grey-coloured with recessed panel lines and details.

Wings: Lower moulded as one-piece to a point just inboard of tip; upper as two separate panels; correct in span and chord; main panel lines match published plans, although some access panels are omitted; radiator units too square in overall shape, rear flaps not separate; cannon blisters too small; centreline details (bulges, scoop etc.) all accurate; cannon barrels moulded with wing and slightly too long (only marginal); fabric effect on control surfaces good, although V-shaped element in flaps omitted; trim tabs nicely moulded; wheel wells correct position/shape; slightly narrow towards outer edge; oleo mounted moulded into inboard bay area, should be in the inside of the upper wing panels to be more accurate; main wheels slightly undersize (only marginal), tyre tread and hub detail all present and accurate; undercarriage doors correct length, but curved section slightly undersized due to error in bay shape; oleo legs about 1mm short, also devoid of accurate details (just 'stepped' tubes); tailwheel moulded with yoke to one fuselage half; tailwheel yoke correct length but wheel very undersize and without any hub detail.

Hasegawa AP9

Fuselage: Overall 2-3mm short, all in proportions of the tail/rudder, which is well undersize; too few ribs in rudder; rudder actuating wires moulded are raised lines on rear fuselage; whole fuselage slightly skinny at front when viewed from above; rear fuselage, towards tail, also slightly skinny when viewed from the side; chin radiator unit not deep enough; exhaust stacks too long (error is all at the front); bulges either side of front/lower nose too small; access step at wing root shown as hole, should just be engraved; all panel lines and hatches match scale plans; gun troughs correct position, length and style; oblong vents forward of troughs too big.

Tailplanes: Correct length and chord; tips

too square; panel lines match published plans; too few ribs in elevators; trim tabs too big and positioned too far inboard.

Engine: None supplied.

Propeller: Propeller diameter less than 0.5mm undersize; blades a little thin in profile; spinner accurate in diameter, length and profile; kit includes both capped and cannon versions.

Interior: Floor/bulkhead unit with 'wedges' for rudder pedals; separate control column, metal seat and instrument panel; sidewall details moulded into fuselage halves is basic; instrument panel devoid of details as relies on decal; no separate (clear) gunsight, just blob moulded to instrument panel; seat in instructions is wrong style, but metal part in kit is more accurate.

Detail: This particular version includes a 300lt drop tank and bomb canister; each comes with separate, accurate rack; control surface mass balances are separate; pitot also separate.

Canopy: Single-piece; accurate in length and profile; armoured windscreen moulded in situ; head armour as separate piece, with cushion detail.

Decals: This version had four options: 'White 12', flown by *Oblt* Joachim Mücheberg of 7./JG26; 'Black <<', flown by *Maj.* Helmut Wick of I./JG2; 'White <', flown by *Maj.* Reinhard Heydrich of Stab III./JG1; S9+RS of 8./ZG1; decal sheet includes swastikas (cut off in those nations where it was banned) and full stencils; national insignia proportions and styles accurate.

Verdict: *Although most would assume this to be one of the best in the scale, nowadays it has been surpassed by a number of others and the errors in the tail area would require replacement from another kit, at the very least.*

Hasegawa, Japan

1/72nd Messerschmitt Bf 109E 'Galland' #AP101
1/72nd Messerschmitt Bf 109E-4' Wick' #00263

Hasegawa replaced their old E-series kit (#JS-17/#A25) in 1992 with a brand new tooling initially released as the Bf 109E-4/7 (#AP9) and followed this with the Bf 109E-3 (#AP8) in 1993, which was subsequently reissued in 1994 as Bf 109E 'Galland' (#AP101), in 1995 as Bf 109E-3 'Spanish Air Force' (#AP114), in 2001 as Bf 109E-4 'Wick' (#00263) and in 2003 as Bf 109E-3 'Swiss Air Force' (#00672). It then remained unavailable for nine years before returning with the Spitfire Mk I as a 'Battle of Britain' set (#01909) in 2010. We have #AP101 and the contents of #00263 here for assessment: See the assessment of #AP9 elsewhere for overall comments on accuracy, as these versions are all based on the E-4/7, all that is listed here are those areas that differ.

Plastic: All medium grey-coloured plastic with engraved panel lines and hatches etc.

Propeller: Galland version (#AP101) used the 'capped' spinner; 'Wick' and 'Swiss' versions used the spinner with the cannon port.

Interior: Swiss version (#00672) does not include the spade-type control column used by this nation.

Canopy: The 'Galland' version (#AP101) needs the periscope sight favoured by this pilot and although included the modeller has to drill the E-4/7 canopy to fit it.

Decals: #AP101 had three options: 'Black <-+-', JG26, France, September 1940; 'Black <-+-', JG26, Audembert, France, December 1940; 'Black <<', III./JG26, France, June 1940 (all flown by Adolf Galland): #00263 had two options: 'Black <<', I./JG2, Belgium, October 1940; 'Yellow 2', 3./JG2, Belgium, September 1940 (both flown by Helmut Wick); the decal sheets include swastikas, although these were trimmed off in those countries where it was banned; full stencils included; all national insignia of correct style and proportions.

Verdict: *As with the E-4/7, although a 'modern' tooling in some respects, the overall accuracy of the whole series is not the best and so it has been surpassed by more modern and accurate examples.*

Heller, France

1/72nd Messerschmitt Bf 109B-1/C-1 #236

This kit was first released in 1978 as #101, it was renumbered in the late 1970s as #236, then again in 1987 as #80236. It was last reissued as #80236 in 1993 and is currently unavailable

Plastic: Light grey-coloured plastic with raised panel lines.

Wings – Lower moulded as one-piece, to a point just inboard of tip; less than 0.5mm too great in span for this section; panel lines match plans; most access hatches also match plans, but also has some associated with the later E-series; centreline detail good, scoop and bulges all correct size/location; oil cooler moulded to wing, slightly too small and overall shape poor (also solid); flaps moulded to lower wing, with rib detail; upper wing two separate panels, same slight error in span; panel lines match plans except one added in the middle running from root to tip; complete (upper/lower) ailerons moulded to upper wing halves; aileron slightly too long inboard; trim tabs correct shape/location; wheel wells correct shape but slightly too long overall; correct outline; undercarriage doors overlong as per bays; interior detail on each door; mounted into lower wing half, not fuselage; oleo legs correct length considering attachment point; angle of wheel to ground correct; separate compression linkage; main wheels correct diameter; no tread detail on tyre; hub shows six spokes but no other detail; tailwheel and yoke moulded as one; overall good shape to yoke and tyre correct diameter.

Fuselage: Less than 1mm too long, all at the tail; panel lines match plans; some access panels missing; radio hatch correct shape/location in port side; no jacking holes in aft fuselage; vertical fin and rudder profile match plans; rudder rib detail matches plans; aerial mast moulded to fuselage, should be attached to rear canopy section; vents in forward nose (side) as half-relief, shape not good and shows the two on each side not applicable to all machines; gun troughs good shape/location but guns moulded to inner edge, should be central in trough; exhaust stacks as blobs, with vents fore and aft too big; chin intake with separate internal matrix, but too long and lacking the flap at the rear; vents in front of nose too big, only half relief and too far round

sides of cowling.

Tailplanes: About 1mm too great in span; overall profile good, cut-back at trailing edge should be rounded at corners; rib detail shown across entire elevator; inaccurate additional panel line in centre of tailplane, other panel lines match plans; trim tabs correct location/size.

Engine: None supplied.

Propeller: Two styles included; wooden propeller diameter too great (1mm per blade), but overall shape and blade profile good; metal propeller correct diameter and blade profile; separate spinner and backplate for metal propeller, both correct diameter/shape.

Interior: Floor/bulkhead, seat, control column and instrument panel; seat inaccurate for a B/C series; instrument panel has raised dial detail, but inaccurate and dials too big for scale; limited sidewall detail moulded inside each fuselage half.

Detail: No ordnance or tank; separate aileron mass balance weights; separate pitot.

Canopy: Three-piece; mid-section more akin to the squarer shape of the later E-series; sliding panel line in main pane; windscreen depicted with external armoured glass.

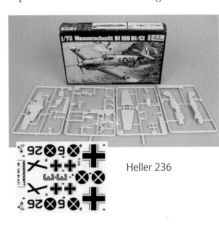

Heller 236

Decals: This kit comes with two decal options: B-1, 6•26, 2./J88, Legion Condor, Spain, 1937; C-1, 'Yellow 3', 9./ZG26, Germany; decal sheet does not include swastikas; no stencils included; national insignia shape/style looks accurate.

Verdict: *Warts and all this is a great kit, OK it has been surpassed in some ways but as a mainstream injected kit of the early series in 1/72nd it still holds top honours. If you cross-kit it with others to overcome the accuracy issues it would make a good model, however it is easier to backdate a really good E-series, so probably this one is now relegated to collectors.*

Heller, France

1/72nd Messerschmitt Bf 109E #234

This kit was first released in 1975 as #089, then renumbered as #234 in the 1979 and as #80234 in 1987. It was also reissued as a 'Rapid Kit' in 2000 as #59772.

Plastic: Light grey-coloured plastic; raised panel lines and access panels

Wings: Lower wing moulded as one, to a point just inboard of the tip; span is about 1-2mm short; panel lines and access panels do not match modern plans; radiators moulded in situ with flaps, the latter having rather heavy rib detail; cannon bulges undersize; cannon

barrels separate but too thick diameter; upper wing as separate panels: same error in span; tip profile too rounded; panel lines do not match published plans; odd set of double lines inboard; missing oval panel towards root, at back of wing; wheel wells are correct location but too long and have a straight edge at 45º at the rear that is incorrect; doors too long due to error with wheel wells; oleo legs also too long; compression links separate; detail on oleo legs at odds with real thing; main wheels correct diameter; hub detail shows correct six spokes, but no other detail; tyres have no rib detail; tailwheel yoke and wheel moulded together; wheel has no hub detail.

Fuselage: Marginally (<1mm) short, all at the front as cockpit and tail all correct; panel lines do not match plans; aft fuselage jacking hole too far forward (by one rib); rudder linkage missing; rudder rib detail at odds with scale plans; exhaust stacks moulded with fuselage halves and are shallow in relief; upper gun troughs too far round the cowling sides as they are also too big overall; radiator intake and overall profile under chin is too sharp, should be more curved; supercharger intake unit separate, but overall shape poor and too short; kit also includes tropical intake, although this too is short in overall dimensions and a little 'skinny'.

Tailplanes: Correct length, but slightly too broad in chord; panel lines do not match plans, elevators too wide and fabric effect is heavy

Engine: None supplied.

Propeller: Slightly short blades; profile also too bulged; spinner correct shape and with cannon port in centre, kit also includes blanked-off version.

Interior: Floor/rear bulkhead with wedges for rudder pedals; separate instrument panel with raised dial detail; separate gunsight, but moulded in grey plastic; separate control column and seat, the seat is generic in shape/detail.

Detail: No racks or bombs included; pitot (#20) under port wing is T-shaped, should be L-shaped; separate aileron mass balances; separate aerial mast.

Canopy: Three-part canopy, with standard and tropical versions; all canopy sections correct shape/length, just a little thick; separate head armour with cushion detail.

Decals: Throughout its life this kit offered one option, that in #234 being for 'Black <<', which is not identified in any way in the instructions but was the machine of Gunther Scholz, III./JG5. The decals have the cross of the JG5 shield being black, they should be blue and it is most likely that the white nose and tail depicted for this machine were in fact yellow. The decal sheet just has the basic markings, no swastikas or stencils

Verdict: *Really, truthfully, there are much better E kits in 1/72nd, so this one is only for the collector with fond memories of building Heller kits in the 1970s/80s.*

ICM, Ukraine

1/72nd Messerschmitt Bf 109E-3 & 4 Series

ICM announced the Bf 109 series in 2002, but it was not until 2004 that they released the E-3 (#72131), followed by the revised E-3 (#72162)

and E-4 (#72163). The E-4 'Nightfighter' (#72134) was released in 2009, and in 2022 two of the the E-3 (#72131) kits were included in the 'Over all Spain, the sky is clear' set (#DS7202). As yet the Bf 109B (#72161) announced way back in 2002 still remains to be released. We have #72134 and the E-3s in DS7202 here for assessment, but as they are all based on common parts, it covers most elements.

Plastic: Medium grey-coloured with engraved panel lines and rivets etc.

Wings: Span OK; trailing and leading edge profiles OK; additional round access panel on underside mid-span towards aileron hinge line; raised ridges on either side of centreline, should not be there; cannon bulges and ejector ports correct shape and location; panel lines do not match published plans with a few panels missing; wheel wells correct squared-off outline; roof ribs moulded into underside of upper wing panels; undercarriage correct length; links moulded to each oleo; main wheels slightly undersize, but so marginal not worth worrying about; hubs have correct style; tailwheel moulded with oleo leg; tailwheel tyre undersize

Fuselage: Correct length and overall profile; panel lines match published plans, although some access panels do not; angle at top of rudder hinge line too steep (forward), this also affects the shape of the separate rudder; aerial mast on top of rudder too big; rudder actuating wires moulded as raised lines on aft fuselage; vents in front of upper cowling too big and blisters either side of gun troughs too pronounced; supercharger intake correct size, shape and location.

Tailplanes: Correct size and profile; panel lines match published plans; support arms underneath are positioned slightly too far outboard, so are therefore too long?

Engine: None supplied, just a square 'block' with no detail.

Propeller: Separate propeller, spinner and backplate; propeller blades correct length and profile; three styles of spinner included, but only one used here: correctly shows version with cannon port in centre.

Interior: Full cockpit interior, with moulded detail in each fuselage sidewall; correct style separate seat unit; floor, bulkheads, instrument panel, control column and gunsight

ICM 72134

moulded in clear plastic.

Detail: No additional items such as bombs or racks included.

Canopy: Two-part canopy, with windscreen separate from canopy and rear section; separate head armour of correct shape; separate armoured glass for windscreen if required (instructions mark item as '?'); can pose canopy open by using the separate rear section (#B3) intended for other versions; earlier E-3 style (curved) canopy included, with this element separate; Montex do masks for this version (#SM72066)

Decals: Each kit came with the following decal options:
#72134
• G9+JV, III./NJG1, Germany 1941. This option was overall black (RLM 22) and the decals are very matt with prominent carrier,

ICM 72135

no swastikas, but stencils are included.
#DS7202
• Bf 109E-3, 6•107, 2.J/88, Legion Condor, spring 1939
• Bf 109E-3, 6•91, 3.J/88 Legion Condor, spring 1939

The decals by this stage are beautifully printed, with perfect register and colour and they are very glossy. The sheet includes all the unique markings, wing crosses and a set of basic airframe stencils.

Verdict: *The E-3 and E-4 are excellent kits that will build into one of the better models of either type in this scale. Probably one of your better options for the type in this scale as far as price and accuracy go.*

ICM, Ukraine

1/72nd Messerschmitt Bf 109E-7 Series

Based on the new-tooled E-3 & 4 series airframe from 2004, the E-7 version was released in 2006 as the E-7/Trop (#72133) and was followed in 2007 by the E-7b/Trop (#72164). This particular version (E-7/b) was released in 2010 and as this kit is the same as the E-3 and E-4 (#DS7202 & #72134) we covered earlier in this chapter, all we will deal with here are note any changes or additional parts.

Plastic: Medium grey-coloured plastic with engraved panel lines and other detail.

Propeller: This version uses the capped spinner that was on the sprue in the E-3 kit

Detail: This is the only real change from the E-3, with a separate sprue for ordnance; ETC50 VII centreline rack with 4x SC50 bombs; ETC rack and SC250 bomb as alterna-

ICM DS7202

tive; fins commendably thin on both bomb types, with one pair moulded to the bomb body and the other separate; bomb crutches separate for SC250; no tail fin braces on SC250.

Decals: There are two options in the kit: 'Black < | 5', flown by *Lt* Heindl, *Gruppe Adjutant* of II./JG54, Yugoslavia, April 1941; S9+CD of III./ZG1, Russia, summer 1942; no swastikas included; full stencils included; decals quite matt with visible carrier film.

Verdict: *The whole ICM series is excellent but strangely has never seemed to evoke much admiration from modellers? As an overall package, in any version, it is probably the best available in the scale.*

Matchbox, UK

1/72nd Messerschmitt Bf 109E-3/4 #PK-17

This kit was first released in 1974 and remained in production until Matchbox ceased kit production in the 1980s (the box art/style was revised in this period, though). The kit was then reissued when the Matchbox brand was leased by Revell in 1991 as #40017 and remained in production until the licence agreement ceased in 1999. The tooling is now owned by Revell, but with their own tooling of the type it has not yet been seen in a Revell box.

Plastic: (1st box) Mustard yellow and light brown-coloured plastic; (2nd box) deep yellow and medium brown-coloured plastic; all with recessed panel lines and other details.

Wings: Port and starboard panels to point inboard of tip, flaps and ailerons moulded with upper wing halves; overall length and width correct; tip profile good; cannon bulges good shape and position; cannon ports in wing leading edge slight too far inboard; panel lines at odds with published plans; no leading edge slots engraved; access panels at odds with scale plans; radiators separate and good overall shape; bulge in flap behind radiator moulded with radiator, so gap between two not defined; no vertical bar in radiator intake; upper wing panels moulded with lower sections of flaps and ailerons; fabric ribs very good, although probably not to modern style (with rib details showing); panel lines at odds with scale plans, also has the double line inboard that is also seen on the Heller kit!; wheel wells correct position and shape; open main and leg elements although no corresponding detail in the upper wing half; sidewalls are very thin, so will not meet top wing half thus allow you to see into the wing; oleos mounted into fuselage, not wing, just like the real thing; oleo legs correct length and axle at correct angle; compression linkage moulded to oleo; main wheel tyres correct diameter but no tread pattern; hub has six-spoke pattern but inaccurate in overall detail; tailwheel and yoke moulded as one, overall dimensions good but just 'generic' in style/detail.

Fuselage: Correct in length; overall shape/profile very good; vertical fin and rudder correct; ribs on rudder very good, although not modern style of depicting this; insufficient panels in fuselage; no jacking holes in aft fuselage; very few access panels depicted and some of those included are spurious; radio hatch on port side is square, should have rounded corners; exhausts separate, but these are located slightly too far aft (overall length of exhaust unit is correct, though); radiator under nose good overall shape; upper cowl is separate, gun troughs too long/wrong shape; oblong vents forward of gun troughs omitted; standard and desert filters included, both are the correct shape/size, the latter has the intake flap open, but is solid.

Tailplanes: Overall shape and dimensions correct; panel lines match published plans; rib detail accurate, although not the modern style of depicting this; trim tabs correct shape and location.

Engine: None supplied.

Propeller: Separate propeller and spinner; propeller correct diameter, blades marginally narrow; spinner only offered with the flat style of cap.

Interior: None, just a 'bench' seat/bulkhead and generic pilot figure.

Detail: No bombs or drop tanks included; aileron counterbalance weights missing; pilot included; cannon barrels separate, although too long.

Canopy: One-piece, correct length and width; no frame mid-pane in opening section; angle of windscreen is slightly too steep.

Decals: Both early and late boxes offered the same two options: E-4/Trop, 'Black 9' of 1./JG27, Derna, Libya, 1941; E-3, 'Yellow 65', Rumanian Air Force, Russia, 1943; the decal sheet includes swastikas; no stencils; dimensions of some of the crosses are dubious.

Verdict: *This is a typical Matchbox kit, yes it does have deep panel lines, but they are not the 'trenches' so often associated with this manufacturer. Detail is limited, but overall accurate so from Revell's point of view this is a better option for reissue than their old (1963-vintage) example!*

MPM, Czech Republic

1/72nd Messerschmitt Bf 109 V1 Upgraded Kit #72128

The original version of this kit (#72029) was released in 1997 then two years later in 1999 the 'upgraded' version was released with resin detail parts. It is the latter version that we have for assessment.

Plastic: Light grey-coloured plastic with engraved detail.

Wings: This is moulded as one, top and bottom; span and chord correct; bulges on upper wings probably slightly too high and too short; panel lines match plans, but a number of access panels omitted; ailerons and flaps feature rib/fabric detail that match scale plans;

trim tabs correct size/location; centreline detail correct although wing bolt bulges look too small; radiator screens on inboard leading edge missing, nor supplied as etched; as the wing is solid this results in the wheel wells having no real detail; overall shape is correct but the dimensions are not, being a little undersized overall; correct round shape to main wheel bay; undercarriage doors are slightly undersize as per wells; main wheels correct diameter; hubs plain: in this upgraded kit replaced with resin ones, but had six-spoke hubs of the production machines; tyre features tread detail (both plastic and resin versions); oleo legs correct length: replaced in upgraded version with resin examples (probably better to stay with plastic parts though!); compression links as etched; tailwheel moulded with yoke, good overall shape/size.

Fuselage: Overall length correct; width of

MPM 72128

vertical fin slightly undersize (marginal), resulting in rudder top hinge line being low; rudder separate, ribs etc. match plans; panel lines match scale plans; hatches match plans; access step in half-relief should be engraved outline; exhaust stacks just dimples, would be better drilled out; twin vents on side of aft cowl correct; lower chin section separate, flaps depicted just as engraved lines and lower vents missing; radiator matrix supplied as etched.

Tailplanes: Pretty close in overall shape, correct in span; too few ribs on elevators; trim tabs too long; tail struts separate.

Engine: None supplied.

Propeller: Correct diameter, blade profile/twist a little suspect; spinner, but no backplate; spinner correct diameter, profile a bit too blunt.

Interior: The original release had a floor/rear bulkhead with separate seat and control column, etched belts, rudder pedals and trim wheel plus an instrument panel that used overlays of acetate film and etched brass (no sidewall detail in fuselage halves except for one bit of etched); upgraded version featured new resin floor/front/rear bulkheads with seat and moulded seat belts; sidewalls and instrument panel with much finer detail; etched and acetate film remained in both kits.

Detail: Two aileron mass balance weights per wing (correct), but supplied as two-dimensional etched-brass.

Canopy: One-piece vacformed plastic; overall length correct; profile of top of windscreen section too pronounced.

Decals: Both versions came with two options: D-IABI, Rechlin, Autumn 1935; D-IABI, Summer 1935; decal sheet includes tail band with partial swastika to get around bans in certain countries; known stencils on rudder and red line on upper wing included, as no other stencils confirmed by period photos.

Verdict: *This is basically an early MPM product, even with the upgraded parts, so the moulding is very much limited-run in quality and as such is hard work to build. That said this still remains the only injected kit of the V1 in the scale and if you want a better one, you can cross it with a good E-series. One for the experienced modeller only, really.*

MPM, Czech Republic

1/72nd Messerschmitt Bf 109T Upgraded Kit #72132

The original basic T-series kit was released by MPM in 1995 and then in 2000 they added resin detail parts and released it as an 'Upgraded Kit' (#72132). Although it remained in production for a few years it has not been seen for quite a while now and is unlikely to be reissued as MPM have come a long way in the quality of their kit production since this very early example of their work.

Plastic: Light grey-coloured plastic with engraved surface detail.

Wings: Moulded as one piece, with top and bottom surfaces combined; less than 1mm short in span; width towards the tip is slightly under and the tip profile too rounded; panel lines do not match scale plans; cannon bulges too small and teardrop shaped; aileron edge too far inboard, resulting in flap outer edge also being too far inboard; rib detail on flaps and ailerons match plans, albeit some are on the other due to the separate point error; radiators separate, good shape, no vertical bar in intake and no interior blanking plate; wheel wells are moulded into solid wing, so a little shallow; generic rib detail moulded into roof; outline and size correct; undercarriage doors correct shape/size; separate oleo legs of correct length (in upgraded kit these were replaced with resin examples); separate etched compression links although injected ones are on the sprues (just

MPM 72132

blobs!); main wheels correct diameter and with six-spoke hubs and tread detail; in upgraded kit these were replaced with resin examples; tailwheel and yoke moulded as one; tailwheel diameter correct but hub lacks detail.

Fuselage: 1mm short, all in tail; panel lines match plans; numerous access panels missing; radio hatch in port side; access step as dimple, should be engraved outline; rudder separate, correct overall shape; ribs on rudder poorly defined; gun troughs too pronounced and no gun barrels; oblong vents ahead of gun troughs masked by sprue gates on one half and only partial on the other; vents in cowl sides only as indents; chin radiator a little shallow and nothing inside to stop you seeing straight through;

Tailplanes: Correct span but too wide; panel lines match plans; trim tabs too big and too far inboard; supports separate.

Engine: None supplied.

Propeller: Separate propeller, spinner and backplate; propeller diameter and profile good; includes cannon and pointed spinners

Interior: Initial release comprised floor/rear bulkhead, seat and control column in plastic, with seat belts, trim wheel, rudder pedals and instrument panel in etched; upgraded version had new resin interior of floor/rear bulkhead, seat with moulded belts; rudder pedals, front bulkhead, sidewalls and instrument panel, plus a gunsight albeit 'solid' not clear.

Detail: Aileron mass balance weights separate in plastic, catapult spools and hook also included; separate pitot; no gun barrels, instructions tell modeller to make from 0.5mm tubing.

Canopy: One-piece vacformed plastic; two supplied; overall shape and length good; vertical line in side panes missing; profile of top of front windscreen section too square.

Decals: Both versions came with the same two decal options: T-2, RB+OP of JG77 (and later NJG101), Wallisheck, April 1941; V-17a, TK-HM at Travemünde test facility; decal sheet includes swastikas split in half due to laws in certain nations; national insignia and codes of correct size/style; no stencils of any kind.

Verdict: As we said at the start, even with new resin parts this is an early kit from MPM and it shows, as it is basic, with lots of flash and other moulding flaws. This one is probably beyond most, but if you have one in the stash then use the resin, etched and vacformed (mid-section only) canopy plus the extended wing tips, hook/spools and decals to convert a sound E-series kit as it will still probably give you a better T than the Face kit.

Revell, USA

1/72nd Messerschmitt Bf 109E #H-612

This is probably one of the oldest Bf 109 kits around, as it was first released in 1963 as #H-61. It was reissued in 1967 as #H-682, in 1969 as #H-684, in 1970 as #H-223, in 1972 as #H-612, in 1974 as #H-63, in 1976 as #H-663 and in 1978-1980 as #H-49. It was not until 2010 that it was to reappear, this time as a 'Bf 109E-4' (see listing elsewhere) as #04679.

Plastic: Light grey-coloured plastic with raised panel lines and loads of rivets.

Wings: In our example, surprisingly as it was factory sealed, the lower wing was short-shot with the tips rounded off instead of

square, as they should be! Checking with the later version we can confirm however that the span is within 1-2mm; narrow in chord, being about 1-2mm at the root narrowing to 1mm at the tip; no panel lines, just lines of rivets and these do not match published plans; no access panels depicted; cannon bulges too big and wrong shape; pitot placed too far outboard; centreline detail omitted except for the wing bolt bulges and centreline scoop, the latter being too big; radiators are separate, overall shape at odds with plans and flap elements moulded with each are misshapen blobs; also engraved flaps in each radiator are the wrong shape/position; cannon barrels too far inboard; wheel wells not bad shape, but oleo leg elements are too short resulting in the well being inboard; straight edge at rear of main bay at too shallow an angle; undercarriage doors moulded with oleo legs, which are just simple rods; door lower profile incorrect; wheels are separate to hubs, but they are simple discs and too small in diameter; separate hubs show 6 spokes but no other detail; tailwheel and yoke moulded as one; tailwheel tyre is too small and has no detail.

Fuselage: Fuselage is about 0.5mm short, overall position of the cockpit is wrong, being 1.5mm too far forward; fuselage when viewed from above is too wide; aft fuselage is too narrow towards the tail; tail profile wrong, rudder profile is incorrect and raised rib detail at odds with plans; radio hatch on port rear fuselage too small and as raised panel; another square panel forward and above the radio hatch, which is incorrect (also repeated on starboard side); exhaust stacks moulded with fuselage, very poor detail; access step as heavy recessed dip; no jacking holes in aft fuselage; gun troughs wrong shape and poorly defined; oblong holes forward of gun troughs are poorly defined dimples.

Tailplanes: Correct span and width; rivet lines do not match plans; rib effect on elevators does not match plans.

Engine: None supplied.

Propeller: Separate propeller and spinner; spinner has cannon hole in centre, but is slightly too small in diameter and length; propeller blades are 1-2mm short and have the wrong profile.

Interior: No interior as such, even has 'Revell' as raised detail on the fuselage sidewall; basic seat/bulkhead unit, nothing like real thing; no instrument panel, floor, rudder pedals, control column or gunsight; generic seated pilot figure.

Detail: None included, no bombs or rack; pitot shown under port wing correctly in instructions, but the part on the sprue is a misshapen rod; aerial mast is separate, but just a basic rod.

Canopy: One-piece; framework is accurate but whole unit is slightly too wide; aerial shown fitted to fuselage dorsal spine, not rear section of canopy.

Decals: Only one option was included in this kit, that of 'Black <-' of a spurious unit, as the eagle head motif is not from any recognised Luftwaffe unit, the only one close being *Regierungstaffel*, which only operated the Fw 200 or Ju 52/3m and even then it was a white shield, not yellow as in this kit. The proportions of the crosses are wrong and the swastika

is too small. The sheet does include two fuel/oil triangles, but no other stencils.

Verdict: One very much for the collector only, as it is very dated in detail and easily surpassed in accuracy by more modern kits.

Revell, Germany

1/72nd Messerschmitt Bf 109E-4 #04679

Note: Now although this is a reissue of H-612 (see entry elsewhere for that tooling), on close inspection we can see that it has at some stage been retooled in certain areas, so below we will cover those aspects that have changed in relation to H-612.

Plastic: Light grey-coloured.

Wings: The lower wing panel is the main area of change and as we found in H-612 that this part was short-shot, maybe this is why it is revised by this stage? The overall span and details remain unchanged (see H-612), but on the centreline, where the over-sized scoop was on H-612, there is now an oblong bulge with two holes in it (See Detail).

Detail: Added to the sprue with the propeller and radiators (unchanged) are a bomb and drop tank; the former is a bit nondescript being neither SC250 or SC500 in overall shape and the fins are thick; the drop tank is good in overall shape, but lacks detail as the retaining strap is an engraved line and the other lines around the unit are also very deep/heavy; both bomb and drop tank plug into the bulge under the wing via two pins.

Canopy: This is now on a sprue and three-part, although strangely the sprue is clearly marked as 'H-612', but was certainly not in H-612 nor shown on the instructions in that kit? Overall dimensions remains the same as H-612, so a little wide; the main canopy does not have the vertical line in the middle of the pane; all parts are thick, and the rear section has an ejector pin mark visible in one clear section.

Decals: This kit also has only one decal option: 'Yellow 10' of 2.(J)/LG2, in the Balkans in the spring of 1941; All the insignia dimensions and proportions are accurate; no swastikas included (banned in Germany, where kit was produced); full set of stencils.

Verdict: Although the tooling looks to have been cleaned up considerably, with the revisions noted, it is still very dated and limited in both detail and overall accuracy, so there are still better options out there in the scale.

Special Hobby, CZ

1/72nd Messerschmitt Bf 109E-series

Special Hobby produced a new E-series tooling in co-operation with Eduard in 2021. Thus far they have released the E-1 'Legion Condor' (#SH72459), E-1 'Lightly-armed Emils' (#SH72454), E-3 (#SH72443) and E-4 (#SH72439), all of which share common components, so we will base this assessment on the E-1 and note any differences in the others as we do along. Special Hobby also intend to offer the E-3 as a 'Simple Set' (#SS018) of just the sprues, along with the E-4 'Night Fighter', Bf 109E-4/B, E-7 and E-7 Trop at a later date.

Plastic: Medium grey-coloured plastic with engraved surface detail including structural rivets.

Wings: This is moulded as a single lower

and two separate upper halves; landing flaps, ailerons and leading edge slats are separate; the quoted 'real' span is 9.90m, when it was 9.87m, so the kits span will be slightly over; surface detail is good and the E-1 kits all have just the MG 17 machine-guns in the wings, whilst the E-3 and E-4 have the MG FF via different wing components that include the bulge in the lower surface, revised leading edge port and exposed gun barrel; the fabric effect on the landing flaps and ailerons are via raised ribs that reflect the structure underneath; the fixed trim tab on each aileron is depicted; the bulge underneath each landing flap is separate; the coolant radiator fairings are separate, but

Special Hobby SH72459

have the exhaust flap moulded in the open position; the radiator blocks themselves are moulded in situ under each wing, so lack any matrix detail; the vertical strut in the front of each coolant radiator is not depicted; the main wheel wells have the roof detail depicted inside each upper half; the inboard section and sidewalls of each main bay are moulded with the lower wing half; the latter lack any depiction of the canvas covers in this region; the oleo legs have the compression linkage moulded in situ, along with the guide rod at the front that most miss; the main wheel doors have engraved detail on the outside, with recessed detail on the inside; the main wheels have a cross-wise tread pattern and the hub is nicely recessed (again resin versions are available from the Quick and Easy range #Q72384) the oil cooler/lower engine cowling is part of the lower wing half, with the shape of the duct and coolant block inside done via a separate component; the front of the oil cooler has the horizontal splitter plate in situ, whilst the rear exhaust flap is separate.

Fuselage: This is moulded with the cowling and rudder separate; rudder has the fabric effect via raised ribs that depict the structure underneath; the fixed trim tab along the lower trailing edge of the rudder is depicted (in this scale it would be impossible to show this at scale thickness); the rear formation light is moulded in situ, so coloured, not clear plastic; aerial mast atop the vertical fin is moulded to each fuselage half; all access panels depicted; the jacking tube in the rear fuselage is only in partial relief; the upper cowling machine guns come with the option of the full set-up, so they can be exposed with the cowling off, or just barrels to be used when the cowling is fixed in place; separate exhaust stacks, although the outlets are solid (Quick & Easy do resin replacements #Q72390); the tailwheel is separate and has nice hub detail (again a resin

replacement is available in the Quick & Easy range #Q72391).

Tailplanes: These are solid each side and moulded with the elevators; rivet detail is good; fabric-effect on elevators is via raised ribs that match the structure underneath, although the engraved line along the rear should just be defined by indentations, as it's caused by the fabric over the structure underneath, not a structural (engraved) line; the support strut under each tailplane is separate and locates via a tab/hole arrangement.

Engine: The basic engine is included, along with the engine bearers and oil header tank; ignition lines and other detail moulded in situ, but quite acceptable for this scale; the separate engine cowling should be able to be put in place or left off (time will tell if that's true though).

Propeller: This is offered as a backplate, spinner and three-blade propeller; the profile and diameter of the latter is good, although once again the Quick & Easy range offer a detailed resin version (#Q72389); three spinner types are included on the sprues (hole for motor-cannon, covered motor-cannon hole and 'pointed' versions).

Interior: This is moulded as a floor, forward bulkhead (without oil tank), rudder pedals (later style, but they are a little 'flat' with the straps moulded in situ), rear bulkhead, control column, trim wheel/seat adjustment lever; seat with decals for the seat harness (correctly depicted with the shoulder straps coming through the hole in the back of the seat), instrument panel and gunsight; the instrument panel is offered with raised detail for a decal overlay and a plain one that can be used with an etched panel that is available separately; the gunsight is clear plastic and has both the lens and cover depicted.

Detail: The aileron mass balance weights and pitot are separate, as is the main radio mast; included on the sprues, but not used in any of the kits thus far released, is a 300lt drop tank and centreline rack.

Canopy: The E-1 and E-3 have the curved

Special Hobby SH72454

style canopy, whilst the E-4 (and E-7) have the square version; each is offered in three separate components; frame lines are raised, with the sliding side panel depicted via an engraved vertical line; both versions of the windscreen come with or without external armoured glass, depending on the variant/option you are building; the E-1s don't have head armour, all other versions do via a separate component.

Decals: Each kit came with the following decal options:

Special Hobby SH72443

#SH72459
- 6•123, flown by *Oblt* Hans Schmiller-Haldy, 3.J/88, Barcienes airfield, Toledo, Spain, March 1939; 6•121, flown by *Lt* Karl-Wolfgang Redich, 2.J/88, La Senia, León, Spain, 1938/39; 6•119, flown by *Hptm.* Siebelt Reents, 1.J/88, La Senia, León, Spain, winter 1938/39

Again the decal sheet includes all the unique and national insignia along with a full set of airframe stencils and decals for the seat belts and instrument dial faces.

#SH72454
- 'Red 16', flown by *Oblt* Fritz Losigkeit, 2./JG26, Werl, spring 1940; W/Nr.1986, 'Black >>', flown by *Hptm.* Hannes Trautloft, Stab III./JG51, St Omer, France, July-August 1940; 'Yellow 14', 6.(J)/Trägergruppe 186, winter 1939-40; 'Black <-', flown by *Oberst* Gerd von Massow, JG2, Schleissheim, Germany, winter 1939-40.

The decal sheet includes all the national and unique markings with the swastikas split in two. There is an extensive set of airframe stencils, including wing walkways and there are also decals for the seat belts and instrument panel dial faces.

#SH72443
- 'Black <<', flown by Werner Mölders, Gruppenkommandeur III./JG53, France, June 1940; 'Yellow 15', flown by *Uffz.* Karl Wolff, 3./JG26, Coquelles, France, August 1940; 'Yellow 1', flown by *Oblt* Josef 'Pips' Priller, *Staffelkapitän* 6./JG51, France, July-October 1940; 'Black 4', flown by *Ofw.* Anton Hacki, 5./JG77, Vaernes, Trondheim, Norway, summer-autumn 1940; W/Nr.3714, 'White 13', flown by Heinz Bär, 1./JG51, France, summer 1940

The decal sheet includes all the national and unique markings with the swastikas split in two. There is an extensive set of airframe stencils along with decals for the seat belts and instrument panel dial faces.

#SH72439
- 'Yellow 1', flown by *Oblt* Gerhard Schöpfel, III./JG26, Caffiers, France, August 1940; W/Nr.4148, 'Yellow 2', flown by *Oblt* Helmut Wick, *Staffelkapitän* 3./JG2, Beaumont-le-Roger, France, August 1940 – The complex camouflage pattern on the fuselage of this option is available as decals separately from Special Hobby as #K72031; W/Nr.4148, 'Black <<', flown by *Hptm.* Wolfgang Lippert. *Kommandeur* II./JG27, Larissa, Greece, April 1942; 'Yellow 8', III./JG52, Rumania, May 1941.

The decal sheet includes all the national and unique markings with the swastikas split

Special Hobby SH72439

in two. A full set of airframe stencils along with decals for the seat belts and instrument panel dial faces are also included.

Verdict: *Special Hobby have really gone to town on this one, as the detail is excellent and going by their more recent 1/72nd scale kits, these should all build with relative ease. They certainly take the top slot for the E-series in 1/72nd, although easier/less complex/detailed builds can be probably found via the Airfix or Tamiya kits, and with the tropical, fighter-bomber, night-fighter and E-7 airframes to follow, they are all well worth adding to your collection.*

Tamiya, Japan

1/72nd Messerschmitt Bf 109E-3 #60750

This new tooling was first released in 2000 and has remained in production ever since.

Plastic: Dark grey-coloured plastic with engraved panel lines and other details.

Wings: Lower section as single-piece to point just inboard of tips; span and chord correct; wing tip profile correct; panel lines match published plans, as do access panels (those inboard near root on the upper panels are all missing); cannon bulges correct size/location; centreline details good, although bulges over wing bolts look a little large; leading edge slats depicted; ailerons and flaps moulded with upper wing halves; radiator correct size/location and separate from fairing on flaps; radiator flap not separate and vertical bar in intake missing; wheel wells correct position and shape; main bay has sidewalls, although probably not deep enough to meet interior of

Tamiya 60750

upper wing; roof detail to main bay moulded into inside of upper wing halves; oleo legs correct length; axle at correct angle to ground; oleo detail correct; compression links moulded with oleo; main wheels correct diameter and with tread pattern; wheel hub detail accurate although a little shallow; tailwheel and yoke moulded as one; tailwheel tyre slightly undersize and with detail.

Fuselage: About 1-1.5mm short; cockpit is 1mm too far aft; panel lines and access hatches match plans; lifting hole in aft fuselage just semi-relief not a hole; all vents etc., in correct semi-relief; exhaust stacks moulded in situ with good detail; bulge under exhaust correct size/shape; rudder actuator wires moulded to fuselage as raised lines; radio hatch in port side correct size/shape/location; oblong vents aft of cowl guns too big; engine cowling separate; gun troughs good shape/location; oblong holes ahead of troughs are too big and have raised

Tamiya 60755

beading around edge; lower chin cowling separate, with separate rear flap and good overall contours; rudder separate, correct shape and rib detail matches plans; fixed trim tab depicted on rudder.

Tailplanes: Correct span and shape; hinge and panel lines match plans; rib detail on elevators match plans; trim tab correct size/location.

Engine: None supplied.

Propeller: Separate propeller, spinner and backplate; propeller correct diameter and blade profile; spinner correct diameter and profile

Interior: Probably the best of the bunch, comprises floor/rear bulkhead, seat, control column, front bulkhead with rudder pedals and instrument panel; moulded sidewall detail in each fuselage half; seat belts supplied as decals; instrument dials supplied as decals; separate gunsight in clear plastic.

Detail: Standard intake filter (tropical on sprue but not used); separate tail struts, aileron mass balance weights, pitot, cannon barrels and aerial mast all separate.

Canopy: Two-piece, thus unable to pose it open; separate head armour (remove the curved top for certain versions) with headrest cushion detail.

Decals: This kit came with three options: "Black <<', flown by Adolf Galland, 9./JG26,

France, August 1940; 'White 5', 4./JG77, Norway, September 1940; 'Black <', II./JG54, France, August 1940; decal sheet includes swastikas (may be removed in certain countries); full set of stencils; seat belts supplied as decals; all national insignia style/size correct.

Verdict: *Being Tamiya this kit will build easily and well, which makes it one of the top choices for the type in this scale.*

Tamiya, Japan

1/72nd Messerschmitt Bf 109E-4/7 Trop #60755

Following on from their E-3 kit released in 2000, this E-4/7 kit was released in 2001 and remains in production. As the parts in this are identical to those in 60750, the assessment of that kit applies here also: all we have included below are those elements that differ.

Detail: Tropical filter with the intake flap closed; 300lt drop tank, with accurate detail including the retaining strap; separate rack for drop tank, basic detail; decals supplied for the matrix in the tropical filter.

Propeller: Three styles of spinner: cannon port and capped flat or pointed; all spinners correct diameter and profile.

Canopy: Separate windscreen armour plate included.

Decals: This kit came with three options: 'White 12' of 7./JG26; 'Black 8' of 2./JG27; 'Black <<', flown by *Maj*. Helmut Wick of JG2; decal sheet includes swastikas (may be removed in certain countries); full set of stencils; white fuselage bands supplied as decals; all national insignia style/size correct.

Verdict: *Just like the E-3, this is a Tamiya so it will build easily and well. It is certainly one of the top choices for the type in this scale.*

1/48th Scale

Academy, Korea

1/48th Messerschmitt Bf 109D #2178

This is the ex-Hobbycraft kit first released in 1992, and Academy released it in 2000. As it is essentially identical to the Hobbycraft kit all we will cover here are any difference in relation to that kit.

Plastic: Medium grey-coloured.

Detail: The sprues actually still contain all the parts for the B, C & D versions.

Decals: Three decal options: D-1, 6•79, flown by *Oblt* Werner Mölders, 3.J/88, Spain, 1938; D-1, 6•56, flown by *Hptm*. Gotthardt Handrick, J/88, Spain, 1938; 'White <<', flown by *Maj*. Hannes Gentzen, JGr.102, Germany, late 1939; no swastika; minimal number of stencils; no walkway markings; national insignia correct size.

Verdict: *Although the base kit is flawed, this one is good value as all the parts for B, C or D are there.*

Academy, Korea

1/48th Messerschmitt Bf 109E-3 'Heinz Bär' #12216

This is the ex-Hobbycraft from 1992 and it was reissued by Academy with Heinz Bär markings

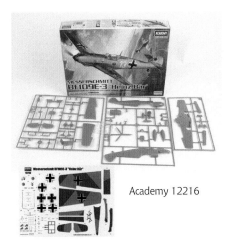

Academy 12216

(#12216) in 2009 (see above for overall assessment of the tooling: the details below only list differences between the two kits).

Plastic: Dark grey-coloured.

Detail: Pitot added (#63); sprues also contain the tropical filter seen in the E-4/7 Trop version (not used here).

Canopy: Still same E-3 style canopy, but sprue now has addition of armoured glass for windscreen as separate part.

Decals: One option: 'White 13', flown by *Oblt* Heinz Bär, 1./JG51, France, September 1940; decal sheet includes complete camouflage decals for upper surfaces (RLM 02/70) with stencils and crosses in situ; also includes canopy frames; separate crosses and walkways also included; full stencils; swastikas split in two.

Verdict: *This is probably a better 'simple' option for the E-series in 1/48th than the original Hobbycraft version, as the overall kit builds well if you can live with the dimensional problems. Apply decals instead of painting, though, not an easier option in our books!*

Academy, Korea

1/48th Meserschmitt Bf 109T-2 #12225

This kit was released in 2010 and it combines the basic E-series kit first released by Academy in 1992 with conversion parts made by Wolfpack Design in Korea. For an overall assessment see the Hobbycraft entry in the download version, all that is covered

Academy 12225

below are those aspects that differ in this version.

Wings: The main parts are as per the original Hobbycraft kit, all that has changed are the tips, which are supplied as resin parts made by Wolfpack Design. No modified parts are included for the radiators.

Fuselage: The only change here is in the front section of the radiator intake, which is again replaced with a resin example of the correct shape/style; no need to include arrestor hook etc., as removed from T-2.

Decals: Two options: 'Black 6', flown by Oblt. Herbert Christmann, JG11, Norway, winter 1944; 'Yellow 7', NJG101, Maching, Germany, spring 1943; swastikas split in two; full set of E-series stencils.

Verdict: *There are other options to convert other kits into the T-series, but this one from the box should look the part and will be a lot easier to build than the MPM example.*

Airfix, UK

1/48th Messerschmitt Bf 109E-1/E-3/E-4 (#A05120) & Bf 109E-3/E-7 'Airfix Club' Limited Edition (#A82012)

Under Hornby's control the new Bf 109E series was released in 2010, with the E-1/E-3/E-4 (#A05120) being followed by the E-1/E-3/E-7 Trop (#A05122). A special Airfix Club edition (#A82012) was offered to members in 2012.

As all these kits use a common set of parts we will assess them as one, pointing out any differences between each kit.

Plastic: Light grey-coloured plastic with engraved panel lines and details.

Wings: Lower moulded as one piece to a point just inboard of tips; less than 1mm too great in span; ailerons, flaps and slats separate; ailerons slightly too long; slats slightly long (marginal); flaps slightly too long, separate bulge; rib details in flaps match plans; main panel lines match plans for underside; most access panels correct, although oval cannon one is too narrow and there is an additional round one mid-span at aileron hinge line; radiators separate and correct shape/profile (although edge inboard should be straight, not at an angle); matrix blocks inside radiators separate; no vertical rib in radiators; centreline detail good, although centre scoop too narrow; cannon bulges separate, but too narrow; upper as two separate panels; tips are undersize overall; indents for tip lights, but no separate clear sections; all panel lines present but not in correct positions in relation to plans; cannon access panel missing oval latch; access panels do not match plans for upper surfaces; cannon ports separate inserts to allow early (E-1) machine-gun or later (E-3/4/7) cannon; wheel wells about 1.5mm too far outboard; overall shape correct; sidewalls in upper and lower wings enclose each well; rib detail in roof of well, although there is also an ejector pin mark in the same area; oleo leg element moulded with wing, but no detail; oleo legs attached to lower wing, not fuselage or inside upper wing half; oleo doors too long, due to dimensional error in wheel well; oleo legs also too long; compression links moulded to oleo leg; wheels slightly too small, also square-edged when they should be rounded; tyre has tread detail; hubs separate with six-spoke and

reasonable detail (probably not deep enough); tailwheel and yoke as one; angle of yoke too steep, resulting in wrong attitude in relation to the oleo.

Fuselage: 2-3mm short, all forward of engine bulkhead; vertical fin top wrong angle (too steep) resulting in it being undersize and aerial post being too far forward; rudder separate, trailing edge profile good, but top angle wrong matching error in vertical fin top; panel lines match plans; those access panels that are present match plans; jacking point hole in half-relief; radio hatch in port rear fuselage; top strip of wing root fillet looks too thick; vents in starboard side, behind engine cowling both the same size, should be different; exhaust stacks separate, but not hollow; tropical filter slightly short (marginal); bulges under exhaust stacks correct; ventral radiator separate with matrix inside, but unit short due to error in nose dimensions; engine cowl separate, but too short; gun troughs also too short; oblong vents in front of troughs are slightly oversized; cowl gun barrels separate and correctly staggered.

Tailplanes: Separate tailplanes and elevators; tailplane length 1mm too great, slightly narrow at inner trailing edge (marginal); panel lines match plans; elevators same length error as tailplane, trim tab too short; rib detail matches plans.

Engine: Basic block moulded to fuselage

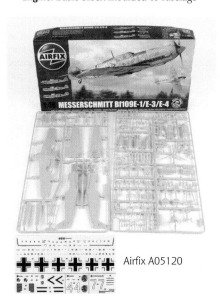

Airfix A05120

halves, suspect undersized to fit in (thick) cowling; separate engine bearers, although these also look undersize.

Propeller: Propeller, spinner and backplate; propeller, each blade about 1.5mm too long; blades too narrow; spinner correct diameter and profile.

Interior: Floor/rear bulkhead, front bulkhead, rudder pedals, seat with moulded belts; trim wheels, instrument panel and control column; throttle box and oxygen bottle separate; separate gunsight in clear plastic.

Detail: 300lt drop tank and rack; SC50, SC250 and SC500 bombs each with rack; bomb fins moulded to main body but commendably thin; separate aileron mass balance weights; separate pitot.

Canopy: Three-piece; offered in early (E-1/E-3) or late (E-4/E-7) styles; windscreen

Airfix A82012

offered for each version plus E-4/E-7 version with or without armoured glass, rear section offered with or without central bar; aerial mast separate.

Decals:

- #A05120 – E-4N, 'Black <-', flown by *Maj.* Adolf Galland, Stab JG26, Audembert, France, late 1940; E-3, 'White 3', flown by Johan Boehm, 4./JG51, France, July 1940; E-1/B, 'White 7', II(Schlact)/LG2, Calais-Marck, France, September 1940; no swastikas; full stencils
- #A82012 – E-3, W/Nr.1304, AE479, No.1426 Flight at A&AEE Boscombe Bown, 1941; E-7 evaluated by the Imperial Japanese Army Air Force in 1941; full national insignia for each option; complete set of original German stencils

Verdict: *It was a surprise to find this one dimensionally inaccurate, but that is one of the problems of working from plans and drawings. Overall the errors are not great and the kit builds well, save for the annoying engine block, so for those working on a budget they are a good alternative, to more expensive ones from Eduard or Tamiya.*

Eduard, Czech Republic

1/48th Messerschmitt Bf 109E-series

Eduard announced a new series of 1/48th Bf 109Es in 2011 and produced the new tooling in 2012 with the release of the E-1 (#8261), E-3 (#8262) and E-4 (#8263, which was reissued in 2021) in their 'ProfiPACK' series and in the same year produced the special 'Royal Class Edition'. The F-7/ Trop 'ProfiPACK' edition (#8264) was released in 2013. The E-1 was released in late 2012 in the simplified 'Weekend Edition' range (#84164) without the inclusion of photo-etched parts and another version of this in the series was produced with different decal options in 2020 (#84158). The E-3 in the 'Weekend Edition' (#84165) range was released in 2013 (#84165), followed by the E-7 Trop (#84167) in 2015 with a different version of the E-3 with revised decal options (#84157) in 2019. The E-4 'Weekend Edition' (#84166) was released in 2013 with another version with different decal options (#84153) produced in 2019. The E-series sprues were also included in the limited edition 'Adlergriff' kit (#11140) released in 2020, which focused on the E-1, E-3 & E-4 during operations from June to October 1940. The E-1/E-3 tooling was also combined with the Roden Heinkel He 51 kit in the limited edition 'Legion Condor' kit (#1140) in 2016. The Bunny Fighter Club also offered the E-4 in the limited edition 'Balthasar' edition (#BFC070) in 2019 by combining #84153 with two additional decal options and this was only

available to club members directly from the Eduard website for a limited period. The most recent release as we write, is the E-7 in the 'Weekend Edition' series (#84178), released in 2022.

As all these kits use a common set of parts we will assess those we have as one, pointing out any differences between each kit.

Plastic: Mix of tan in the early releases and tan and dark grey-coloured plastic in the later ones, all with recessed panel lines and other details.

Wings: One-piece lower to point inboard of tip; panel and rivet detail matches plans; access hatches match plans, although again, some devoid of detail; cannon bulges look undersized (not wide enough); ejector ports only in partial relief; radiators separate, correct size/shape/location; ailerons, flaps and slats separate: uppers moulded as two panels; overall length correct; tip profile at trailing edge too narrow/pointed, resulting in ailerons being too long (>1mm); panel lines and hatches exactly match plans (although some hatches without detail such as push-buttons); also has subtle rivet detail that again matches plans; separate slats, slightly too long (>1mm) inboard; tip lights moulded as bulges, but with wing so not clear; wheel wells correct size/shape/location; separate 'liner' to give correct detail to well interior; oleo legs correct length, mounted into top (inside) of upper wing panels; good overall detail to oleo legs, linkage moulded in situ; undercarriage doors feature interior detail; main wheel tyres separate from hubs, slight undersize (diameter) though; thread pattern in tyres; hubs split in two, with separate outer spoke ring to give more depth; tailwheel has separate yoke and tyre/hub; extremely fine detail to oleo; tyre is plain, but hub has detail.

Fuselage: Correct length, rear fuselage slightly too deep along lower edge, mainly from trailing edge of wing to mid-length; vertical fin shape correct; panel lines match plans; filler, on upper spine on port side shown as oblong, should be oval; hand-hold aft of cockpit on port side undersize; all other access panels match plans; exhaust slot correct size/location (exhaust stacks separate); chin radiator correct size/shape, separate intake and exhausts; engine cowl separate, correct shape; gun troughs correct size/location; oblong vents forward of troughs too big; supercharger intake duct panel separate, rear of unit looks too short; panel on starboard side aft of cowling separate, correct size/location vents (x2); upper cowling, forward of windscreen, separate with correct detail/vents etc.; tail struts separate

Eduard 8261

Eduard 8262

with lower element moulded to fuselage to alleviate any with alignment.

Tailplanes: Correct span and profile; panel lines match plans, ribs in elevators match plans, trim tabs correct size/location; cut-back on aileron inner face correct angle; rudder is separate; correct size/shape; rib details match plans; moulded (solid) rear light; fixed trim tab correct shape/location.

Engine: A complete engine is included, in both ProfiPACK and Weekend Edition kits, the latter without any etched detail parts; inclusion of engine near to scale makes fitting cowling very difficult (a problem all kits would have

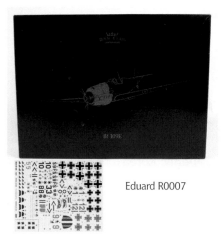

Eduard R0007

due to thickness of plastic); the exhaust stacks are separate, and individual(!), with semi-recessed outlets.

Propeller: Separate propeller, spinner and backplate; propeller correct diameter and blade profile; spinner correct diameter and profile; kit includes cannon port or capped (pointed or blunt) spinners dependant on the versions.

Interior: Full interior comprising floor/ rear bulkhead, seat, control column, oxygen regulator, rudder pedals, instrument panels, seat adjustment handle and trim wheels, plus moulded detail inside each fuelage half; the ProfiPACK versions have the addition photo-etched seat belts, chains for the trim wheels, rudder pedals (replacements for plastic parts) and instrument panels (pre-painted); the gun-sight is separate and moulded in clear plastic.

Detail: The over-engine machine guns are included; in the ProfiPACK versions you get photo-etched screens for the radiators, linkage for the rudder; aerial lead connector for the rudder post; the canopy-mounted periscope is included in some versions; SC250 bomb and rack, 300lt drop tank and rack; ETC 50 rack and SC50 bombs with etched fins (latter parts not included in all versions).

Canopy: Moulded in three sections; separate armoured windscreen; slightly undersize, but less that 0.5mm overall; framework matches plans; side panels separated by double line; aerial post mounted correctly in upper framework of rear section; vertical line/frame moulded into port side windscreen panel, not shown on any plans?; ProfiPACK versions have different sprue to Weekend Editions with two styles of main canopy element for opened or closed; separate (etched) head armour and canopy stays, plus canopy latch; head armour in all versions in plastic with moulded cushion, two styles, but only later (curved top) version; die-cut self-adhesive masks included for the canopy in ProfiPACK versions.

Decals: The options in all the versions we had to hand are as follows:

- #8261 – Five options, all E-1s: 'Red 13', flown by *Ofw.* Kurt Ubben, 6(J)./Trager-

Eduard 84164

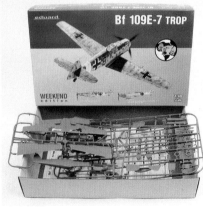

Eduard 84167

Eduard 84178

Eduard 8263

Eduard 8263 (2021 reissue)

gruppe 186, Wangerooge, Germany, March 1940; 'Red 1', flown by *Hptm.* Hannes Trautloft, 2./JG77, Juliusburg, Germany, September 1939; 'Yellow 2', 6./JG52, Husum, Germany, 1940; 'Yellow 11', flown by *Fw.* Artur Beese, 9./JG26, Caffiers, France, August 1940 (x2 schemes with or without yellow nose/tail)

- #8261 – Five options, all E-3s: 'Yellow 15', flown by *Uffz.* Karl Wolff, 3./JG52, Pihen/ Calais, France, August 1940; 'Yellow 1', flown by *Oblt* Josef Priller, 6./JG51, France, Autumn 1940; 'Black <-', flown by *Obstlt* Hans-Hugo Witt, JG26, Dortmund, Germany, April 1940; 'White 7', 1./JG2, Bassenheim, Germany, May 1940; 'Yellow 3', 3./JG51, Mannheim-Sandhofen, Winter 1939-40

- #8263 – Five options, all E-4s: 'Yellow 10', flown by *Ofw.* Fritz Beeck, 6./JG51, Wissant, France, 24th August 1940; 'Black <-', flown by *Maj.* Helmut Wick, JG2, Beaumont, France, November 1940; 'Yellow 13', 9./ JG54, The Netherlands, August 1940; 'Black <', flown by *Oblt* Franz von Wera, Ii./ JG3, Wierre-au-Bois, France, 5th September 1940; 'Black <-', flown by *Obstlt* Adolf Galland, JG26, Audembert, France, December 1940

- #8263 (2021 reissue) – W/Nr.5587, 'Yellow 10', flown by *Ofw.* F. Beeck, 6./JG51, Wissant, France, 24th August 1940; W/Nr.5344, 'Black <-', flown by *Maj.* H. Wick, CO of JG 2, Beaumont, France, November 1940; 'Yellow 13', flown by *Lt* J. Eberle, 9./JG54, The Natherlands, August 1940; W/Nr.1480, 'Black <', flown by *Oblt* F. von Werra, *Gruppenadjutant* II./JG3, Wierre-au-Bois, France, 5th September 1940; W/Nr.5819, 'Black <-', flown by *Obstlt* A. Galland, CO of JG 26, Audembert, France, December 1940

- #84164 – One option: E-1, 'Yellow 2', 6./JG52, Husum, Germany, 1940

- #84165 – One option: E-3, 'Yellow 1', flown by *Oblt* Josef Priller, 6./JG51, France, Autumn 1940

Each kit has the swastika split in two; only the ProfiPACK versions include a full set of stencils

- #84178 – E-7/B, S9+AS of 8./ZG1, Belgorod, Russia, June 1942; E-7/Z, W/Nr.7677, 'White 8', flown by *Oblt* Josef Priller, CO of 1./JG26, St Omer, France, June 1941; E-7/Trop, 'Black 1', flown by *Hptm.* Erich Gerlitz, CO of 2./JG27, Ain-el-Gazala, Libya, summer 1941; E-7, W/Nr.3523, 'Red 6', flown by *Lt* Wolf-Dietric Widowitz, 5./JG5, Petsamo, Finland, April 1942

The decal sheets, which are printed by Eduard, are excellent and have perfect register and colour density. You get all the unique markings plus a set of national insignia, although the Nazi swastikas are included in two forms; those in the main body of the sheet are in two parts, whilst those on the lower right hand corner are complete, but will be clipped off in those nations that ban the Nazi symbol. There is also a separate sheet containing a complete set of airframe stencils.

Verdict: *THE choice in 1/48th for accuracy and detail. If you want cheaper go with the 'Weekend Edition' version, if you want easy to build and cheaper, go with Tamiya, if you just want cheaper go with Airfix, but if you want the best option currently in 1/48th then this is the only game in town.*

Hasegawa, Japan

1/48th Messerschmitt Bf 109E-series

Hasegawa first released their new 109 kit as the E-3 in Japan as #U9 in 1988 but most modellers outside of Japan will have first come across it in 1989 as #J1. At the same time this basic tooling was also released as the E-4/E-7 (#J2), E-4/7 Trop (#J3) and Bf 109E 'Galland' (#J4). The tooling was revised and reissued in 1994 as #JT8, with the E-4/7, E-4/7 Trop and 'Galland' being reissued as #JT9, #JT10 and #JT11 respectively at the same time. Since then, the basic tooling has been reissued numerous times as follows: Bf 109E 'Luftwaffe Experten' (#JT112) in 1995, Bf 109E-3 'Swiss Air Force' (#JT104) & Bf 109E 'Bulgarian Air Force' (#JT123) in 1996, Bf 109E-3 'Condor Legion' (#JT169), Bf 109E-4/7 'Jabo' (#JT161) & Bf 109E-4/7 'Superdetail' (#CH24) in 1998, Bf 109E-1 (#09369) & Bf 109E-3 (#JT8) in 2001, Bf 109E-1 'Sitzkrieg' (#09482) in 2003, Bf 109E-3 'Rumanian Air Force' (#09624) & Bf 109E-3 'Spanish Civil War' (#09601) in 2005, Bf 109E 'Hahn' (#09746) in 2007, Bf 109E-4 'Battle of Britain' (#09823) in 2008, Bf 109E 'Marseille' (#09892) & Bf 109E 'Galland w/figure' (#09879) in 2010 and Bf 109E-4/E-7b 'Jabo' (#07316) in 2012. A study of the parts has shown that this kit was not revised once, as always thought, but twice, the second revision being in 1995, as JT112 from that year shows the second series of revisions.

As all these kits use a common set of parts, in their 1st, 2nd and 3rd generation forms, so we will assess them as one, pointing out any differences between each kit.

Plastic: (1st & 2nd generation) light grey-coloured plastic with engraved panel lines and details: (3rd generation) medium-grey colour plastic with engraved panel lines and details

Wings: (1st, 2nd & 3rd generation) Upper

Hasegawa 09892

Hasegawa 09624

moulded as one from tip to tip; correct span and chord; leading edge slats, flaps and ailerons separate; slats slightly too long (inboard); radiators moulded in situ, no front bar and overall shape at odds with plans; cannon bulges too narrow and too long; main panel lines match plans; access panels do not match plans, and most are too big; centreline scoop too narrow; wingtip lights moulded to wing and not correct style/shape; lower moulded as two halves; ailerons in situ, correct rib detail; tip too narrow resulting in aileron being slightly too long; trim tab correct size/location; gun barrels correct length but moulded into wing; panel lines match plans; access panels do not match plans and correct ones are too big; gun access hatch too wide; flaps slightly too long (1mm) and rib detail does not match plans (missing inboard); correct bulge on underside, aft of radiator; wheel wells are about 1-2mm too far outboard due to leg element being too long; shape correct; oleo pick-up moulded into lower wing, not fuselage sides or inside upper wing; limited sidewall in lower halves only and two raised dual lines inside upper wing half; oleo legs correct length; separate compression links; main wheels correct diameter; six-spoke hubs with excellent detail; tread pattern on tyres; tailwheel and yoke moulded together on one fuselage half; tailwheel diameter correct but hub lacks any detail and is too big; in the 2nd generation kit the tailwheel tyre was revised in size with the hub edges not as pronounced; in the 3rd generation kits the tailwheel reverted to the same size/hub detail as seen in 1st generation kit.

Fuselage: (1st generation) Less than 1.5mm short, all between the 1st and 2nd ribs behind the cockpit; also slightly skinny, mainly

towards the tail, but it is marginal; decking forward of windscreen too steep, resulting in engine cowl being too short and upper nose profile being wrong; wing root bulge wrong position; panel lines match plans, as do all access panels; jacking hole in rear fuselage in deep relief; rib detail on rudder match plans; fixed trim tab and rear light on rudder; aerial post on top of vertical fin too long and wrong shape; exhaust stacks correct length and depict six stacks, but detail is basic and inaccurate; bulge under exhaust correct size/shape/location; chin intake good shape and interior detail via etched; no rear flap in chin radiator; supercharger intake slight short and too pointed profile at rear; cowl gun troughs slightly short, but engraved outline correct; oblong vents in front of troughs too big; vents in side of nose aft of engine cowl too big on starboard side.

Fuselage: (2nd generation) This is where the revisions took place; now correct length to within 0.4mm; access panels revised (still not 100% but most in correct place); upper section of starboard fin that was moulded with

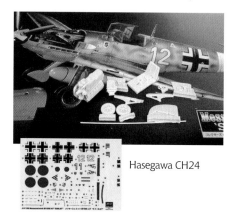

Hasegawa CH24

the port half in the 1st generation kit, now with starboard half; wing root fillet contour revised to curved, but on port side only!; bulge on wing root moved to correct location; upper contours forward of windscreen revised; engine cowl revised to show correct height and thus profile (gun troughs and vents remain the same though); side vents aft of engine cowl on starboard side revised to correct size/location; exhaust stacks revised to six; exhaust outlet and engraved flap added to chin radiator; area that was raised on the base of the vertical fin leading edge is now just engraved lines but

only on port fuselage half!

Fuselage: (3rd generation) Again this is the area of revision; area at base of vertical fin that was shown as engraved outline on port half and raised detail on starboard in 2nd generation kit, is now raised on both halves; the revisions to the wing root fillet edge that were only on the port half have also been removed so they now match the starboard half; the rear fuselage has been increased in diameter slightly to deal with the 'skinny' lower edge profile; rear fuselage also extended slightly once again to make it accurate in length.

Tailplanes: (1st, 2nd & 3rd generation) Correct span and chord; slightly too square at tip, all at trailing edge; trim tab too short; cut-back on elevator should be rounded at corners; ribs across entire elevator; panel lines match plans.

Engine: (1st, 2nd & 3rd generation) None supplied.

Propeller: (1st, 2nd & 3rd generation) Separate propeller, spinner and backplate; propeller correct diameter, although tips slightly too broad; spinner shape and size correct; E-4/7 kit also contains pointed spinner.

Interior: (1st, 2nd & 3rd generation) Floor/rear bulkhead, seat with moulded belts (very short), front bulkhead, rudder pedals, control column, instrument panel. sidewalls and trim wheel; separate gunsight in clear plastic; no decal for instrument panel.

Detail: (1st, 2nd & 3rd generation) The E-3 has no bombs or drop tank, although parts remain on sprues; separate aileron mass balance weights; separate pitot; E-4/7 kits include 300lt drop tank and rack (overall shape good) and SC250 bomb; bomb rack pretty basic in shape and detail; SC250 bomb fins thick as moulded with bomb halves; E-4/7 Trop kits include

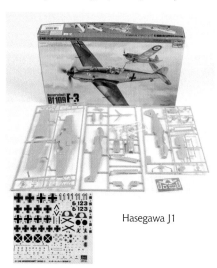

Hasegawa J1

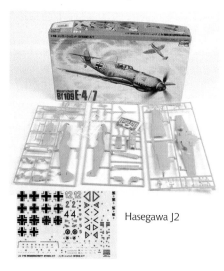

Hasegawa J2

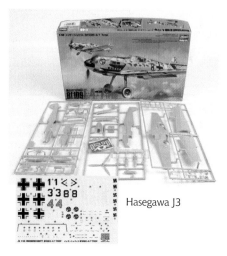

Hasegawa J3

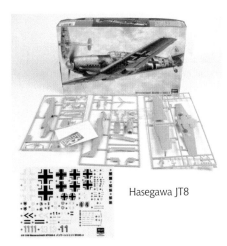

Hasegawa JT8

desert filter for supercharger intake (moulded with flap closed).

Canopy: (1st generation) Three-part; correct length and profile, but windscreen section too wide at base; separate armoured glass windscreen; framework matches plans; vertical line in main panel shown as frame, should be single line; head armour separate as etched, although only early (flat) style in all kits; head armour cushion also as etched, not very effective; different style main canopy in E-3 and E-4/7 kits (correct); Galland kit (#J4) included both E-3 and E-4/7 style canopies, the latter with hole for the periscope sight.

Canopy: (2nd & 3rd generation) This is a complete new tooling and whilst the aft and main sections remain the same, the windscreen has been revised to match the new forward/upper cowling profile; revised separate armoured glass as well to match new windscreen; note that although the sprue layout for the E-3 and E-4/7 kits are different, both have been revised in the same manner.

Decals: (1st generation) #J1: 'White 1', flown by *Oblt.* Otto Bertram, 1./JG2, France, May 1940; 'yellow 1', flown by Josef Priller,

Hasegawa JT112

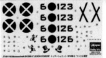

Hasegawa JT169

6./JG51, Belgium, 1940; 'Yellow 11', flown by *Lt* Waldemar Wübke, 9./JG54, 1940; 'Black <', JG53, Summer 1939; 6•123, flown by *Oblt.* Hans Haldy, 3.J/88, Spain, Spring 1939; 'White 5', JG135, Juterbolg-Damm, 1937: #J2: E-4, 'Black <<', flown by *Maj.* Helmut Wick, 1./JG2, Belgium, 1940; E-7/N, 'White 12', flown by *Oblt.* Joachim Mücheberg, 7./JG26, Sicily, 1941; E-4, 'Yellow 2', flown by *Oblt.* Helmut Wick, 3./JG2, France, September 1940; E-4B, 'Black <|', flown by *Lt* Steindl, II./JG54, Leningrad, 1942; E-4, ''Black <', flown by *Hptm.* Hans Hahn, I./JG3, France, 1940; E-4, 'Black 4', flown by *Hptm.* Günther Rützow, I./JG3, France, 1940: #J3: E-4 Trop, 'Black 8', flown by *Lt* Werner Schroer, 2./JG27, North Africa, 1941; E-4/N Trop, 'White A', flown by *Oblt* Ludwich Franzisket, *Stab* JG27, North Africa, 1941; 'E-4 Trop, 'Black 3', 2./JG27, North Africa, 1941; E-7/N Trop, 'Black 1', 2./JG27, North Africa, 1941; E-4/B Trop, 'Black 1', 3./JG27, North Africa, 1941; E-4/N Trop, 'White 6', 1./JG27, North Africa, 1942: #J4: E-4N, 'Black <', JG26, France, September 1940; E-4N, 'Black <-', JG26, Audembert, France, December 1940; E-3, 'Black <<', III./JG26, France, June 1940; E-3, 'Black <<', III./JG26, Marquise, France, August 1940; E-3, 'Black <', flown by Werner Mölders, III./JG53, France, May 1940 (the first four options all flown by Adolf Galland).

Decals: (2nd generation) #JT8: 'Yellow 1', flown by Josef Priller, 6./JG51, Belgium, 1940; 'Yellow 11', 6./JG54, summer 1941; 'White 13', flown by Heinz Bär, 1./JG51; 'Black <-1', flown by the *Kommandeur* of JG2.

Verdict: *What really strikes you about the 1st Generation kit is just how 'similar' the Hobbycraft kit is in comparison! Hasegawa at least made the effort and retooled the kit (twice!), as the first generation was definitely below bar for them, even then. There is not much to choose between this and the Airfix or Tamiya examples for top honours, although for detail the Eduard kits win that accolade.*

Hobbycraft, Canada

1/48th Messerschmitt Bf 109C (#HC1567) and Bf 109D (#HC1568)

This is another of the toolings that were released in 1992 by Hobbycraft and which we believe are now all owned by Academy in Korea. As both kits are essentially the same, with just a few alternative parts, we will cover them together identifying the differences.

Plastic: Light grey-coloured plastic with recessed panel lines and details.

Wings: Lower is one piece; span just over 1mm short; note that overall this wing is identical to that used in the E-series kit with the exception of the radiators that are removed form the B, C & D versions probably by means of inserts in the tooling; wing tips too narrow at trailing edge; wing marginally narrow along entire leading edge; wing bolt bulges too small; panel lines match plans; access panels present but all too big and some that should not be present; scoop on centreline too small/narrow; cannon access panels wrong size/location; ailerons too short (flaps too long); aileron rib detail does not match plans; flaps separate with bulge behind radiator, ribs do not match plans; oil cooler

included for D, unit the correct length but the wrong shape front and rear; uppers moulded as two parts, same dimensional errors as lower wing (again, same wings as used in E-series kits); aileron rib detail does not match plans; no trim tab on aileron; main panel lines match plans; cannon access panel too big; access panels do not match plans and are all too big; cannon port correct location; no tip light; wheel well has the leg of bay slightly too long, resulting in wheel bay being too far outboard; overall shape of wheel bay does not match plans, as angle cut-back at rear is too pronounced; oleo leg section moulded into wing and has some detail, oleo legs themselves fitted into bay, not to fuselage or into upper wing; rib lines moulded into inside of upper wing, although these are not accurate; undercarriage doors reflect same shape errors as seen in the wells; some detail inside doors, but not consistent with real thing; oleo legs correct length; separate compression links; main wheels correct diameter; hub had six spokes and other detail; tyres have tread detail; tailwheel and yoke moulded to one fuselage half; tailwheel oleo lacks compression link; tailwheel tyre diameter correct although hub is devoid of detail.

Fuselage: 4.5mm short; if cockpit lined up with plans, fuselage is 1mm short at the nose and 3.5mm short forward of the tail; profile of upper decking forward of canopy is flat, should be sloped; vertical panel line between gun access panel and cowling is too

Hobbycraft HC1567

far forward, resulting in guns and troughs also being wrong; rear fuselage skinny along entire length, top and bottom; vertical fin profile good, but rudder slightly undersize at trailing edge; rudder rib detail does not match plans; rudder top hinge line, wrong angle (too steep); rudder actuator horn moulded to rudder and hole for control cables in rear fuselage; main panel lines match plans; access panels do not match plans; round access panel on lower starboard fuselage side missing, as is one below cockpit on port side; has four vents in starboard fuselage sides aft of engine cowling, there should only be the two, and the shape/size of all of them are wrong; vents in port side shown inline, although some machines had these staggered; panel lines for chin radiator do not match plans; exhaust stacks separate insert for both C or D, neither hollow and lack vents front and rear; C-version of exhausts are square outlets, should have rounded corners; chin intake area too solid and without detail; three oblong vents in upper cowling are too close together; air scoop on starboard upper nose solid part; gun troughs too short; no projecting barrel tips for cowl guns.

Tailplanes: About 1mm too long and trailing edge profile is 1mm undersize along entire length; trim tab correct position but slightly too short overall; panel lines match plans; rib detail does not match plans and too few ribs depicted; tail support strut mount slight too far outboard (marginal)

Engine: None supplied

Propeller: C has two-blade wooden propeller moulded as one with spinner; diameter and blade profile correct, but moulding process results in excess wedges at base of both blades that need to be removed and reshaped; D has two-blade metal propeller with separate spinner and backplate, propeller correct diameter but blade profile suspect; spinner diameter

Hobbycraft HC1568

correct, profile slightly too long (marginal).

Interior: Comprises floor/rear bulkhead, seat with moulded cushions and belts, control column, sidewalls, front bulkhead, rudder pedals and instrument panel (all identical to that used in E-series kits); separate gunsight in clear plastic, not accurate shape for this version; detail very good, although kickplates missing from floor; raised detail on instrument panel good, although not 100% accurate and no decal included for dials.

Detail: Drop tank and bomb, plus separate racks; drop tank shape not bad, but retaining strap as deep recessed furrow; bomb not bad for SC250 but fins very thick and no support rods between each are supplied; rack for bomb includes shackles but is not accurate for any version; rack for drop tank is too wide and lacks detail; aileron mass balance weights separate; no pitot; cannon barrels separate, but too short and muzzle brakes too long.

Canopy: One-piece; curved upper main canopy section; accurate in length and profile; framelines match plans; no line in main pane for sliding panel.

Decals: Two decal options: ER+16 of Jagdfliegerschule 1, Germany, 1940; J-310, Switzerland, 1940; swastikas split in two; no stencils.

Verdict: *It is a surprise to find this one so far out dimensionally and annoying, as we still don't have a replacement mainstream injected kit in the scale. With a lot of work and a bit of cross-kitting you can probably correct this one, but be prepared for the work.*

Hobbycraft, Canada

1/48th Messerschmitt Bf 109E-3 (#HC1569) and Bf 109E-4 (#HC1570)

Hobbycraft released their new series of Bf 109 kits in 1992 and they remained in production for a number of years. We are led to believe that these toolings are now owned by Academy, who reissued the E-3 version with Heinz Bär markings (#12216) in 2009 (see separate listing), then added resin conversion parts to the basic E to offer the T-2 (#12225) in 2010 (see separate listing).

As all these kits use a common set of parts we will assess them as one, pointing out any differences between each kit.

Plastic: Light grey-coloured plastic with recessed panel lines and details.

Wings: Lower wing is one piece; span just over 1mm short; wing tips too rounded; wing marginally narrow along entire leading edge; radiator shape too square, no vertical bar in intake; panel lines match plans; access panels present but all too big; wing bolt bulges slightly too small; scoop on centreline too small; cannon bulges separate but wrong shape/size and have to be fitted over panel lines that are still partially visible; ailerons too short (flaps too long); aileron rib detail does not match plans; flaps separate with bulge behind radiator, ribs do not match plans; upper wing moulded as two parts, have same dimensional errors as lower wing; aileron rib detail does not match plans; no trim tab on aileron; main panel lines match plans; cannon access panel too big; access panels do not match plans and are all too big; cannon port correct location and barrels separate; no tip light; leg section of wheel wells slightly too long, resulting in wheel bays being too far outboard; overall shape of wheel bay does not match plans, as angle cut-back at rear is too pronounced; oleo leg section moulded into wing and has some detail, oleo legs themselves fitted into bay, not to fuselage or into upper wing; rib lines moulded into inside of upper wing, although these are not accurate; undercarriage doors reflect same shape errors as seen in the wells; some detail inside doors, but not consistent with real thing; oleo legs correct length; separate compression links; main wheels correct diameter; hub has six spokes and other detail; tyres have tread detail; tailwheel and yoke moulded to one fuselage half, correct length and tyre diameter although hub is devoid of detail.

Fuselage: 4mm short, all in the rear fuselage and tail; rear fuselage skinny along entire (bottom) edge; vertical fin profile good, but rudder slightly undersize at trailing edge; rudder rib detail does not match plans; rudder top hinge line, wrong angle (too steep); rudder actuator horn moulded to rudder and hole for control cables in rear fuselage (no raised 'cable' moulded to fuselage like most kits, so this can be easily and accurately added); main panel lines match plans; access panels on mid/aft fuselage correct, those at front are not; two vents either side on top of nose, forward of windscreen, should be just one per side; side vents present and correct location, but too long; exhaust stacks moulded in situ and only have five stacks; two bulges below exhausts, should be one (that is bigger); supercharger intake slightly skinny overall due to pointed profile; gun troughs correct overall size and

position, but panel lines do not match plans; oblong vents forward of gun trough too wide and only partial relief; cowl guns supplied separately, but shown staggered the wrong way round in instructions and not at all on the actual part; separate engine cowling devoid of access panels.

Tailplanes: About 1mm too long and trailing edge profile is 1mm undersize along entire length; trim tab correct position but slightly too short overall; panel lines match plans; rib detail does not match plans and too few ribs depicted; tail support strut mount slight too far outboard (marginal).

Engine: None supplied.

Propeller: Propeller with separate spinner and backplate; propeller correct diameter and blade profile; spinner diameter and profile correct; cannon spinner in E-4 and capped version in E-7.

Interior: Comprises floor/rear bulkhead, seat with moulded cushions and belts, control column, sidewalls, front bulkhead, rudder pedals and instrument panel; separate gunsight in clear plastic; detail very good, although kickplates missing from floor; raised detail on instrument panel good, although not 100% accurate and no decal included for dials

Detail: Drop tank and bomb, plus separate racks; drop tank shape not bad, but retaining strap as deep recessed furrow; bomb not bad for SC250 but fins very thick and no support rods between each are supplied; rack for bomb includes shackles but is not accurate for any version; rack for drop tank is too wide and lacks detail; aileron mass balance weights separate; no pitot; cannon barrels separate, but too short and muzzle brakes too long.

Canopy: One-piece; different styles for E-3 and E-4 kits; accurate in length and profile for both versions; framelines match plans; no line in main pane for sliding panel; no separate armoured glass for windscreen; aerial separate and attached to rib in top.

Decals: E-3 (#HC1569) offered two decal options: 'Yellow 11' of 9./JG54, Channel front, 1940; 'Red 5' of I./JG52, France, 1940. E-4 (#HC1570) offered two decal options: 'Red 3' of 2./JG3, Channel Front, 1940; 'Yellow 3', 9./JG26; decal sheet has swastikas split in two; no stencils; red lion of 9./JG26 poorly depicted and later style *Tatzelwurm* of 2./JG3 should have a yellow tongue; 9./JG54 shield proportions at odds with photos resulting in demon head looking too large; background to I./JG54 shield at odds with photos, should be blue overall behind the boar in a wash, not a solid band curved above it.

Verdict: *Not bad but not great, this is a basic tooling that has nice touches like the interior, but various dimensional issues. The kits are not readily available at present, and although they offer a nice basic kit they have been surpassed even in that role by more modern toolings.*

Monogram, USA

1/48th Messerschmitt Me 109E #PA74-98

Monogram, USA 1/48th Messerschmitt Bf 109E & Hurricane 'Air Combat Series' #6082.

This kit was first released in 1962 and had been renumbered as #6800 by the early 1970s. It was last seen in 1988 when it was reissued with the Hawker Hurricane as 'Air Combat Combo #4' (#6082). It is difficult to determine the exact version this kit depicts, as in some aspects it looks pre-E series, whilst in others it looks like an E, for the purposes of this assessment we will judge it as an E-1/-3 as it has the curved canopy of that series.

Plastic: (#PA74-98 & #6800) moulded in dark green-coloured plastic for the main components with all the detail parts in black; raised panel lines and rivets etc.

Wings: Lower moulded as one piece; overall span about 0.5mm too great either side; also too narrow, less than 0.5mm at root, but over 3mm by tip: error all in trailing edge; wing tips too rounded, mainly due to narrow wing; radiators correct overall dimensions, but shape wrong, no vertical bar in intake and placed too far outboard; ailerons too long, flaps too short; too many raised ribs on control surfaces; cannon blister present, but wrong shape; centreline detail inaccurate, square bulges at front, centreline scoop too small and wing bolt bulges too far outboard and too small; panel lines do not match plans; various access panels missing; no wing tip lights; upper wing moulded as separate port and starboard panels, same overall dimensional errors as lower wing; panel lines do not match plans; most access panels missing; raised ribs on ailerons and flaps do not match plans; flaps only have ribs for half their span; no trim tab; if cannon barrels fitted into wing they will be too short; wheel wells extend too far inboard and square edged, should be at angle; overall shape not bad, but main wheel well area slightly too big; no detail or sidewalls inside bays (open to wing interior); undercarriage doors too long due to error in well size; oleo legs designed to retract, but slightly too long; no compression links; main wheels correct diameter and have treads, but they are raised; hubs too big diameter, have six spokes but little detail; axle has to be heated and flattened to secure wheels.

Fuselage: 5.5mm short, with 0.5mm in the front cowling area and the remaining 5mm at the aft fuselage/vertical fin joint; rear fuselage also too 'skinny'; jacking point in aft fuselage just a raised ring; radio hatch correct position/size; another oblong panel forward of radio hatch shouldn't be there; fuel filler on port dorsal spine is round, should be oval; access hatches on starboard side missing; supercharger intake too short and narrow; exhaust stacks too short and only five stacks depicted; gun troughs correct position and overall .shape; no oblong vents forward of gun troughs; bulges below exhaust stacks too small; chin radiator good shape but solid front and back.

Tailplanes: Moulded as one piece that goes through fuselage; overall shape good, but tip slightly short by about 0.5mm; trim tabs too long (clip inboard area); ribs on elevators do not match plans; panel lines do not match plans; tailplanes covered in raised rivets; rudder correct height but angle at top too steep and profile at base not rounded enough; raised rib detail on rudder does not match plans; separate supports.

Engine: None supplied.

Propeller: Supplied as propeller with tip of spinner, plus rear section of spinner; propeller diameter and blade profile correct; spinner diameter and profile correct.

Interior: None as such, just a rear bulkhead with a slot to take the tab moulded into the back of the generic pilot figure; moulded ledge in fuselage halves acts as instrument panel; decal for instrument panel, not accurate; no raised detail inside fuselage halves.

Detail: Separate pitot, but depicted as 'T' instead of 'L' shaped; no aileron mass balance weights; aerial mast mounted into rear fuselage, but does project through canopy.

Canopy: One-piece; correct length but about 1-2mm too short; frame detail good, but one on top of rear section missing; depicted with armoured glass on windscreen.

Decals: #PA74-98 offered one decal option: 'Black <-' of II./JG26; #6800 offered one option: 'White 4' of 4./JG26; no swastikas for either kit; overall dimensions of tactical markings too big/too broad character stroke in original issue, corrected for #6800; the JG 26 shield not accurate for #PA74-98; no stencils in #PA74-98; some stencils but no walkways in #6800.

Verdict: *The age of this kit shows and although in its day it was probably the best about, nowadays it is best left to the collector in any incarnation.*

Revell, Germany

1/48th Messerschmitt Bf 109E-4/7 Trop #04572

This is a reissue of the 3rd generation ex-Hasegawa kit and it was released in a Revell box in 2002. See the comments for the 3rd generation Hasegawa versions elsewhere for an overall assessment, as all that is included below are those elements that differ in this release.

Lower **Wings:** As no etched parts are included in this kit, the matrix for each radiator is missing, resulting in them being 'see-through'

Fuselage: No etched parts, so matrix for chin radiator is missing.

Canopy: No etched parts, so the head armour is omitted, even though a template to make one from plasticard is included in the instructions.

Decals: E-7 Trop, 'Yellow 13', flown by *Lt* Hans-Joachim Marseille, 3./JG27, North Afrika, April 1941; E-4, 'Black <<', flown by *Hptm.* Helmut Wick, I./JG2, Beaumont-le-Roger, France, October 1940; E-4, G9+JV, III./NJG1, Germany, 1941; no swastikas; complete stencils.

Verdict: *As the third generation tooling this is the most accurate from Hasegawa and, at the time, this version was far cheaper than in a Hasegawa box, so it was well worth investing in. Overall the same comments made for the Hasegawa example/s apply here.*

Tamiya, Japan

1/48th Messerschmitt Bf 109E-3 (#61050) and E-4/7 Trop (#61063)

Tamiya did the Bf 109E-3 first in 1997 and followed it with the E-4/E-7 Trop (#61063) in 1999. Both kits remain in production and as they are basically the same tooling we will cover them as one, pointing out any differences between them.

As both of these kits use a common set of parts we will assess them as one, pointing out any differences between each.

Plastic: Dark grey-coloured plastic with engraved panel lines and details.

Wings: Lower is one-piece; correct span; wing tip profile too rounded at trailing edge; aileron ribs match plans; trim tab too far inboard; wing tip light moulded as 'pimple'; cannon bulges too narrow; panel lines match plans; some hatches match plans but additional one mid-span near trailing edge; none of the hatches have detail in them; upper wing as port and starboard panels; panel lines match plans; cannon access hatch too wide; access hatches do not match plans; trim tab too far inboard; wheel wells about 1mm too far outboard; overall shape and outline correct; detail moulded into inside of upper wing; sidewalls moulded in lower wing half, but not enough to meet upper wing; oleo mounts moulded to upper wing halves; oleo legs correct length; compression linkage moulded to oleo; wheels correct diameter and tyre profile; tyre has tread detail; separate wheel hubs, six-spoke and good detail; tailwheel and yoke moulded as one; yoke oleo diameter too thin; tyre undersize, hub detailed but too big resulting in tyre being thin.

Tamiya 61050

Fuselage: Marginally short, all in fuselage aft of rib directly behind the cockpit (1-1.5mm); angled edge for top of rudder too steep; jacking point in half relief; panel lines match plans albeit in wrong place due to short fuselage; access panel match plans; rudder separate, top trailing edge too bulged and forward top hinge line follows incorrect line of vertical fin; rib details in rudder match plans, but too pronounced/deep; gun troughs correct position and size; oblong vents forward of troughs too big; separate gun barrels, nice muzzle detail and correctly staggered; ventral chin radiator separate, correct shape, exhaust with engraved flap detail and intake has separate radiator matrix and flap; supercharger intake correct shape/size /location; exhaust stacks separate, correct six stacks, but unit slightly too long; tropical filter included in E-4/7 kit, correct size/shape, front flap depicted open (hollow inside).

Tailplanes: Slightly too broad (marginal); tip profile too square; panel lines match plans; inboard cut-back should have rounded corners; ribs of elevator not a complete match to scale plans, also a bit too pronounced; trim tab slightly short; support in correct position.

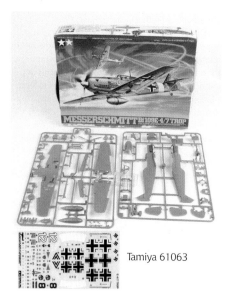

Tamiya 61063

Engine: None supplied.

Propeller: Propeller, spinner and back plate; propeller correct diameter; blade profile a little too pointed at tip; spinner diameter and profile correct; cannon and capped (blunt and pointed) spinners included.

Interior: Floor/rear bulkhead, seat, control column, rudder pedals, front bulkhead and instrument panel; separate clear gunsight; trim wheel and oxygen bottle separate for sidewalls.

Detail: 300lt drop tank parts on sprues in both kits, but only used in E-4/E-7; detail/shape is good; aileron mass balance weights separate; pitot separate; wing gun barrels separate, nice muzzle detail.

Canopy: Three-piece; E-3 correct style with single line for separate panels in side pane; windscreen with separate armoured glass; aerial mounted in rear section; head armour plate separate with cushion detail, only depicts later version with angled top.

Decals:
- E-3 – 'Black <<', flown by Adolf Galland, II./JG26, France, August 1940; 'White 3', II./JG77, Norway, October 1940; 'Black <', II./JG54, France, autumn 1940
- E-4/E-7 – 'White 12', 7./JG26; 'Black 8', 2./JG27; 'Black <<', flown by *Maj.* Helmut Wick, JG2

Verdict: *Both of these kits build beautifully and will pose no problem to anyone, regardless of experience. Recommended as the 'nicest' 1:48 kit, but not the most detailed or accurate.*

Wingsy Kits, Ukraine

1/48th Messerschmitt Bf 109E-1/3/4

This firm released their all-new E-series kits in 2021 with the E-1 (#D5-07) and E-3 (#D5-08) released first, followed by the E-4 (#D5-10) and special E 'Legion Condor' (#D5-09), which contained two complete kits. We only have #D5-07 here for assessment, but they all share common components.

Plastic: The kit is moulded in a dark grey-coloured plastic with finely engraved surface detail including all the structural rivets.

Wings: Span is quoted as being 206mm, which is probably just rounded up from the 205.6mm conversion of the real thing; moulded as lower half with two upper halves and separate wing tips; the tip lights are

moulded in situ though, so coloured, not clear plastic; leading edge slats, ailerons and landing flaps all separate, although no option to depict them deflected is depicted in the instructions; fabric effect on latter two are again via subtle raised ribs, that are almost invisible, plus with the landing flaps these do not reflect the structure that was underneath; fixed trim tab on the ailerons depicted, with the linkage underneath in etched and the balance weight as a separate (plastic) part; bulge aft of radiator under each landing flap is separate; coolant radiators multi-part built into recesses in wing; there are etched splitter plates (#PE26) fitted into the intake of each coolant radiator that don't match any period diagrams or preserved E-series airframes; the coolant radiator exhaust flaps are separate and etched; armament in the E-1 is the single MG17 in each wing, whilst the E-4 and E-7 will have revised wing components to depict the bulges and relocated port for the barrel of the MG FF; the main wheel wells have the roof detail moulded inside each upper wing half, with the remainder of each bay depicted via two separate components; these latter parts whilst enclosing the bay do not depict the canvas liners of the E-series (the side are actually depicted curved); main wheel doors separate and have internal detail; main oleo legs have the compression linkage separate, although these latter items are just solid and lack the recess caused by the flanges on the real thing (a lot to ask); main wheels are solid and have a cross-wise tread pattern plus sidewall detail.

Wingsy Kits D5-07

Fuselage: Overall length is quoted as 183mm, which is a little over the 180mm conversion of the real thing; rudder separate and fabric effect is done raised ribs that are so subtle as to be almost invisible; rear formation light is depicted, but it's grey-coloured, not clear plastic; upper and lower engine cowlings separate inserts and whilst the rearmost section of the upper cowling follows a panel line, there is no corresponding panel line in the mid and front portion, so you are going to have to hide that without filling in all the engraved structural rivets; lower cowling has much the same problem, although the mid to front seam is actually less of an issue as the side of the oil cooler radiator fairing are part of each fuselage half, so only the seams to these on the underside will need to be filled (again their are structural rivets to contend with though); exhaust flap for oil cooler is a separate etched component, as is the splitter plate at the front; main access panels depicted, along with the slots either side of the nose and

the jacking tube in the rear fuselage is depicted via an open hole each side; aerial mast on top of the vertical fin is moulded in situ with the port fuselage half; supercharger intake is separate but a single piece, which seems pointless, but at least means the raised flange at the base is well defined; complete cockpit sill and rear bulkhead region separate, again odd, as the sills are devoid of any detail; raised flanges around exhaust stacks are separate etched components; exhausts are single unit per side and acceptable, but each stake outlet is not angled enough and they are also solid; the tailwheel is a separate component and the definition between the wheel hub and yoke is pretty poor/soft.

Tailplanes: The tailplanes are split into upper and lower halves with the support struts and elevators are separate components; elevators have the fabric effect as raised ribs, but these are so subtle as to be almost invisible plus they don't reflect the structure underneath; elevator trim tab is depicted; tail support struts fit into a recess in the rear fuselage and under the tailplane, so hopefully their location/alignment should not be an issue

Engine: Just a bare upper portion of the engine block is included, so the exhausts have something to mount onto.

Propeller: This is moulded as a backplate, spinner and three-blade propeller; blade diameter and profile are good, but the boss is solid, so the motor-cannon option is not truly depicted (use the CMK replacement); the sprues contain four styles of spinner (with motor-cannon port, capped motor-cannon and two styles of the 'pointed' version).

Interior: Bucket seat with etched lap and shoulder straps (not convinced by the layout of the latter though); early style rudder pedals with separate etched straps; trim wheel and seat adjustment lever as a separate sub-assembly; cockpit floor well detailed, but regardless of what the instructions show, the separate oxygen bottle lacks the perforated cover and our example had a sink mark in the middle; separate sidewalls with the map case an etched component; instrument panel in upper and lower section with all dials as raised rings whilst the dial faces are done with decals; separate gunsight in clear plastic, but again the instructions show it with the lens and cover, but the part itself only has the lens; front firewall includes the tank and feed pipe.

Detail: The pitot is separate under the port wing, but the vertical element is much too long; separate main aerial mast with the option of a pennant via a photo-etched component if needed.

Canopy: This comes in three sections and in the E-1 it depicts the early rounded shape, whilst the E-4 and E-7 kits will have the squarer version; the external armoured glass for the windscreen is separate, should the option you build need it; the head armour is made up of three etched and one plastic component; a rearview mirror is also included as etched, should your option require it; regardless of the separate canopy elements, the instructions do not depict an 'open' option; die-cut, self-adhesive vinyl masks are included for the canopy.

Decals: #D5-07 comes with the following decal options:
- 'Black <', flown by Josef 'Pips' Priller,

Stab I./JG51, Speyer, Germany, 1939
- 'White 13', flown by Heinz Bär, I./JG51 during the early stages of the Battle of France
- 'Red 16', flown by *Staffelkapitän* Frotz Losigkeit, II./JG26, Germany, 1940
- 'Black 5', flown by *Lt* Hans Krug, 5./JG26, Marquise, France, 1940

The accompanying decal sheet is well printed and includes all the national and unique markings, although the swastikas are only depicted in two parts; The images have a satin finish, but excess carrier film is limited and that which can be seen in the smaller stencils will hopefully disappear once applied. Decals are included for the instrument faces of the two instrument panel, plus the electrical distribution boxes on the sidewalls in the cockpit.

Verdict: *Although not truly 'limited run' these kits are not mainstream injected either and to produce a Bf 109E in this scale is bold, when there is such stiff competition from the likes of Eduard, Hasegawa or Tamiya. The nature of the tooling system limits what can be achieved, plus you also have the complexity of the overall assembly, which when combined with a UK retail price greatly in excess of a 'ProfiPACK' version from Eduard and easily twice that of the 'Weekend Edition', will probably have a lot of modellers side-lining this series. We have shown you what they contain so, as always, the ultimate choice is entirely down to the individual.*

1/32nd Scale

Cyber-Hobby, Hong Kong

1/32nd Messerschmitt Bf 109E-3 (#3222) & E-4 (#3204)

This is a brand name used by Dragon and they released the E-4 (#3204) version first in early 2011, followed by the E-3 (#3222) in late 2012. These were followed by the E-7 Trop (#3223) in 2013 and the E-4/B in 2015. The E-7/B (#3221) was announced initially, but to date it has not been released. We have the E-3 (#3222) here for assessment. These toolings were also reissued by Hobby 2000 in 2022 as #32004 (E-3), #32005 (E-4) and #32006 (E-7).

Plastic: Light grey-coloured plastic with recessed panel lines and other details.

Wings: Supplied as upper and lower halves; span correct; slightly narrow; panel lines match plans; access hatches correct and with detail; cannon bulge correct shape and separate cover; complete MG FF cannon and ammo drum for each wing; radiators separate but round hatch that is within the boundary of the edge is moulded into the wing as a whole, so no joint through centre; cannon ejector ports open; cannon port/panel in wing leading edge separate; separate ailerons, flaps and slats, all correct length/location; rib detail matches plans; control surface linkage uses etched brass parts; slats have retaining bar that allows them to be opened or closed; separate clear tip lights; tip correct width/profile; undercarriage bays correct location/size; inner canvas liner as separate flexible plastic parts; raised ribs in inside of wing for bay roof; oleo leg correct length; wheels of correct diameter and hub detail both sides; separate brake lines; detail

inside undercarriage doors; Venturi in back of radiator; radiators do not have separate flaps; vertical bar in front; centreline area under fuselage separate part; wing spars (partial) included to give strength to chosen parts breakdown of wing/fuselage join (see Interior); detail on underside centreline panel matches plans; two styles of scoop offered for the centreline panel.

Fuselage: Moulded from aft of the engine to the rudder hinge line; length is correct; panel lines match plans; access hatch aft of cockpit on starboard size wrong size/style; reinforcing plates at front corrected moulded as raised detail; jacking tube holes in rear fuselage; engine cowl separate; gun troughs short; small bulges on either side of cowl elongated, should also be flatter; oblong slots forward of troughs are slightly narrower at one end than the other; separate lower chin cowl with radiator detail; bulges on side of lower nose correct shape/location; separate exhaust stacks with outlets in partial relief; separate rudder with control arms and linkage in etched brass; rib detail matches plans; separate clear tail light.

Tailplanes: Separate elevators; correct profile; panel lines match plans; rib detail matches plans although 'V' wedges are too big; no rivet detail on main part of tailplanes, just on the tips?; trim tab correct length but one

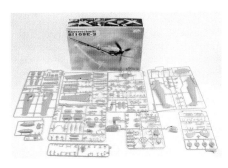

Cyber-Hobby 3222

rib too far outboard; separate support struts, although placed slightly too far outboard under tailplanes (marginal).

Engine: Complete engine; parts (sprue) actually comes from their Bf 110 kit; has the oil booster tank only applicable to the E-4 onwards (kit part #E6).

Propeller: Separate hub, blade rings, blades, backplate and spinner; blade length correct; tip profile looks slightly too broad; spinner correct diameter/profile; includes four styles of spinner, cannon, blunt, pointed and very pointed, although the latter ones only really apply to the E-4 onwards (use #J13 for options 1 to 7 and #A9 for 8 and 9).

Interior: Full cockpit interior built up on a floor/front bulkhead unit that also includes partial wing spars; separate seat with etched belts, control column, rudder pedals, instrument panel, oil tank and drain cover, rear bulkhead and ribs; trim wheel, oxygen regulator and various sidewall panels are all separate parts (some with decals); separate gunsight with clear plastic projector glass.

Detail: The upper cowl guns are included along with the canvas cover over the back of the instrument panel in this area; the ammo boxes below are there, but moulded all as one with the pipework on the port side etc.; 300lt drop tank and rack included but not used in

this version; 1,000kg bomb with a superbly detailed rack and separate cover on the sprues, but again not used in this version.

Canopy: Moulded as three parts; correct length/profile; overlap of panes in main canopy moulded as raised line; vertical seam in side panel of windscreen also moulded as raised lines, should only be on port side, though; separate part to make rib above windscreen and add a rear-view mirror, although instructions give no indication of which options this applies to; separate windscreen armour; sprue with windscreen to take the periscope used by Galland included, but not used in this version; separate head armour, offered in early and late styles; canopy retaining strap included as etched brass.

Decals: There are nine decal options: 'Yellow 7', flown by *Uffz.* H. Grabow, 3./JG3, France, 1940; 'Black <', flown by *Maj.* A. Galland. III./JG26, Marquise, France, 1940; 'Red 1', flown by *Oblt* G. Framm, JG27, Krefeld, 1940; 'Yellow 11', flown by *Oblt* W. Schuller, JG27, Plumetot, 1940; 'Black <-', flown by *Maj.* H. Witt, JG26, Dortmund, 1940; W/Nr.4101, DG200 as captured and tested in the UK, 1940; 'Black 5', flown by H Bennemann, 1./JG52, France, 1940; 'Black 1', flown by H. Tietzen, 5./JG51, Marquise-West, 1940; 'Black 11', flown by *Uffz.* F. Mias, 5./JG3, Brombos, 1940.

The decal sheet does not include swastikas; full stencils only.

Verdict: *Today you really have two options for THE best kit in this scale, the Eduard one for a basic version and this one if you want to show/add a lot of detail. This is a superb kit and the extra cost is all down to the extra parts. Cyber-Hobby/Dragon obviously did good research on this one, probably using the one in Munich as the basis, although we suspect they failed to get the cowl off, so that erroneous oil tank on the port side is understandable (and easily fixed).*

Eduard, Czech Republic

1/32nd Messerschmitt Bf 109E-series

Eduard announced their new series of Bf 109Es in this scale in 2008 and began releasing them in 2009 with the E-1 'ProfiPACK' (#3001). This was followed by the E-4 (#3002) and E-3 (#3003) in the 'ProfiPACK' series the same year and the E-7 Trop (#3004) in 2010. Simplified versions without photo-etched parts were released in the 'Weekend Edition' series in 2010 (E-1 [#3401] and E-4 [#3403]) and 2011 (E-3 [#3402]). In 2011 they also offered the basic E-series toolings with additional resin parts as the limited-edition Bf 109E 'Over the Balkan Peninsula' (#1156). The E-1 and E-3 parts were included in the limited edition 'Legion Condor' (#11105) kit in 2019, with an 'Overtrees' version (#3009X) that did not include the wings, as both E-1 and E-3 wings were in #11105 released at the same time directly from the Eduard website only. E-1 'Overtrees' (#3001X) were also offered directly in 2019, with the E-1, E-3 and E-4 parts included in the limited edition 'Adlerangriff' kit (#11107) released in 2020.

As all these kits use a common set of parts we will assess those we have as one, pointing out any differences between each kit.

Plastic: Light olive-coloured plastic for all to date, with recessed panel lines and other details.

Eduard 3001

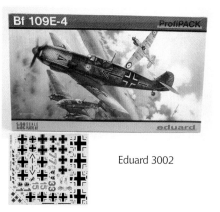

Eduard 3002

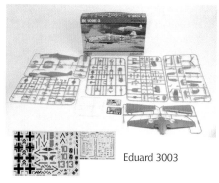

Eduard 3003

Wings: Lower moulded as one piece; span about 2mm too great; tip slightly too thin at trailing edge; tip lights moulded with wing half, so solid, not clear; panel lines match plans; access panels match plans with exception of two round ones mid-span at leading edge, which are side-by-side, when should be staggered; radiators separate, correct size/shape; ProfiPACK kits come with etched matrix inside and vertical bar in front (nothing supplied in Weekend Edition kits for these areas); bulges over wing bolts have too exaggerated 'point' at rear; other centreline detail as per plans; upper wings as port and starboard panels; panel lines match plans; access panels match plans although none have any detail; gun access panels slightly raised detail; slats, flaps and ailerons separate; flaps and ailerons rib detail matches plans, bulge on underside of flaps separate; tips as per lower section; gun ports open, no detail inside; wheel wells correct size/shape/location; separate inserts

Eduard 3004

for main bay sidewalls and leg elements; oleos mount into block moulded into underside of upper wing panels; oleo legs correct length; compression links moulded to legs; brake pipes included; wheels slightly small diameter (marginal); thread detail correct; hubs separate, but detail is shallow; tailwheel and yoke separate; tailwheel tyre features ribs and hub detail; no detail inside fuselage halves within tailwheel bay, just mounting block.

Fuselage: About 1mm too long; panel lines match plans; access panels match plans and all have details such as fixtures etc.; upper decking forward of windscreen and both side panels, aft of engine cowl, are separate, all show correct vents and other detail; engine cowling separate, gun troughs correct shape/size/location, oblong vents ahead too big(?); chin radiator correct size/shape; matrix for chin radiator as etched in

ProfiPACK versions, nothing supplied in Weekend Editions; exhaust with separate individual stacks, all the semi-relief holes as outlets; aerial mast on vertical fin too long; supercharge intake correct size/location; rudder actuating rod as etched part in ProfiPACK versions, nothing in Weekend Editions.

Tailplanes: Correct span and shape; separate elevators; rib detail matches plans; trim tab slightly too far inboard (marginal) and tab a bit too big; cut-back on rear of elevator correct angle and edges curved; panel lines match plans (as do rivets); separate support struts with moulded bottom lug on fuselage side to easy this joint.

Engine: Complete engine and bearers included; fit of this does make getting the cowl on extremely difficult, although really designed to have engine in and cowls off, or no engine and cowls on (lug for propeller included for latter option).

Propeller: Separate propeller, spinner and backplate; propeller correct diameter; blade profile correct; spinner correct diameter and profile; sprues include cannon port or capped (pointed) style spinners.

Interior: Made up of sidewalls, floor/rear bulkhead, seat and support frame, seat adjustment lever, rudder pedals, oxygen regulator; two-part instrument panel; ProfiPACK versions also include the trim wheel chains, seat belts and instrument panels in pre-painted photo-etched; gunsight separate and in clear plastic.

Detail: The sprues contain a 300lt drop tank of correct shape/size, plus its rack, although only suitable for certain versions; aileron mass balance weights separate; guns above engine along with their associated ammunitions boxes and bulkhead also included,

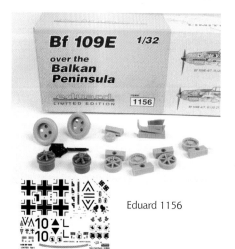

Eduard 1156

pitot separate; #1156 as a limited edition included the resin main wheels plus tailwheel and yoke previously released separately under the Brassin label.

Canopy: Four-piece; separate armoured windscreen glass; head armour depicts mid/late version with curved top; armour supports and canopy retaining strap as etched in ProfiPACK versions, nothing in Weekend Editions; different sprues for E-1/E-3 and E-4/E-7 versions (for 'curved' and 'square' canopies), the latter includes the windscreen with periscope version; all panel lines match plans; single vertical line to denote side panes; ProfiPACK versions include die-cut, self-adhesive paint masks for the canopy and wheels.

Decals: These are the decal options in the various versions we have to hand:

- #3001 – E-1, 'Yellow 11', flown by *Fw.* Artur Beese, 9./JG26, Caffiers, France, August 1940; E-1, 'Red 1', flown by *Hptm.* Hannes Trautloft, 2./JG77, Juliusburg, Germany, September 1939 ; E-1, 'Red 13', flown by *Ofw.* Kurt Ubben, 6(J)./*Tragergruppe* 186, Wangerooge, Germany, March 1940; E-1, 'Yellow 2', 6./JG52, Husum, Germany, 1940

- #3002 – E-3, 'Yellow 1', flown by *Oblt* Josef Priller, 6./JG51, France, Autumn 1940; E-3, 'Yellow 3', 3./JG51, Mannheim-Sandhofen, Winter 1939-40; E-3, 'White 7', 1./JG2, Bassenheim, Germany, May 1940; E-3, 'Black <-', flown by *Obstlt* Hans-Hugo Witt, JG26, Dortmund, Germany, April 1940; E-3, 'Yellow 15', flown by *Uffz.* Karl Wolff, 3./JG52, Pihen/Calais, France, August 1940

- #3003 – E-4, 'Black <-', flown by *Maj.* Helmut Wick, JG2, Beaumont, France, November 1940; E-4, 'Yellow 10', flown by *Ofw.* Fritz Beeck, 6./JG51, Wissant, France, 24th August 1940; E-4, 'Yellow 13', 9./JG54, The Netherlands, August 1940; E-4, 'Black <', flown by *Oblt* Franz von Wera, II./JG3, Wierre-au-Bois, France, 5th September 1940

- #3004 – E-7 Trop, 'Yellow 4', 3./JG27, Ain-el-Gazala airfield, Libya, spring/summer 1941; E-7 Trop, 'Black <A', flown by *Oblt* Ludwig Franziset, Stab I./JG27, Ain-el-Gazala airfield, Libya, June 1941; E-7 Trop, 'Black 8', 2./JG27, Ain-el-Gazala airfield, Libya, 1941; E-7 Trop, 'Black 3', 2./JG27, Ain-el-Gazala airfield, Libya, 1941

- #1156 – E-4, flown by *Hptm.* Max Dobislav, III./JG27, Belica airfield, Yugoslavia, April 1941; E-7, 'Black 10', III./JG77, Belgrad-Semlin airfield, Yugoslavia, May 1941; E-4, 'White 11', III./JG77, Greece or Rumania, May 1941; E-4, 'Black <<', flown by *Hptm.* Wolfgang Lippert, II./JG27, Larissa airfield,

Eduard 3401

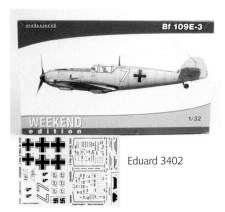

Eduard 3402

Eduard 3403

Greece, April 1941
- #11105 – E-1, 6•123, flown by *Oblt* H. Schmoller-Haldy, 3. J/88, Spain, 1938; E-1, 6•119, flown by *Oblt* S. Reents, CO of 1. J/88, León, Spain, spring 1939; E-3, 6•107, 2. J/88, Catalunyan Front, Spain, early 1939; E-3, 6•19, flown by *Uffz.* H. Schob, 3. J/88, Barcience, Spain, March 1939; E-3, 6•111, flown by *Lt* W. Ursinus, 2. J/88. La Cenia, Spain, spring 1939
- #11107 – E-3, W/Nr.5102, flown by *Lt* Herbert Kunze, Stab I./JG77, Döberitz, Germany, June 1940; E-4, W/Nr.5274, 'White 15', flown by *Lt* Werner Machold, 1./JG2, Marigny, France, June 1940; E-1, W/Nr.3413, 'Black 5', flown by *Lt* Hans Krug, 5./JG26, Marquise, France, July 1940; E-4, W/Nr.3709, 'White 1', flown by *Oblt* Josef Fözö, 4./JG51, Desvres, France, July 1940; E-3, flown by *Maj.* Adolf Galland, III./JG26, Caffiers, France, August 1940; E-3, 'Black <<', flown by *Maj.* Adolf Galland, III./JG26, Caffiers, France, late August 1940; E-1, W/Nr.3771, 'Yellow 12', flown by *Fw.* Ernst Arnold, 3./JG27, Peuplingues, France, August 1940; E-1, W/Nr.3417, 'White 2', flown by *Gefr.* Erich Mummert, 4./JG52, Peuplingues, France, September 1940; E-4, W/Nr.5375, flown by *Hptm.* Wilhelm Meyerweissflog, Stab JG53, Etaples, France, September 1940; E-4, W/Nr.3709, 'White 1', flown by *Oblt* Josef Fözö, 4./JG51, Desvres, France , second half of September 1940; E-4, W/Nr.5153, 'Yellow 5', flown by *Oblt* Egon Troha, 9./JG3, Desvres, France, October 1940; E-4, W/Nr.4869, flown by *Lr* Bernhard Malischewski, Stab II./JG54, Campagne-les-Guines, France, October 1940; E-4/B, W/Nr.3726, 'Yellow M', flown by *Fw.* E. Pankratz, 6.(S)/LG2, Calais-Marck, France, October 1940
- #3401 – E-1, 'Red 1', flown by *Hptm.* Hannes Trautloft, 2./JG77, Juliusburg, Germany, September 1939
- #3402 – E-3, 'White 7', 1./JG2, Bassenheim, Germany, May 1940
- #3403 – E-4, 'Yellow 13', flown by *Lt* Josef Eberle, 9./JG54, The Netherlands, August 1940

Verdict: *Today this is THE choice for the E-series in 1/32nd if you want a simple and effective model. The Cyber-Hobby one offers more from the box as far as detail goes, but Eduard also offer a lot of extras for this one should you want to spend the extra cash. Overall it surpasses the Hasegawa one in detail and is more accurate than the Trumpeter examples.*

Hasegawa, Japan

1/32nd Messerschmitt Bf 109E #ST1

Hasegawa first produced the E in this scale in 1973 as #JS-073 and it remained in production until 1977. It was also issued under the Minicraft/ Hasegawa label in the USA as #073 during this period. At some later date it was renumbered #S5, and was reissued for the last time in 1993 as #ST1. It is the last version that we have here for assessment.

Plastic: Medium grey-coloured plastic with raised panel lines and rivets.

Wings: Lower half moulded as one-piece; about 2mm short in span; ailerons and flaps moulded in situ; control surfaces covered in a fabric effect, not considered accurate nowadays; ribs on ailerons accurate, too few on flaps; ailerons and flaps slightly too wide on underside half, correct on upper halves; trim tab too far outboard; panel lines do not match plans; cannon bulges oval; no ejector port (even are raised outline); radiators moulded to lower wing half, wrong shape/profile; matrix only at front of radiator; bulge aft of radiator moulded to wing, too shallow; vertical bar moulded into radiator intake; wing bolt bulges too small; centreline scoop too long/ narrow; upper surface in two halves; panel lines do not match plans; access hatches do not match plans; leading edge slats too wide at tip, slightly too wide (>0.5mm) inboard; tip lights moulded (solid) with wing; the cut-out on the underside, mid-span in the flaps is shown on the upper surface; wheel well length OK but the wheel section is elongated; no depth to wheel wells, nor any detail; oleo leg slightly too long, angle of tyre to ground also wrong (shown vertical to ground, not at angle); separate compression linkage; no detail inside undercarriage doors; main wheels slightly undersize; tyre rib detail too pronounced; hub detail shallow and inaccurate; tailwheel and oleo as one unit; oleo leg too short; tailwheel tyre too small; no detail on tyre or hub.

Fuselage: About 3mm short; panel lines match plans; rivet lines do not match plans; line of rivets at angle under cockpit area, should not be there; jacking tube hole in half-relief and too far round fuselage side; cross-sections of aft fuselage good; cockpit opening correct size/location; aerial mast moulded to fuselage; bulge mid-wing root too large; all vents on nose/side half-relief and to on starboard side equal lengths (top one should be smaller); engine cowl separate, but front section also separate (should be one unit); front profile of cowling too curved; bulged at

(top) back of engine cowling wrong, shown as two separate blisters; gun troughs slightly too wide, overall shape not bad and shown as slightly raised; exhaust moulded as single unit each side, correct length but panel above outlet in cowl is too thick; chin radiator has matrix inside and inlet door, but no exhaust flap, not even as raised lines; standard and tropical filters on sprue, latter one with inlet flap open but just blocked off inside (no detail)

Tailplanes: Correct span and overall profile; panel lines match plans; rivet lines match plans; trim tab too big and too far inboard; elevators have that 'fabric' effect again; some undulations for the ribs, but too few and thus wrong location; support struts mount too far outboard and are thus too long

Engine: None supplied

Propeller: Separate propeller, spinner and backplate; propeller blades each 2mm short; blade profile too wide; spinner diameter correct but profile wrong, cannon one has pronounced 'curve' to it; both cannon port and capped spinner types included; profile of capped one neither 'blunt' or 'pointed' style.

Interior: Cockpit floor/rear bulkhead, seat, sidewalls, instrument panel, control column, trim wheel and rudder pedals; seat style/shape inaccurate; sidewall detail a bit generic and inaccurate; rudder pedals not correct shape, just simple oblongs; instrument panel has raised detail, but limited and thus not that accurate; fuel tank (bag) below the cockpit is also included.

Detail: 300lt drop tank and rack, basic shape OK but engraved detail too heavy and strap missing/shown as another engraved line; drop tank rack totally wrong shape/size; cluster bomb and rack; overall shape good but fins thick and sway braces on rack over-simplified; pitot separate; aileron mass balance weights separate; guns included for wings and above engine, but all look very 'skinny' and lack detail/definition.

Canopy: Offers both early (E-1/E-3) 'curved' and later (E-4/E-7) 'square' units, both as three-piece; no separate armoured glass (nor moulded in situ); shape of rear section in each version is wrong, being curved at the top/sides, instead of flat, also has odd 'wedge' profile visible when viewed from above; odd raised line inside rear of 'square' version for head armour to mount on; separate head armour, but no support arms (hence mounting to canopy interior), just 'floats about'; frame lines match plans, but the one in the centre/top of the aft section is missing on both versions; the periscope and revised windscreen is missing for the Galland option.

Decals: The example we had came with the following options: E-4N, 'Black <-', flown by Adolf Galland, JG26, France, September 1940 (see Canopy); E-4N, 'Black <<', flown by *Maj*. Helmut Wick, Belgium, October 1940; E-3, 'White 1', flown by *Oblt* Otto Bertram, 1./JG2, France, May 1940; decals include swastikas, but at the side of the sheet so they can be removed in countries where it is banned; full set of stencils; national crosses correct dimensions; Galland insignia also correct size

Verdict: *Not that bad considering the age, but easily surpassed by both Trumpeter and Eduard today, making this really one only for the collector. Odd to note that many of the errors in this kit, even including the decals and lack of periscope, were duplicated by Trumpeter!*

Trumpeter, China

1/32nd Messerschmitt Bf 109E-3 (#02288), E-4 (#02289) and E-4 Trop (#02290)

Trumpeter announced their Bf 109E series in 2009, but the E-3 was not actually released until 2010. At the same time the E-4 Trop version (#02289) was released, with the standard E-4 (#02289) going on sale in 2011.

As all these kits use a common set of parts we will assess them as one, pointing out any differences between each kit.

Plastic: Medium grey-coloured plastic with engraved panel lines and other details; rubber tyres for main and tail wheels; photo-etched detail parts.

Wings: Lower wing moulded as one piece; span 1-2mm too great; panel lines match plans; most access panels correct, but one in outer section has a line of rivets running through it(!); none of the access panels have any detail (fixtures etc.); trailing edge of tip looks too pointed and narrow; ailerons slightly too long as result of tip (marginal); gun ports in leading edge separate, difficult joint on panel lines; cannon drum access panels separate, blister shape looks too narrow cross-wise; radiators moulded with lower wing, forward profile too curved making fronts too narrow; etched matrices included for radiators; rear flaps separate for radiators; radiator fronts lack vertical bar, although it is shown in the instructions; centreline scoop too long/too narrow; wing bolt blister good; wing tip lights moulded (solid) with lower wing half; ailerons, flaps and slats separate; bulges on inboard (lower) flaps moulded with flap; rib details on flaps not accurate, as 'V' in middle too wide and lacking central rib; aileron ribs

Trumpeter 02288

Trumpeter 02290

correct but trim tab too far outboard; wheel wells correct shape/location; inner edges have etched detail with canvas covers; leg section of wheel wells also have etched detail; wheels mounted into lower wing half; undercarriage doors have some interior detail, but lacking others; oleo legs slightly too long (>1.5mm); oleo legs have top swivel point just like real aircraft; main wheel hub 1mm undersize; tyre diameter also small; rubber tyres may fail over time; tyres feature rib details; tailwheel tyre also rubber/separate, correct diameter; tailwheel hub detailed; separate yoke/oleo for tailwheel.

Fuselage: Length correct; panel lines match plans; access panels match plans although one under tailplanes too big; fuselage profile when viewed from side OK, but from top the taper to the tail is too pronounced, resulting in the cockpit area not having parallel sides (see canopy); radio hatch separate; vents in upper/side of nose forward of cockpit in half-relief; separate scoop on starboard nose, forward/below windscreen, too big; handhold aft of canopy too big and footstep at wing tailing edge too small; angle at top of vertical fine slightly too shallow; opening for canopy slightly too long (2mm); rudder separate, rib detail matches plans but upper (forward) angle too shallow as per vertical fin; separate aileron linkage; chin radiator separate with etched detail, separate intake and outlet flaps plus radiator flap linkage inside; bulges under chin correct size/location; small flap intake forward of radiator is present and a separate part; tropical filter included in E-4/trop kit, with separate inlet flap.

Tailplanes: Correct span and profile; separate elevators; panel line and rivet detail matches plans; support struts are slightly too far inboard (>1mm).

Engine: Complete engine with bearers; exhaust stacks all separate and hollow at tips; kit cannot be built without engine, as separate lug to mount propeller not included; engine cowls do not fit in the closed position well

Propeller: Separate propeller, spinner and backplate; propeller correct diameter; blade profile correct; spinner correct diameter and profile; sprue includes three spinner types – cannon port and capped (blunt or pointed); propeller held in place by cannon tube with separate 'plug' for end like the real thing.

Interior: Full interior comprising floor, seat, rear bulkhead, rudder pedals, control column, trim wheels and instrument panel; gunsight separate with two clear lenses; cannon breech cover depicted is for later marks; etched details included for rudder pedals and straps; radio equipment included for aft fuselage; fuel tank under cockpit floor also included.

Detail: 300lt drop tank with separate rack

and retaining strap in etched; cluster bomb with rack and separate braces; separate pitot; separate mass balance weights for ailerons; full armament in wings and over nose, latter with ammunition boxes etc; cannon access panels in lower wing supplied in clear plastic; separate aerial lead insulator for the dorsal spine and etched pick-up for top of fin.

Canopy: Three-part; no separate windscreen armour; profile of canopy is OK from side, as are dimensions, but the errors in cross-section from above means that canopy sides taper (should be parallel) and the canopy reflects this (very noticeable in middle section); no (larger) frame below aerial mounting point; separate 'edge' hoop for front of mid-section difficult to fit and unnecessary/inaccurate; canopy release lever etched part; grab handles inside windscreen; vertical line in the port side of the windscreen (just like the Hasegawa 1/48th kit!); split line for side panels extends over the top, which is incorrect; this error is not present in the E-4 kits, as they have a different mid-canopy section; the E-4 (#02289)

Trumpeter 02289

lacks the periscope and revised windscreen for Galland's machine, even though the box art shows it.

Decals: The decal options for those we had to hand are as follows:
- #02288 – Three options, all E-3s: 'Yellow 1', flown by Josef Priller, 6./JG51, Autumn 1940; 'White 13', flown by *Fw*. Heinz Bär, 1./JG51, Pihen, September 1940; J-371, Swiss AF, early 1940
- #02289 – Three options: E-4/N, 'Black <-', flown by Adolf Galland, JG26, 1940 (see Canopy); E-4, 'Black <<', flown by *Hptm*. Hans von Hahn, 1./JG3, Colombert, August 1940; E-4, 'White 9', *Escadrille de Chasse*, Bulgarian AF, 1943
- #02290 – Two options, both E-4/Trops: 'White 3' of JG27 and 'Black 8', flown by *Lt* Werner Schroer, 2./JG27, both in North Africa during 1941 (although instructions tell you none of this).

Swastikas split in two; full stencils; decals for instrument panel; crosses are all slightly too big (marginal >1mm); Galland's Mickey Mouse emblem is too big.

Verdict: *An odd one to call this, as the Eduard examples are more accurate thanks to that odd cross-section error in the fuselage on these, but the level of detail included here is better? Overall they have to fall into third behind Cyber-Hobby and Eduard although we suspect their lower retail price and ease of availability will have more buying (and building) them.*

1/24th Scale

Airfix, UK

1/24th Messerschmitt Bf 109E
#1202/09321-1, #12002-9 & #12002

Airfix's 'Super Kit' of the Bf 109E (#Patt. No.1202) was first released in 1972 and in 1973 it was renumbered as #09321-1 (box also still carried the number #1202). It was renumbered again in 1976 as #12002-9 (although the actual boxes are marked as '9-12002') and it was a few years before it was reissued in 1989 as #12002. It reappeared again in the mid-1990s once again as #12002, but in a much larger box, then it was reissued/renumbered in 2008 as #A12002 before being reissued once again with the same number in 2010. The most recent reissue of this kit took place in 2020 when it was reissued with the original artwork as part of the 'Airfix Classics' series (#A12002V).

As all these kits use a common set of parts we will assess them as one, pointing out any differences between each kit.

Plastic: Original ones were in light blue-coloured plastic, whilst later ones were in grey-coloured plastic, all with raised panel lines and other details.

Wings: Moulded as upper and lower halves, port and starboard; with the correct span at 412.5mm here it is some 12mm too great(!) and it's all in the wing panels as the fuselage width on the underside is correct; panel lines match plans; rivet lines do not match plans; access panels all present, although one is far too close to a rivet line to be accurate; ailerons separate; flaps moulded in situ; rib detail on underside of ribs does not match plan (mirror-image of upper surface); bulge aft of radiator moulded to flap; flaps too long due to over-size span; ailerons correct length; radiator units separate; correct shape/size; rear flap separate; interior detail in radiators but no flap linkage at rear; separate bar in front of radiator; the round access panel that overlaps the radiator flange on the outer edge is just truncated, it does not continue on the radiator piece; wheel well length and shape correct; no detail inside bays (open to wing interior); wheels mounted to fuselage side and can be articulated; under-carriage doors have internal detail, none on outside except rivets; no join/split of upper section of door; oleo legs about 3mm short; rear brake plate and compression link moulded to oleo, latter is wrong shape/no detail; no brake pipes; tyres rubber, correct diameter/ tread detail; two-part hubs of correct diameter/ good detail; tailwheel with separate yoke and hub; tyres diameter correct, tailwheel oleo with two-part yoke mounted to bulkhead inside rear fuselage, overall shape/detail good; wing tip

Airfix 1202

Airfix 12002
larger box

Airfix 12002
smaller box

lights supplied in clear plastic

Fuselage: About 4-5mm too long in main fuselage component, all the error seems to be in the length of the cockpit aperture (approx. 2mm too long at front and back – rear corner should line up with vertical panel line in this area, but is aft of it); chin radiator unit too shallow; panel lines match plans; rivet detail does not match plans; some access panels present, others missing; spurious square panel below cockpit on either side, crossed by rivet line; hand-holds behind rear cockpit section shown as wrong shape (half-circle instead of inverted D-profile); exhausts moulded in situ, lack any detail/separation from surround or hollow outlets; engine cowling separate, no interior detail; gun troughs correct length/shape/location; panels aft of engine cowling separate, port side

Airfix 12002-9

has correct shape/location supercharge intake duct, starboard has two vents or correct size/ location; centreline underside smaller detail missing; scoop depicted but solid; wing bolt bulges separate; no panel lines or rivets in centreline underside; rudder separate, correct size/shape; rib details match plan, but each rib probably too wide; no fixed trim tab on rudder; no clear element for rear light.

Tailplanes: Correct span and width; elevators separate, rib number correct, but too wide; trim tab correct size/location; panel lines and rivets match plans; support struts separate/correct location.

Engine: Complete engine; designed to make small electric motor to spin prop (not mentioned in later releases, although motor now available once more – will need modification/ extra parts to work, though); engine bearers separate; oil cooler unit separate/included; no wiring or other pipework; gun ammo boxes moulded to rear of engine block, not very effective/accurate.

Propeller: Separate propeller, spinner and backplate; propeller diameter correct; blade profile too wide; spinner diameter and depth correct; tip profile of spinner too rounded,

should be flatter; propeller hub separate but no cannon barrel or tube blanking piece included (you can see inside/back of rear propeller hub component through front of spinner).

Interior: Full interior comprising floor, rear bulkhead, seat, trim wheel, seat frame and adjusting arm, sidewalls, oxygen bottle, rudder pedals, control column and instrument panels; separate gunsight but not in clear plastic(!); instrument panels in clear plastic; no decals for instrument panel.

Detail: Wing and fuselage armament with ammo feeds included; gun barrel muzzles solid; underside wing cannon bulge access panels separate, as are the leading edge panels; separate pitot, separate aileron mass balance weights; separate tie-down eyelets under each wing tip, which is probably a post-war addition to the one they studied (?); all versions came with the three-part display stand and battery holder moulded in black plastic.

Canopy: Three-piece; supplied as early (E-1/E-3) 'curved' and later (E-4/E-7) 'square' versions; overall length too great due to error in fuselage (See Fuselage); separate late style head armour with curved top, with support arms; windscreen armour moulded in situ, looks a little thin; framework matches plans; vertical split in side panels shown as raised line (like frames); separate aerial post correctly mounts into flange in upper sections.

Decals: The decal options in the ones we have are as follows:
- #09321-1 & Cat No.1202 – E-4, 'Black <<', flown by *Maj.* Helmut Wick, JG2; E-3, 'Yellow 10' of 9./JG26
- #9-12002 – E-4, 'Black <<', flown by *Maj.* Helmut Wick, JG2; E-3, 'Yellow 10' of 9./ JG26
- #12002 (1989 copyright, smaller box) – E-4, 'Black <|', JG53; E-3, 'Yellow 1' of 6./JG51
- #12002 (1989 copyright, large box) – E-4, 'Black <|', JG53; E-3, 'Yellow 1' of 6./JG51
- #12002V: – E-4, 'Black <<', flown by *Maj.* Helmut Wick, 1./JG2, France/Belgium, October 1940; E-3, 'Yellow 10' of 9./JG26, France, July 1940

The early decal sheets have no swastikas or stencils, while the later ones still have no swastikas but do now have a full set of stencils.

Verdict: *It is odd to see some dimensional errors in this one, but I suppose that was down to the drawings of the era. It is really the only game in town in 1/24th, as the Bandai one is very difficult to obtain and will thus come at a premium even though it is the same vintage. With a little work this one can be built into an impressive model, just don't think about those dimensions.*

Chapter 9: Building a Selection

Having looked at what kits are and have been available of the early Bf 109 series in the four major scales, we thought it would be a good idea to build a selection in 1/72nd, 1/48th and 1/32nd. Apologies that this is not a large section and we have not done the Hasegawa or Tamiya ones in 1:48, but we only have so many pages.

The main components, showing the basic nature of this kit in its original form, prior to the upgrade with resin

MPM 1/72nd
Bf 109 V1

by Libor Jekl

The prototype Bf 109 is fairly well covered in 1/72nd, as there are several available kits on the market, although the majority of them are complete resin kits from the likes of LF Models or HR Model. The only injection moulded kit of the V1 powered by the Rolls-Royce Kestrel was released by MPM. This kit first appeared in 1997 and later was followed by its reissue with complementing resin parts as an 'Upgraded Kit'. Although the kit has been out of

production for a long time it regularly appears on the auction websites for a reasonable price. I got my kit at a swap meet without the box and instructions, but this wasn't a serious problem as the kit is quite simple and photographs of the V1 airframe can be easily found. The kit consists of a single sprue containing 24 parts, another 17 parts are on the small etched fret plus there is a printed acetate film for the instruments, a single vacformed canopy and decal sheet with all the unique marking. Quality-wise the kit corresponds to the contemporary short-run standards, which means nice moulding of the larger parts with fine engraved panel lines, but substantial amounts of flash, gritty surface texture in places and poorly defined or malformed smaller parts. The cockpit offers only very basic equipment with all the parts being on the crude side, no sidewall details and not even the inclusion of several etched items could improve the overall look of this area (the upgraded version fortunately addresses this as a complete resin interior is included). The landing gear does not look the part either, as the main legs suffer from flash and poor definition and the wheels do not correspond to the V1's type at all. The ravages of time had caused yellowing

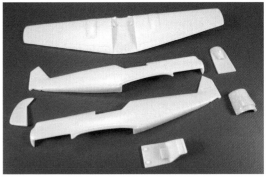

of the vacformed canopy, but fortunately after a bath in Future varnish it was usable. Overall, the kit's proportion and dimensions look fine; maybe the engine cowling should be more bulbous above the rocker covers whilst other smaller omissions are mentioned later.

I commenced the build with preparation of the main parts, which were sanded down with finer Micro-mesh pads and all damaged or missing panel lines were restored. The missing cockpit details were scratchbuilt using strips of Evergreen plastic stock and brass wire; the kit parts were either refined (seat) or replaced (control stick). The cockpit was then sprayed RLM 02 (Gunze-Sangyo H70) and the control boxes, levers and buttons were brush-painted in their corresponding colours. After closing the fuselage halves I could deal with the exhausts. These were of oval shape and slightly protruded from the airframe

Some additional detail from the etched fret livens up the cockpit interior

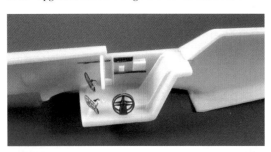

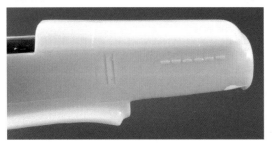

The exhaust stacks as moulded just won't do...

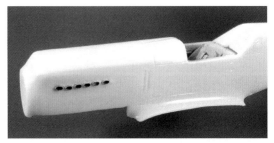

New pipes made from flattened brass tubing look a lot better

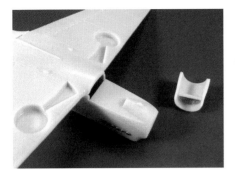

The complex shape of the nose is achieved with this odd breakdown of parts – it works, though

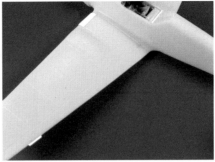

Plasticard was used to reproduce the radiators on the inboard wing leading edges, plus the aileron and elevator trim tabs

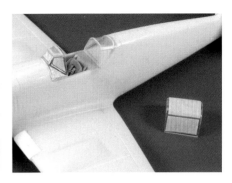

The canopy was cut into three parts, secured and then masked ready for paint

Once the canopy frames are sprayed RLM 02 the model receives an overall coat of Mr Surfacer primer

With the overall scheme applied and sealed with varnish, the panel lines are highlighted with a wash

contours, but the kit offers only a simplified version of flat, vaguely defined stubs. They were therefore sanded off, the apertures opened with a fine drill bit and scalpel blade and twelve new exhaust stacks were cut from brass tubing and gently pressed in pliers to give them the correct oval shape. The cowling lower part with the radiator has a fairly complex shape that the kit addresses via the assembly of several parts. First, a blanking plate with shaped inlet body has to be glued to the bottom fuselage followed with the radiator assembly. Fit of these parts is a little bit tricky and at the end of the day some putty was needed to blend all the joints in. On the cowling I added apertures and vents as shown in the period photographs as well as the oil cooler inlets in the wing roots. The wing is one-piece with perfectly thin trailing edges and its assembly to the fuselage was straightforward, just a smear of filler was need on the rear joint at the trailing edge. However the kit completely omits the wing oil cooler plates located on the leading edges, so these were added from 0.13mm Evergeen plastic strips. From the same material I also added the control surface trim tabs then I focused my attention on the canopy. The vacformed part was carefully cut into three pieces using a fresh scalpel blade and a JLC fine razor saw, then the windscreen and rear section were

glued to the fuselage with thin cyanoacrylate, then they were both masked off using Tamiya tape.

The kit was now primed with Mr Surfacer 1000 and any blemishes that appeared were sorted out and the surface was polished to a high shine using nail polishing pads. Based on period photographs of the V1 I believe the plane was painted in a overall light grey color, which I don't feel matches the often quoted RLM 02, so I opted for a light grey based on Gunze-Sangyo H311 toned down with a touch of white and light green. I intended to build

Detail in things like the wheel wells is non-existent, although any Bf 109E etched update for this area would work

The radiators on the wing leading edges were finally picked out in a metallic (buffable) brass colour

The kit undercarriage on the left was replaced with new parts from various sources (see accompanying text)

the prototype in its very early appearance before any markings were applied, so after the gloss varnish I applied a Neutral Wash from MIG Productions along all the panel lines followed by a final coat of semi-matte varnish. The final painting task was to paint on the wing oil coolers using Agama Brass compound applied with a brush and then polished.

The landing gear parts were completely replaced, the main struts being sourced out of the Avis Bf 109B kit that was used for a conversion, so I had many spare parts left, and the main wheels were replaced with items I found in my spares box (these are probably not 100% accurate, but still look better than the kit wheels, which seem to be Bf 109G wheels). The malformed tailwheel was replaced

with a part from the Tamiya Bf 109E kit, which fits exactly due to it being of a smaller diameter. Finally I added the Venturi tube made of thin wire and brass tubing onto the starboard fuselage side.

Verdict

To sum things up, the MPM kit is a typical short-run kit with all the good and bad points this type of kit offers. Due to its age it is obvious it cannot match the recent short-run kit standards, but it represents a reasonably good basis for building the V1.

Tamiya 1/72nd
Bf 109E-3 converted to a Bf 109A

by Libor Jekl

The first job is to separate the nose from the both kits

The selection of the early Bf 109 versions in 1/72nd has been for a long time limited to the Heller Bf 109B kit. With the advent of new short-run manufacturers quite a few new kits have appeared, for instance those from Amodel, AML, Avis or Sword covering all the early Jumo-powered variants. In all cases these were typical products of limited-run technology with overall accurate shapes and good details, however they needed a lot of work to reach at least an average standard in comparison with mainstream products and therefore they appealed only to a limited group of modellers. One of the latest additions to the market are two AML kits containing, as their basis, the Avis mouldings supplemented with etched and resin parts and decals for machines employed in the Spanish

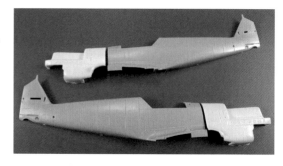

Civil War. One of these reboxings labelled 'Messerschmitt Bf 109B in the Legion Condor' offers two guises of the example coded 6-10. Anyway the designation 'B' may seem to be confusing and needs a little explanation, 6-10 was one of the first production batch of approximately 20 and the majority of these were sent to Spain where they

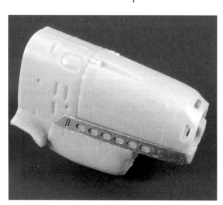

The Avis kit nose with the etched exhaust surround

With the moulded detail removed from the interior of the Tamiya kit fuselage halves, the resin and etched parts from the AML set could be installed

The completed resin and etched interior once painted

received codes 6-3 to 6-18 and according to company records these machines were designated as 'A', while there are doubts about the 'B-2', as this seems to never be mentioned in the factory documents? Fortunately, the appearance of these machines can be pretty accurately reconstructed based on period photographs, no matter what official designations they wore.

On inspection of the AML kit it is quite distinct from the original Avis moulding, having deteriorated somewhat as all parts feature quite an amount of flash, there are damaged panel lines in places and the smaller parts have suffered too, many being malformed. The single-piece canopies are too thick, cloudy and my examples suffered from additional scratches. The kit contains two styles of engine cowling (with and without cooling apertures), two propellers (wooden Schwarz and variable-pitch VDM items) and the wing corresponds to the early production standard with long slats and no wing weapons. The AML etched and resin parts look excellent, offering a complete cockpit, wheel well inserts and other useful parts. The decal sheet comprises all unique marking including the alternative rendition of the 2.J/88 emblem, and the well drawn instructions contain full-colour camouflage schemes.

For my build I opted for the late appearance of 6-10, after undertaking an upgrade (the aircraft had the metal VDM propeller and late style of undercarriage covers with the typical slope at bottom rear part) and it received a new camouflage comprising RLM 63 light grey and RLM 65 light blue. This plane with 15 kill marks on the fin is often mentioned as being Günter Lützow's personal mount, but since he achieved only five victories in Spain, it had to have been flown by other successful pilots too. The machine still wore the original wing with long slats and no armament, cowlings with cooling apertures and, as was often the case with the majority of the first production batch, it had the rear fuselage panel lines completely filled in. My original intention was to combine this kit with the Tamiya Bf 109E parts, utilizing the AML front cowling part and the Tamiya E wing that would be completely reworked to the early production standard. However, close comparison of both kits showed the original Avis moulds were in some way cloned from the Tamiya kit which meant I could use part of the AML wing and this saved me substantial work (e.g. removing the wing radiators), whilst the Jumo cowling could be more easily fitted due to its having practically the same cross-section of the front fuselage bulkhead. I commenced

the build by cutting the engine cowlings at the relevant bulkhead line off both fuselage halves followed by filing and sanding the resulting joint lines. The cowling halves were assembled together and the etched exhaust plates from the Part detail set (designed for the Heller kit, but very useful for this build indeed) were added, which replaced the rather soft rendition of the kit parts; from the set I also used the radiator matrix. The cockpit was assembled from several extremely finely cast resin parts and then painted RLM 02 *Grau* with the exception of the instrument panel that may have been painted in a mid-blue/grey colour on early Bf 109s. Despite the resin parts not being intended for the Tamiya kit they fitted inside with only a little adjustment required. After closing the fuselage halves I glued on the cowling and with some two-part epoxy putty the joints to the etched exhaust plates were blended in, sanded smooth and the panel lines were renewed. The individual exhaust stacks were made of brass round stock with 1mm outer and 0.7mm inner diameter cut to about 2mm lengths that were gently pressed in flat pliers to get the oval shape. These items were then secured in the openings with thin cyanoacrylate and eventually aligned with a fine flat file to protrude about 1mm.

The bottom part of the wing came from the AML kit whilst the upper halves were from the Tamiya kit and

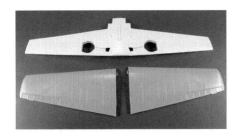

The Avis lower wing half (top) will accept the two Tamiya upper wing halves (bottom)

The prominent join in the Avis cowl will have to be filled – the joint between the Tamiya and Avis parts was reinforced with two-part epoxy

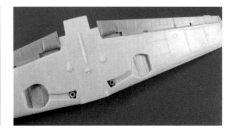

The ease with which the two kits parts fit together shows that the Avis kit learned a lot from the Tamiya tooling!

More filling and sanding is needed at the wing and nose/fuselage joints

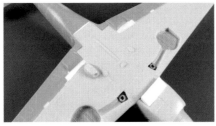

The gaps in the backs of the wing are filled with plasticard, which is also used to make a new rear flap for the chin cowling

Finally a good overall finish is achieved on the nose

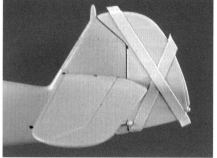

The black areas of the cross on the tail are applied then masked so that the white can be reapplied

With the decals on, the model was sealed with varnish, then rivets were lightly engraved prior to a wash being applied

The front and rear sections of the Tamiya canopy are installed, then masked and sprayed RLM 02 before the wing tips are picked out in white and the rest of the airframe is primed with Mr Surfacer

the rather shallow detail in the wheel bays was improved with the addition of the etched roofs from the AML kit. While the wing halves matched together fairly well, some filling with thick cyanoacrylate was necessary to hide the redundant cannon bay panel lines on the upper wing, the rectangular openings in front of the flaps and the airfoil shaped items on the flaps itself. Newly rescribed were the longer slots on the leading edge. The oil cooler below the wing should be located on this particular plane closer to the wheel bay than on later variants as the original position at about the wing root meant the flow was disturbed when the landing gear was down, causing issues with oil overheating

(Gunze-Sangyo H67) was applied straight from the bottle, while the upper RLM 63 light grey seemed to be quite elusive as it is often interpreted in different ways from very pale up to darker grey/green (according to some sources this colour is identical with RLM 02). I decided on the paler variant with a slight green tint that was achieved by mixing Gunze-Sangyo H311 light grey with a few drops of RLM 02. Both lower and under surfaces were locally post-shaded with darker shades of the main colours and then I masked off the exhaust plates and sprayed them black. The decal sheet is printed by AML and looks fine, but in the past I have had troubles with the rigidity of their decals and their lack of ability to adhere to the surface contours. The temperature of the water used is fundamental, as it should be higher than 90°C as this ensures that the decals soften a bit and with the help of Gunze-Sangyo decal solutions they eventually adhered without trouble. Finally I applied a Neutral Wash from the the MIG Production range along all the panel lines and I brushed on fine paint scratches using Vallejo dark grey acrylics.

Now I could continue with the final assembly. First I assembled the landing gear, improving them with hydraulic lines added from thin lead wire, and dusted the wheel treads and the hubs with Light Dust pigment from MIG Productions. The cowl gun barrels were from the Quick-boost range and were brush-painted black then polished to a dark metal shine with Gunmetal pigment before being finally glued into pre-drilled holes. The last task was to install the canopy centre sections and the propeller, which was attached to the cowling with an imperceptible gap between the spinner cowl panel, just like the real thing.

Verdict

A shortage of good quality early Bf 109 kits in 1/72nd is still persisting despite there being a few new short-run kits available on the market. However, the Avis example clearly shows that these kits are intended only for a narrow group of modellers willing to invest considerable effort in the build because the kit would require a complete reworking of the surface details, panel lines, scratchbuilding of small parts and a replacement canopy. From this point of view the conversion using the excellent Tamiya kit is not that complex and addresses the most troublesome features of the short-run kit. I have no hesitation recommending it even to moderately skilled modellers.

The canopy from the Avis kit was no use other than to act as a mould to crash-form a replacement mid-section over it

(unfortunately, I noticed that detail on a period photograph too late, as I had placed it in the later position). Attaching the wing to the fuselage required corrections mainly at the front wing root, where the joints were levelled with Tamiya epoxy putty. On the bottom fine plasticard strips filled the gap at the rear joint where the AML wing met the Tamiya fuselage, and that was it. The tail assembly went on quickly, followed by putty to the rear fuselage panel lines with Gunze-Sangyo Mr White Putty. The Tamiya canopy was cut into three parts and since the AML canopy was useless and the Tamiya part seemed to be too thick to be posed open (although being perfectly clear), I made a new part from heated thin acetate sheet using the kit part as a former.

After an overall coat of Mr Surfacer primer all blemishes were sorted out, especially those on the filled fuselage where the putty sank down in a few places. I started the painting with the black and white cross on the rudder and continued with the wing tip bands that were then all subsequently masked off. The lower RLM 65 light blue colour

Tamiya 1/72nd
Bf 109E-3 backdated to E-1

by Libor Jekl

Tamiya kits have earned themselves an outstanding reputation thanks to first class quality, and their Bf 109E kit is no exception. Despite being on the market for more than 10 years now it is still one of the best 'Emil' kits in 1/72nd, at least from as far as engineering, ease of build and levels of detail are concerned. However, for any modeller that persists in matching a model with scale drawing there is a minus point as the fuselage is about 1.5mm short. The kit was released in two boxes covering the E-3 and E-4/E-7/E-7 Trop versions, which differ only in the appropriate canopy parts (this means there are useful leftovers such as an ETC rack, 250kg bomb, belly drop tank

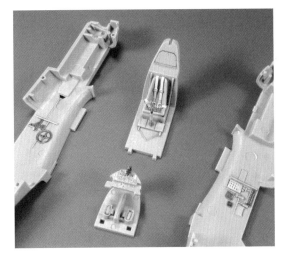

and a tropical filter). About 50 parts in a grey-coloured plastic are offered on a single sprue, all perfectly moulded with no signs of flash or sink marks, while the ejector pin marks are located in places where they do not show. The engineering of the kit is well thought out and despite quite a number of separated parts, especially the engine cowling, the fit is faultless throughout – this can be proved by trial assembly of almost the complete model! The engraved panel lines are fine and crisp and raised surface features such as braces on the fuselage or cannon covers are well defined. The rendition of the fabric-covered control surfaces and flaps is also very subtle. The cockpit is adequately equipped and includes the basics needed including a decal for the instrument panel (although raised dials are featured on the panel as well) and seat belts. Nicely done are the cockpit sidewalls, control boxes and ribs, although they look a little on the shallow side and I would recommend you rework them or replace them with resin or etched aftermarket bits if you open the canopy. The landing gear is particularly well done with sufficiently deep wheel bays with raised internal bracing and cleverly designed attachment points for the oleos that ensure the right angle. The small clear sprue includes a two-part

canopy that unfortunately cannot be posed open, but the parts are crystal clear and despite being a little on the thick side they do not distort the view inside the cockpit.

Although the kit offers the late versions with cannon armament, the conversion to the early E-1 version with the machine-gun armed wing is a simple matter. I commenced the work with the wing modification, which consisted of grinding off the cannon ammo drum bulges using a Dremel motor tool with ultra fine head, filling the panel lines on the leading edge and bottom wing surface with thick cyanoacrylate and blanking off the holes for the cannon barrels. Once all this was sanded smooth I engraved new machine gun access panels and drilled the new gun apertures inboard of the cannon ones. Since I planned to model the kit with a closed canopy I did not improve the interior in any way, with the exception of Eduard pre-coloured seat belts and a Revi C/12D gunsight from the Quickboost range, as the kit item although moulded from clear plastic does not look that well defined. The complete interior was sprayed RLM 02 *Grau* with any contours of individual details picked out with a dark wash in order

The only additions to the interior were the pre-painted Eduard seat belts

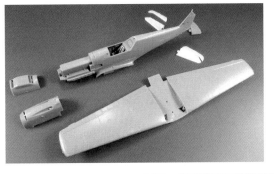

Main assembly is quick and straightforward – the tailplanes are replacement resin parts

The kit wing depicts the later cannon-armed version, so the bulges etc. would have to go

The upper wing and leading edges need modification to depict the early machine-gun-armed E-1

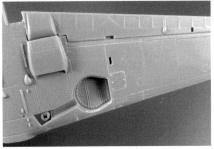

A new access panel will need to be engraved on the wing underside, as seen here

The excellent resin tailplanes and elevators are direct replacements for the kit parts

In next to no time the model was together and masked, ready for spraying

Once the canopy frames are sprayed RLM 02 the rest of the airframe can be primed with Mr Surfacer

The underside blue was applied over a post-shading of the panel lines

After masking, the upper surface RLM 02 was applied and weathered

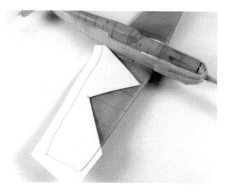

Paper masks, held off the model surface with Blu Tac, were used to get a straight, but soft-edged demarcation

to give them depth under the closed canopy. I used the instrument panel decal sheet, which perfectly copied the raised surface with the help of a little Mr Mark Softer decal solution. Mating the fuselage halves was easy, the joints had a few light passes of Mr Cement S and the fuselage was then put aside to dry overnight. The subsequent wing and fuselage assembly was equally straightforward and again super thin Mr Cement S was used. I found in my spares box the Aires tailplane resin set with separated elevators, so opted to use them here. They are flawless

and matched perfectly the plastic parts including the holes for the bracing struts; additionally they are designed as direct replacements, so no surgery was needed. Next I closed the fuselage cowling and installed the compressor air inlet. The fuselage machine gun barrels looked fine, but I opened their muzzles with a fine drill bit. Attaching the canopy and masking it off with Eduard paint masks meant the main assembly steps were done, the build had taken me so far just three short evening sessions.

After some speculations about the markings I eventually decided on *Uffz*. Leo Zaunbrecher's 'Red 14' machine of 5./JG 52 (W/Nr.3367) that took part in Battle of Britain operations and was shot down on 12th August 1940 by Plt Off McClintock from No.615 Squadron. I used the decals printed by Techmod and included in the 'Battle of Britain Part II' book by Kagero. I started off spraying the canopy framing with RLM 02 followed by Mr Surfacer 1000 primer. The kit was next gently riveted and the surface then sanded with fine grade Micro-mesh pads and polished with Gunze Sangyo Mr Grinding Cloths. The camouflage colours consist of a combination of RLM 02 and RLM 71 on the upper surfaces with RLM 65 underneath, and Gunze-Sangyo Mr Aqueous

The revisions to the panels on the wings are not drastic, but effective

Hobby Color acrylics were used throughout, all lightened for scale effect. The transition of the upper colours should be soft and gently diffuse, not sharp, so I used a paper mask attached to the kit with pieces of Blu Tack so they were about 2mm above the surface. The second camouflage colour was then sprayed on keeping the airbrush at approximately 45° to give the right, soft-edged effect. After a coat of gloss varnish the decals went on; the insignia were sourced from my decal bank as they are not included on the Kagero sheet and the Tamiya decals seemed to be little bit thick – I did use a couple of kit stencils. The weathering was reproduced with silver pencil and after a dark oil wash in all the panel lines the kit received its final semi-matt varnish coat.

Although the landing gear parts are well detailed, I decided to replace the main wheels with resin ones from North Star Models, which I had just received and was

The overall camouflage scheme applied and the masking removed

You can see how small the wheel of the kit tailwheel (right) was in comparison with the Quickboost example (left)

The kit wheels were replaced with these superb resin ones from North Star Models

The propeller was built and painted RLM 70 with a red spinner

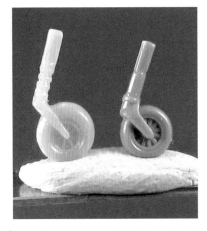

impressed with the wheel hub's excellent 3D details; in my opinion these are the best Bf 109 aftermarket wheels I have ever seen. I also replaced the tailwheel with the Quickboost part as the kit part is about 1mm under size in diameter and that is quite evident. This machine was equipped with a rear mirror fitted on the upper part of the front canopy. These parts were made of plastic scraps and copper wire, whereas the mirror is a piece of silver self-adhesive tape. The propeller was painted, assembled and pushed into place on the poly cap, then I made the aerial lead from black fishing thread with an insulator cut out of thin plastic stock.

Verdict

The Tamiya kit is in my opinion the best Bf 109E kit in 1/72nd on the market. It is precisely engineered in every aspect in typical Tamiya manner, so any possible omissions are hard to find. As stated in the introduction, this kit is often criticized for the fuselage length error, but I doubt if this is really the sort of shortcoming that devalues the kit overall. The conversion to the early E-1 version is simple enough to be managed even by less experienced modellers.

Special Hobby 1/72nd
Bf 109E-4

by Libor Jekl

The Bf 109E series of kits from Special Hobby were launched in 2020. They have been produced in collaboration with Eduard, who provided the data from the 3D design of their existing 1/48th kits. Looking at the advertising materials and judging from the way in which the kit is designed, I believe it is more than obvious that Special Hobby will progressively cover all main sub-version of the Emil from E-1 up to the E-7 ,including the tropicalised variants, export E-3a, and naval T-series. As I write this article, some of them were or are just about to be released and Eduard have done their own release of the tooling as the 'Adlerangriff' dual combo kit with markings from the Battle of Britain period, plus they also offered the bare sprues for a limited period in their 'Overtrees' range. This E-4 kit contains two sprues of more than seventy parts and a single clear sprue with seven components, some of which won't be used as they are intended for other versions. First inspection of the parts reveals the perfect surface and exceptionally high level of details, which is

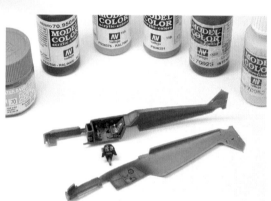

The interior is primed black then painted RLM 02 with all the various details picked out in Vallejo acrylics

rarely seen in this scale. This is supported with high quality moulding without any signs of sink marks, flash, thick sprue gates or visibly located ejector pin marks. Only on the smallest parts like the cannon barrels or aileron weight balances are there subtle moulding seam lines. The panel lines are hair thin, but sufficiently deep and of note are other surface details such as fasteners, the gently raised fairing on the fin, stiffeners on the fuselage sides etc. The fabric effect with finely raised ribs on the control surfaces look very nice as well. Fans of rivets will appreciate the delicate and precise rendition of the engraved rivet lines, which I doubt any of the regular modelling rivet tools would ever be able to reproduce. Anyway, despite being a fan of riveting the kits, I'm unsure whether this feature will be appraised by the broader modelling audience? The kit provides detailed cockpit, armament compartment and engine unit, possible thanks to the separately moulded engine cowling and fuselage side panels. The engine with its bearers and auxiliaries is decently detailed however, overall this part looks a little simplified and considering the thickness of the cowling walls I assume the size of engine must be reduced to fit inside the given area. Special Hobby addressed by offering separately several resin sets for the engine, wing armament, radio compartment etc. The MG17 machine guns in the box looks pretty nice having finely perforated barrels and nicely done magazines compartment. The wheel wells are also highly detailed, as are the radiators, which include an open outlet flaps. The wing is moulded separated from the ailerons and landing flaps, which can be posed offset, as can the leading edge

From the box the interior is nicely detailed, the sidewall items are moulded pretty shallow though, so as not to cause sink marks on the outside of the fuselage

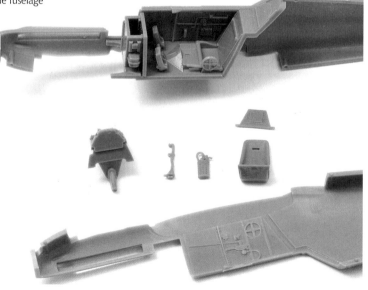

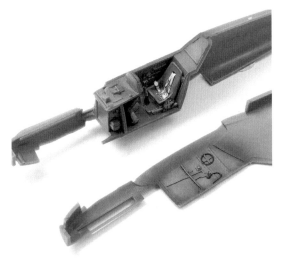

The completed cockpit interior, just the seat belts were aftermarket etched versions

The kit comes with separate cowls and and engine that would need careful painting and additional detailing to really work, even in this small scale

The canopy parts are slightly too wide, so here you can see the fuselage assembled, but with the region aft of the cockpit left unglued, so that it can be aligned once the canopy sections are in place

slats. The clear parts are flawless and without distortion however, they are a bit on the thick side and honestly I can't recommend posing them open - a vacformed replacement would definitely be a better option. Comparison the mouldings with the scale drawings proves them to be very accurate. I only noticed the depth of the separately moulded slats seems to be some 0.3 - 0.5mm greater than they should be (although this assessment depends on the plans you use). Whilst assembling the undercarriage I also found out that the landing legs were too long so they would give the kit an unnaturally high sit, the correction is quite simple though. The kit offers camouflage schemes for four machines all flown by Luftwaffe aces; these are personal mounts of Gerhard Schöpfel from III./JG26, Oblt. Helmut Wick from 3./JG2, Hptm. Wolfgang Lippert from II./JG27 and Obfw. Leopold Steinbatz from III./JG52 (although in this case it not certain it was his personal machine). For the stippled camouflage of Wick's machine you could use the separately available decal sheet. Talking of decals these are another example of the cooperation with Eduard as they are printed by them with good register (perhaps except for the smallest stencilling having the background white colour slightly off), opaque colours and extremely fine carrier film, which can hardly be seen by the naked eye – that's because the decal sheet is not produced using traditional screen printing, but on a digital printer. This fact brings another interesting feature as a side effect of the print process, as it is possible to peel off the upper clear layer from the individual decal items, thus making each image look even more convincing.

Construction

The base of the cockpit assembly forms the floor moulded integrally with the rear fuselage bulkhead on which

goes the individual components. Provided separately are the oxygen bottle/regulator and the control wheel (in fact this was a double wheel) for the the flaps and horizontal stabiliser, while the other details are moulded directly onto the sidewalls. These look rather flat, but that fact actually reduces the likelihood of them creating sink marks on the exterior of the fuselage. I replaced the seat belts provided as decals with etched ones from the Eduard set (#73034 Seatbelts Luftwaffe II Fighters - Steel) while the decals intended for the instrument panel worked fine for me considering I was leaving the canopy closed. The parts were all primed with Mr. Finishing Surfacer 1500 (black) followed by H70 RLM 02 Grau and the details were brushed painted with Vallejo Model Color acrylics. Despite the cowling and armament compartment being split from the fuselage, I do not think it is mandatory to use some of the internal parts that won't be visible if you decide to do the kit with all the covers on. The upper gun decking has to be used since it holds the instrument panel, but with the engine, bearers and other parts you can omit them and save yourself some

All the separate parts of the cowling - in reality you could omit a lot of the interior detail if you are closing up the cowlings

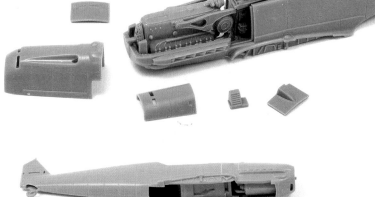

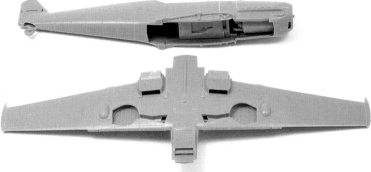

The oil cooler radiator under the nose has a separate insert to stop it being see-through

The assembled wings and fuselage before the two are joined - note the detail moulded at the wing root

The assembly of the tailplanes and their support struts is very straightforward thanks to good overall fit

Next to no filler is needed anywhere on this kit

The windscreen is secured in place first, later the rear section will also be added spreading the fuselage to the correct width at that point

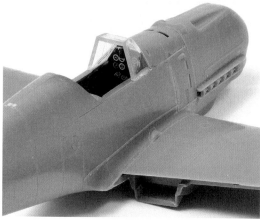

With the mid-canopy section sanded to fit, it can be added and the dorsal spine seam secured with cement - any small gaps can be filled with superglue

work (I used them on this build just to check the overall fit). In the nose you need to insert at least the gear casing with shaft (#B40) because eventually you have to attached the propeller/spinner to it. I did not use the supplied machine guns and modified #B49 by cutting off the barrels and drilling out the holes to later accept replacement brass barrels that were inserted at the end of the construction phase. Next, I joined the fuselage halves, omitting glue along the dorsal spine. That was because the trial fit with the canopy revealed the canopy as being fractionally wider than the fuselage, so this had to be adjusted only once the canopy was finally fixed in place. I continued with the cowling and side panels, which do need some careful fine trimming, but overall their fit was very satisfactory.

The wing assembly started with the attachment of the oil cooler body and control flaps in the front section and matching them together with the fuselage; thanks to their perfect fit, this step was easy. I continued with attaching the separate radiators, again these settled precisely in the wing openings and then I could join the wing to the fuselage. All matched very well with just a few strokes of a sanding stick needed here and there and after snapping the wing into its final position the joints were secured with a small amount of super thin Mr Cement S. The installation of the tailplanes with their brace struts was also straightforward and whilst the ailerons were already glued into the wing at this step, the landing flaps were easier to paint separately and attached at the end of the build. Now I focused my attention on the canopy that comes in three sections. First, I cemented the windshield and the rear part in place and carefully aligned them with the fuselage sections, then finished the job with the central element, which needed a little sanding with a flat file in order to fit tightly. Only now could I cement the fuselage dorsal spine joint line and having spread the fuselage width in the cockpit area slightly the joint was secured with super thin cement without any need for filler or a spacer. The clear parts were then masked off using the canopy masks (#M72009) available separately and the kit received a single thin layer (in order not to swamp the fine surface details) of Mr Surfacer 1000 (grey) which helped to detect any surface imperfections or damaged rivet lines, which were subsequently restored with a razor saw and fine needle.

Camouflage & Markings

From the supplied options my attention was taken by Gerhard Schöpfel's machine in which he shot down four No.501 Squadron Hurricanes over Canterbury on the 18th August 1940. I therefore started with H70 RLM 02 Grau sprayed in the slat bays and wheel wells, and continued with the yellow elements airbrushed with H24 Creamy Yellow applied over a H11 white background. The under surfaces and fuselage sides were then sprayed in H67 RLM 65 Lichtblau that partially overlapped on the wing's upper surfaces. These were then airbrushed freehand with fine transitions using H70 RLM 02 Gau and H64 RLM 71 Dunkelgrun. Eventually, I separated the trim tabs on the control surfaces with strips of masking tape and sprayed them H414 RLM 23 Rot. The paint was then sealed in with a couple of thin coats of Mr Color GX Super Clear III thinned with Mr Color Levelling Thinner in order to achieve a high gloss and hard background for the decals. As I mentioned, the decals are printed using different technology that allows the removal of the upper clear layer; this is possible thanks to fact the upper layer does not merge with underlying colours (as is the case when done by screen printing). Obviously, the decals can be applied in the usual way too, but in this case I recommend you trim off the individual decals as the upper clear film is printed with rather large overlapping areas. Since I already had a positive experience with this type of decal, I decided to remove the

Stage one of painting is to mask the canopy and spray the frames RLM 02, then the whole model is primed

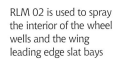

RLM 02 is used to spray the interior of the wheel wells and the wing leading edge slat bays

Yellow is notoriously 'weak', so all the regions to be that colour are first primed with white

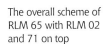

The overall scheme of RLM 65 with RLM 02 and 71 on top

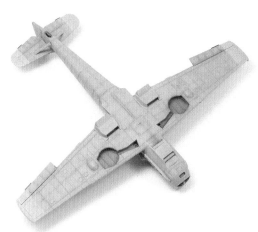

Tonal variations in the camouflage are done by using slightly darkened versions of the base colour

Super Clear III is applied to create a smooth and hard base for the decals

The underside blue is also given some tonal effect with a slightly darkened version

upper layer as it completely eliminates the possibility of the decals silvering, as well as removing the usual 'step' around each image caused by the layers, plus each image itself is thinning. The decals were therefore applied in the usual manner using softening solutions (Microscale Set and Sol in this case) to ensure the best adhesion to the surface. I did not trim the decals at all in fact the large overlapping areas helped to easily later grab the clear film with tweezers. After sufficient drying time, ideally overnight, I carefully lifted up the clear layer using pointed tweezers and gently pulled it off. This method works well also for the smallest items such as stencils and wing walkways and again this greatly improves their final

appearance. At the end I applied a dark wash in the panel lines mixed from black and brown oil paints and wiped off any excesses with a cotton bud.

Final Details

First I prepared the undercarriage components and based on the trial assembly and judging from drawings and photographs, I reduced the height of each legs by about 2 mm, cut from the top. These were then glued in with the correct track width and slope to ensure the proper 'sit' for the Bf 109. The gun barrels were replaced with brass items from Master (#AM-72-009), which were first darkened with AK Interactive brass burnishing agent. To

The undercarriage (each oleo leg was shortened by 2mm) and propeller ready to be attached

Freaky or what! The printing method used to make the decals allows the carrier film to be pulled off once the decals are dry

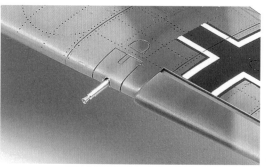

The gun barrels were replaced with the brass ones from Master, which would be darkened with burnishing fluid before they were finally secured

the radio mast I glued the commander's pennant, which unfortunately drooped a bit after drying. In reality such pennants were made thin metal sheet, so I would recommend replacing it with a piece of thin plastic or paper. Next, I attached the pitot, weight balances, propeller unit and put on the aerial lead cut from thin elastic thread. At the very end I secured the extended slats, so that I could safely manhandle the model during the final assembly stage.

Verdict

Despite a number of good to excellent Bf 109E kits available on the market, including the Tamiya kit which is considered as the best option so far, Special Hobby's brand-new E-series is in my opinion pointed straight at that top spot. This kit does not have competition as far as the level of detail and surface treatment is concerned, so only if you do not desire an extremely detailed kit

the Tamiya kit may be a better option. Special Hobby will most likely continue in offering plenty of interesting reissues with reasonable coverage of individual sub-variants and interesting decal options, another point in their favour, as Tamiya traditionally tends to ignore such things.

Airfix 1/72nd
Bf 109E-7 Trop

by Libor Jekl

Airfix, having had a successful rebirth, keeps the modeller busy with a fair number of new releases. One of these is their Bf 109E kit, one of the latest additions to the 'Emil' range in 1/72nd. This first appeared as the E-3 version but was then followed by E-7/E-7 Trop variant. The latter kit is supplied in a rather larger box than the original E-3 issue and again features catchy computer-generated box artwork. The kit consist of three sprues done in a light grey-coloured plasic and one in clear plastic, and a high quality decal sheet printed by Cartograph containing all the unique markings (including stencils) for the well known 'Black 8' of JG27 and the less well known but an equally attractive Bulgarian Air Force option. The moulding corresponds to Airfix's recent standards being clean with subtle surface details and offering overall easy assembly. The panel lines are restrained and when compared to previous kits their finer rendition is obvious; the fabric effect of the control surfaces is also very delicate. The parts have traditionally thick sprue attachment points, which means fine cutters are appropriate for their removal from the sprues. Some of the surface features still look a little bit on the thick side, though, namely the rims of wing radiators and gun covers, but a little sanding will sort them out. The radiator bodies have over-thick walls that need to be trimmed down a bit. The smaller parts look fine, maybe just the exhausts could be improved by being hollowed out to better represent the real thing and the fuselage machine gun barrels have an odd oval cross-section. A nice bonus is the separately moulded landing flaps that can be posed either up or down. In contrast, the main wheels are quite ugly with shallow hub detail and heavy tread patterns. The tailwheel looks suspicious too, having a simplified yoke with a wheel that has a small diameter. The fuselage halves are moulded integrally with the engine bay, however the engine proper is considerably under-size and I'm afraid it can not be left exposed without substantial reworking. Anyway, at least it is visible through the cooling apertures, which gives the right impression.

Comparing the kit with scale drawings shows the main dimensions and proportions are satisfactory, only some details on the wing upper surface seem to be redundant and the fuel filler on the port fuselage spine is omitted, but these are nothing serious. More serious, however, is the shape of the propeller blades, which are too narrow and pointed. The transparent parts are perfectly thin and

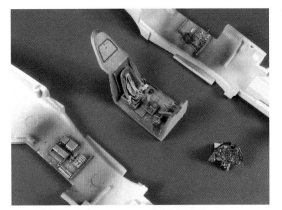

The cockpit interior was enhanced with the addition of the pre-painted photo-etched set from Eduard

Assembly is straightforward and quick, with only a few bits of filler needed

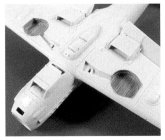

The etched details for the wheel wells cover up the gaps in this area; you can also see the small amounts of filler used at nose and tail

The canopy put in place, with the armoured windscreen made from clear plastic stock

The option of the flaps in the up or down positions is a neat one

After priming, the first markings are the tactical ones – white under the wing tips and around the aft fuselage, and yellow under the nose

The upper surface RLM 79 was weathered with a mix of sand yellow, brown and red

Once all the colours are on the masking can come off and gloss varnish is applied

The underside is also weathered with lightened tones of the overall colour

Both upper and lower surfaces had a Neutral Wash applied

Once the wash had dried out, the excess was wiped off in the direction of the airflow

Pastel dust was applied to the wheel bays and underside, then fixed using the Pigment Fixer from MIG Productions

clear, however they look odd in places, for example the triangular side windows are not flat as they should be and also the pins on the middle canopy look disturbing. The cockpit equipment looks rather generic with missing or too-shallow details on the sidewalls. I think the instrument panel is undersize and without any raised details (the instruments are provided on the decal sheet); I did not like the moulded seat belts on the seat either. Compared to the E-3 kit the E-7 boxing includes an additional sprue with a tropical filter, two styles of propeller spinner, 250kg bomb and drop tanks with racks.

My intention was to approach this build with more detail so I acquired aftermarket sets that address the majority of the kit's weak points; namely the Eduard pre-painted etched, North Star Models wheels, Quickboost gun barrels and Revi C12/D gunsight, AML propeller, plus the Rising Decals sheet as I wanted to build anything other than 'Black 8"! I commenced the cockpit assembly with the addition of the etched parts as well as cutting a rectangle-shaped hole in the seat backrest for the belts.

The 'pointy' propeller from the kit (left) was replaced with the resin example from Quickboost (right)

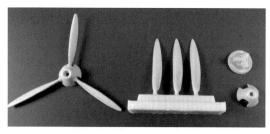

Then I sprayed the parts with a base coat of black and continued with RLM 02 (Gunze-Sangyo H70), that was sprayed on with varying intensity – more saturated on the flat areas and less around raised details and ribs, which helps to create a naturally shaded look. After gluing the pre-painted bits in position I applied a dark wash to the recesses and sealed the paint job with matt varnish. The fuselage halves as well as the cowling and oil radiator assembly fit perfectly; to the latter item I added an etched screen. With the tip of a scalpel blade I removed the oddly shaped gun barrels and drilled out holes for the replacement resin parts. Also the wing halves matched together nicely, however there is a gap around the wheel bay circumference that is quite distinct and difficult to fill. Fortunately the Eduard set addresses this issue with the etched bay inserts that imitate the canvas or leather covers that were fitted to the sides of the wheel bays. Joining the fuselage with the wing required a little sanding on the fuselage so that the wing could be easily snapped on whilst retaining the correct dihedral. However, I still feel the wing tips should be few degrees higher as the wing seems to sit a little 'flat' on the fuselage. Assembly of the tailplanes, wing radiators, landing flaps and canopy went without trouble and all the parts were secured in place with a few drops of thin cyanoacrylate. Overall, the assembly was pretty straightforward and, as with the Tamiya kit build, I managed it after a couple of evening sessions.

After cleaning all the joint lines and polishing the surface I continued with the painting. From the Rising Decals sheet 'Deutsche über der Wüste' I opted for the Bf 109E-7 Trop from III./ZG1 that operated out of Libya in 1942 and was adorned with a unique motif of the African continent on a white band. The machine was camouflaged in the tropical scheme comprising RLM 79 sand yellow on the upper surfaces and RLM 78 bright blue underneath with white and yellow theatre markings. First I applied a coat of Mr Surfacer 1000 primer followed with a gentle application of rivet lines according to scale drawings, then a general fine sanding and polishing. After spraying the white wing tips, fuselage band and yellow cowling I continued with the RLM 78 under surfaces (Gunze-Sangyo H418). Then the upper RLM 79 was given a light application of H79 sandy yellow and H310 brown with a small amount of H23 red to give a gentle pinkish hue caused by sun bleaching. Both under and upper surfaces were locally post-shaded with darker versions of the original shades along the panel lines and other surface details. The gloss varnish sealed the paints and prepared the surface for the decals, which all went on without any fuss. From the kit decals I used several stencils and these worked beautifully, too. The panel lines then received a dark brown oil wash that was mixed from brown oil paints to suit the sandy yellow camouflage; after about 30 minutes the superfluous wash was wiped off the surface with cotton buds in the direction of the airflow. The hot and dusty climate quickly caused paint deterioration, so this was imitated with a light overspray of dust colour H314 (Radome Tan) in a few thin layers along the bottom fuselage and wing roots. The wheel bays were dusted with MIG Productions Light Dust pigment fixed inside with few drops of Pigment Fixer; this solution was gently brushed into the wheel treads and hubs, too. Then I sprayed on the exhaust staining from heavily thinned black acrylics, and with some AK Interactive Engine Oil and Fuel Stains enamels I brushed on the fluid leaks. A few paint scratches on the wing and around the grab handles were applied with a silver pencil.

Now I assembled the replacement propeller unit including the spinner (according to a photograph this machine wore the older style of spinner with the central hole) and then sprayed it with the corresponding RLM 70 black-green and white colours. From the kit's undercarriage parts I used only the main legs, the wheels were sourced from North Star Models, the covers from the etched set (but the kit parts look fine and are usable) and the tailwheel with the correct diameter from Quickboost. The head armour assembly again looked too thick and was replaced with pre-painted etched; by the way these parts are cleverly designed and cover up the holes in the hood. The external armoured glass that was fitted to this machine was cut from 2mm thick acetate sheet and secured in front of the windshield with drops of Future varnish. Finally I glued on the antenna wire made from black-coloured fishing line.

Verdict

The Airfix kit represents a worthy alternative to the Tamiya example and it offers in 1/72nd the best value without doubt, being priced at about half that of the Japanese kit. The other positive points are accurate shapes, easy assembly, dropped flaps option and excellent decals. It is pretty evident though that even after ten years, Tamiya is still the market leader as far as kit engineering for ease of assembly is concerned. From my personal view I really regret those errors with the wheels and propeller which spoil an otherwise very impressive kit.

All the various sub-assemblies and parts painted and awaiting final assembly – the tailwheel is a Quickboost resin replacement

Airfix 1/48th
Bf 109E-1/E-3

by Steve A. Evans

There's no doubt that Airfix are trying hard these days and it's no surprise that they're also playing safe with one of the 'Big Boys' of the Second World War. The kit's box is a sturdy affair with some neat art on the top and sides, hiding two large sprues of light grey-coloured plastic and a single impressive sprue of transparent parts, more of which later. There is also a single decal sheet, a very well drawn and printed, 12-page instruction booklet and a 4-page full-colour painting and marking guide. The plastic looks to be well formed with good detail work. The panel lines are fully etched and are even and sharp edged, although maybe a little on the large side, it's nothing to get upset about. There are very few rivets on show which is going to please some modellers and horrify others so that's either good or bad, depending on your point of view. There is very little flash, although there are a few sink-holes around the location pegs but most notable of all is the fully moulded engine, injected as part of the fuselage. This is a very neat touch allowing for instant detail although it has the drawback of being drastically undersize and obviously over-simplified, but it's nice to see that Airfix are doing things their own way again.

The build begins with the interior, as you'd expect. It's not superdetailed but it's more than adequate for most, with all the major components on show. The smaller parts are well detailed and locate positively with the minimum of trimming and fettling. The only real minus point as far as I am concerned are the hideous moulded seat belts, which need to be carved off and replaced with some photo-etched or home-made items, I have to mention here the sprue layout, which is logical and a joy to use after

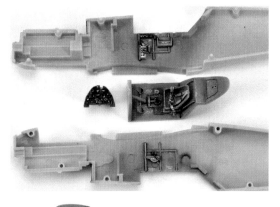

The interior isn't massively detailed but it's a very good start. The parts location is positive and minimum trimming is required

Airfix's normal habit of random parts placement. It starts at #1 in the top left corner and works up and down, left to right, to finish at #82 in the bottom right hand corner, simple. OK, so far so good, but there are a couple of problems ahead, thankfully nothing major, though. First of all there are some really poor positions for the ejector pins and injection gates, which need careful removal/filling/sanding, made worse by the fact that the plastic is hard and a little brittle. The detail is also a little on the inconsistent side, some of it is very fine and beautifully done, while other bits are clumsy and not well produced. Really good bits are the subdued fabric effects and the control linkages for the rudder, bad bits are the wing leading edge inserts and the 'no-fit' engine cowling. That cowling was never going to fit over the engine as it's about half a yard thick in places but with careful, extensive thinning of the

plastic, it does eventually slot into place. No such hassles with the chin oil radiator, which is a superb fit, as are the radiator baths and the cannon bulges under the wings (if you're doing the 'E-3/E-4' versions). Following on with a true Airfix tradition is the supply of all of the control surfaces as separate pieces, in this case not movable, but very welcome anyway. This allows full artistic control over how you wish to pose the machine, especially as the Messerschmitt looks good with the flaps dropped. All of which fit without complaint, needing only the minimum of trimming and dry runs to get a good joint. Special mention has to go to the clear parts, though. These are beautifully moulded in some of the clearest, ripple-free plastic I've seen in ages and you get a mass of versions, including no fewer than FOUR different types of windshield, two main canopies and two rear canopies to choose from, marvel-

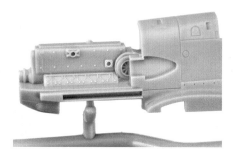

The moulded engine is a nice touch, even if it is about 1/50 scale, at least Airfix are making the effort to be different

The engine is reasonably detailed but if you want it to be on show then there's a lot to do, especially as all of the nose gun equipment is missing

The wing gun inserts are a bit clumsy, why they didn't use some flashed-over holes I don't know

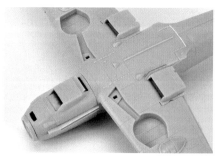

No such problems with the undersurface parts, which all go together very neatly indeed. You can see that there is a tiny fillet of plasticard at the wing trailing edge joint under the fuselage. That's nothing to do with the kit, I'm afraid that was me being clumsy with the knife!

Fit of the wings is just about perfect with only minor trimming required to get the wing anhedral right

The RLM 04 Gelb nose is applied first, over a coat of primer

The RLM 02 Grau is applied next, followed by the hard-edged masking. Airfix have done their homework where the pattern is concerned because they've got it spot on

RLM 71 Dunkelgrün is added next and very handsome it looks too. The RLM 65 Hellblau underside will finish the pattern

Weathered and glossed it's beginning to get a bit more character

lous stuff. Be warned, though, they are very brittle and need careful cutting from the sprue.

In this particular box you get three versions to choose from, each one being utterly typical of the breed. The first is for Adolf Galland's E-4/N, complete with full *Geschwader Kommodore* markings, the second is one of the most well-known in the UK as it's the machine that was shot down over Badbean, Kent in 1940, while the third is for a Jabo 'E-1/B' with distinctive cross-hatched camouflage pattern. All in all a great spread of choices.

The upper surface disruptive pattern was applied

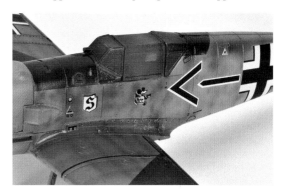

first in RLM 02 and RLM 71, all neatly hard-edged. The paints for this one were of course the White Ensign Colourcoat enamels, which have an excellent Luftwaffe collection. Just make sure they've had plenty of drying time between coats and everything will turn out just dandy. The RLM 65 underside colour was then applied and it's here that you have to make a choice, the White Ensign version of this colour is for the grubby looking Hellblau, but if you're looking for the cleaner, brighter version of this colour then may I suggest the LifeColor acrylic version, which is has an excellent pale cast to it; it's nice to have options, isn't it? Mottling along the fuselage sides and tail are thinned out RLM 02 and RLM 71 sprayed on in a very fine mist pattern to almost completely cover the RLM 65 beneath. This lot was then allowed to set for a couple of hours before some weathering was applied. In this case I kept it looking pretty grubby as they were hard-worked machines. This means plenty of pastel dust, especially around the control hinges and the engine bay, some silver pencil chipping at the wing roots and a fine spray of dark brown paint along many of the panel lines. All of which was sealed in under a coat of Johnson's Klear in preparation for the decals.

Aaah, Airfix decals, always the Achilles Heel of their kits and I'm sorry to say that this, one of their later releases, is no better than anything that's gone before it. They are thick, they are brittle, they have that horrid dot-matrix style print and are completely unresponsive to any kind of decal solution, including Microscale, Mr Mark Setter and even the brutal Daco Strong. Worst of all,

though, Airfix are still printing decal sheets that are out of register! I don't mean to be rude here but come on Airfix, how many times do you have to read that the decals were rubbish before you do something about it? However, I do have to say that in their defence, once on the model they move around well and eventually settle down, at least over the larger details and into most of the panel lines. They 'silver' a bit as well but that's a decaling hazard anyway, isn't it? The whole lot was given a coat of Johnson's Klear to seal them in and a quick spray with some thinned-out dark brown enamel to blend them in a bit. Then it was on to all the bits and pieces that complete the model.

The undercarriage is pretty good with weighted wheels (marvellous) and very positive location for the oddly angled main gear legs (equally marvellous). There are quite a few odd little bits as well, including the aileron mass balance weights, the aerials and wires, the guns and the propeller, all of which fit without any problems whatsoever. Then it's a case of the final coats of Xtracolor XDFF flat varnish and sort out the canopy fitment, which included a little retaining strap made from a length of fishing line. The last bit of all was to mix up a very dark brown enamel and lightly spray it along the exhausts and down the fuselage side. The DB 601 engines ran pretty mucky so you can go to town with this bit if you like.

Verdict

This kit goes together really well, with components that fit properly and it has good levels of detail. There are lots of good options in the box and it's all well produced. The decals are a serious minus point but then there are already a LOT of aftermarket ones for this machine, so that's no worry. Shape-wise the propeller is a bit dubious and I'm not 100% sure about the nose profile and the undercarriage is a tiny bit too tall, but those are just niggles about what is basically an excellent kit and one that's very good value for money to boot.

Airfix and its decals, love them or loathe them, there can be no excuse for printing out of register these days

The sturdy box is well designed with a very nice bit of art on the lid

The cockpit isn't overly detailed but it's more than serviceable

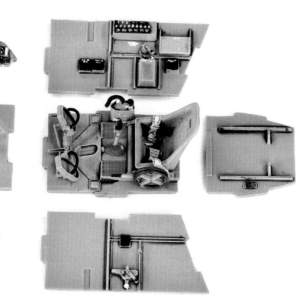

Wingsy Kits 1/48th
Bf 109E-1 'Emil' (#D5-07)

by Steve A. Evans

Wingsy Kits from the Ukraine are relatively new to the kit making world, having started production in 2016. They're definitely new to my workbench as well because this is the first one of their kits I've seen. First impressions are very good as it starts with a neatly decorated box, with plenty of technical bits on the sides and art from all the decal options inside, which I love to see. The plastic comes on six sprues of dark grey-coloured plastic and a single transparent sprue. There are 115 plastic bits, accompanied by 43 parts on the little etched fret provided. The decals have options for four very good looking machines and the instruction book is neatly printed over ten, fold-out pages. There's also a four-page, full-colour guide for the paint and markings. Sadly you only get three-view drawings of the aircraft, so the camouflage pattern on the right hand side of the fuselage is a mystery. Considering this is considered a 'short-run' product, the detail is exceptional, with cleanly moulded parts, very little flash and no distortions. The exterior has a lot of rivet detail, which won't please some but I love it, and although the fabric effect on the control surfaces is almost non-existent it is in scale for the real thing. The etched parts include seat belts, armour plating and radiator louvres, as well as a number of small but important details and optional parts. Talking of which there are no options as such in the kit, other than having the armoured headrest in place, or a rear-view mirror, or a mast pennant, depending on your choice of decals.

Construction

It all begins in the cockpit, as usual and there are no surprises here, with some etched parts adding scale detail where needed and decals for the separate upper and lower instrument panels. Everything fits properly and the instructions give plenty of proper directions, although calling for RLM 66 as the interior colour is a bit suspect to me. The seat is probably the only let down in here. Even though it's the correct shape it looks a little clumsy and could do with thinning out a bit as well as making the edges more rounded. The seat belts work well though and also include are the upper shoulder strap sometimes seen on the early Bf 109s.

On to the fuselage now and the detail is very good on its exterior and the interior is catered for too with a neat little engine section that connects the two halves together and gives a sense of there being a DB601 in there on the finished item. The cockpit slots into this from underneath and fits perfectly, along with the upper cowlings for the guns and the lower nose section where the oil cooler sits. There are some cooling pipes in there as well, which can also be seen from outside so they have certainly been doing their homework.

The wings carry on the excellent design work, with sharp panel lines and details. The undercarriage bays are boxed in by separate pieces and although there are inserts for the access panels on the upper surface, the E-1 gets its own wing without the canon bulges of the later E-3s and E-4s. The wing does have separate control surfaces, which is good news for those of us who love to pose the main

A nice touch is the top section of the engine, which can be seen through the cooling slits on the finished model

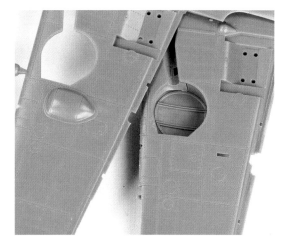

Wingsy Kits do a number of Emils and they do this by new sprues as opposed to inserts. That's the kit E-1 wing on the right and the wing from their E-4/7 on the left

The cockpit, complete with belts is in place. Notice the belts have the rarely seen shoulder strap as well

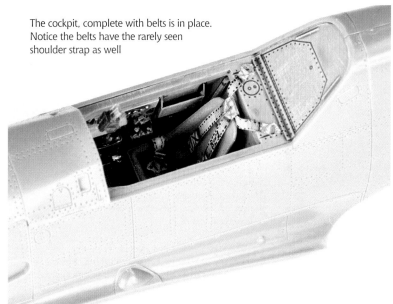

Wingsy Pic 05. One odd bit is the separate wing tip. Odd that is until you remember that the Bf 109T with extended wingspan could be on the cards

flaps in the 'down' position. There are also separate wing tips, which could allow the Bf 109T to be produced as the first of these were converted from E-1 airframes. The fit of the wing to the fuselage isn't just good, it's great! Especially as Wingsy have also thought about the attachment point at the rear because it's extended backwards along the lower fuselage to the next frame, meaning the joint falls along the panel line. It's a pity then that completing the wings are not quite so much fun. The main radiator units are the culprits here, with the sides (E4, E5, E7 & E8) just not fitting into their slots very well. Quite a bit of trimming is needed to get them into the right place. Oh well, it can't all be perfect can it? There is also a lot

The upper wing has the correctly moulded gun access panels made as inserts, so make sure you get the right ones. They fit perfectly by the way

Another great bit of planning is the wing connection to the lower fuselage. It's extended back further than most other kits and falls squarely on a panel line: good thinking'

of detail work to be added here with the internal matrix parts, etched louvres and doors as well as a couple of bits that I just don't think should be in there, namely parts PE 26. These are horizontal dividers for the radiators that I just couldn't see at all in the photographs I had available. Maybe I'm wrong but I left them out anyway.

With the tail built, another easy job with the excellent mouldings, and the flaps and ailerons in place it's getting close to paint so it's time to put the clear bits in place.

The clear plastic is very nicely formed, with good clarity and sharp framework. The bits fit perfectly and even though you only get the early, rounded windscreen, you do get the armoured section to add if your chosen version has it fitted. The armoured headrest is built with a mix of etched and plastic parts and there is also a rear-view mirror to add, once again, check the references for both of these bits. The kit provides some vinyl masks for the

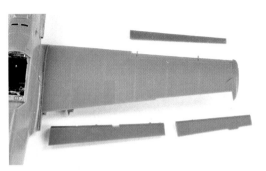

The main wing has separate control surfaces too and the lack of fabric effect is noticeable here as well. Notice the excellent fit at the wing root though

The main radiator assemblies are a one of the few trouble spots on this kit, as they need careful trimming to get them to fit in the right spot

The tail is made of completely separate fixed and moveable sections but it's a pity that the fabric effect wasn't a little more pronounced

canopy, which includes the internal ones as well, which is good to see. I wouldn't advise using any of the masks that go over the external curved sections though, as they will peel away all too easily.

Colour & Markings

In the box you get four different marking choices. There are 2 in the early RLM 65/70/71 and two in the classic Battle of Britain look RLM 65/02/71. Each of the choices has plenty to offer, as they're all very different, with personal badges and JG emblems on show. I would have gone with the lighter schemes, especially 'Black 5', which looks gorgeous but we've already got a few in that kind of scheme in the book, so a darker one it is. The decals look good, with very sharp printing, good density and perfect registration. I'm not a fan of the matt look decals like these as they're usually less responsive to softening solutions, but we'll see.

Paint start with a clean down and some primer, to show up all my mistakes, which in this case are few and far between. Then the RLM 65 is applied in layers to get a graduated effect and then faded with a few lighter tones;

no pre-shading for me anymore thank you. Masking tape is applied to keep the demarcation lines clean and then it's on with the top colours. Here there is a little poetic license as even though I used the paints straight from the jars (Mr Hobby Aqueous) the contrast between them is a little high. In reality the RLM 71 should be a shade darker but it does look good in this scale. Once again, a few shades of lightened paint are used to get some variation in the panels but weathering is very simple here, as these machines seemed to be kept quite clean. This means a little paint chipping at the wing root, some dirtier looking splotched of paint and of course the underside gets a much muckier application of pastels and brown pencils to show oil streaks and such like. All of this is sealed in under a good coat of Johnson's Klear (yes I still have some of it) and we're ready for the decals.

What an excellent surprise these were. Not only are they well printed and obviously the four choices all look good, but also in use they are nothing short of brilliant. Thin and a little brittle, so they need careful handling but that's a tiny price to pay for the results as they easily conformed to all the detail work and had almost no silvering to speak of. A quick coat of softener finished them off and really smoothed them over so when they were sealed in under a light coat of the Klear they practically melted into the paintwork.

Oil washes were next, with a dark grey for the underside and black for the top surface. A little Burnt Umber oil around the engine and along the underside centre line for extra grime and it's all looking pretty good.

Final Details

Thankfully there's not too much to do at this point. The undercarriage is always the biggest part of this process and it's here that the kit's only real weak spot is apparent. The main undercarriage legs are well detailed and only need a brake line to finish them off but the fit into

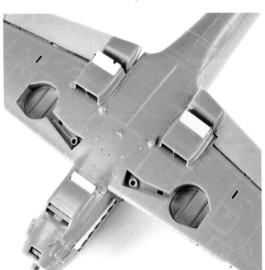

The etched fret in the box contains plenty of little bits for the radiators and exhausts, which gives excellent scale thicknesses

The transparent bits are an excellent fit and it's almost ready for the painting to begin

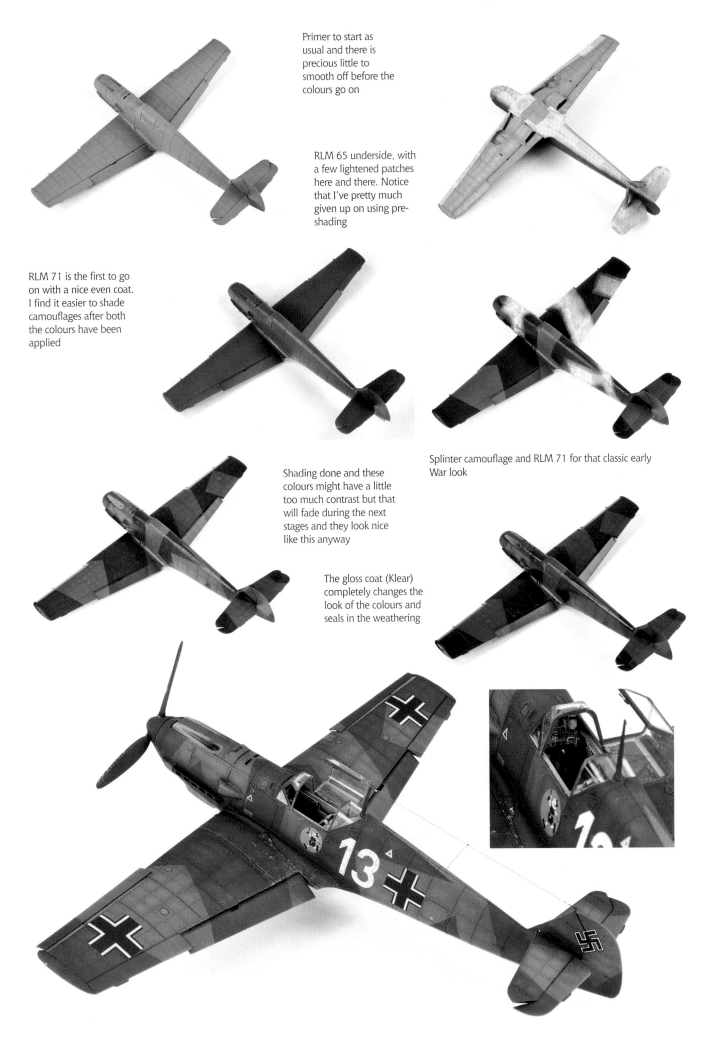

Primer to start as usual and there is precious little to smooth off before the colours go on

RLM 65 underside, with a few lightened patches here and there. Notice that I've pretty much given up on using pre-shading

RLM 71 is the first to go on with a nice even coat. I find it easier to shade camouflages after both the colours have been applied

Splinter camouflage and RLM 71 for that classic early War look

Shading done and these colours might have a little too much contrast but that will fade during the next stages and they look nice like this anyway

The gloss coat (Klear) completely changes the look of the colours and seals in the weathering

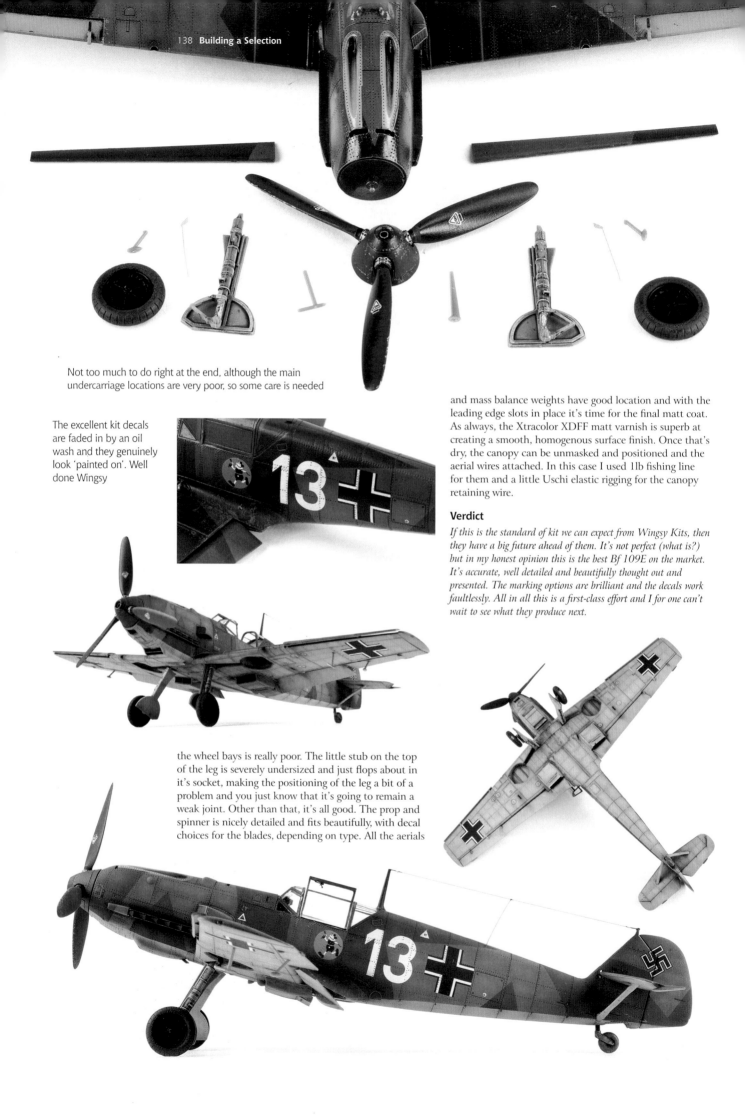

Not too much to do right at the end, although the main undercarriage locations are very poor, so some care is needed

The excellent kit decals are faded in by an oil wash and they genuinely look 'painted on'. Well done Wingsy

and mass balance weights have good location and with the leading edge slots in place it's time for the final matt coat. As always, the Xtracolor XDFF matt varnish is superb at creating a smooth, homogenous surface finish. Once that's dry, the canopy can be unmasked and positioned and the aerial wires attached. In this case I used 1lb fishing line for them and a little Uschi elastic rigging for the canopy retaining wire.

Verdict

If this is the standard of kit we can expect from Wingsy Kits, then they have a big future ahead of them. It's not perfect (what is?) but in my honest opinion this is the best Bf 109E on the market. It's accurate, well detailed and beautifully thought out and presented. The marking options are brilliant and the decals work faultlessly. All in all this is a first-class effort and I for one can't wait to see what they produce next.

the wheel bays is really poor. The little stub on the top of the leg is severely undersized and just flops about in it's socket, making the positioning of the leg a bit of a problem and you just know that it's going to remain a weak joint. Other than that, it's all good. The prop and spinner is nicely detailed and fits beautifully, with decal choices for the blades, depending on type. All the aerials

The raw materials; the E-1 version is perfect because that minimises the work needed to backdate it. The Alley Cat set is just one of a number dealing with early Bf 109s

Eduard 1/32nd
Bf 109D conversion

Bf 109E-1 converted to Spanish Civil War Bf 109D using the Alley Cat conversion set

by Steve A. Evans

There's plenty of scope out there in the modelling world for the Bf 109 in 1/32nd, especially if you want any of the wartime versions. But what if you want one of the earlier marks? One of the best ways to get a 'B', 'C' or 'D' is by using one of Alley Cat's excellent resin conversion sets for Eduard's first rate Bf 109E. The donor kit can be anything in the Eduard range but the most obvious choice is to use the E-1 version as this needs the minimum of alterations to the plastic pieces. If you use the 'Weekend Edition' version as well it means you keep the cost to a minimum and as I'm cheap, that's just what I did.

The Alley Cat conversion comes in a number of different sets (six in all thus far), each with their own character. I opted for the B & D 'Spanish' set #AC32006C, which gives four good alternatives, straight out of the little white box. The box is a sturdy affair that protects the delicate resin within and that resin is dark grey-coloured and comes in two bags, all very neatly cast with the minimum of casting blocks and no obvious imperfections. There are

32 parts as well as a couple of spares in case you break or lose any of the bits, which is a neat touch. The detail work is very good, with even panel lines and recessed detail along with a fine collection of parts to allow a conversion to either a 'B' or a 'D'. You get three instruction sheets, one with written instructions and diagrams, one with pictures to direct you and a full-colour paint and marking guide. All three sheets are very well reproduced on good quality paper with concise directions and lots of hints and tips to help along the way. The photographs are well shot and really do help with getting the donor kit parts modified to suite the new bits. The last bits are the decal sheets, two supplied, printed by Fantasy Printshop and they look beautiful, so more on them later.

If you follow the instructions during the build you won't go far wrong with the conversion as Alley Cat have obviously done their homework and got most of the new bits fitting correctly. The most noticeable change is of course the new engine section, replacing the DB 601 of the Emil with the earlier Jumo 210D. This engine produced far less power and used a single cooling radiator under the chin as opposed to the later twin radiators installed under the wings. All of this needs the appropriate modifications to the donor kit plastic so it's a good bit of slicing and dicing to begin with, which makes this kind of

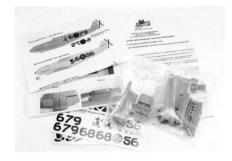

The Alley Cat resin, instructions and decals, all produced to very high standards. I couldn't ask for a better start

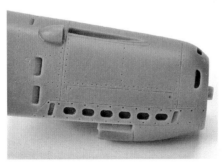

The main attraction is that Jumo engine and the casting is very neat and tidy, it's hollow too

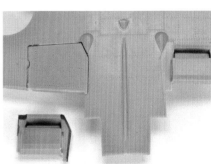

The wing radiators need to be sliced out and replaced with the resin inserts – no troubles yet

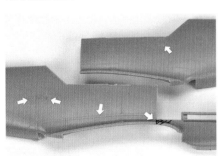

There are a number of modifications necessary on the fuselage to backdate the 'Emil' to a 'Dora'

The forward part of the lower wing section needs to be hacked about a bit too and this needs a careful touch to keep it all together

The lower wing joint is a little tricky but with trimming and alignment it's not a huge problem. Note the little inserts in the trailing edge to stop it being see-through when the flaps are in position

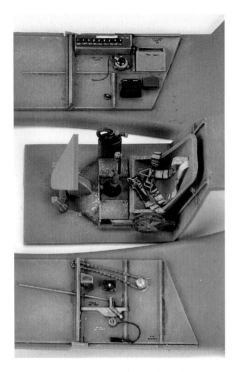

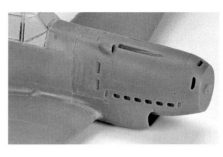

The engine and radiator fit very well indeed with the minimum of fuss and filler, just what we need

The interior is almost identical to that of the later Bf 109s, the most obvious difference being the spade grip on the control column

Grey primer fills the little blemishes and keys the surface for later painting

Main colours applied and it's a very characteristically 'Spanish' look

I couldn't resist the chipping and weathering of the paint, even though I know Mölders' aircraft were usually kept much cleaner

operation not for the squeamish. The trickiest part of the enterprise is the removal of the wing radiator baths, which must be done with a fair supply of patience and care as the replacement inserts will require cautious trial fits and trims. Luckily the new parts are well cast and have a very accurate shape, following the lines of the original kit very well. This doesn't mean you get away without any filler but at least it's kept to a minimum. The same can also be said for the replacement engine section, which comes in a multi-part set of castings that require just the minimum of clean-up to fit the fuselage. That fuselage has to be modified itself, of course, with the addition of some new panels and access hatches and the filling of others as well as the removal of the reinforcing plate along the wing root fillet. Once again, all of this is clearly pointed out in the Alley Cat instructions so there's nothing to worry about. If you use the E-3 version of the kits you'll also have to do quite a bit of wing modification as well as there are a number of panels to fill and rescribe as well as the removal of the underwing bulges for the MG FF cannon. All of which make it a much better option to use an E-1 as the donor kit. Don't forget, this kind of major alteration to a kit requires lots of trial fits and constant trimming and

fettling of the parts. Modification to this degree isn't the easiest thing to get right, so I wouldn't recommend this for complete beginners but it's not beyond the scope of reasonably seasoned model makers.

Once all the major modifications are done the remainder of the plastic is built up around them and now it's time for some paint, so I'm going to quote you a passage from the Alley Cat instructions; " ...this period of aviation in Spain is very vague and there are still many discussions on this period…" No kidding. Every single reference for these aircraft and this time period seems to have its own way of thinking and belief about the colours and markings. Hopefully other information in this book will set things a lot straighter for us all, but for now I just followed the instructions (mostly) and hoped they were about right. The conversion set gives you four different aircraft, three in the light grey version of RLM 63 and one in RLM 02. I fancied doing Mölders' RLM 02-painted machine as it has that crazy looking mouse on the side as well as a full rudder scoreboard. The only variation from the instructions I made was for the red spinner, which many references have on Mölders aircraft. This is inconsistent with his being the 3rd *Staffel* leader as red was the 2nd *Staffel* colour, but I thought it looked good and added a splash of colour to it, so why not? I also added the black area around the exhaust that strangely enough

the paint guide omits, but is quite prominent on the real aircraft and is actually one of the characteristic markings from this period.

I used White Ensign Colourcoat enamels for the main colours as they look to have the right kind of shades to my eyes. Even though I may have over-weathered it a bit, with pastels and Tamiya X-19 Smoke, combined with some silver paint chips courtesy of Alclad and masking fluid, this makes it all look suitably dirty. The markings supplied in the box are a good little selection of Spanish Bf 109s and the decals actually work very well indeed. They are a little thin and delicate but settle down on a gloss surface very well. There is a touch of silvering to deal with along some of the panel lines but a drop or two of setting solution sorted that out. They are all in perfect register and have good colours with the only negative being that the wing roundels are a little too small, but it's hardly noticeable. The markings are quite striking and I have to admit, they do look good against the plain colour of the model. There is the minimum of stencil work to apply as most of these machines were repainted at some time, so the whole process takes very little time at all. The entire lot is blended in with a thin overspray of Tamiya Smoke and it's on to the usual final bits and pieces.

These take up the final phase of the build; undercarriage, control rods, balance weights and propeller are the main items. The propeller is OK but nothing special, with the locking rings at the base of the twin blades being cast rather poorly, actually. Some careful painting made them look alright, but you might be better off modifying the donor kit blades to fit. The final finish is Xtracolor XDFF varnish that further settles everything in and then the

cockpit is demasked and repositioned with the additions of the locking handle and retention wire. Then it's time to sit back and see what we've got.

Verdict

The donor kit from Eduard is excellent, it has lots of detail, good shapes and is easy to build. In its standard form it gets the full engine and nose guns as well, remember. Using the Alley Cat conversion set changes its whole character and considering the major alterations, is surprisingly easy to do. Full credit to Alley Cat for making it this easy, with an excellently thought-out and produced set. Apart from the poor casting of the propeller hubs it's just about faultless. This conversion set is highly recommended to anyone with an interest in the Spanish Civil War, or wants their Messerschmitt looking just a little bit different.

The decals are beautiful made by Fantasy Printshop and although you do have to watch out for a bit of silvering, they work very well indeed

---

Eduard 1/32nd
Bf 109E-1

by Steve A. Evans

The first thing anyone notices about this Eduard 1/32nd version of the Bf 109E is the artwork on the lid, just how gorgeous is that? This is what box-top art is all about: dramatic images, beautifully drawn. Take note Trumpeter, Airfix et al., this is how you do it! Inside, the 'wow' factor continues as you are greeted with six large sprues of light olive green-coloured plastic and a single sprue of transparent parts. The detail work is very neat indeed with fine recessed panel lines, all very crisp and clean. You also get a pack of pre-painted, photo-etched parts for the cockpit and a few external bits, as well as a large decal sheet and a 16-page, full-colour instruction book. There are four versions on offer in the box and each of them is very different and an excellent set of choices from Eduard, but a little more on that later when we come to put the stickers on.

First of all let's start with the interior. It's not as crisply and cleanly moulded as some of the Hasegawa 1:32 kits

are but then you get the amazing photo-etch to really liven things up in there. Painting the interior is one of the easy jobs to do here because of the good moulding, not to mention the pre-painted bits. The basic interior is RLM 02 and I used LifeColor acrylic for that. When dry this has a black oil wash and then a drybrush with Humbrol 90 Beige-Green. The details are picked out in various acrylics and a few chips are added with a silver pencil, simple really. The engine assembly is done in much the same way although the basic colour is matt black but the oil washes and drybrushing is the same basic process to bring the mechanical bits to life. The engine itself is made up of a dozen or so parts and they fit together reasonably well, although some careful adjustments do need to be made on the smaller parts. The fit of the major sub-assem-

Put on a lick of paint and add the pre-painted photo-etch and you've got yourself an excellent pilot's office

Wires, stretched sprue and little off-cuts of plasticard make all the difference once the paint is on

blies into the fuselage is reasonable, although once again it needs careful trimming and lots of trial fits. You get another option here of not using the engine parts at all, with a separate backing plate to mount the spinner onto, as well as exhaust mounting plates. Good work by Eduard as that would mean a much simpler and straightforward build if all you want is the basic shape of the 'Emil' and aren't interested in all that engine detail. Talking of which, the separate exhaust stubs are very cleverly moulded so that they appear almost hollow but without the use of slip moulds, which would have upped the cost factor even more. The wings go together very well without any kind of fuss, and of course you get a full set of separate control surfaces. The leading-edge automatic slats are moulded so that they fit in the slightly 'drooped' position often seen

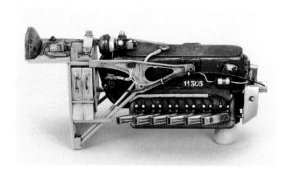

of fish as it could have been a nightmare but Eduard have got it spot on with positive location for all the parts. You also get fully poseable control surfaces, again with the doped fabric effect and raised tape lines.

The Bf 109 went through a whole raft of different colour schemes during its service life and Eduard has provided a fine selection for us from its early years. There are four versions in the box, all with their own characteristics. Versions A and C are the classic early Battle of Britain look with RLM 02/71/65 colours and high demarcation. Version B is for Hans Trautloft's machine from the Polish campaign in RLM 70/71/65 and version D is again in RLM 70/71/65 but with the fuselage sides mottled over with RLM 65 and a yellow nose. Painting starts with a good wash and brush-up to get rid of all the building detritus, followed by a coat of Grey Primer, Halfords finest, of course. There's no pre-shading on a subject this big so it's straight on with the paint and because the upper surface is the smallest area and the easiest to mask, it gets done first. I used White Ensign Colourcoat enamel for this one and first out of the airbrush is ACLW11 RLM 71 *Dunkelgrün*, lightened with about 10% light grey. This is applied in a couple of thin coats and given heavier applications along all the panel lines and the rivet lines as well, so you get a nice variation in tone. Masking for the fairly simple pattern of ACLW12 RLM 02 *Grau* is done with paper masks, held just off the surface of the kit with

Location in the fuselage is a little tricky around the engine, so careful trial fits are the order of the day

in photos of the aircraft on the ground, while the trailing edge bits get a very nice fabric effect. The raised support tapes over the ribs may be a little overdone but under a couple of coats of paint these are going to soften into the details anyway. The fit of the wings to the fuselage always seems to be a bit of a problem for many manufacturers, even Eduard still have their troubles. I'm sorry to say that they haven't got it quite right with this one either and it is a bit of a hassle getting everything to line up. In the end I added a little reinforcing/filling plate at the trailing edge on the underside of the joint to tidy up the worst of it. The empennage (posh word for tail) is a different kettle

Wing-to-fuselage joint is pretty good along the wing root itself

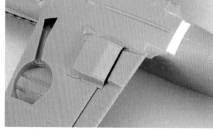

The wing-mounted radiator baths were new to this version of the '109 (the previous 'D' had the radiator under the nose) and they're well represented by Eduard with photo-etched bits for the radiator matrices

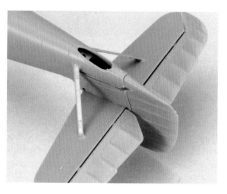

Tailplane fit is exemplary, with the struts holding everything at just the right angle, as it should be of course

The first coat of paint is the RLM71 for the upper surfaces; lots of masking will follow

Paper masks with Blu Tack holding them proud of the kit surface will give excellent semi-soft demarcation lines; this really is one of the oldest techniques in the book

The RLM 02 splinters are a really classic Bf 109E look

thin rolls of Blu Tack. The paper mask method is used again for the lower surface RLM 65 (ACLW03 *Hellblau*) demarcation line. The light blue is applied in a couple of coats allowing the paint to be a little heavier toward the centre of each panel, this time the grey primer acting as a shading undercoat. The masks are then ceremoniously removed and the weathering can begin. For this particular aircraft that was going to be kept to a minimum because it was still early on in the war and very little wear and tear had taken place. This meant that I kept the application of Tamiya Smoke limited to the major panel lines and along the hinge lines for the controls. Of course, the engine area and the underside got a much heavier dose as these areas would get mucky in an instant. Pastel dust swiftly followed, as well as a very limited application of soft silver pencil for paint chipping at the wing roots and along some of the more removable panels.

The decal sheet in the box is a real peach; designed and printed by Cartograf of Italy, it looks good with excellent colour density and perfect register. In use the decals release quickly from the backing paper and are easy to move around on the glossy surface. Settling down is a bit of a problem, although a few applications of Mr Mark Softer and some gentle persuasion over the deeper recesses had the decals behaving themselves but they still have one major problem: my goodness, they're bright! This calls for a double-edged approach at calming them down. First of all I scrubbed a little bit of grey pastel dust into any area where the decal crossed over a panel line. Then I mixed up a very thin Ocean Grey mix of enamel paint (10% ACRN07 to 90% thinners) and with some caution, sprayed a little onto each decal. This toned it all down a fraction and took the edge off the contrast allowing the markings to fade back into the paintwork a little. After that it was a coat of Klear to seal it all in and then

the final matt top coat of White Ensign Matt Varnish. This varnish needs some serious mixing, much more than any other type of varnish I use, but when thinned out properly it sprays very well and dries to a tough finish. But be warned, the thicker you make it, the more matt it becomes, so if you want a sandpaper type finish you can do that too.

This kit is all about the little bits and pieces that make up the final 'look' of the machine and there's a lot to do. The undercarriage units are well moulded and I was pleased to see separate tyres, although unhappy to see that they're unweighted. Even though they all fit well enough, the angles and rather odd camber of the main units need careful adjusting as the glue dries. The propeller and the spinner get to be painted in RLM 70 Black-Green and here I use the good old Humbrol 91 for that as it still looks just about perfect to me. The propeller boss and the backplate for the spinner get a quick spray of Alclad II Aluminium followed by black and brown oil washes. These parts fit so well together that glue is almost unnecessary, although I did bottle out and add a drop of superglue to the joint to make it a bit more permanent. The last bit of kit detailing comes with the upper nose

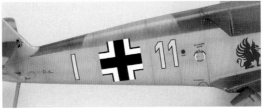

How bright are my numbers? This is supposed to be RLM 04 Gelb, you know. Toning down definitely required

decking and the MG17 7.92mm machine-guns. This area is as well detailed as can be expected in a plastic moulding but there are acres of room to add lots more bits and pieces here. I elected to complete the interrupter gear with the addition of a few wires and tubes but that was about it. One thing to mention here is that if you've decided, like me, to open up this area, then there's no going back; the panels won't fit back into place unless you rip the guns and engine out and fit the alternative pieces. The added parts are then given another coat of the matt varnish and allowed to dry while I look at the final bits. This means unmasking the cockpit and fitting it into the open position and getting the aerial wires into place. This last bit also entails making the little conical wind deflectors on the wire and the insulator for the upper rear fuselage, all from drilled-out and shaped stretched sprue. With these in place that's one 'Emil' complete.

Verdict

First off, this is a great kit, even without the magic of the etched frets this would still be pretty good value for money, considering what you get in the way of plastic in the box. It's a little tricky to build at times and some of the part locations are a touch on the vague side, but if you leave out the engine and guns those difficulties would completely vanish. However you look at it, this is a good looking, accurately shaped Bf 109E-1.

With the RLM 65 masked and sprayed it's time for some weathering, beginning with the chipped paint at the wing roots followed by pastels and Tamiya Smoke

Chapter 10: **Building a Collection**

With so many versions of the early Bf 109 series as potential modelling subjects we thought it would be useful to show you the differences between prototype and production machines to assist you in making them.

Note – this list only includes those machines actually built, not projects or unbuilt production/prototype machines, see Chapters 1 through 6 for details of these machines.

Original artwork ©Jacek Jackiewicz 2013 & 2022
Additional artwork ©Juraj Jankovic, 2022

Bf 109 V1

Some form of probe can be seen fitted to each wing tip in early photos, this is probably a pitot of some type, but is fitted directly into the end of the wing projecting outwards by about 18in, then turning through 90° at the extreme tip to face forward – probably associated with stall and spin testing it undertook

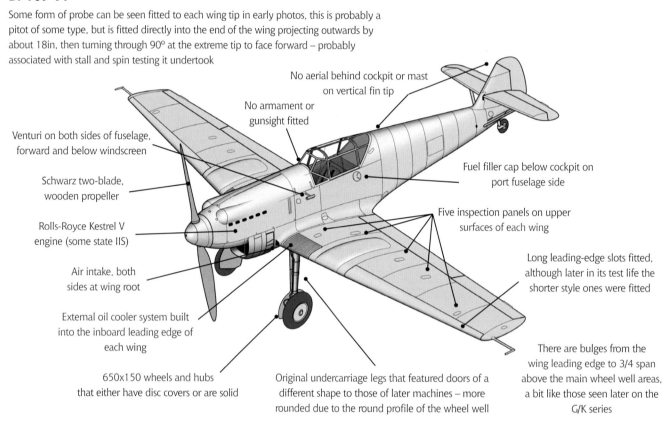

No aerial behind cockpit or mast on vertical fin tip

No armament or gunsight fitted

Venturi on both sides of fuselage, forward and below windscreen

Schwarz two-blade, wooden propeller

Rolls-Royce Kestrel V engine (some state IIS)

Air intake, both sides at wing root

External oil cooler system built into the inboard leading edge of each wing

650x150 wheels and hubs that either have disc covers or are solid

Original undercarriage legs that featured doors of a different shape to those of later machines – more rounded due to the round profile of the wheel well

Fuel filler cap below cockpit on port fuselage side

Five inspection panels on upper surfaces of each wing

Long leading-edge slots fitted, although later in its test life the shorter style ones were fitted

There are bulges from the wing leading edge to 3/4 span above the main wheel well areas, a bit like those seen later on the G/K series

Bf 109 V2

Same as V1 except:

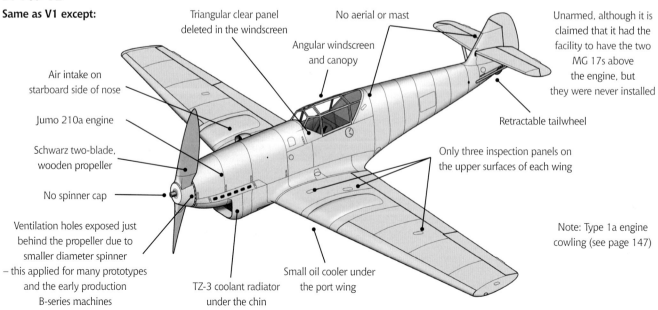

Triangular clear panel deleted in the windscreen

Angular windscreen and canopy

No aerial or mast

Unarmed, although it is claimed that it had the facility to have the two MG 17s above the engine, but they were never installed

Air intake on starboard side of nose

Jumo 210a engine

Schwarz two-blade, wooden propeller

No spinner cap

Ventilation holes exposed just behind the propeller due to smaller diameter spinner – this applied for many prototypes and the early production B-series machines

TZ-3 coolant radiator under the chin

Small oil cooler under the port wing

Retractable tailwheel

Only three inspection panels on the upper surfaces of each wing

Note: Type 1a engine cowling (see page 147)

Bf 109A W/Nr.808 D-IIBA
Same as the Bf 109 V4 except:

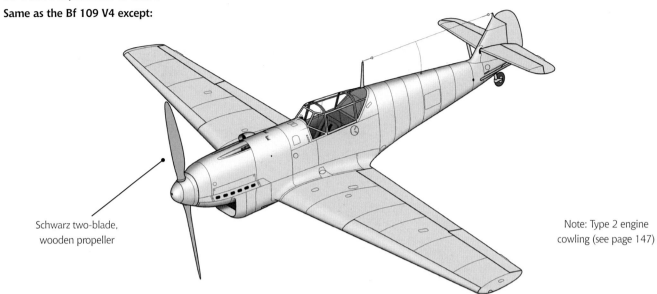

Schwarz two-blade,
wooden propeller

Note: Type 2 engine
cowling (see page 147)

Bf 109A W/Nr.809 D-IUDE
Same as the Bf 109 V4 except:

Bf 109A W/Nr.810 D-IHNY
Same as the Bf 109A W/Nr.809 D-IUDE except:

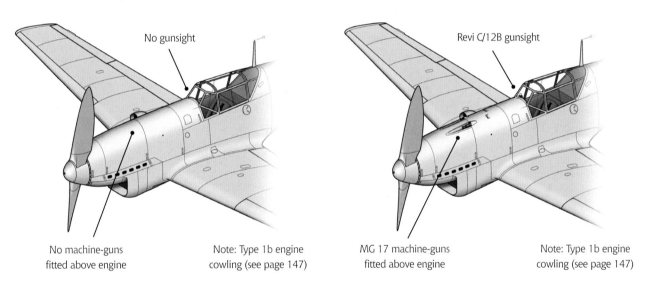

No gunsight

Revi C/12B gunsight

No machine-guns
fitted above engine

Note: Type 1b engine
cowling (see page 147)

MG 17 machine-guns
fitted above engine

Note: Type 1b engine
cowling (see page 147)

Bf 109 V3
Same as V2 except:

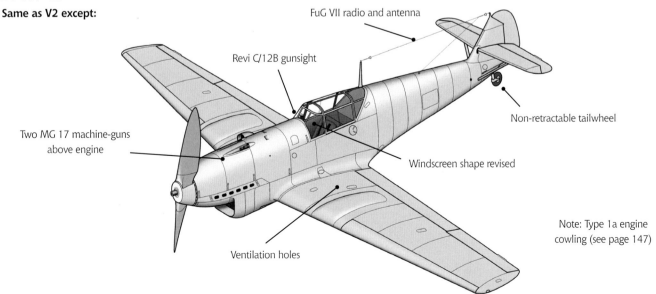

FuG VII radio and antenna

Revi C/12B gunsight

Two MG 17 machine-guns
above engine

Non-retractable tailwheel

Windscreen shape revised

Ventilation holes

Note: Type 1a engine
cowling (see page 147)

Bf 109 V4 W/Nr.878 D-IALY (Bf 109B-01)
Same as the Bf 109 V2 except:

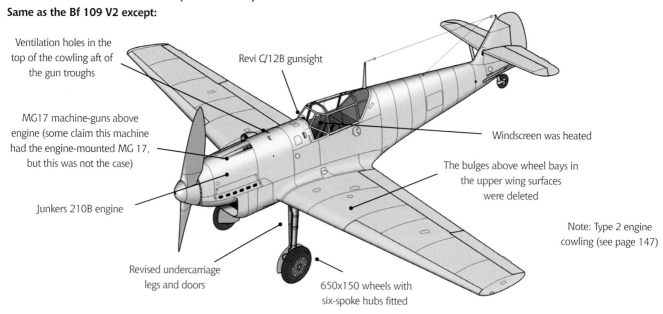

Ventilation holes in the top of the cowling aft of the gun troughs

Revi C/12B gunsight

MG17 machine-guns above engine (some claim this machine had the engine-mounted MG 17, but this was not the case)

Junkers 210B engine

Windscreen was heated

The bulges above wheel bays in the upper wing surfaces were deleted

Note: Type 2 engine cowling (see page 147)

Revised undercarriage legs and doors

650x150 wheels with six-spoke hubs fitted

Bf 109 W/Nr.879 V5 D-IIGO (Bf 109B-02)
Same as the Bf 109 V4 except:

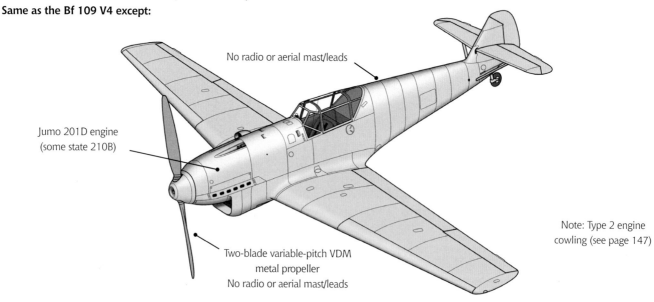

No radio or aerial mast/leads

Jumo 201D engine (some state 210B)

Note: Type 2 engine cowling (see page 147)

Two-blade variable-pitch VDM metal propeller
No radio or aerial mast/leads

Bf 109 V6 W/Nr.880 D-IHHB (Bf 109B-03)
Same as the Bf 109 V4 except:

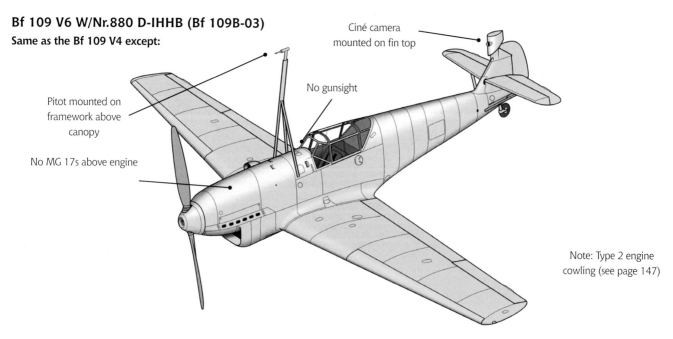

Ciné camera mounted on fin top

Pitot mounted on framework above canopy

No gunsight

No MG 17s above engine

Note: Type 2 engine cowling (see page 147)

Bf 109 V7 W/Nr.881 D-IJHA (Bf 109B-04)
& Bf 109 V8 W/Nr.882 D-IMQE (Bf 109B-05)
Same as the Bf 109 V5 except:

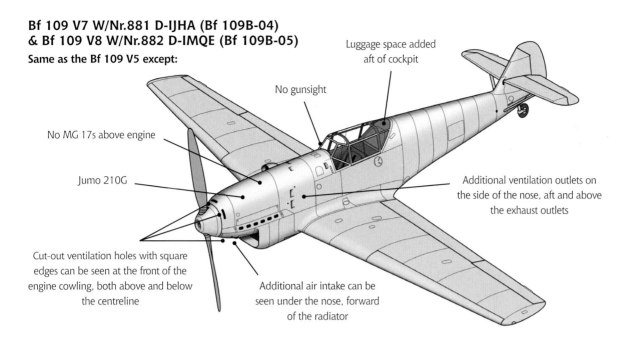

Luggage space added
aft of cockpit

No gunsight

No MG 17s above engine

Jumo 210G

Additional ventilation outlets on
the side of the nose, aft and above
the exhaust outlets

Cut-out ventilation holes with square
edges can be seen at the front of the
engine cowling, both above and below
the centreline

Additional air intake can be
seen under the nose, forward
of the radiator

Bf 109 V9 W/Nr.883 D-IPLU (Bf 109B-06)
Same as the Bf 109 V8 except:

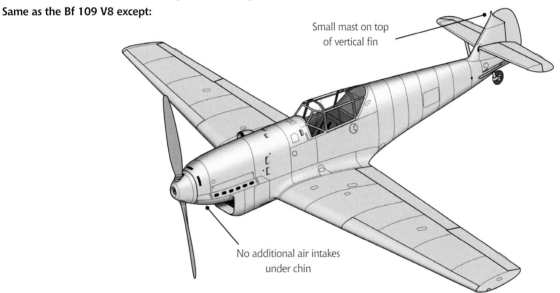

Small mast on top
of vertical fin

No additional air intakes
under chin

Bf 109 V10 W/Nr.883 D-IXZA (Bf 109B-07)
& Bf 109B-2 W/Nr.0320 D-IEKS
Same as the Bf 109 V9 except:

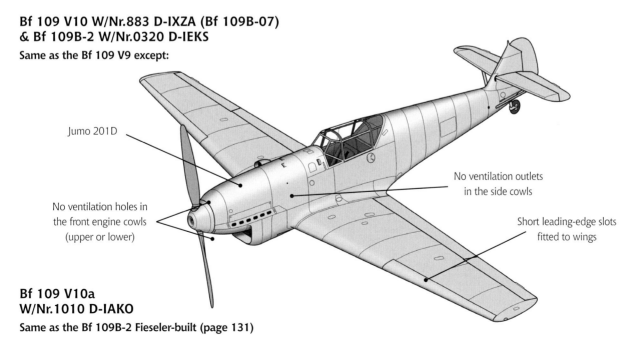

Jumo 201D

No ventilation outlets
in the side cowls

No ventilation holes in
the front engine cowls
(upper or lower)

Short leading-edge slots
fitted to wings

Bf 109 V10a
W/Nr.1010 D-IAKO
Same as the Bf 109B-2 Fieseler-built (page 131)

Bf 109 V11 W/Nr.1012 D-IFMO (Bf 109B-08)
Same as the Bf 109 V10 except:

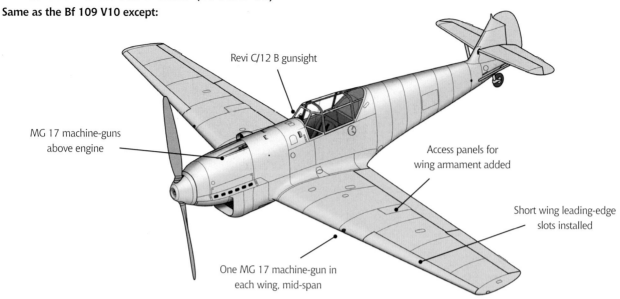

Revi C/12 B gunsight

MG 17 machine-guns
above engine

Access panels for
wing armament added

Short wing leading-edge
slots installed

One MG 17 machine-gun in
each wing, mid-span

Bf 109 V12 W/Nr.1016 D-IVRU (Bf 109B-09)
Same as the Bf 109 V11 except:

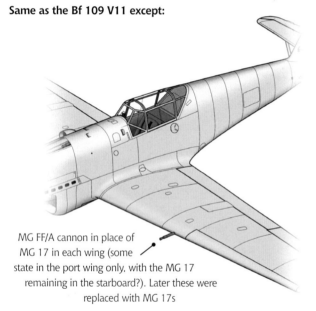

MG FF/A cannon in place of
MG 17 in each wing (some
state in the port wing only, with the MG 17
remaining in the starboard?). Later these were
replaced with MG 17s

Bf 109B-0 W/Nrs.0994, 0995, 0996 & 0997 D-IMRY, P-IPLA, D-IVSE & D-IZQE
Same as the Bf 109 V4 except:

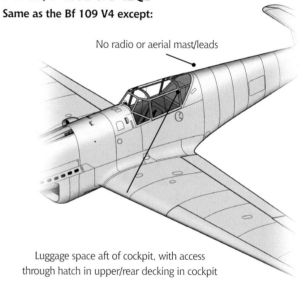

No radio or aerial mast/leads

Luggage space aft of cockpit, with access
through hatch in upper/rear decking in cockpit

Bf 109B-1
Same as the Bf 109B-0 except:

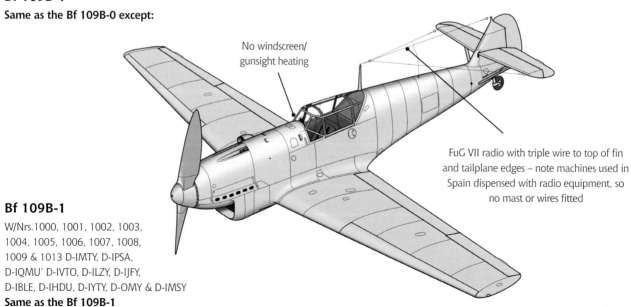

No windscreen/
gunsight heating

FuG VII radio with triple wire to top of fin
and tailplane edges – note machines used in
Spain dispensed with radio equipment, so
no mast or wires fitted

Bf 109B-1
W/Nrs.1000, 1001, 1002, 1003,
1004, 1005, 1006, 1007, 1008,
1009 & 1013 D-IMTY, D-IPSA,
D-IQMU' D-IVTO, D-ILZY, D-IJFY,
D-IBLE, D-IHDU, D-IYTY, D-OMY & D-IMSY
Same as the Bf 109B-1

Bf 109B-2 BFW-built
Same as the Bf 109B-0 except:

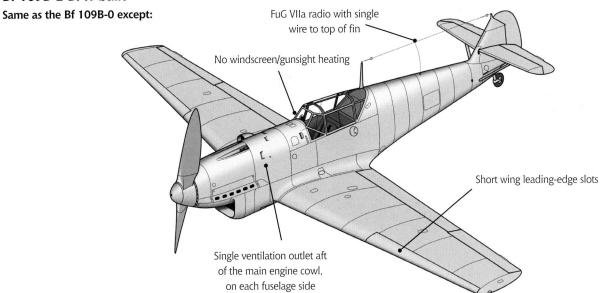

FuG VIIa radio with single wire to top of fin

No windscreen/gunsight heating

Short wing leading-edge slots

Single ventilation outlet aft of the main engine cowl, on each fuselage side

Bf 109B-2 Fieseler-built
Same as the Bf 109B-2 (BFW-built) except:

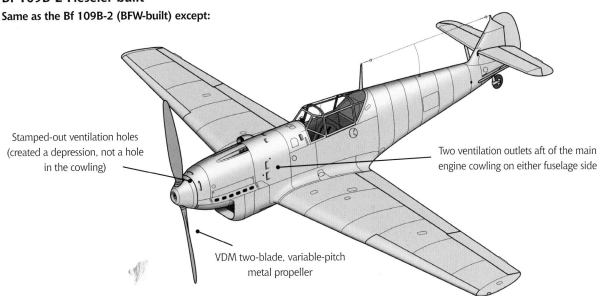

Stamped-out ventilation holes (created a depression, not a hole in the cowling)

Two ventilation outlets aft of the main engine cowling on either fuselage side

VDM two-blade, variable-pitch metal propeller

Bf 109B-2 Fieseler-built 'Late production'
Same as the Bf 109B-2 (Fieseler-built) except:

Bf 109B-2 Erla-built
Same as the Bf 109B-2 (Fieseler-built, late production) except:

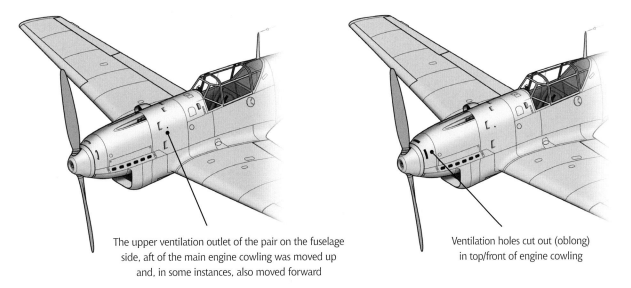

The upper ventilation outlet of the pair on the fuselage side, aft of the main engine cowling was moved up and, in some instances, also moved forward

Ventilation holes cut out (oblong) in top/front of engine cowling

Bf 109 V18 W/Nr.1731 D-ISDH (Bf 109C-0)
& Bf 109 V19 W/Nr.1720 D-IVSG (Bf 109C-0)
& Bf 109C-1

Same as the Bf 109B-2 Fieseler-built, late production except:

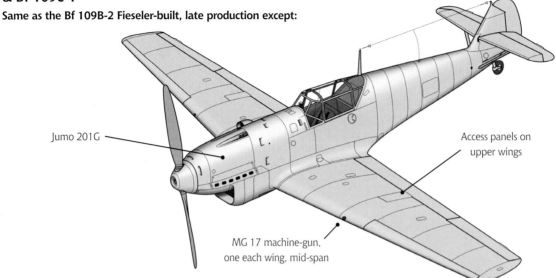

Jumo 201G

Access panels on
upper wings

MG 17 machine-gun,
one each wing, mid-span

Bf 109C-2 – Project only

Same as the Bf 109C-1 except:

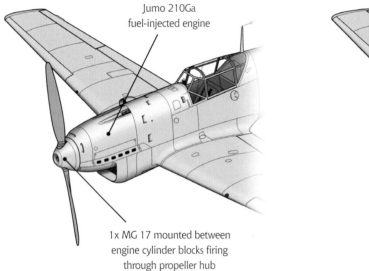

Jumo 210Ga
fuel-injected engine

1x MG 17 mounted between
engine cylinder blocks firing
through propeller hub

Bf 109C-3 (converted from C-1)

Same as the Bf 109C-1 except:

2x MG FF/A replaced MG 17s,
one in each wing at mid-span

Bf 109C-4 – Project only

Same as the Bf 109C-1 except:

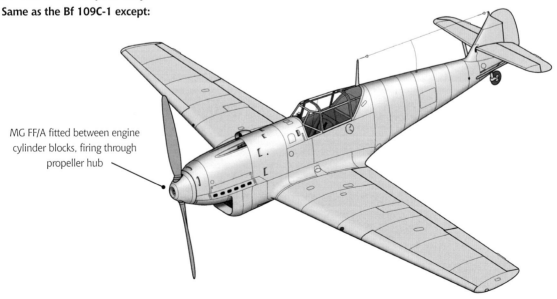

MG FF/A fitted between engine
cylinder blocks, firing through
propeller hub

Bf 109D-1
Same as the Bf 109C-1 except:

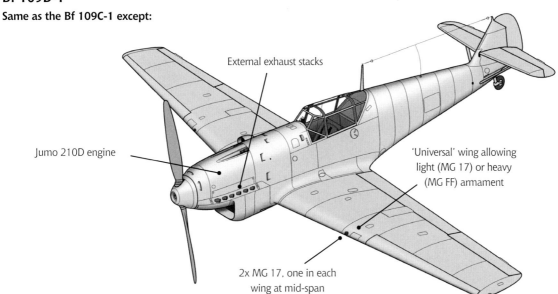

External exhaust stacks

Jumo 210D engine

'Universal' wing allowing light (MG 17) or heavy (MG FF) armament

2x MG 17, one in each wing at mid-span

Bf 109 V16 W/Nr.1775 D-IDXG (later CE + BI)
Same as the Bf 109D-1 except:

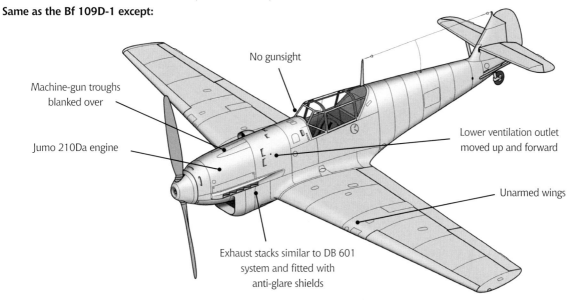

No gunsight

Machine-gun troughs blanked over

Jumo 210Da engine

Lower ventilation outlet moved up and forward

Unarmed wings

Exhaust stacks similar to DB 601 system and fitted with anti-glare shields

Bf 109D-1 (Last production series)
Same as the Bf 109D-1 except:

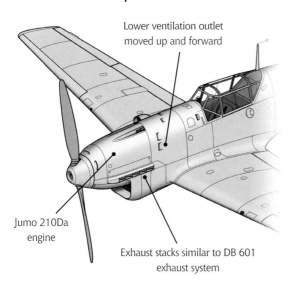

Lower ventilation outlet moved up and forward

Jumo 210Da engine

Exhaust stacks similar to DB 601 exhaust system

Bf 109D-1 Night Fighter
Same as the Bf 109D-1 (Last production series) except:

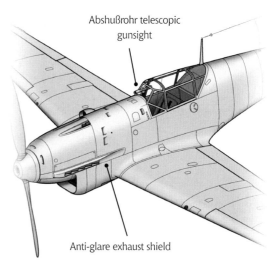

Abshußrohr telescopic gunsight

Anti-glare exhaust shield

Bf 109D-1 (Swiss version)
Same as the Bf 109D-1 except:

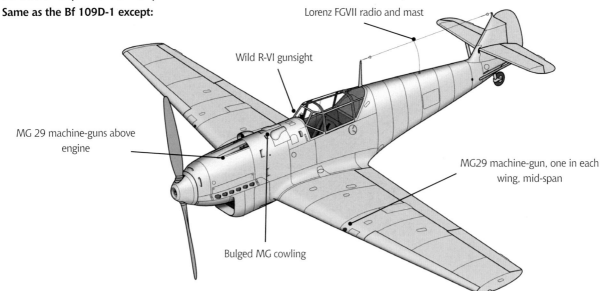

Lorenz FGVII radio and mast

Wild R-VI gunsight

MG 29 machine-guns above engine

MG29 machine-gun, one in each wing, mid-span

Bulged MG cowling

Bf 109D-1 W/Nr.2303 Swiss version (J-308)
Same as the Bf 109D-1 (Swiss version) except:

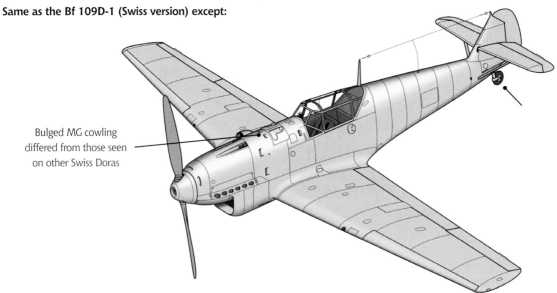

Bulged MG cowling differed from those seen on other Swiss Doras

Bf 109 V13, W/Nr.1050 D-IPKY (Bf 109E-01)
& Bf 109 V14 W/Nr.1029 D-ISLU (Bf 109E-02)

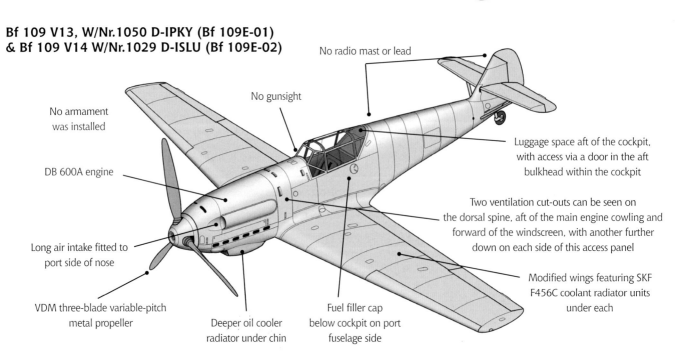

No radio mast or lead

No gunsight

No armament was installed

DB 600A engine

Long air intake fitted to port side of nose

VDM three-blade variable-pitch metal propeller

Deeper oil cooler radiator under chin

Fuel filler cap below cockpit on port fuselage side

Luggage space aft of the cockpit, with access via a door in the aft bulkhead within the cockpit

Two ventilation cut-outs can be seen on the dorsal spine, aft of the main engine cowling and forward of the windscreen, with another further down on each side of this access panel

Modified wings featuring SKF F456C coolant radiator units under each

Bf 109 V13 (Record Attempt)

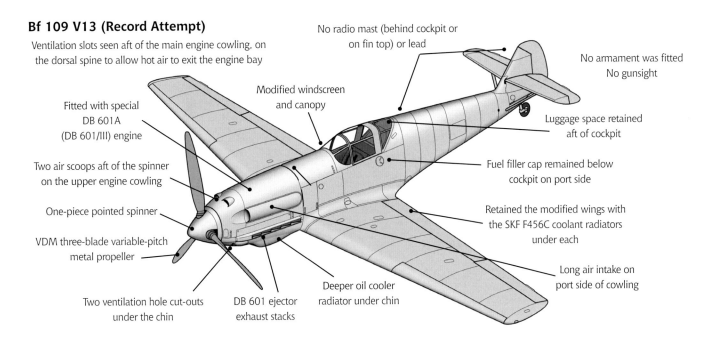

Ventilation slots seen aft of the main engine cowling, on the dorsal spine to allow hot air to exit the engine bay

No radio mast (behind cockpit or on fin top) or lead

No armament was fitted
No gunsight

Fitted with special DB 601A (DB 601/III) engine

Modified windscreen and canopy

Luggage space retained aft of cockpit

Two air scoops aft of the spinner on the upper engine cowling

Fuel filler cap remained below cockpit on port side

One-piece pointed spinner

Retained the modified wings with the SKF F456C coolant radiators under each

VDM three-blade variable-pitch metal propeller

Long air intake on port side of cowling

Two ventilation hole cut-outs under the chin

DB 601 ejector exhaust stacks

Deeper oil cooler radiator under chin

Bf 109 V15 W/Nr.1773 D-IPHR (Bf 109E-03)

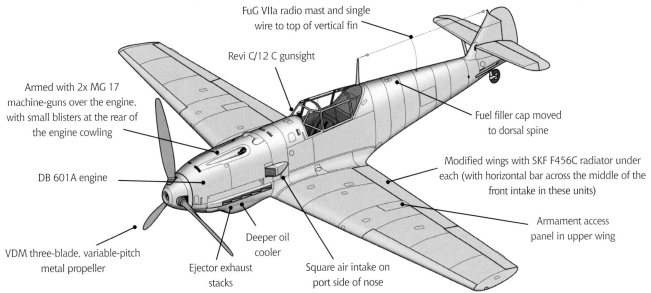

FuG VIIa radio mast and single wire to top of vertical fin

Revi C/12 C gunsight

Armed with 2x MG 17 machine-guns over the engine, with small blisters at the rear of the engine cowling

Fuel filler cap moved to dorsal spine

DB 601A engine

Modified wings with SKF F456C radiator under each (with horizontal bar across the middle of the front intake in these units)

VDM three-blade, variable-pitch metal propeller

Armament access panel in upper wing

Deeper oil cooler

Ejector exhaust stacks

Square air intake on port side of nose

Bf 109 V15a W/Nr.1774 D-ITPD
Same as Bf 109 V15 except:

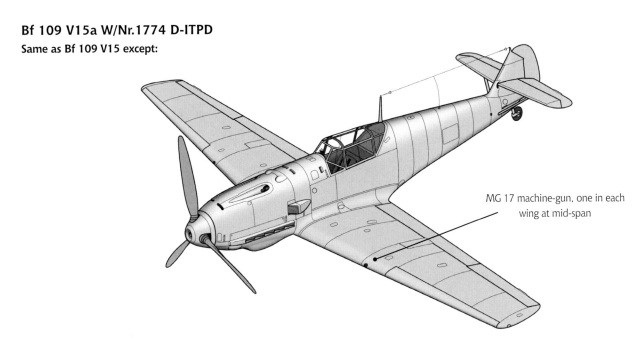

MG 17 machine-gun, one in each wing at mid-span

Bf 109E-0 W/Nrs 1784 & 1787
Same as the Bf 109 V14 except:

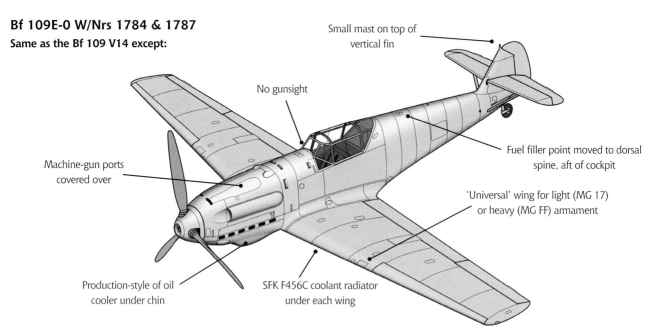

Small mast on top of vertical fin

No gunsight

Fuel filler point moved to dorsal spine, aft of cockpit

Machine-gun ports covered over

'Universal' wing for light (MG 17) or heavy (MG FF) armament

Production-style of oil cooler under chin

SFK F456C coolant radiator under each wing

Bf 109E-0 W/Nr.1783, 1781 and another D-IDFD, D-IECY and another
Same as Bf 109E-0 W/Nrs.1784 and 1787 except:

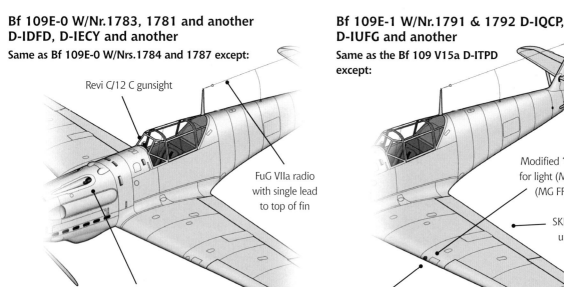

Revi C/12 C gunsight

FuG VIIa radio with single lead to top of fin

MG 17 machine-guns over the engine

Bf 109E-1 W/Nr.1791 & 1792 D-IQCP, D-IUFG and another
Same as the Bf 109 V15a D-ITPD except:

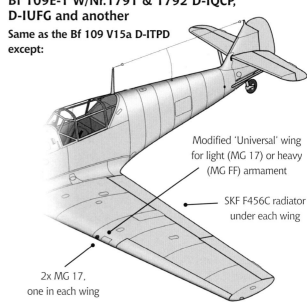

Modified 'Universal' wing for light (MG 17) or heavy (MG FF) armament

SKF F456C radiator under each wing

2x MG 17, one in each wing

Bf 109E-1/U3
Same as the Bf 109E-1 except:

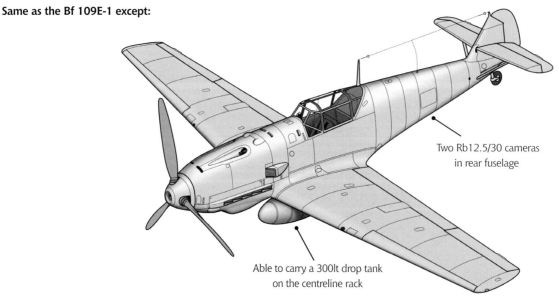

Two Rb12.5/30 cameras in rear fuselage

Able to carry a 300lt drop tank on the centreline rack

Bf 109E-1/B
Same as the Bf 109E-1 except:

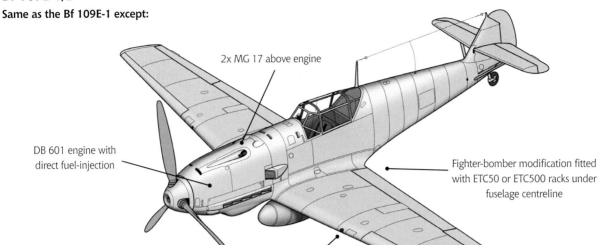

2x MG 17 above engine

DB 601 engine with
direct fuel-injection

Fighter-bomber modification fitted
with ETC50 or ETC500 racks under
fuselage centreline

2x MG 17,
one in each wing

Bf 109 V20, W/Nr.1779
Same as the Bf 109E-1 except:

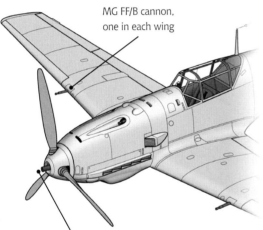

MG FF/B cannon,
one in each wing

Type did not have the engine-mounted MG as some
claim, projecting tube in hub centre was cable
pick-up for towing experiments

Bf 109E-3 W/Nr.1797, N/K & N/K D-IRTT, WL-IGKS (previously D-IGKS) and another
Same as the Bf 109E-1 except:

MG FF/B cannon,
one in each wing

Bf 109 V26 W/Nr.1361 CA+NK
Same as the Bf 109E-1 except:

Centreline ETC500
bomb rack

Bf 109E-3b
Same as the Bf 109E-1 except:

Centreline ETC50/VIII or
ETC500 bomb rack

Bf 109E-3 (Swiss Version)
Same as the Bf 109E-1 except:

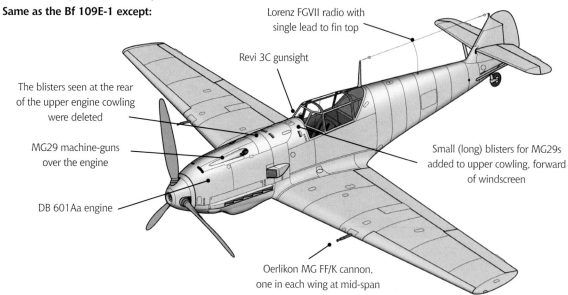

Lorenz FGVII radio with
single lead to fin top

Revi 3C gunsight

The blisters seen at the rear
of the upper engine cowling
were deleted

MG29 machine-guns
over the engine

DB 601Aa engine

Small (long) blisters for MG29s
added to upper cowling, forward
of windscreen

Oerlikon MG FF/K cannon,
one in each wing at mid-span

Bf 109E-3 W/Nr.2442 (Swiss Version – J-369)
Same as the Bf 109E-3 (Swiss Version) except:

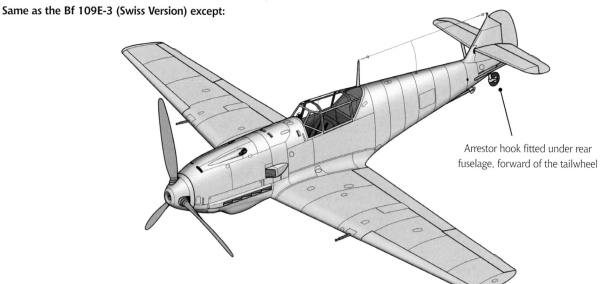

Arrestor hook fitted under rear
fuselage, forward of the tailwheel

Bf 109E-3 W/Nr.2198 and 2359
(Swiss Version – J-340 'Super S.F.R' and J-378 'U-boot')
Same as the Bf 109E-3 (Swiss Version) except:

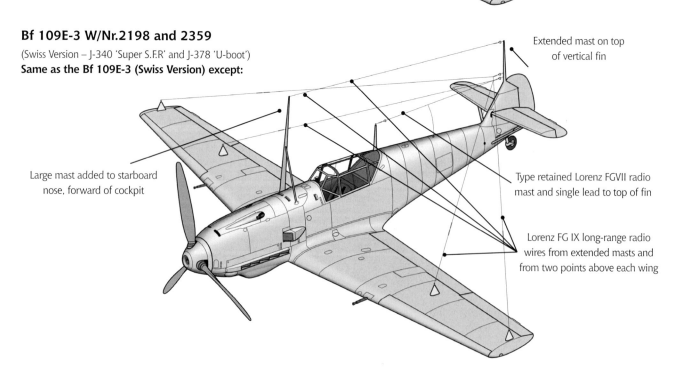

Extended mast on top
of vertical fin

Large mast added to starboard
nose, forward of cockpit

Type retained Lorenz FGVII radio
mast and single lead to top of fin

Lorenz FG IX long-range radio
wires from extended masts and
from two points above each wing

Bf 109E-3 (Doflug-built)
Same as the Bf 109E-3 except:

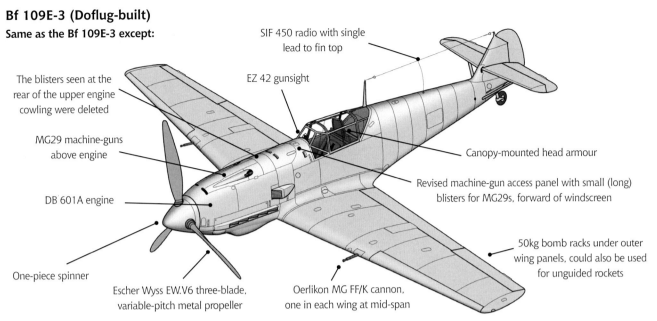

SIF 450 radio with single lead to fin top

EZ 42 gunsight

The blisters seen at the rear of the upper engine cowling were deleted

MG29 machine-guns above engine

DB 601A engine

One-piece spinner

Escher Wyss EW.V6 three-blade, variable-pitch metal propeller

Canopy-mounted head armour

Revised machine-gun access panel with small (long) blisters for MG29s, forward of windscreen

50kg bomb racks under outer wing panels, could also be used for unguided rockets

Oerlikon MG FF/K cannon, one in each wing at mid-span

Bf 109E-4 & E-4N
Same as the Bf 109E-3 except:

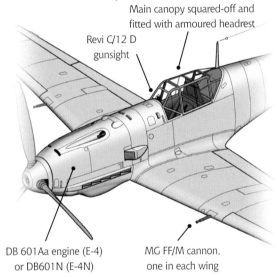

Main canopy squared-off and fitted with armoured headrest

Revi C/12 D gunsight

DB 601Aa engine (E-4) or DB601N (E-4N)

MG FF/M cannon, one in each wing

Bf 109E-4 with Peil IV
Same as the Bf 109E-4 & E-4N except:

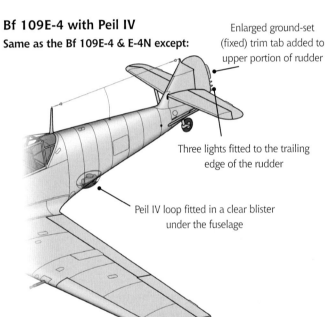

Enlarged ground-set (fixed) trim tab added to upper portion of rudder

Three lights fitted to the trailing edge of the rudder

Peil IV loop fitted in a clear blister under the fuselage

Bf 109E-4b
Same as the Bf 109E-4 except:

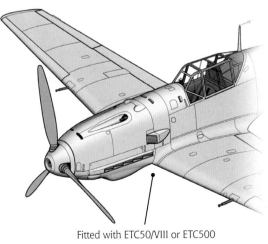

Fitted with ETC50/VIII or ETC500 racks under fuselage centreline

Bf 109E-4 Trop & E-4N Trop

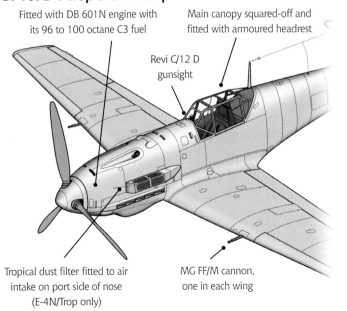

Fitted with DB 601N engine with its 96 to 100 octane C3 fuel

Main canopy squared-off and fitted with armoured headrest

Revi C/12 D gunsight

Tropical dust filter fitted to air intake on port side of nose (E-4N/Trop only)

MG FF/M cannon, one in each wing

Bf 109E-4N W/Nr.5819 (ZRF-4 tests)
Same as the Bf 109E-3 except:

Tested the ZFR-4
telescopic gunsight

Fitted with DB 601N
engine with its 96 to
100 octane C3 fuel

Bf 109E-4 W/Nr.2574 CI+EJ 'Doppelreiter'
Same as the Bf 109E-4 except:

Fitted with DB 601N
engine with its 96 to
100 octane C3 fuel

Experimentally fitted with
overwing fuel tanks
(Doppelreiter)

Bf 109E-4 (Ground training airframe)
Same as the Bf 109E-4 & E-4N except;

Lower engine cowling removed to
expose oil cooler radiator (to improve
cooling effect as airframe only used
for taxing training), this would have
required much modification, as the
oil cooler was built into the lower
engine cowling, which was removed,
so it would have had to be fixed
below the engine and all pipework
re-installed once the cowling section
was removed

Undercarriage locked down and
struts added between oleos

Metal hoop with support strut
added under each outer wing panel

Undercarriage door removed

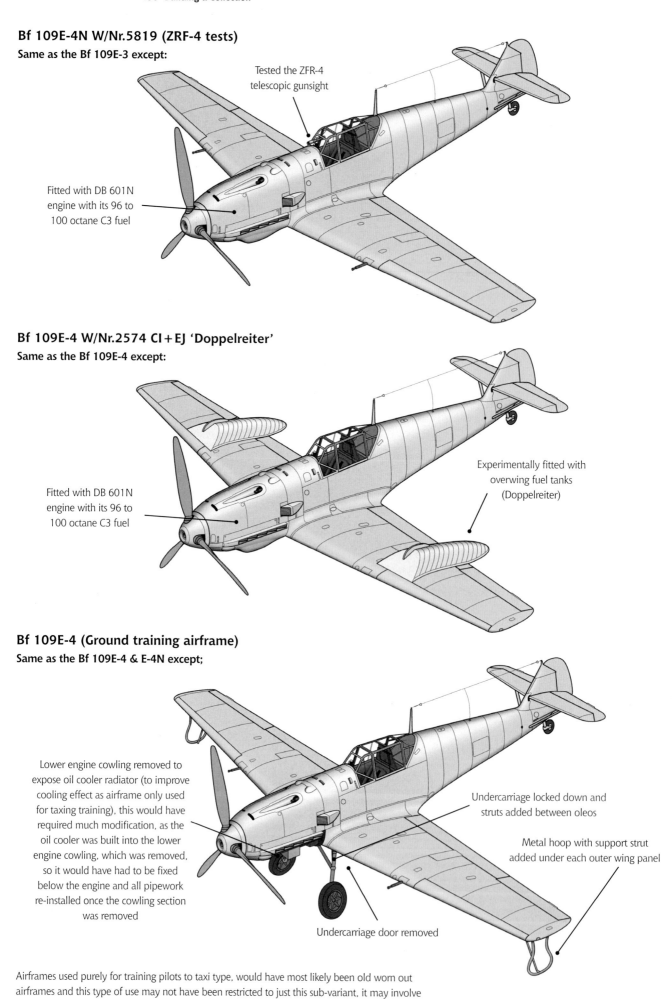

Airframes used purely for training pilots to taxi type, would have most likely been old worn out
airframes and this type of use may not have been restricted to just this sub-variant, it may involve
earlier or later variants as well; depicted here as an E-4 for illustration purposes only.

Bf 109E-5 & E-6 (converted from E-1)
Same as the Bf 109E-1 except:

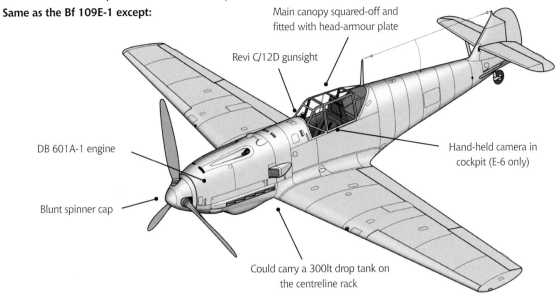

Main canopy squared-off and fitted with head-armour plate

Revi C/12D gunsight

DB 601A-1 engine

Blunt spinner cap

Hand-held camera in cockpit (E-6 only)

Could carry a 300lt drop tank on the centreline rack

Bf 109E-5 Trop
Same as the Bf 109E-1 except:

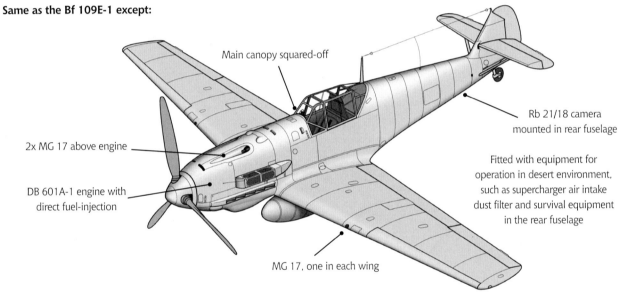

Main canopy squared-off

2x MG 17 above engine

DB 601A-1 engine with direct fuel-injection

Rb 21/18 camera mounted in rear fuselage

Fitted with equipment for operation in desert environment, such as supercharger air intake dust filter and survival equipment in the rear fuselage

MG 17, one in each wing

Bf 109E-7 & E-7N
Same as the Bf 109E-4 except:

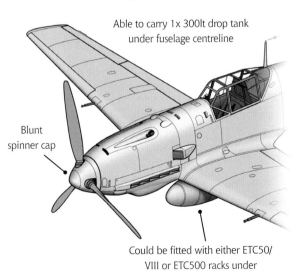

Able to carry 1x 300lt drop tank under fuselage centreline

Blunt spinner cap

Could be fitted with either ETC50/VIII or ETC500 racks under fuselage centreline

Bf 109E-7b
Same as the Bf 109E-7 & E-7N except:

Could be fitted with either ETC50/VIII or ETC500 racks under fuselage centreline

Bf 109E-7 Trop and E-7N Trop
Same as the Bf 109E-4 Trop except:

Able to carry 1x 300lt drop tank
under fuselage centreline

Bf 109E-7Z
Same as the Bf 109E-7 except:

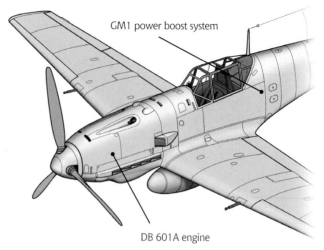

GM1 power boost system

DB 601A engine

Bf 109E-7Z Trop
Same as the Bf 109E-4 Trop except:

DB 601A engine

GM1 power boost system

Able to carry 1x 300lt drop tank
under fuselage centreline

Bf 109E-8
Same as the Bf 109E-5 & E-6 except:

Fitted with DB 601N
engine with its 96 to
100 octane C3 fuel

Able to carry 1x 300lt drop tank
under fuselage centreline

Bf 109E-8 with skis
Same as the Bf 109E-8 except:

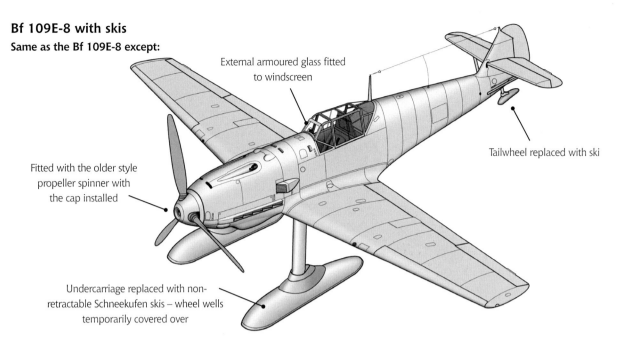

External armoured glass fitted to windscreen

Tailwheel replaced with ski

Fitted with the older style propeller spinner with the cap installed

Undercarriage replaced with non-retractable Schneekufen skis – wheel wells temporarily covered over

Bf 109E-9 and E-9N
Same as the Bf 109E-7 except:

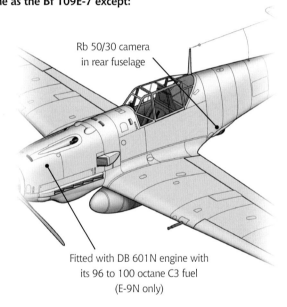

Rb 50/30 camera in rear fuselage

Fitted with DB 601N engine with its 96 to 100 octane C3 fuel (E-9N only)

Bf 109E-9 Trop and E-9N Trop
Same as the Bf 109E-7/Trop except:

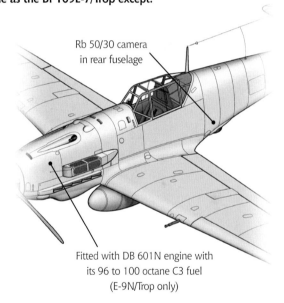

Rb 50/30 camera in rear fuselage

Fitted with DB 601N engine with its 96 to 100 octane C3 fuel (E-9N/Trop only)

Bf 109S
Same as Bf 109E-3 W/Nr.1797, N/K & N/K D-IRTT, WL-IGKS (previously D-IGKS) and another except:

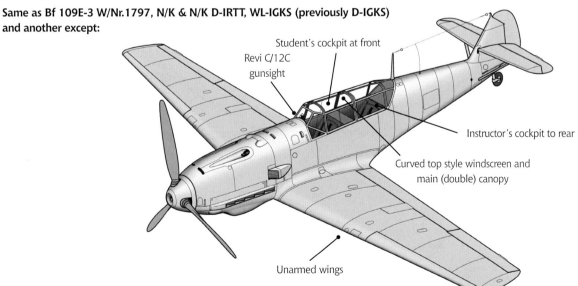

Student's cockpit at front

Revi C/12C gunsight

Instructor's cockpit to rear

Curved top style windscreen and main (double) canopy

Unarmed wings

Bf 109 V19 W/Nr.1776 D-IYMS (later TK+HK)
Same as Bf 109 V19 W/Nr.1720 D-IVSG (Bf 109C-0) except:

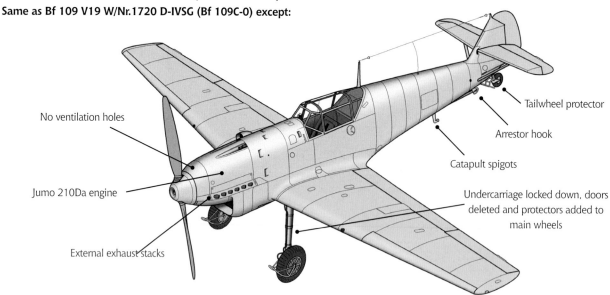

No ventilation holes

Jumo 210Da engine

External exhaust stacks

Tailwheel protector

Arrestor hook

Catapult spigots

Undercarriage locked down, doors deleted and protectors added to main wheels

Bf 109 V17a W/Nr.301 D-IKAC (late TK+HN)
Same as Bf 109 V19 W/Nr.1720 D-IVSG (Bf 109C-0) except:

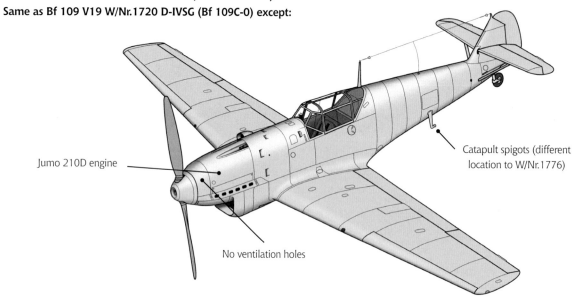

Jumo 210D engine

Catapult spigots (different location to W/Nr.1776)

No ventilation holes

Bf 109E-0 W/Nr.1781 and 1783 WL-IECY (later TK+HL) & GH+NT
Same as Bf 109E-0 W/Nrs.1784 & 1787 except:

Framed style windscreen and canopy without armour plate

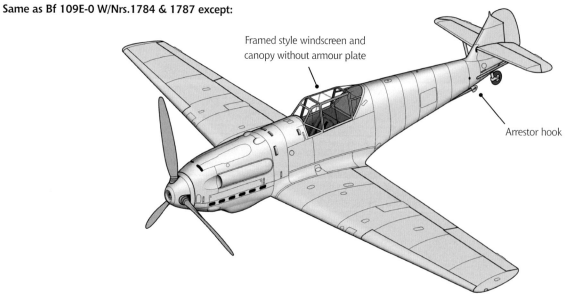

Arrestor hook

Bf 109E-3 W/Nr.1946 GH-NU
Same as Bf 109E-3 W/Nr.1797, N/K & N/K D-IRTT, WL-IGKS (previously D-IGKS) and another except:

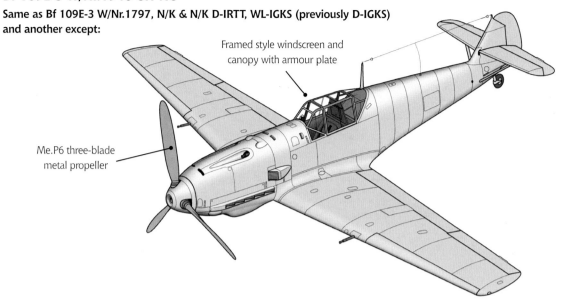

Framed style windscreen and canopy with armour plate

Me.P6 three-blade metal propeller

Bf 109 V15 W/Nr.1773 CE+BF
Same as Bf 109 V15 W/Nr.1773 D-IPHR (Bf 109E-03) except:

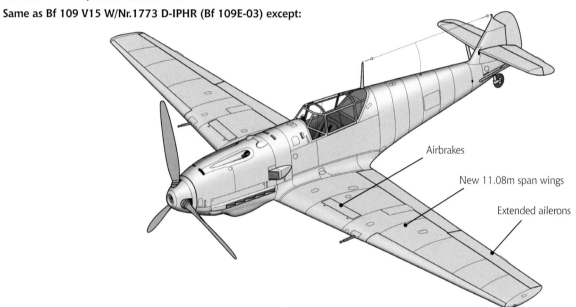

Airbrakes

New 11.08m span wings

Extended ailerons

Bf 109T-0 W/Nr.6153 CK+NC
Same as Bf 109 V15 W/Nr.1773 CE+BF except:

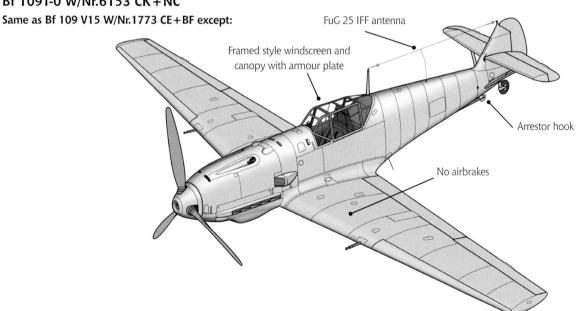

FuG 25 IFF antenna

Framed style windscreen and canopy with armour plate

Arrestor hook

No airbrakes

Bf 109T-1
Same as Bf 109T-0 W/Nr.6153 CK+NC except:

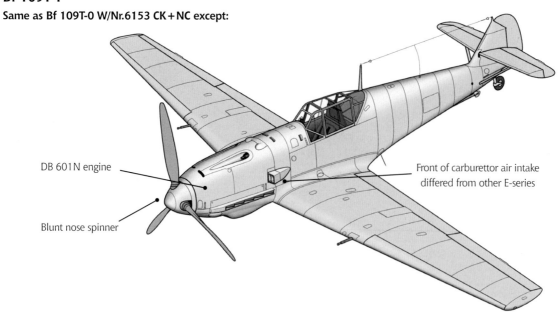

DB 601N engine

Blunt nose spinner

Front of carburettor air intake
differed from other E-series

Bf 109T-2 (converted from T-1)
Same as Bf 109T-1 except:

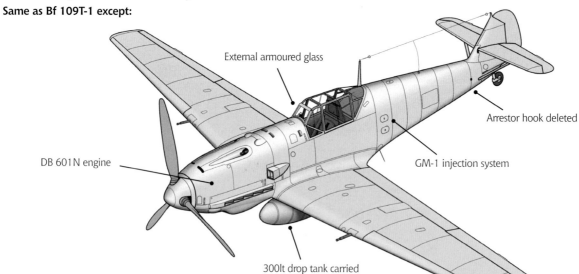

External armoured glass

DB 601N engine

Arrestor hook deleted

GM-1 injection system

300lt drop tank carried
as standard

Bf 109E-1 (6•119 Spanish conversion)

Same as Bf 109E-1 W/Nr.1791 & 1792 D-IQCP, D-IUFG and another except:

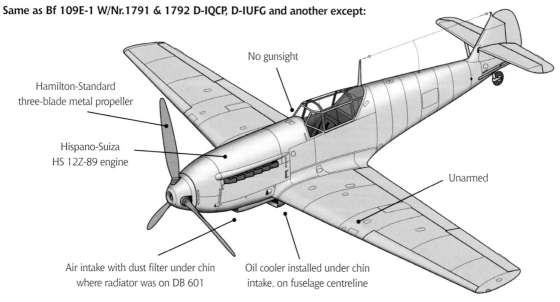

No gunsight

Hamilton-Standard
three-blade metal propeller

Hispano-Suiza
HS 12Z-89 engine

Unarmed

Air intake with dust filter under chin
where radiator was on DB 601

Oil cooler installed under chin
intake, on fuselage centreline

Bf 109 V21 W/Nr.1772

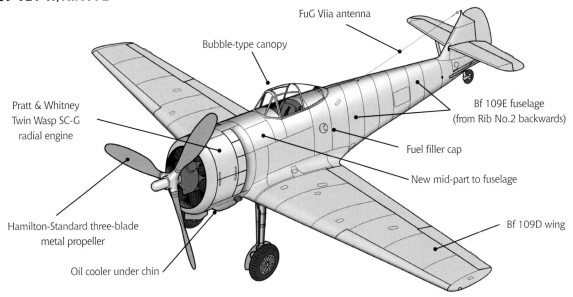

FuG Viia antenna

Bubble-type canopy

Pratt & Whitney
Twin Wasp SC-G
radial engine

Bf 109E fuselage
(from Rib No.2 backwards)

Fuel filler cap

New mid-part to fuselage

Hamilton-Standard three-blade
metal propeller

Bf 109D wing

Oil cooler under chin

Engine cowling shape comparison

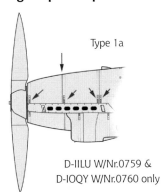

Type 1a

D-IILU W/Nr.0759 &
D-IOQY W/Nr.0760 only

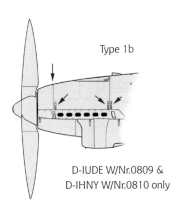

Type 1b

D-IUDE W/Nr.0809 &
D-IHNY W/Nr.0810 only

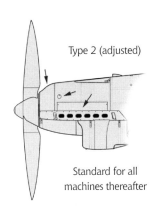

Type 2 (adjusted)

Standard for all
machines thereafter

Additional armour protection of cockpit

E-1 & E-3. Armoured plate
behind pilot's head, no
armoured glass

E-1 & E-3. Armoured plate
behind pilot's head, plus
armoured glass

E-4 to E-9. Armoured plate
behind pilot's head, no
armoured glass

E-4 to E-9. Armoured plate
behind pilot's head, plus
armoured glass

E-4 to E-9. Armoured plate
behind pilot's head (curved
top), plus armoured glass

D/F Loop Installation

This ventral D/F loop housing was
added to some E-series machines used
in the night-fighter role

FuG VIIIc

The three-wire antenna array was seen
on some machines

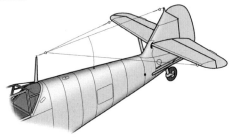

Chapter 11: **In Detail**

What follows is an extensive selection of images and diagrams that will help you understand the physical nature of the early Bf 109 series.

Cockpit & Canopy

Bf 109B-1

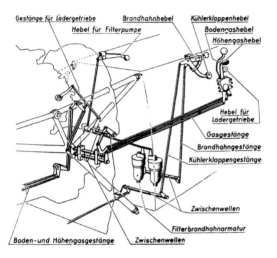

The upper rear decking of the canopy, showing the tubular structure inside, the luggage compartment and the retaining wire. The tubular item on the windscreen frame is a cockpit light

This diagram shows how the throttle and radiator flaps control are installed and linked

Taken from the Russian report, this image gives an overall view of the B-series cockpit, it is pretty much unchanged up to the E-series

Viewed from a little further back, this does show you the early style control column and how little equipment there is on the starboard side at this stage, although the oxygen bottle has been removed by this stage

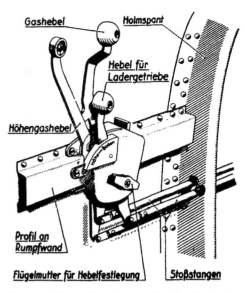

Further up and forward on the port sidewall is the throttle box, this is simplified in the early versions in comparison with the unit that will be used in the E-series

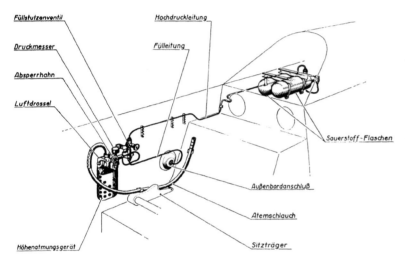

This is the oxygen system in the B, the hatch in the bottom of the luggage rack seen in a previous image is to gain access to the bottles mounted under it

With the luggage hatch open this is what is inside, the inner tube is obviously just put there, while the strap you can see on the side holds the oxygen bottle used to blow this rear section off in an emergency

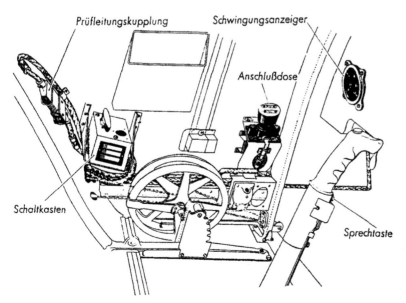

On the port sidewall there is a lot more going on, apart from the trim wheel most of the area contains the radio control boxes as seen in this diagram

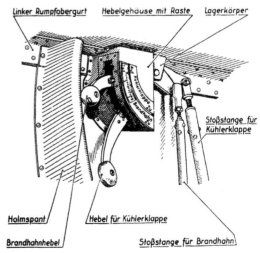

Above the throttle box is the control linkage for the radiator shutters

Teil

1 Spornarretierungshebel
2 Betriebsdatenkarte
3 Einspritzbehälter
4 Absperrhahn am Atemgerät
5 Fernbedienungsventil
6 Fahrwerksschalter
7 Feststellhebel für Festlegung von Landeklappen- und Höhenflossen-Verstellrad
8 Flügelmutter für Festlegung des Gashebels
9 Brandhahnhebel
10 Hebel für Kraftstoffhandpumpe
11 Kraftstoff-Druckmesser
12 Ferntrennschalter
13 Zündschalter
14 Gashebel
15 Höhengashebel
16 Hebel für Ladergetriebe
17 Einspritzpumpe
18 Anlaßschalter
19 Schmierstoffdruckmesser
20 Hebel für Kühlerklappe
21 Borduhr
22 Kühlwasser-Wärmemesser
23 Schmierstoff-Doppelwärmemesser
24 Drehzahlmesser
25 Schalter für Heizdüse
26 Schauzeichen für Heizdüse
27 Anzeigegerät für Fahrwerksüberwachung
28 Verstellschraubenschalter
29 Steigungsanzeiger
30 Schalter für Kennlichter
31 Schalter für Gerätebrettbeleuchtung
32 Verdunkler
33 Ladedruckmesser
34 Kabinengriff
35 Fensterriegel
36 Sitzverstellhebel
37 Gurtverstellhebel
38 Statoskop-Variometer
39 Landeklappenverstellrad
40 Höhenflossenverstellrad
41 Schauzeichen für Höhenflossenverstellung

42 Mechanisches Anzeigegerät für Fahrwerksüberwachung
43 Handhebel für Kabinenbelüftung
44 Wendezeiger
45 Empfindlichkeitsregler
46 Kraftstoff-Vorratsmesser
47 Pumpen-Handknopf für Kraftstoff-Vorratsmesser
48 Auslösegriff für Fahrwerksnotauslösung
49 Netzausschalter
50 Handhebel für Kabinenabwurf
51 Kompaß
52 Fahrtmesser
53 Höhenmesser
54 Sicherungskasten

Overall diagram of the B-series instrument panel layout

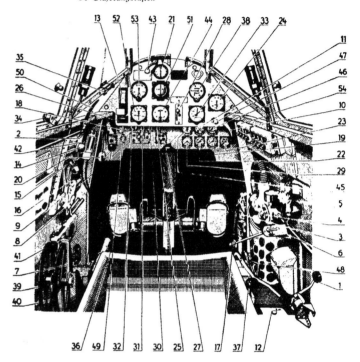

With the Russian test pilot in the cockpit ready to test this recently captured machine, you can see the style and shape of the canopy and how it opened. This is common to all versions through to the E-3

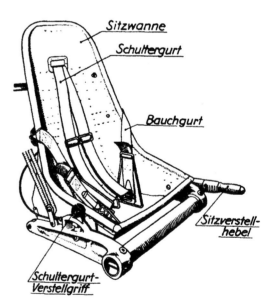

The pilot's seat, this remained constant until the E-series

Nice side view of the cockpit area on the B-1 captured in Spain, showing the refuelling point under the round access panel as well as the framework detail

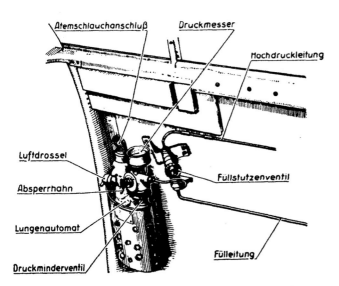

Atemschlauchanschluß
Druckmesser
Hochdruckleitung
Luftdrossel
Absperrhahn
Füllstutzenventil
Lungenautomat
Druckminderventil
Fülleitung

The oxygen bottle usually side on the starboard sidewall, as shown here

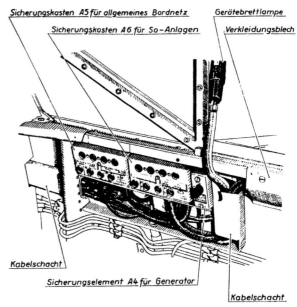

Sicherungskasten A5 für allgemeines Bordnetz
Sicherungskasten A6 für So–Anlagen
Gerätebrettlampe
Verkleidungsblech
Kabelschacht
Sicherungselement A4 für Generator
Kabelschacht

The electrical distribution box on the forward starboard sill is seen here, along with the cockpit light, which in the early versions was mounted vertically up the canopy frame

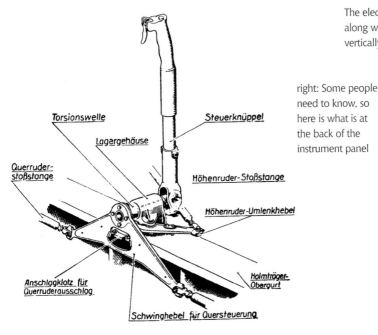

Torsionswelle
Steuerknüppel
Lagergehäuse
Querruder-stoßstange
Höhenruder-Stoßstange
Höhenruder-Umlenkhebel
Holmträger-Obergurt
Anschlagklotz für Querruderausschlag
Schwinghebel für Quersteuerung

right: Some people need to know, so here is what is at the back of the instrument panel

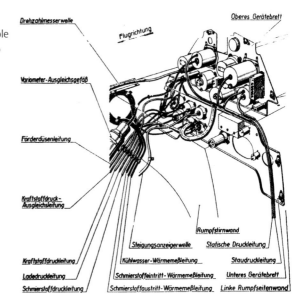

Drehzahlmesserwelle
Flugrichtung
Oberes Gerätebrett
Variometer-Ausgleichsgefäß
Förderdüsenleitung
Kraftstoffdruck-Ausgleichsleitung
Rumpfstirnwand
Steigungsanzeigerwelle
Statische Druckleitung
Kraftstoffdruckleitung
Kühlwasser-Wärmemeßleitung
Staudruckleitung
Ladedruckleitung
Schmierstoffeintritt- Wärmemeßleitung
Unteres Gerätebrett
Schmierstoffdruckleitung
Schmierstoffaustritt- Wärmemeßleitung
Linke Rumpfseitenwand

The manual diagram of the B-series control column, the one captured in Spain certainly had the round grip installed, so it would seem that early machines had that type, then later they went to this style of column and grip

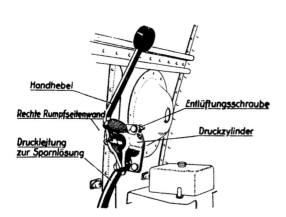

Handhebel
Rechte Rumpfseitenwand
Entlüftungsschraube
Druckleitung zur Spornlösung
Druckzylinder

Towards the rear bulkhead on the starboard sidewall is this hand pump for the tailwheel retraction

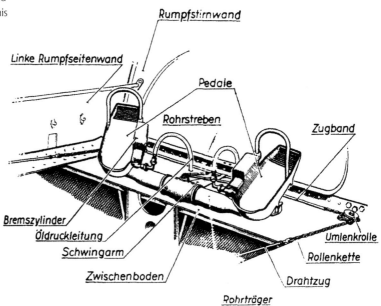

Rumpfstirnwand
Linke Rumpfseitenwand
Pedale
Rohrstreben
Zugband
Bremszylinder
Öldruckleitung
Schwingarm
Zwischenboden
Umlenkrolle
Rollenkette
Drahtzug
Rohrträger

The rudder pedal assembly in the B-series

Bf 109C & D

The instrument panel layout for the Bf 109C

The hydraulic pump unit also moved down the sidewall for the Bf 109C and D series

Aufstellung zur Abb. 3

1 Höhenflossenverstellrad
2 Landeklappenverstellrad
3 Sitzwanne
4 Sitzverstellhebel
5 Schauzeichen für Höhenflossenverstellung
6 Einspritzbehälter
7 Einspritzpumpe (Anlaßpumpe)
8 Flügelmutter für Festlegung des Luftdrosselhebels
9 Hebel für Ladergetriebeschaltung
10 Hebel für Kühlerklappenverstellung
11 Luftdrosselhebel
12 Brandhahnhebel
13 Betriebsdatenkarte
14 Verriegelungsgriff für Windschutzaufbau
15 Anlaßschalter
16 Abwurfhebel für Windschutzaufbau
17 Schauzeichen für Staurohrheizung
18 Fensterriegel
19 Netzausschalter
20 Zündschalter
21 Fahrtmesser
22 Höhenmesser
23 Wendezeiger
24 Kompaß
25 Borduhr
26 Handhebel für Führerraumbelüftung
27 Luftschraubenverstellschalter
28 Ladedruckmesser
29 Kraft- und Schmierstoffdruckmesser
30 Drehzahlmesser
31 Elt. Fahrwerkanzeigegerät
32 Steigungsanzeiger
33 Fahrwerkschalter
34 Hebel für Kraftstoffpumpe
35 Schalter für Kennleuchten
36 Schalter für Gerätebeleuchtung
37 Schalter für Staurohrheizung
38 Mechanisches Fahrwerkanzeigegerät
39 Griff für Fahrwerksnotauslösung
40 Kühlwasser-Temperaturmesser
41 Druckmesser für Sauerstoff
42 Absperrhahn am Atemgerät
43 Spornarretierungshebel
44 Fernbedienungsventil (für Sauerstoffflaschen)
45 Gurtverstellhebel
46 Einschaltgriff für Selbstschalter mit Fernauslösespule
47 Druckknopf für Schmierstoff-Temperaturmesser
48 Schmierstoff-Temperaturmesser
49 Reststandswarnlampe
50 Kraftstoffvorratsmesser

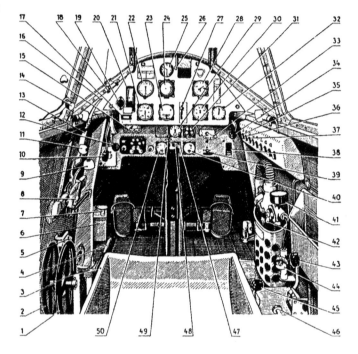

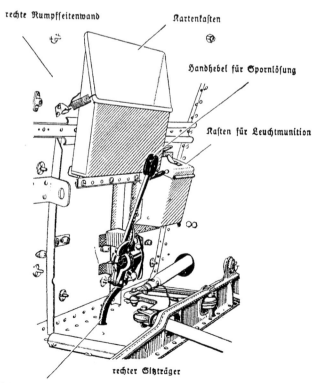

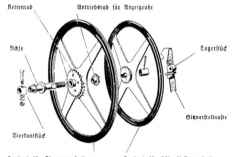

The trim wheel for the B, C & D series remained unchanged

Aufſtellung

1 Sitzwanne
2 Höhenflossenverstellrad
3 Landeklappenverstellrad
4 Sitzverstellhebel
5 Schauzeichen für Höhenflossenverstellung
6 Einſpritzbehälter
7 Einſpritzpumpe (Anlaßpumpe)
8 Flügelmutter für Festlegung der Gashebel
9 Hebel für Ladergetriebeschaltung
10 Höhengashebel
11 Gashebel
12 Betriebsdatenkarte
13 Hebel für Kühlerklappenverstellung
14 Brandhahnhebel
15 Verriegelungsgriff für Windschutzaufbau
16 Anlaßschalter
17 Abwurfhebel für Windschutzaufbau
18 Schauzeichen für Staurohrheizung
19 Fensterriegel
20 Netzausschalter
21 Zündschalter
22 Fahrtmesser
23 Höhenmesser
24 Borduhr
25 Handhebel für Führerraumbelüftung
26 Kompaß
27 Wendezeiger
28 Ladedruckmesser
29 Luftschraubenverstellschalter
30 Kraftstoff-Differenzdruckmesser
31 Drehzahlmesser
32 Schmierstoff-Druckmesser
33 Steigungsanzeiger
34 Elektrisches Fahrwerksanzeigegerät
35 Hebel für Kraftstoff-Handpumpe
36 Schalter für Kennleuchten

37 Schalter für Gerätebrettbeleuchtung
38 Schalter für Staurohrheizung
39 Fahrwerksschalter
40 Mechanisches Fahrwerkanzeigegerät
41 Griff für Fahrwerknotauslösung
42 Druckmesser für Sauerstoff
43 Abſperrhahn am Atemgerät
44 Spornarretierungshebel
45 Fernbedienungsventil (für Sauerstoffflasche)
46 Selbstschalter mit Fernauslösespule
47 Gurtverstellhebel
48 Kühlwasser-Temperaturmesser
49 Druckknopf für Schmierstoff-Temperaturmesser
50 Schmierstoff-Temperaturmesser
51 Reststandswarnlampe
52 Kraftstoffvorratsmesser

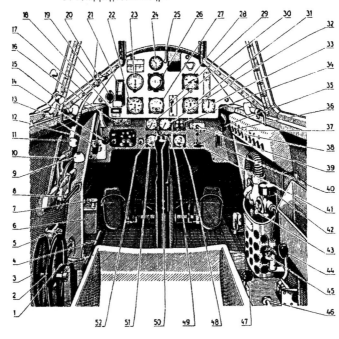

The instrument panel layout for the Bf 109D

An overall shot of the instrument panel etc. in a Swiss Bf 109D. Note the Wild R-VI gunsight, plus the two toggles (with ball ends) in the panel centre that were used to manually cock the guns

Teil

1	Sitzwanne	28	Ladedruckmesser
2	Höhenflossenverstellrad	29	Verstellschraubenschalter
3	Landeklappenverstellrad	30	Kraftstoff-Druckmesser
4	Sitzverstellhebel	31	Drehzahlmesser
5	Schauzeichen für Höhenflossen-	32	Schmierstoff-Druckmesser
	verstellung	33	Steigungsanzeiger
6	Einspritzbehälter	34	Elektrisches Anzeigegerät für
7	Einspritzpumpe		Fahrwerksüberwachung
8	Flügelmutter für Festlegung	35	Hebel für Kraftstoffhandpumpe
	der Gashebel	36	Schalter für Kennlichter
9	Hebel für Ladergetriebe	37	Schalter für Gerätebrett-
10	Höhengashebel		beleuchtung
11	Gashebel	38	Schalter für Heizdüse
12	Betriebsdatenkarte	39	Fahrwerkschalter
13	Hebel für Kühlerklappe	40	Mechanisches Anzeigegerät
14	Brandhahnhebel		für Fahrwerksüberwachung
15	Kabinengriff	41	Auslösegriff für Fahrwerks-
16	Anlaßschalter		notauslösung
17	Handhebel für Kabinenabwurf	42	Druckmesser für Sauerstoff
18	Schauzeichen für Heizdüse	43	Absperrhahn am Atemgerät
19	Fensterriegel	44	Spornarretierungshebel
20	Notausschalter	45	Fernbedienungsventil
21	Zündschalter	46	Ferntrennschalter
22	Fahrtmesser	47	Gurtverstellhebel
23	Höhenmesser	48	Kühlwasser-Wärmemesser
24	Borduhr	49	Druckknopf für Schmierstoff-
25	Handhebel für Kabinen-		Wärmemesser
	belüftung	50	Schmierstoff-Wärmemesser
26	Kompaß	51	Reststandswarnlampe
27	Wendezeiger	52	Kraftstoff-Vorratsmesser

Tafel zur Anlage 1

This is the instrument panel layout diagram for the Bf 109C-1 and D-1

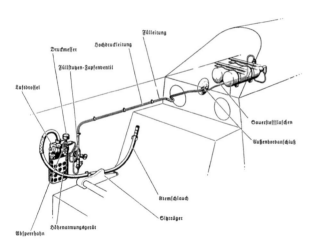

The only change to the oxygen system in the Bf 109C and D series was the movement of the external filler point, which went further aft on the starboard fuselage side

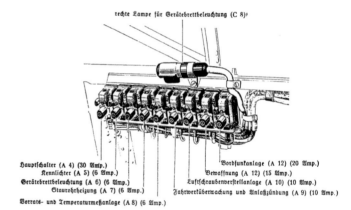

The electrical distribution panel on the starboard sill was revised slightly in the Bf 109C and D series, the cockpit lamp was also mounted horizontally

Bf 109E

The cockpit canopy for the E-1 through to the E-3 featured the curved main section

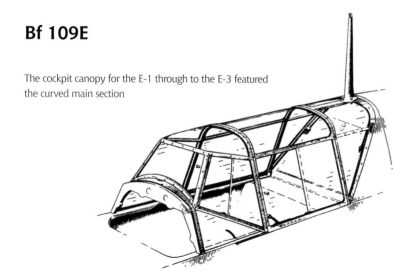

Some E-series machines had a rearview mirror added over the windscreen, this image shows you one example although there are many versions as it was often only done at unit level

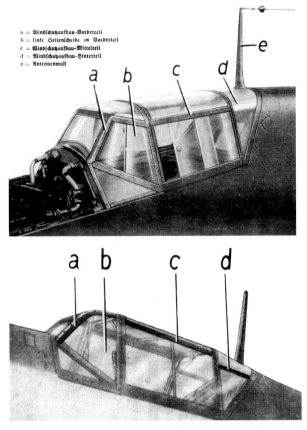

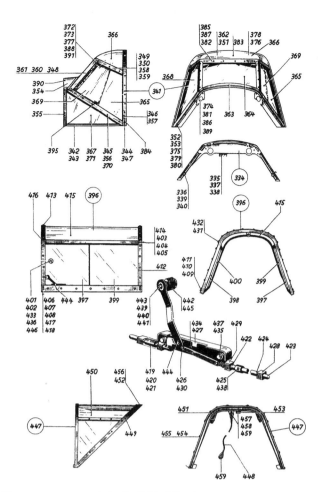

In comparison with the square canopy used from the E-4 there is little other change than the rear inner bracing bar (marked as 'd' in each diagram), which moved from inside the perspex for all versions prior to the E-3, to outside for the E-4 onwards

The canopy components for the E-1 to E-3 series

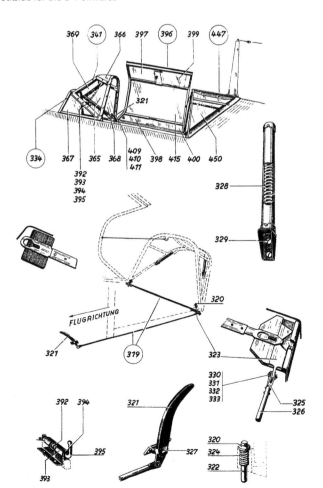

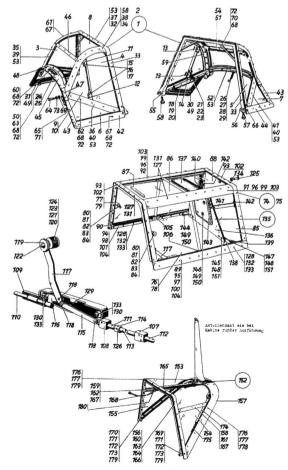

This shows how the canopy is opened as well as the hold-back strap

The canopy components for the E-4 onwards

Nice overall shot of the upper instrument panel and gunsight in the E-3 in Munich
(© Josef Andal)

The upper instrument panel and gunsight in the E-4/b at the Battle of Britain Museum
(© Author)

The lower section of the BofB Museum machine, including the bomb selector panel in the lower/centre

The head armour in this E-7 Trop is the flat-topped one, as there is another version with a curve-over at the top

This is the Swiss AF Museum example and you can see the sliding side panels plus the fact that the vertical join seen in the forward side windscreen panel on the port side does not occur on the starboard side, this is the same for all versions of the Bf 109
(© George Papadimitriou)

Here is a close-up of that join in the port forward side panel in the windscreen – this is the E-3 in Munich
(© George Papadimitriou)

Inside the canopy, on the port side only, is this release latch. The knob above is to slide the panel rearwards
(© Josef Andal)

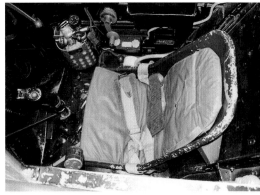

The pilot's seat in the B, C, D and early E-series remained unchanged, this is the one in the E-3 in Munich
(© Josef Andal)

The lower section of the instrument panel in the E-3 in Munich, of note is the cover missing from the oil tank breather tubes you can see in the centre, between the rudder pedals
(© Josef Andal)

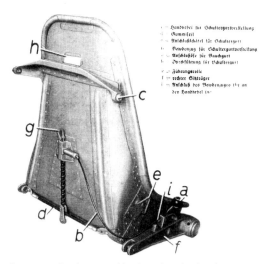

The seat used a clever combination of ratchet bar, bungee and chain to tension the pilot's seat harness

a = Handhebel für Filterpumpe   b = Handkurbel für Kühlstofffühlerklappe   c = Einspritzbehälter
d = Einspritzpumpe   e = Kartenkasten   f = Leuchtmunitionsbehälter
g = Höhenatemgerät   h = Druckmesser am Atemgerät   i = Luftdrossel
k = Fernbedienventil   l = Atemschlauch   m = Rollenkette für Kühlstofffühler-
Klappenverstellung

Overall diagram of the starboard sidewall for the E-series

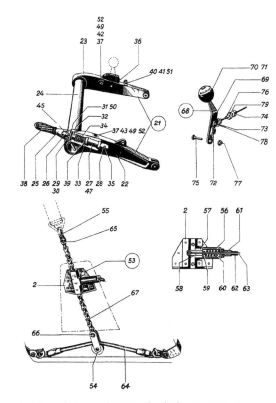

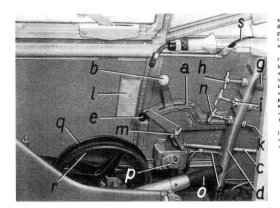

a = Hebelkasten
d = Holmspant
g = Brandhahnhebel
i = Handgriff für Kerzenabbrennung
m = Knebelmutter für Festlegung des Gashebels
r = Handrad für Höhenflossenverstellung
b = Gashebel
e = Hebel für Schmierstoff-Kühlerklappe
h = Startzeug
k = Ölzug für Schnellstoppvorrichtung
n = Handgriff für Schnellstoppvorrichtung
p = Anzeigegerät für Höhenflossenverstellung
s = Hebel für Windschutzaufbau-Abwurfvorrichtung
c = Gasstoßstange
f = Bowdenzug für Schmierstoffkühler-
Klappenverstellung
l = Betriebsdatenkarte
o = Handgriff für Radverstellung
q = Handrad für Landeklappenverstellung

A diagram showing the port sidewall for the E-series

This diagram shows a bit more clearly the seat tensioning components

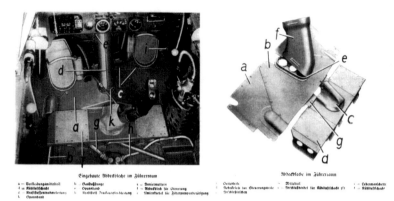

An odd diagram but useful as it shows the separate panels in the E-series cockpit floor, including the cover for the oil tank breather pipes (marked as 'f')

A clear shot of the starboard sidewall in the E-3 in Munich
(© Josef Andal)

The Swiss Bf 109Es used the KG 11 control column unit

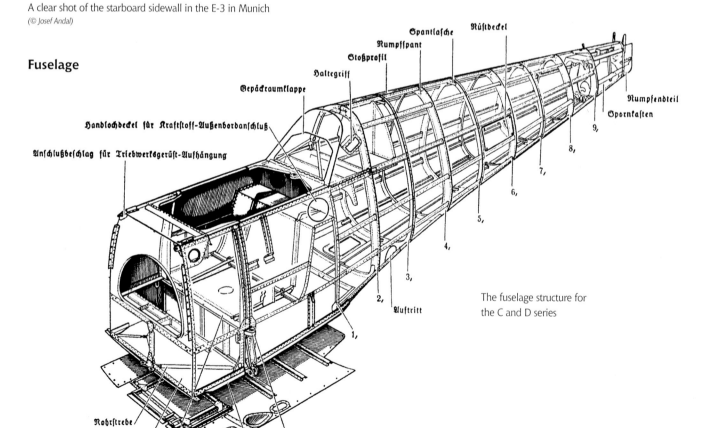

Fuselage

The fuselage structure for the C and D series

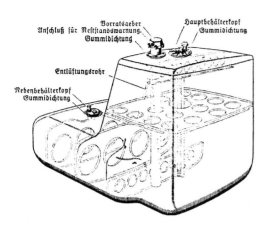

The fuselage fuel tank for the C and D series

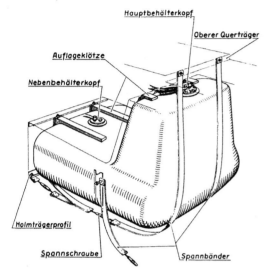

The fuselage fuel tank in the B-series

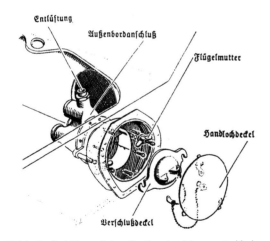

This is the fuel filler point on the B-series, it is mounted below the cockpit sill on the port side

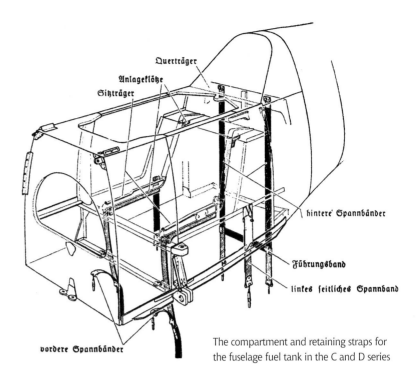

The compartment and retaining straps for the fuselage fuel tank in the C and D series

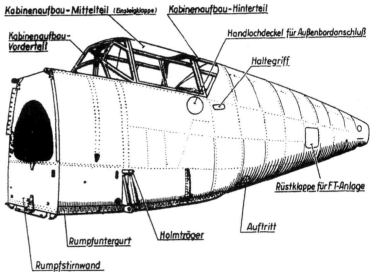

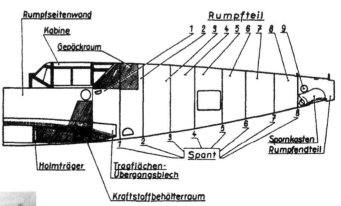

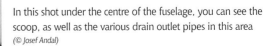

The fuselage structure and access panels for the B series

In this shot under the centre of the fuselage, you can see the scoop, as well as the various drain outlet pipes in this area
(© Josef Andal)

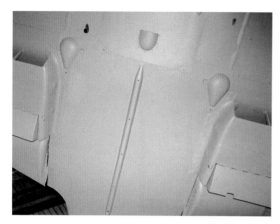

In this shot under the E-3 at Berlin you can see the scoop mentioned previously, as well as the teardrop-shaped bulges over the wing spar bolts

(© George Papadimitriou)

The interior of the rear fuselage is pretty conventional for the era

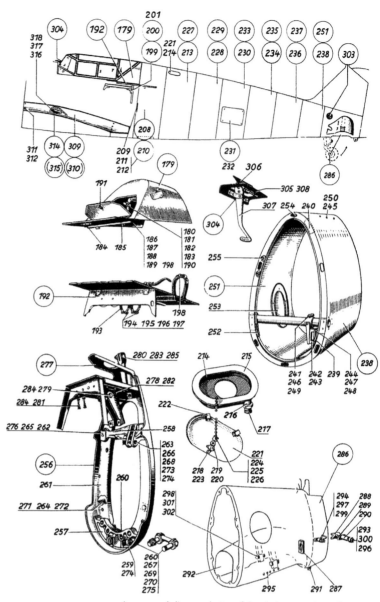

An unusual diagram but useful as it shows various elements in the fuselage of the E-series including the framework that holds the tailwheel (bottom left hand corner)

On the port fuselage side you have the access step at the wing trailing edge

(© Josef Andal)

Higher up on the dorsal spine on the port side is the repositioned fuel filler point

(© Josef Andal)

a = Außenbordanschluß
b = Fülleitung
c = Überlaufleitung
d = Entlüftungsleitung
e = Leckleitung
f = Kraftstoffvorratgeber
g = Kraftstoffbehälter
h = Hauptbehälterkopf
i = Druckausgleichsleitung
k = Nebenbehälterkopf
l = Brandhahnfilter
m = Brandhahnfilterpumpe
n = Anschlüsse an Kraftstofffförderpumpe
o = Rücklaufleitung von Einspritzpumpe
p = Anlaßpumpe (Einspritzpumpe)
q = Kraftstoffdruckmesser
r = Einspritzleitung
s = Kraftstoffdruck-Meßleitung
t = Entnahmeleitung vom Hauptbehälterkopf
u = Einspritzbehälter
v = Entnahmeleitung vom Nebenbehälterkopf
w = Entnahmeleitungen von den Filterbrandhahn-Armaturen

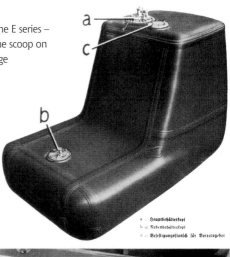

The fuselage fuel tank for the E series – the pipe 'e' lines up with the scoop on the underside of the fuselage

a = Hauptbehälterkopf
b = Nebenbehälterkopf
c = Befestigungsflansch für Vorratgeber

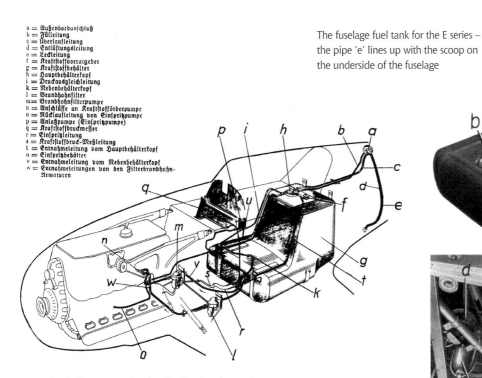

a = FB-Armatur b = FBH-Armatur c = Verbindungswelle der Brandhahnventile
d = Signalhorn e = Kühlluftschacht

Here is the fuel system, as fitted to the E-series, the previous versions are very similar

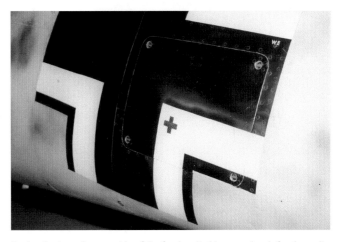

On the starboard side, behind the cockpit on the E-series are these two access points, the larger is for oxygen charging, whilst the smaller red one is for connection of a ground power unit
(© Author)

Further back on the port side of the fuselage is this access hatch for the radio equipment and first aid kit
(© Author)

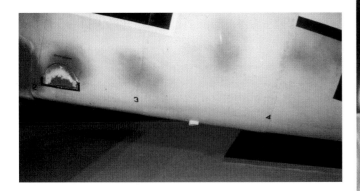

Between frames 3 and 4 on the lower edge of the port side is this drain outlet, it is for the batteries in the radio compartment aft of it
(© Author)

Just aft of the canopy on the port side is this handhold
(© Josef Andal)

Engine, Radiator, Cowls & Propeller

Bf 109B

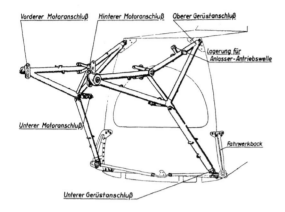

The engine bearers for the B-series

Nice shot by the Russians examining the Jumo taken out of the B-1 captured in Spain

Lovely shot of a restored Jumo 210

(© P. Skulski)

The shot of the captured B in Russia gives you an idea of how all the cowl elements fit, as well as showing why the area around the radiator was often painted black (it discoloured quickly)

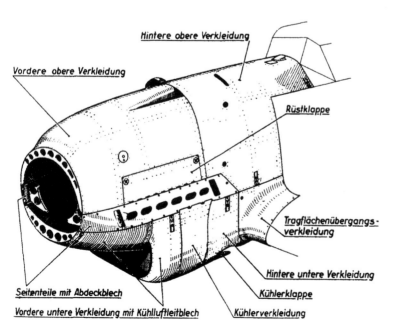

The engine cowls for the B-series

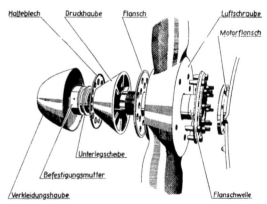

The propeller boss assembly for the B-series

The big two-blade wooden propeller of the B-1

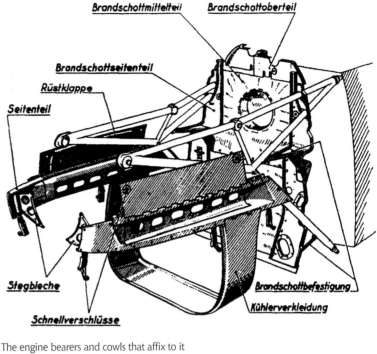

The engine bearers and cowls that affix to it

The front of the B-series, with the coolant header tank visible, as well as the very top of the radiator

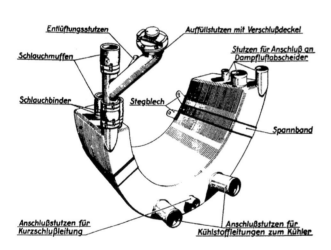

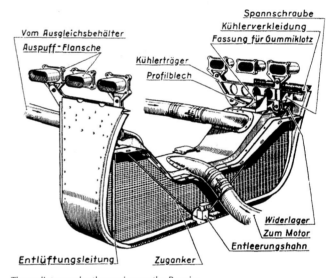

The radiator under the engine on the B-series

The coolant header tank on the B-series was unique to the type

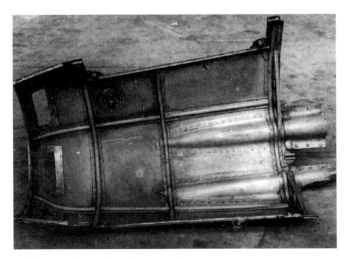

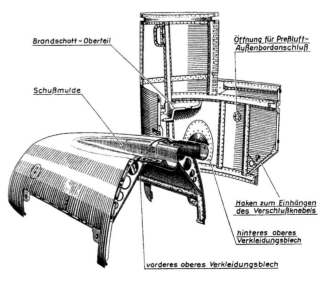

Inside the engine cowl on the captured B-1

This diagram shows the two upper cowls of the B-series

Bf 109C & D

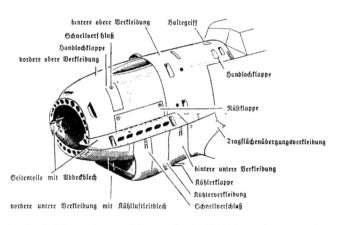

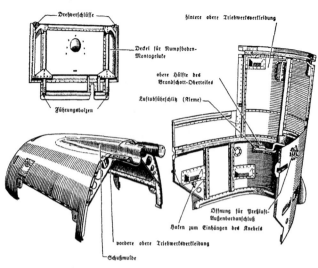

Details of all the cowls around the nose for the Bf 109C-1 and D-1, note the additional access panels etc. in comparison with the B-series

The engine cowls for the Bf 109C-1 and D-1

Bf 109E

The starboard side of the DB 600 engine
(© P. Skulski)

All the ancillary equipment at the back of the DB 600
(© P. Skulski)

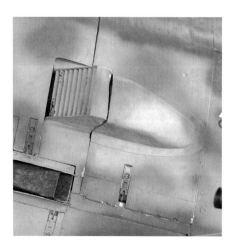

The supercharger intake is fitted on the port side of the engine cowl
(© George Papadimitriou)

With the supercharger intake on the port side, on the starboard it just has air vents from the engine bay and the access for the starter handle
(© George Papadimitriou)

The coolant header tank is much larger on the E-series

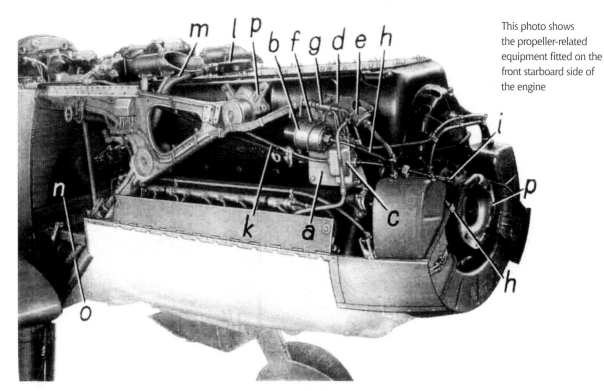

This photo shows the propeller-related equipment fitted on the front starboard side of the engine

a = Lagerblech
d = Befestigungsſchild für Ausgleichsventil
g = Schußrohr für Elt-Leitungen
k = biegſame Welle für Stellungsanzeiger
m = Entlüftungsrohr für Kurbelgehäuſe
p = rechte vordere Lagerbraße

b = Verſtellmotor
e = Druckausgleichsventil
h = biegſame Welle für Luftſchrauben
     Verſtellgetriebe
n = Entlüftungsrohrleitung

c = Endbegrenzungsſchalter
f = Befeſtigungsſchelle für Verſtellmotor
i = biegſame Welle für Endbegrenzungsſchalter
l = Kurbelgehäuſe-Entlüftungsſtußen
o = Befeſtigungsſchelle

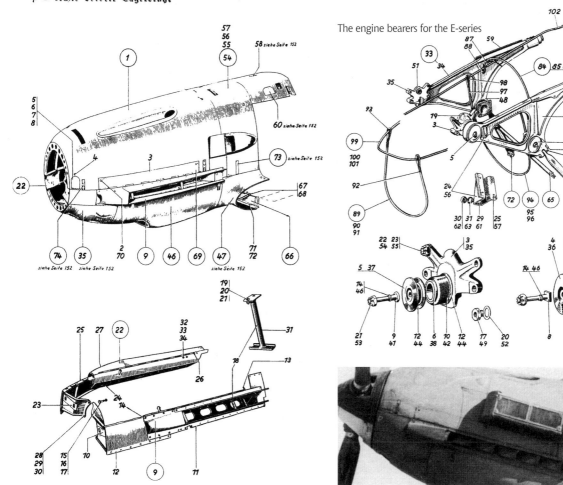

The engine bearers for the E-series

This diagram shows the engine cowls and exhaust surrounds for the E-series

The tropical versions of the E-series all used this dust screen on the supercharger intake

Here you can see the access panel above the exhausts open
(© Josef Andal)

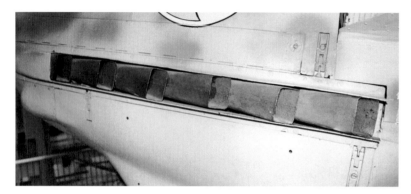

The exhaust stacks are oblong in cross-section
(© Josef Andal)

The front profile of the cowling is distinctive, as are bulges for the scavenger pumps on either side of the nose
(© George Papadimitriou)

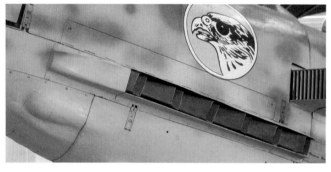

The exhaust stacks on the E, above which that long access panel allows you to reach the spark plugs
(© George Papadimitriou)

Here is an exhaust stack on its own, to show you the overall shape

The supercharger intake on the T-series was a completely different shape

The Swiss E-series machine had revised cowls due to the fitment of MG29 guns
(©George Papadimitriou)

The big three-blade propeller of the E-series, complete with hole in the hub centre for the motor-cannon

A closer look at the hub and blade root detail on the Swiss E-3
(© George Papadimitriou)

Swiss Bf 109E J-399 fitted with the Escher-Wyss propeller and pointed spinner, this was the last E-series built in Switzerland

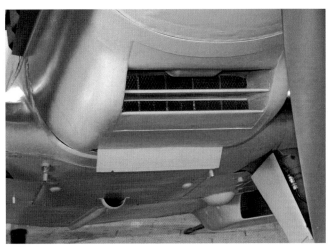

The chin intake on the BofB E-4/b lacks the crosswise bar, probably due to damage over the years rather than anything else
(© Author)

A detailed look into the intake for the chin radiator on the Swiss E-3
(© George Papadimitriou)

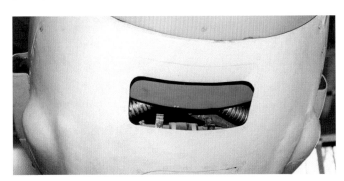

The coolant header tank can be seen through the vent under the chin cowl
(© Josef Andal)

The area just aft of the gun port on all MG17-armed machines had this distinctive double bulge, it was removed on the Swiss machines
(© George Papadimitriou)

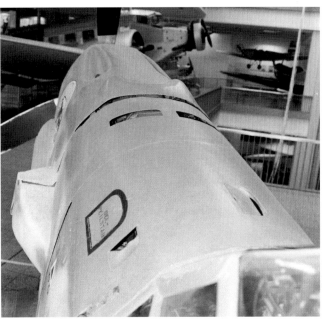

A quick look at the vents etc. in the upper cowling on the Munich example
(© Josef Andal)

Oil, Fuel and Coolant Systems

Bf 109B

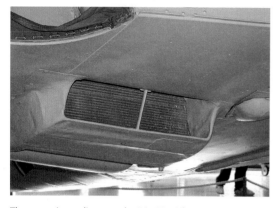

The port wing radiator on the E in Munich
(© George Papadimitriou)

The E-7 and E-8 series had an oil booster system that resulted in the fitment of this extra tank on the front, port side of the engine

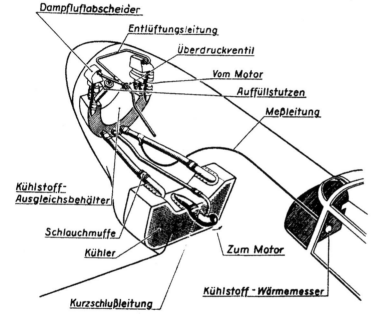

This is the coolant system for the B-series

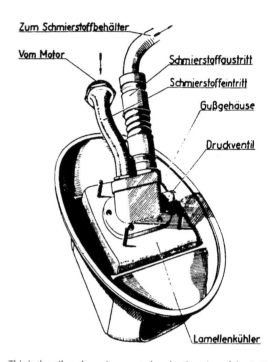

This is the oil cooler unit mounted under the wing of the B, C & D series

The booster system of the E-7 and E-8 series meant it carried extra oil in a standard 300lt drop tank

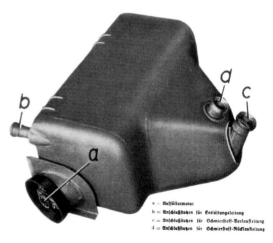

The oil tank for the E-series

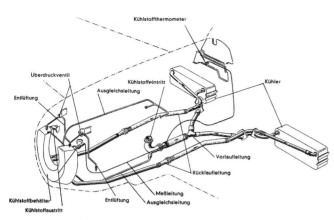

The coolant system on the E-series is a little larger, hence the two radiators under the wing

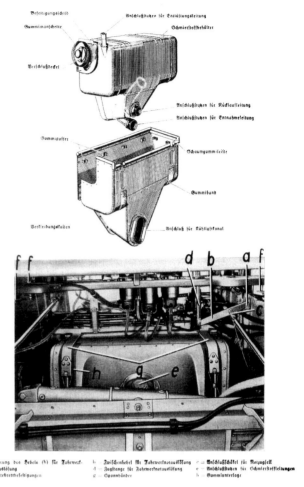

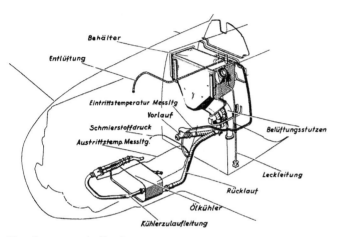

The oil system on the E-series

The oil tank installation in the E-series, this is below the cowl gun breeches

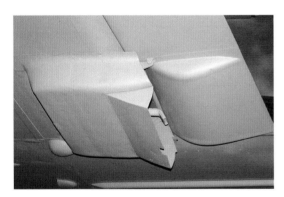

This view from the back of the port radiator shows the bulge on the flaps and the vent tube that projects out the back
(© George Papadimitriou)

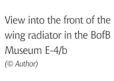 View into the front of the wing radiator in the BofB Museum E-4/b
(© Author)

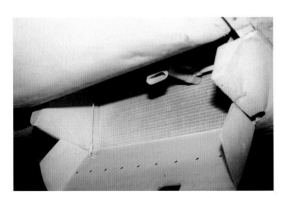

The back of the wing radiator in the BofB Museum E-4/b
(© Author)

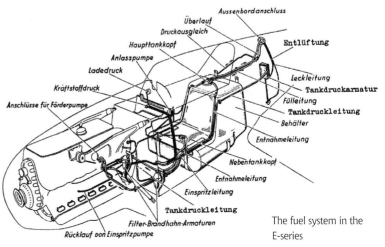

The fuel system in the E-series

Wings & Flight Controls

Bf 109B

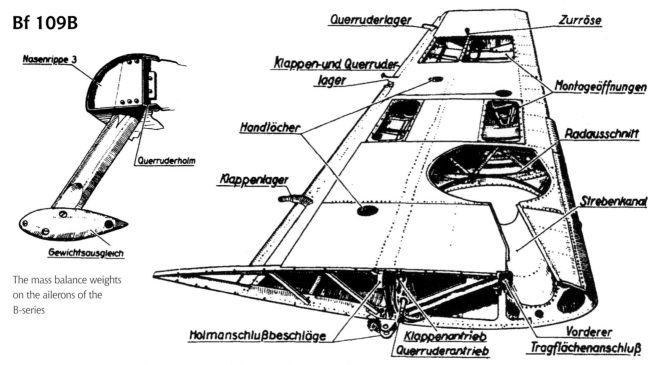

The mass balance weights on the ailerons of the B-series

The wing structure and skinning on the underside for the B-series

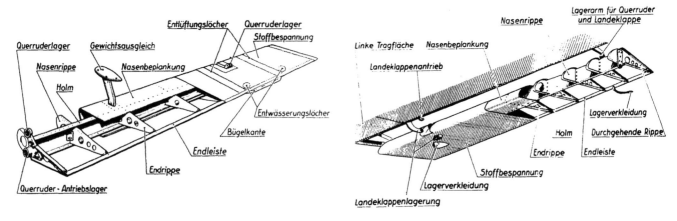

Aileron construction for the B-series

Flap construction for the B-series

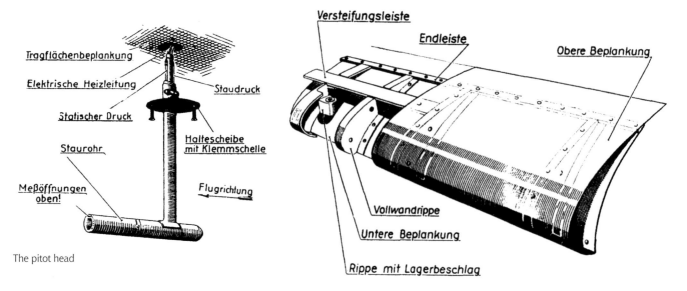

The pitot head

The leading-edge slats of the B-series

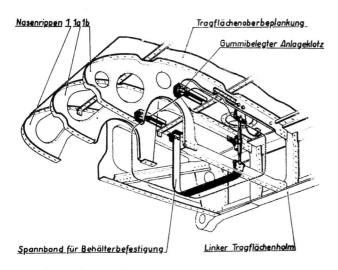

Nasenrippen 1, 1a 1b
Tragflächenoberbeplankung
Gummibelegter Anlageklotz
Spannband für Behälterbefestigung
Linker Tragflächenholm

The bay for the oil tank in the wing

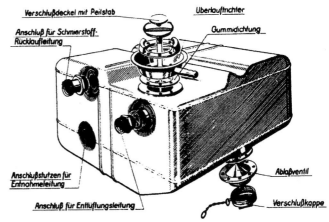

Verschlußdeckel mit Peilstab
Überlaufrichter
Anschluß für Schmierstoff-Rücklaufleitung
Gummidichtung
Anschlußstutzen für Entnahmeleitung
Anschluß für Enttüftlungsleitung
Ablaßventil
Verschlußkappe

The oil tank that goes into the wing

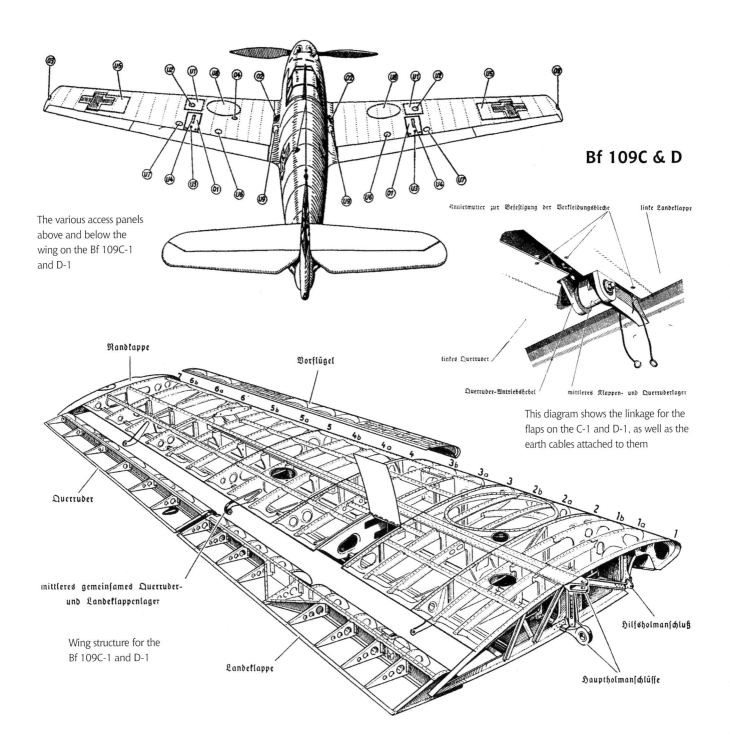

The various access panels above and below the wing on the Bf 109C-1 and D-1

Bf 109C & D

Annietmutter zur Befestigung der Verkleidungsbleche
linke Landeklappe
linkes Querruder
Querruder-Antriebshebel
mittleres Klappen- und Querruderlager

This diagram shows the linkage for the flaps on the C-1 and D-1, as well as the earth cables attached to them

Randklappe
Vorflügel
Querruder
mittleres gemeinsames Querruder- und Landeklappenlager
Landeklappe
Hilfsholmanschluß
Hauptholmanschlüsse

Wing structure for the Bf 109C-1 and D-1

Bf 109E

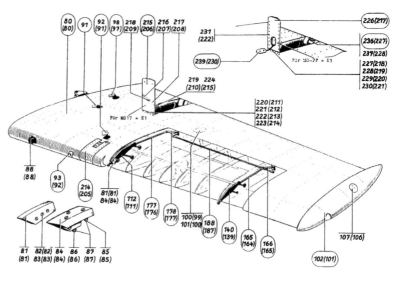

Some of the access panels under the wing of the E-3 opened
(© Josef Andal)

The upper surface of the wing for the E-1 and E-3, including access panels

Flap construction [starboard]

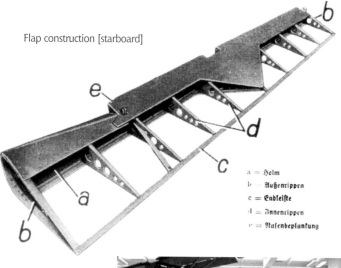

a = Holm
b = Außenrippen
c = Endleiste
d = Innenrippen
e = Nasenbeplankung

The shape of the wing tip lights does not seem to match, this is the port wing tip of the Munich example (see starboard wingtip image on opposite page)
(© George Papadimitriou)

The underside view of the E-3 in Munich showing the linkage for the aileron and the mass balance
(© George Papadimitriou)

Fester Einbau: Austauschfläche

1 Preßluft-Außenbordanschluß
2 Preßluftflasche für linkes Rumpf-MG 17
3 Preßluftflasche für linke Flächenwaffe
4 Füllleitung zum rechten Flaschenpaar
5 Betriebsleitung zum linken Rumpf-MG 17
6 Betriebsleitung zur linken Flächenwaffe
7 Montagetrennstelle
8 Preßluftanschluß an Rippe 3 für Flächenwaffe
9 Verteilerstecdose an Rippe 1
10 Elt. Zuleitung vom SVK
11 ESK-Leitung

12 Blindsockel mit ESK-Winkelstecker
13 Leitung mit Winkelstecker zum FVK 17-FF
14 Flächenverteilerkasten FVK 17-FF
15 Leitung zur Verteilerstecdose bei Rippe 3
16 Verteilerstecdose für ZVKS -FF-Anschluß
17 Rohr für Ziellinienprüfer
18 Abspeerventil der Preßluftflasche
19 Verschlußdecel für MG 17-Ausschußöffnung
20 Bedienungsklappe für Flächen-MG 17 mit Schnellverschlüssen
21 Abdecblech zwischen Rippe 3 und 3b (unten), aufschraubbar
22 EPD-Leitung, blind gehalten
23 Lagerbock für MG-FF

Zusätzlicher Einbau: Flächen-MG 17

24 Große Gurtrolle
25 Innerer unterer Gurtschacht
26 Innerer oberer Gurtschacht
27 Vordere Lafette
28 Hintere Lafette
29 Äußerer oberer Gurtschacht
30 Äußerer unterer Gurtschacht
31 Kleine Gurtrolle

32 Befestigungsprofil
33 Schußkanal
34 Vordere Lagerung 17
35 Hintere Lagerung 17
36 Linkes Flächen-MG 17 mit EPAD 17 und ESi 17 und Preßluftschlauch

Wing structure for the E-1

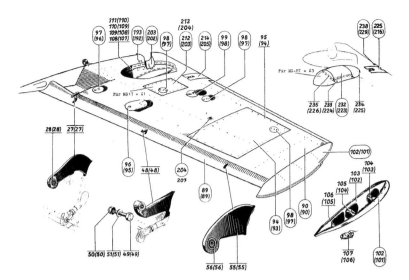

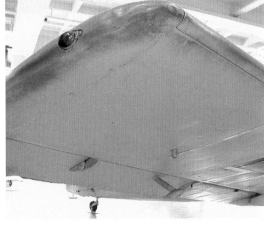

This is the starboard wing tip of the Munich example
(© George Papadimitriou)

The lower surface of the wing for the E-1 and E-3, including access panels

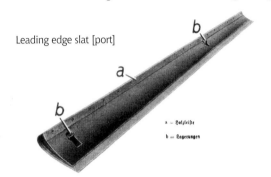

Leading edge slat [port]

a = Holzleiste

b = Lagerungen

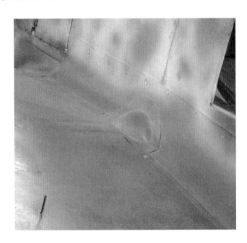

A closer look at the spar pick-up bulge on the port wing root of the Munich example, the red post is the undercarriage lock-down visual indicator
(© George Papadimitriou)

The starboard wing root of the E-4/b at Hendon, the fillet and bulge over the spar pick-ups are evident
(© Author)

Aileron construction [port]

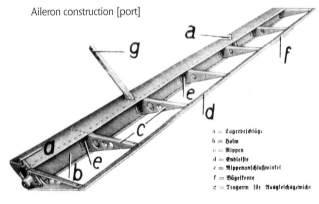

a = Lagerbeschläge
b = Holm
c = Rippen
d = Endleiste
e = Rippenanschlußwinkel
f = Bügelkante
g = Tragarm für Ausgleichsgewicht

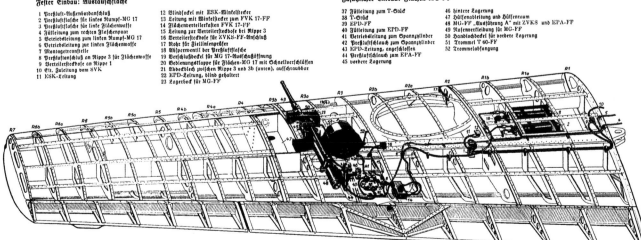

Fester Einbau: Austauschfläche

1 Preßluft-Außenbordanschluß
2 Preßluftfläche für linkes Rumpf-MG 17
3 Preßluftfläche für linke Flächenwaffe
4 Füllleitung zum rechten Flächenwaffenpaar
5 Betriebsleitung zum linken Rumpf-MG 17
6 Betriebsleitung zur linken Flächenwaffe
7 Montagetrennstelle
8 Preßluftanschluß an Rippe 3 für Flächenwaffe
9 Verteilersteckdose an Rippe 1
10 elt. Zuleitung vom SVK
11 ESK-Leitung
12 Blindsockel mit ESK-Winkelstecker
13 Leitung mit Winkelstecker zum FVK 17-FF
14 Flächenverteilerkasten FVK 17-FF
15 Leitung zur Verteilersteckdose bei Rippe 3
16 Verteilersteckdose für ZVKS-FF-Anschluß
17 Rohr für Ziellinienprüfer
18 Absperrventil der Preßluftfläche
19 Verschlußdeckel für MG 17-Ausschußöffnung
20 Bedienungsklappe für Flächen-MG 17 mit Schnellverschlüssen
21 Abdeckblech zwischen Rippe 3 und 3b (unten), aufschraubbar
22 EPD-Leitung, blind gehalten
23 Lagerbock für MG-FF

Zusätzlicher Einbau: Flächen-MG-FF

37 Füllleitung zum T-Stück
38 T-Stück
39 EPD-FF
40 Füllleitung zum EPD-FF
41 Betriebsleitung zum Spannzylinder
42 Preßluftschlauch zum Spannzylinder
43 EPD-Leitung, angeschlossen
44 Preßluftschlauch zum EPA-FF
45 vordere Lagerung
46 hintere Lagerung
47 Hülsenableitung und Hülsenraum
48 MG-FF „Ausführung A" mit ZVKS und EPA-FF
49 Nasenverkleidung für MG-FF
50 Handlochdeckel für vordere Lagerung
51 Trommel T 60-FF
52 Trommelabfangung

Wing structure for the E-3

Tail

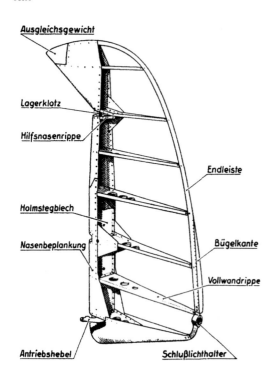

Diagram showing the construction of the rudder of the B-1

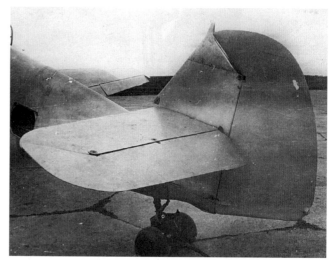

Tail, rudder and tailplane construction for the Bf 109C and D-series

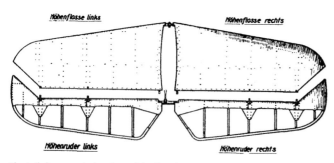

The tailplanes and elevators of the B-series

A photo showing the tail of the B-1 captured in Spain and evaluated in Russia

Overall view of the tail on the E-3 at Munich
(© George Papadimitriou)

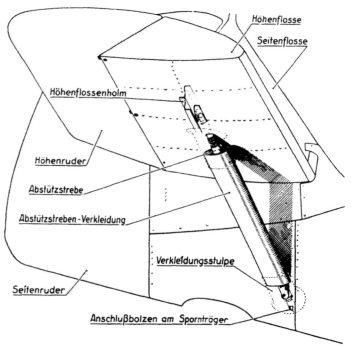

The tailplane support struts for the B-series

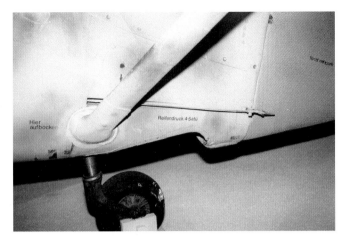

The bottom tail strut mounts, along with the rudder control cables on the tail of the E-4/b at Hendon
(© Author)

Here you can see the rudder actuating horns and control cables, as well as the tail light
(© George Papadimitriou)

In this overall shot of the tailplane on the Swiss E-3, you can see the ribs on the elevator, plus the fixed trim tab and the difference in the texture of the tailplane skinning
(© George Papadimitriou)

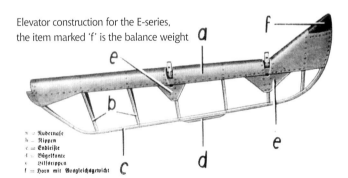

Elevator construction for the E-series, the item marked 'f' is the balance weight

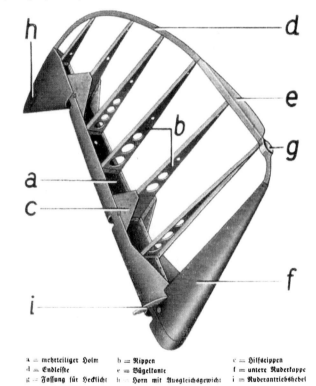

Rudder construction for the E-series

A close-up of the hole in the vertical fin, through which you can see the jack for the tailplane trim mechanism
(© Author)

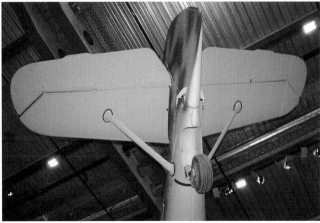

Useful view up under the tail of the example at Berlin, of note is the liner within the tailwheel well
(© P. Skulski)

Undercarriage

Bf 109B

Taken from the Russian test report on the B-1 they evaluated after capture in Spain, this image gives an overall view of the B-series undercarriage

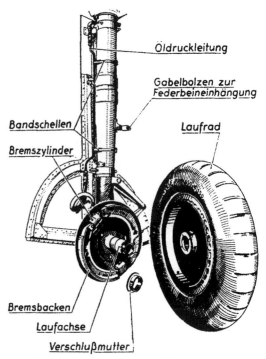

Main wheel, hub, oleo and door detail for the B-series

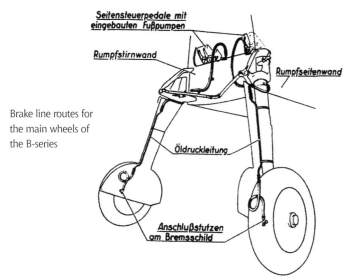

Brake line routes for the main wheels of the B-series

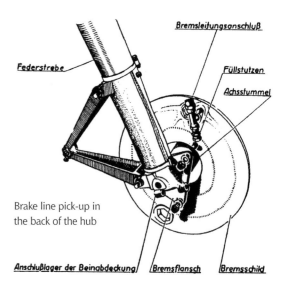

Brake line pick-up in the back of the hub

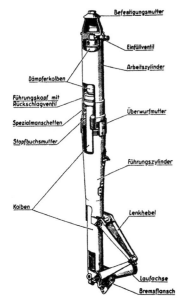

Main oleo construction for the B-series

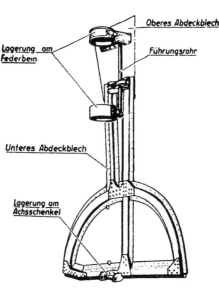

Detail inside the undercarriage door on the B-series

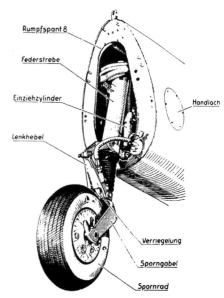

The tailwheel assembly in the B-series

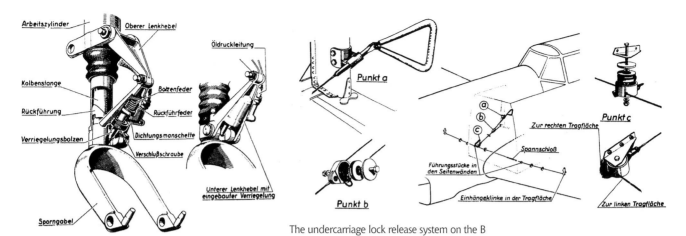

The yoke for the tailwheel on the B-series

The undercarriage lock release system on the B

Bf 109C & D

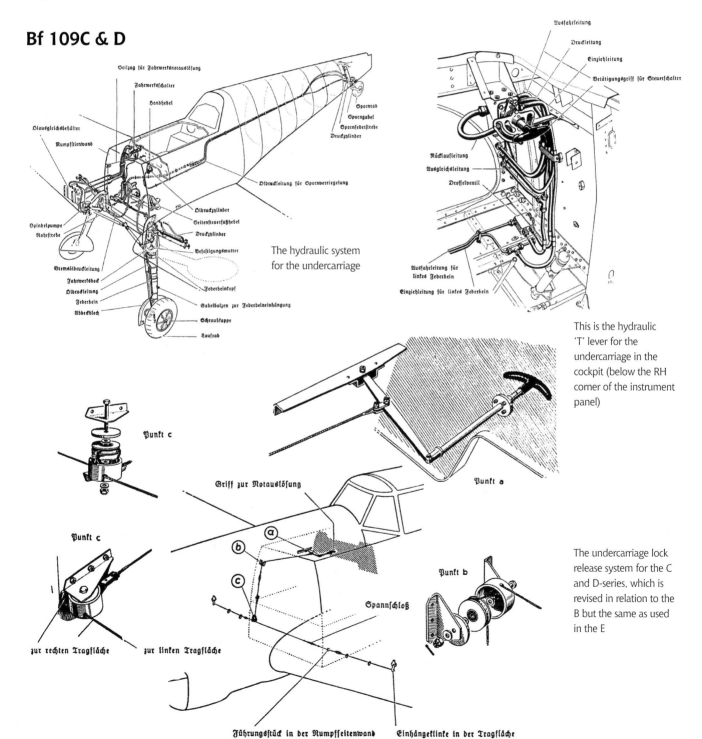

The hydraulic system for the undercarriage

This is the hydraulic 'T' lever for the undercarriage in the cockpit (below the RH corner of the instrument panel)

The undercarriage lock release system for the C and D-series, which is revised in relation to the B but the same as used in the E

Bf 109E

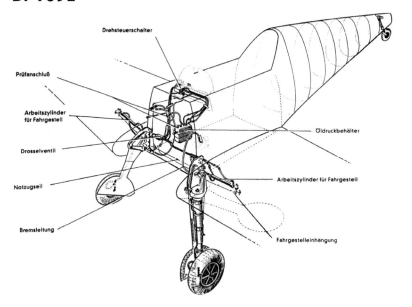

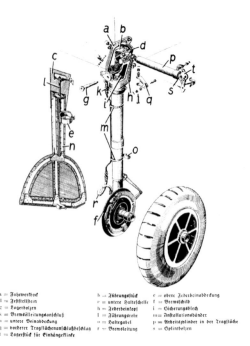

Hydraulic system for the E-series, note the lack of anything for the tailwheel, which was fixed

Main wheel, hub, oleo and door detail for the E-series

Main wheel tyre and hub detail of the example at Berlin
(©George Papadimitriou)

The wheel wells in the B, C, D & E series all had these canvas liners, that zipped shut but which is seen partially open here
(© George Papadimitriou)

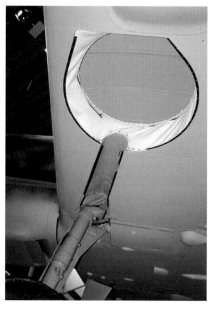

Although a bit bright due to their new nature, this shot of the bays in the E-3 at Berlin are accurate
(© George Papadimitriou)

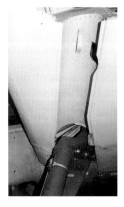

The oleo leg sits within a bay in the inner section of the wheel well
(© Josef Andal)

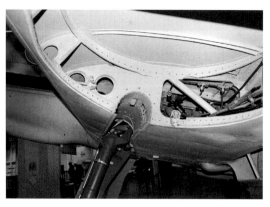

With no canvas liner the interior of the wing structure can be seen
(© Josef Andal)

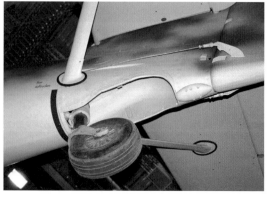

There was a bay still inside the rear fuselage, even though the tailwheel did not retract
(© P. Skulski)

Armament, Ordnance & Drop Tanks

Bf 109B

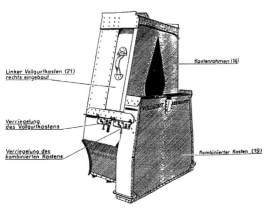

The containers for the ammunition and spent cartridges

This shot of the example evaluated in Russia shows the cowl guns of the B-series

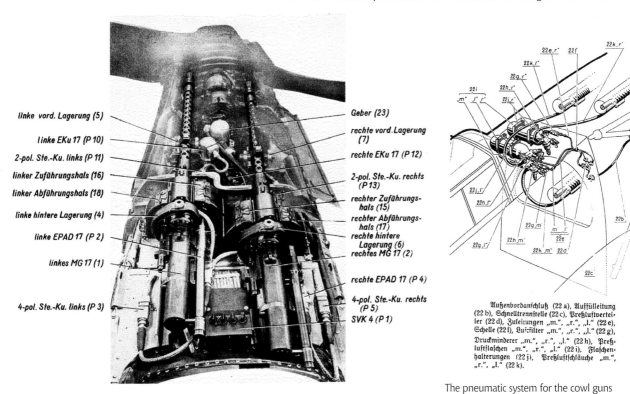

linke vord. Lagerung (5)
linke EKu 17 (P 10)
2-pol. Ste.-Ku. links (P 11)
linker Zuführungshals (16)
linker Abführungshals (18)
linke hintere Lagerung (4)
linke EPAD 17 (P 2)
linkes MG 17 (1)
4-pol. Ste.-Ku. links (P 3)

Geber (23)
rechte vord.Lagerung (7)
rechte EKu 17 (P 12)
2-pol. Ste.-Ku. rechts (P 13)
rechter Zuführungshals (15)
rechter Abführungshals (17)
rechte hintere Lagerung (6)
rechtes MG 17 (2)
rechte EPAD 17 (P 4)
4-pol. Ste.-Ku. rechts (P 5)
SVK 4 (P 1)

This diagram from the manual shows the cowl guns of the B-series

Außenbordanschluß (22 a), Auffülleitung (22 b), Schnelltrennstelle (22 c), Preßluftverteiler (22 d), Zuleitungen „m.", „r.", „l." (22 e), Schelle (22 f), Luftfilter „m.", „r.", „l." (22 g), Druckminderer „m.", „r.", „l." (22 h), Preßluftflaschen „m.", „r.", „l." (22 i), Flaschenhalterungen (22 j), Preßluftschläuche „m.", „r.", „l." (22 k).

The pneumatic system for the cowl guns

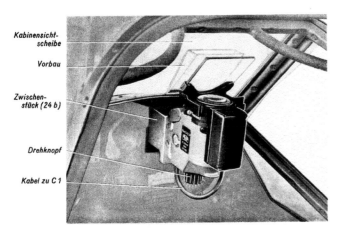

Kabinensichtscheibe
Vorbau
Zwischenstück (24 b)
Drehknopf
Kabel zu C 1

The B-series initially had the Revi C/12-B gunsight

vorschaltbares Farbglas
Führung des Farbglases
Schalthebel für das Farbglas
Drehknopf

Later the C/12-B gunsight was replaced by the C/12-C version

Bf 109C & D

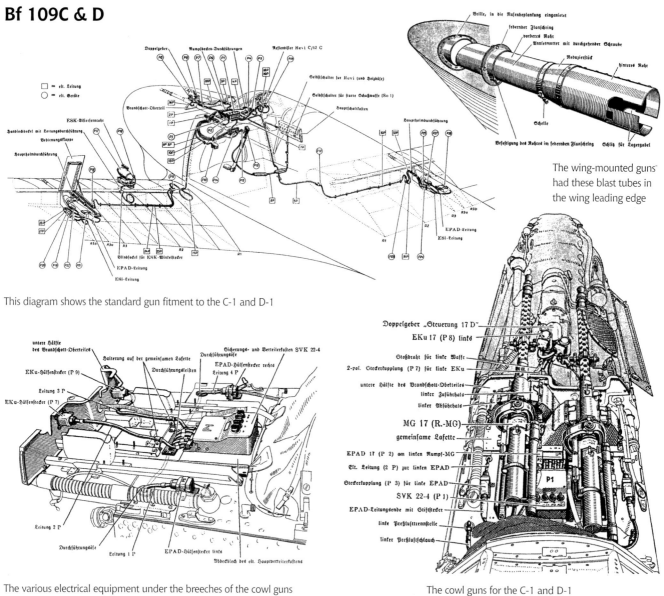

The wing-mounted guns had these blast tubes in the wing leading edge

This diagram shows the standard gun fitment to the C-1 and D-1

The various electrical equipment under the breeches of the cowl guns

The cowl guns for the C-1 and D-1

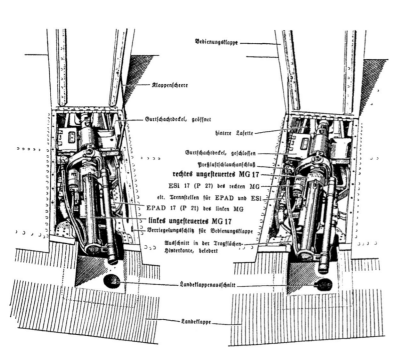

The wing-mounted MG17s of the C-1 and D-1

The ammo boxes for the cowl guns were loaded from underneath

Bf 109E

This colour shot of AE479 in the USA does show how the cowl and motor-cannon were mounted

Each cowl gun had this blast tube secured to the end

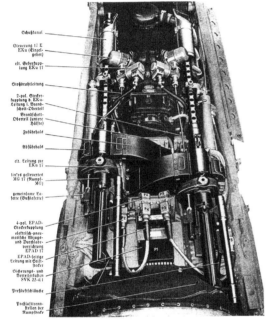

The cowl gun installation for the E-series

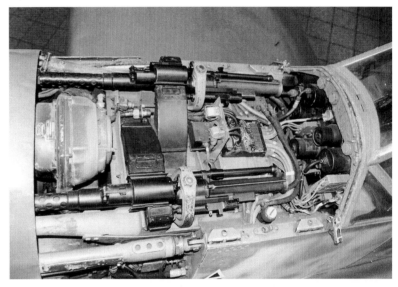

above: These are the cowl guns in the E-3 in Munich
(© Josef Andal)

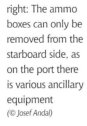

right: The ammo boxes can only be removed from the starboard side, as on the port there is various ancillary equipment
(© Josef Andal)

left Here you have the ammo boxes on the Munich machine, the forward one has been removed
(© Josef Andal)

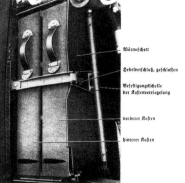

The ammo boxes were loaded from the starboard side

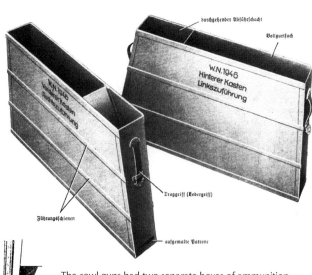

The cowl guns had two separate boxes of ammunition

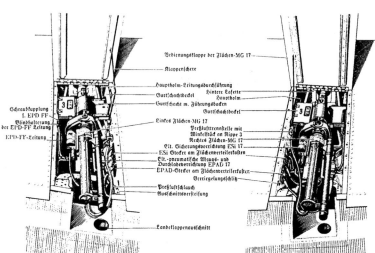

These are the MG17 wing bays for the E-1 series

Here is the barrel of the wing-mounted MG FF exposed with the access cover removed
(© Josef Andal)

Here is the ammo drum, with the access hatch off, in the starboard wing of the example at Munich
(© Josef Andal)

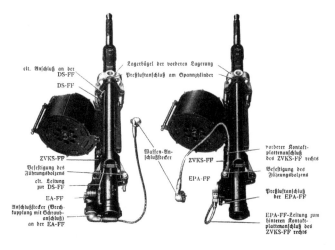

The E-3 and above could carry the MG FF 20mm cannon in the wing, this diagram shows the type versions ('A' and 'B') that could be used in the starboard wing

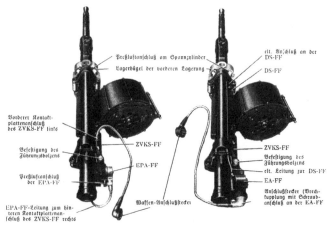

This shows the 'A' and 'B' versions of the MG FF that could be used in the port wing

The MG29 cowl guns were much more compact than the MG17, so this is why the cowls were revised

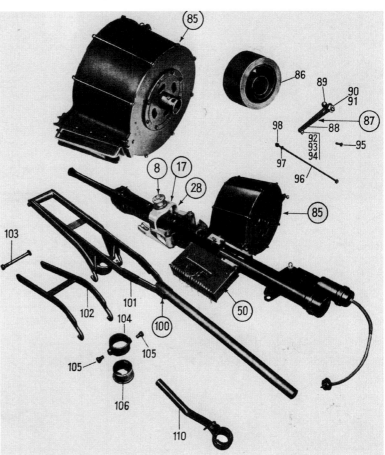

In the wings, the Swiss Bf 109Es used the MG FF-K with 60-round ammunitions drums

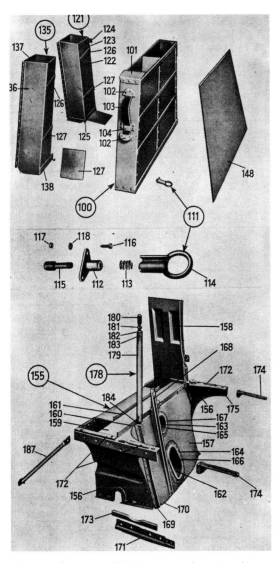

The Swiss Bf 109Es used MG29 guns over the engine, this resulted in different ammunition boxes, holding 480 rounds per gun

The oval access panel on the wing underside, aft of the ammunition drum access panel exposed the rear of the MG FF

(© Josef Andal)

Here you can see the bulge that clears the ammunition drum of the wing-mounted MG FF. The covered (round) hole inboard of the barrel is where the MG 17 barrel was on the earlier machines

(© George Papadimitriou)

Here is the revised cowl shape of the Swiss Bf 109Es, note the lack of the distinctive double bulge on top seen on all Luftwaffe machines

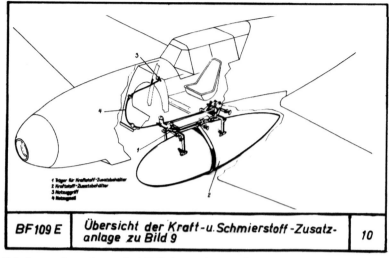

BF 109 E Übersicht der Kraft-u. Schmierstoff-Zusatz-anlage zu Bild 9 10

This diagram shows the standard 300lt drop tank system for additional fuel

The pick-ups for the ETC rack ('c'), plus the fuel pipework ('a' and 'b') and strap ('d') and release mechanism ('e') for the drop tank

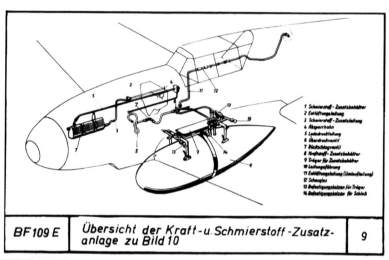

BF 109 E Übersicht der Kraft-u. Schmierstoff-Zusatz-anlage zu Bild 10 9

This diagram shows how the 300lt drop tank was used to carry oil for the booster system used in the E-7 and E-8

Here are the cowl gun troughs, with that distinctive double bulge on the back cowl

(© George Papadimitriou)

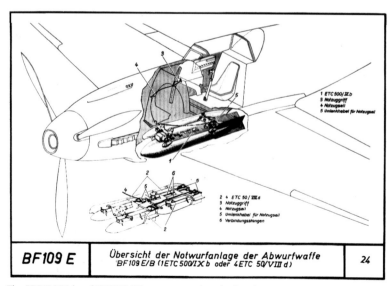

BF 109 E Übersicht der Notwurfanlage der Abwurfwaffe BF 109 E/B (1ETC 500/IXb oder 4ETC 50/VIIId) 24

The ETC50/VIIId and ETC500 IXb systems used on the E-series

BF 109 E Angebauter Bombenträger 4x ETC 50 BF 109 E/B 26

The ETC 50 used on the fighter-bomber versions of the Bf 109E

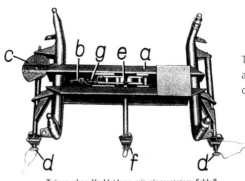

This is the standard rack and cover used when carrying a drop tank

Träger ohne Verkleidung mit eingesetztem Schloß
a Träger   b Notzughebel   c Führungsrolle für Notzugseil   d Befestigungsbolzen
e Schloß   f Befestigungsbolzen für Schloß   g Auslösebolzen für Notzughebel

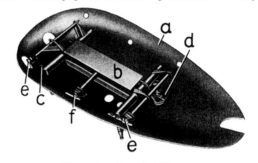

Träger mit angebauter Verkleidung
a Verkleidung   b Träger   c Befestigungsschrauben für Verkleidung   d Führungsrolle
für Notzugseil   e Befestigungsbolzen für Träger   f Befestigungsbolzen für Schloß

The ETC 500 IXb rack under an E-7/b

The E could also carry this special rack and 96 of the SD-2 butterfly anti-personnel bombs

An E-7/b of III./JJG27 with a 250kg bomb on an ETC500 IXb rack

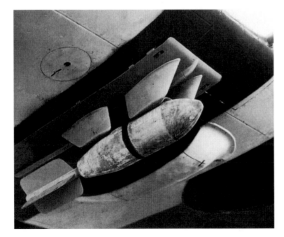

The Swiss bomb rack was fitted to a plate that mounted on to the wing. Here is carries a single 12kg practice (concrete) bomb with the tip painted dark green

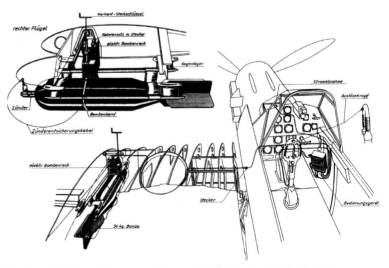

The Swiss Bf 109Es had their own unique system of wing-mounted bomb racks

Electrical & Radio Systems

Bf 109B

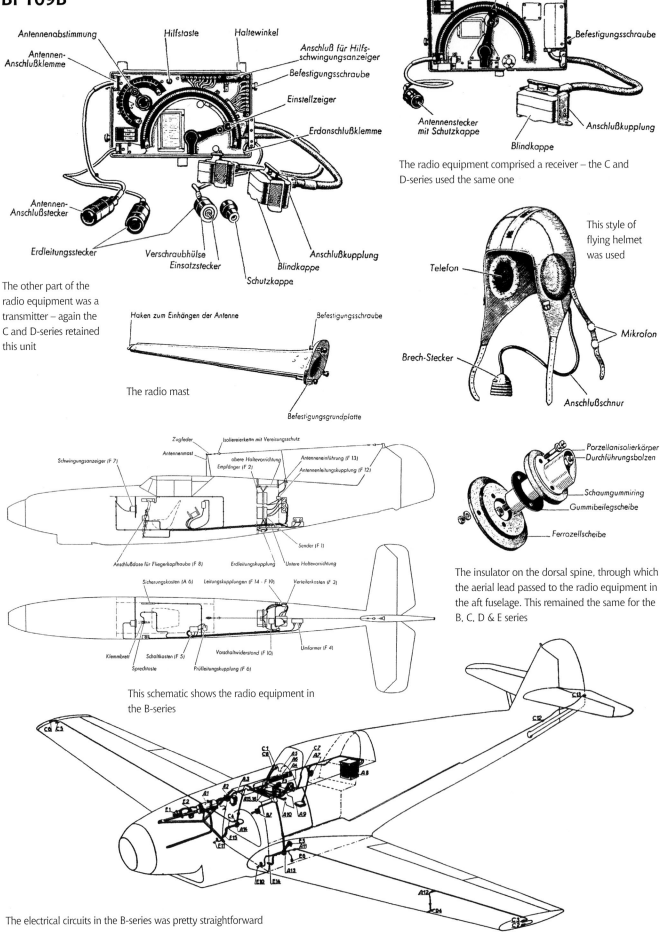

Antennenabstimmung
Hilfstaste
Haltewinkel
Antennen-Anschlußklemme
Anschluß für Hilfsschwingungsanzeiger
Befestigungsschraube
Einstellzeiger
Erdanschlußklemme
Antennen-Anschlußstecker
Erdleitungsstecker
Verschraubhülse
Einsatzstecker
Schutzkappe
Blindkappe
Anschlußkupplung

The other part of the radio equipment was a transmitter – again the C and D-series retained this unit

Einstellzeiger
Haltewinkel
Befestigungsschraube
Antennenstecker mit Schutzkappe
Blindkappe
Anschlußkupplung

The radio equipment comprised a receiver – the C and D-series used the same one

Haken zum Einhängen der Antenne
Befestigungsschraube
Befestigungsgrundplatte

The radio mast

Telefon
Mikrofon
Brech-Stecker
Anschlußschnur

This style of flying helmet was used

Zugfeder
Isoliereierketten mit Vereisungsschutz
Antennenmast
obere Haltevorrichtung
Schwingungsanzeiger (F 7)
Empfänger (F 2)
Antenneneinführung (F 13)
Antennenleitungskupplung (F 12)
Anschlußdose für Fliegerkopfhaube (F 8)
Erdleitungskupplung
Sender (F 1)
Untere Haltevorrichtung

Sicherungskasten (A 6)
Leitungskupplungen (F 14 - F 19)
Verteilerkasten (F 3)
Klemmbrett
Schaltkasten (F 5)
Sprechtaste
Vorschaltwiderstand (F 10)
Prüfleitungskupplung (F 6)
Umformer (F 4)

This schematic shows the radio equipment in the B-series

Porzellanisolierkörper
Durchführungsbolzen
Schaumgummiring
Gummibeilegscheibe
Ferrozellscheibe

The insulator on the dorsal spine, through which the aerial lead passed to the radio equipment in the aft fuselage. This remained the same for the B, C, D & E series

The electrical circuits in the B-series was pretty straightforward

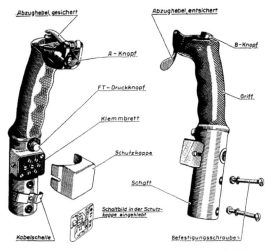

With no wing or motor-cannon, the early machines had the transmitter 'talk' button on the control column

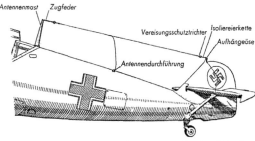

Just a single lead was needed from mast to the tip of the fin, the C & D series were the same

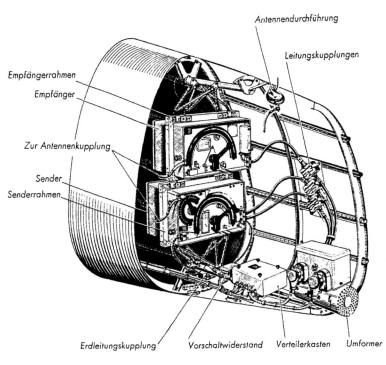

All the radio equipment was mounted in the rear fuselage like this, the C and D-series retained this system

Bf 109C & D

A schematic of the radio and electrical systems in the Bf 109C and D-series

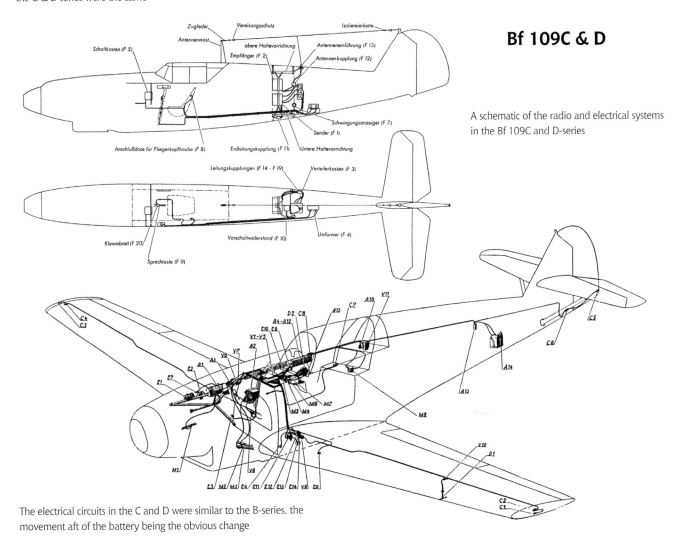

The electrical circuits in the C and D were similar to the B-series, the movement aft of the battery being the obvious change

Bf 109E

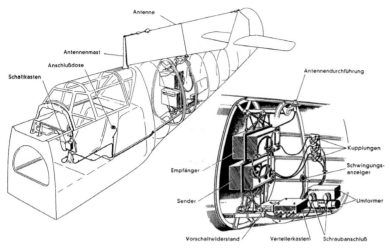

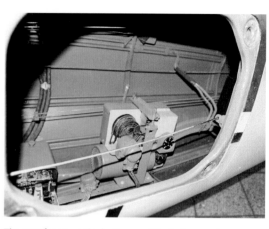

The transformer at the bottom and the battery on top (sectioned in this example) are aft of the transmitter and receiver
(© Josef Andal)

The basic radio transmitter/receiver was the same as in previous versions

The aerial mast of the E-4/b at Hendon, note the way the lead attaches to a tab in the top of the mast
(© Author)

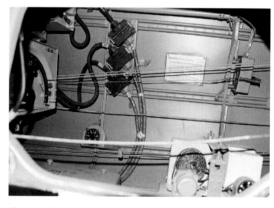

Through the access hatch on the rear, port fuselage you can see the connectors on the starboard fuselage interior
(© Josef Andal)

Here you can see the transmitter and receiver in the rear fuselage of the E at Munich
(© Josef Andal)

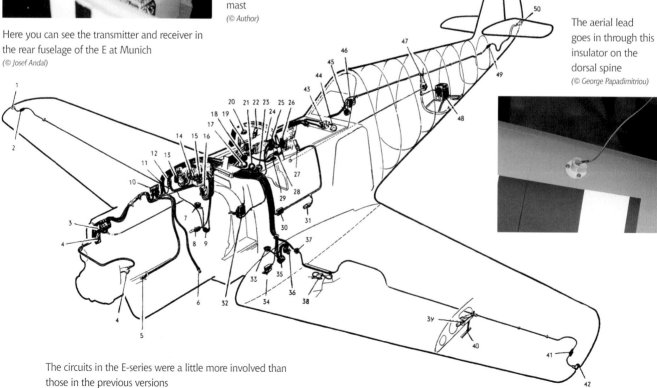

The aerial lead goes in through this insulator on the dorsal spine
(© George Papadimitriou)

The circuits in the E-series were a little more involved than those in the previous versions

Miscellaneous Equipment

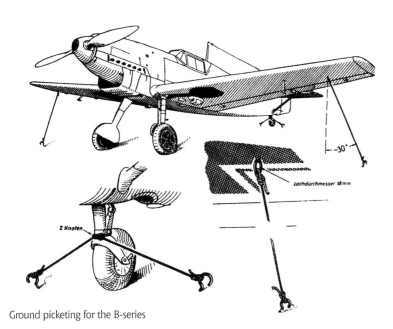

Ground picketing for the B-series

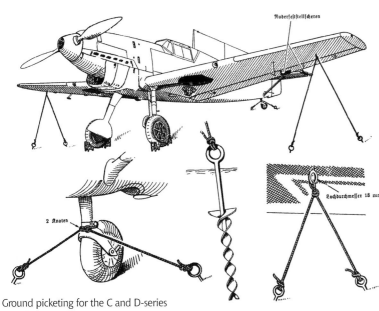

Ground picketing for the C and D-series

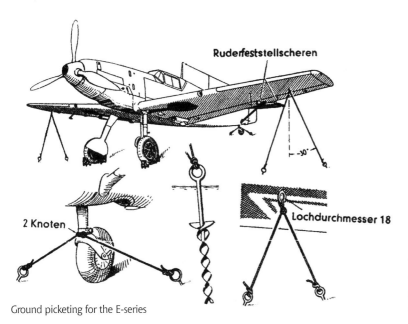

Ground picketing for the E-series

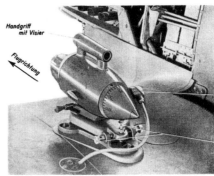

All versions from the B through to the E could have this ESK2000 camera gun installed on the port wing

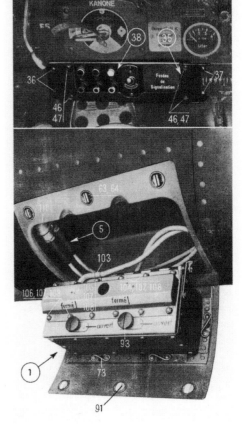

The Swiss Bf 109E had a system of signal rockets fitted into the lower rear fuselage on the starboard side, a bit like that seen on the Me 262 much later. Here you can see the unit open, as well as the control unit in the cockpit

a Handgriff für Absperrhahn b Absperrhahn c Ladedruckleitung

The GM-1 system required extra oil for the engine, so this dilution switch was added to the instrument panel

Had the Bf 109T series gone into service on board a carrier, it had to be hoped the dinghy installation would have been better that that used on the initial airframes as seen here

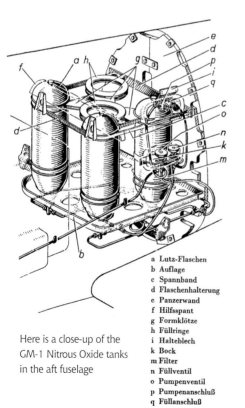

Here is a close-up of the GM-1 Nitrous Oxide tanks in the aft fuselage

a Lutz-Flaschen
b Auflage
c Spannband
d Flaschenhalterung
e Panzerwand
f Hilfsspant
g Formklötze
h Füllringe
i Halteblech
k Bock
m Filter
n Füllventil
o Pumpenventil
p Pumpenanschluß
q Füllanschluß

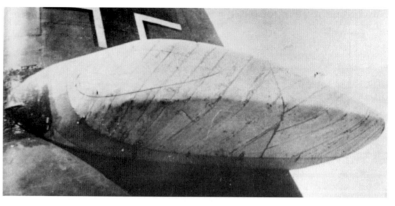

To extend the range of the Bf 109E the double-rider (Doppelreiter) system was tested, comprising fuel tanks on the upper wings housed in aerodynamic bulges

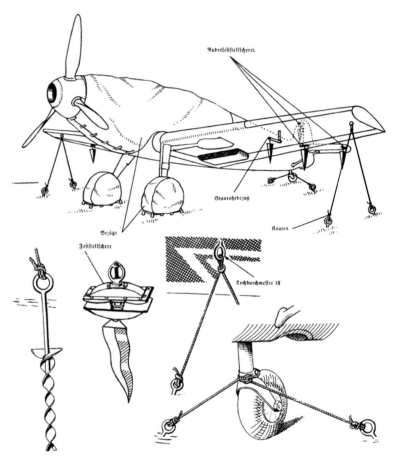

This diagram shows the various covers that could be fitted to the E-series

Here you can see the Doppelreiter tank installed on the wing of an E-series airframe for testing

Appendix: I   **Bf 109 V1 to E-9** (inc. T-series) **Kits**

Below is a list of all static scale construction kits produced to date of the early Bf 109 series. This list is as comprehensive as possible, but if there are amendments or additions, please contact the author via the Valiant Wings Publishing address shown at the front of this title.

Note: All kits are injection moulded plastic unless stated otherwise.

1/87th or smaller

- Academy-Minicraft (ex-Crown) 1/144th Bf 109E #4436 (1995)
- AHM (ex-Cox) 1/87th Bf 109E #SK-10 (mid-1970s)
- AHM (ex-Mitsuwa) 1/144th Bf 109E #K-406 (mid-1970s)
- Airfix (ex-Doyusha) 'MiniKit' 1/100th Bf 109F #A50072 (2008)
- AMG 1/144th Bf 109A #14421 (2016)
- AMG 1/144th Bf 109B 'Luftwaffe Service' #14423 (2016)
- AMG 1/144th Bf 109C 'Luftwaffe Service' #14425 (2019)
- AMG 1/144th Bf 109D 'Luftwaffe Service' #14427 (2019)
- Armory 1/144th Bf 109A/B #AR14104 (2016) – *Two kits in the box*
- Armory 1/144th Bf 109E-3/E-4 'WWII: in the beginning' #AR14303 (2019) – *Two kits in the box*
- Armory 1/144th Bf 109E-3/E-4 'Battle of Britain Aces' #AR14304 (2019) – *Two kits in the box*
- Armory 1/144th Bf 109E 'Mediterranean TO Aces' #AR14305 (2019) – *Two kits in the box*
- Armory 1/144th Bf 109E 'Foreign Service Aces Pt.1 – Spain, Switzerland, Yugoslavia & Serbia' #AR14306 (2019) – *Two kits in the box*
- Armory 1/144th Bf 109E 'Foreign Service Pt.2 – Eastern Front' #AR14307 (2020) – *Two kits in the box*
- Atlantic Giocattoli S.p.A. 1/100th Bf 109E #458 (1970s-80s) – *Poor quality, made of rubber-like plastic*
- Cornerstone Models 1/87th Bf 109E #N/K
- Eldon 1/100th Bf 109E #021 (1968)
- Eko 1/150th Bf 109 #5003 (1978) – *Probably a copy of the Busch kit?*
- F-Toys 1/144th Bf 109E #FT60104 (2011) – *Included in 'Wings Collection Vol.7'*
- Mitsuwa 1/144th Bf 109E & Me 262A #105 (1970s-mid 80s)
- Mitsuwa 1/144th Bf 109E-4 #1009 (1970s-mid 80s) – *Also issued as #1008*
- Pegaso (ex-Busch?) 1/132nd Bf 109 #P106 (mid-1980s)
- Revell 1/144th Me 109 #H1017 (1973) – Reissued in 1992 as #4045 and as #04916 in 2012
- Revell/Congost (ex-Revell) 1/144th Me 109 #H1017 (1973)
- Revell Japan (ex-Revell) 1/144th Me 109 #H1017 (1973)
- Revell/Kikoler (ex-Revell) 1/144th Me 109 #H1017 (1976)
- Sankyo 1/148th Bf 109E-4 #10 (late 50s-1968)
- Sanwa/Tokyo Plamo 1/109th Bf 109E #189 (1950s-60s)
- Sanwa/Tokyo Plamo 1/95th Bf 109E #128 (1950s-60s)
- Sram [res] 1/144th Bf 109E-4/E-7 Trop {2x kits} #201 – *Announced 2007, not released to date*
- Tomytech 1/144th Bf 109E-3 #22894 [& WW101] (2012) – *Pre-painted parts*
- Tomytech 1/144th Bf 109E-3 'Rumania' #22898 [& WW105] (2011) – *Pre-painted parts*
- Tomytech 1/144th Bf 109E-3 'Swiss' #22899 [& WW106] (2011) – *Pre-painted parts*
- Tomytech 1/144th Bf 109E-3 'Night Fighter' #WW105 (2011) – *Pre-painted parts*
- Tomytech 1/144th Bf 109E-4/B 'JG54' #22895 [& WW102] (2012) – *Pre-painted parts*
- Tomytech 1/144th Bf 109E-7/Trop 'JG27' #22896 [& WW103] (2012) – *Pre-painted parts*
- Walthers Inc. 1/87th Bf 109E #1171 (1999->)

1/62nd to 1/72nd

All 1/72nd scale unless otherwise stated
- Academy-Minicraft Bf 109E #1668 (1990)
- Academy-Minicraft Bf 109E-3/4 #2133 (1993) – *Retooling of #1668*
- Academy Bf 109E-3/4 'Heinz Bär' with Kettenkrad #2214 (2003) – *Also issued as #12499*
- Aero Plast (ex-Face/RPM) Bf 109T #90019 (1999)
- Aero Plast (ex-RPM) Bf 109B #00257 (1999->)
- Aero Plast (ex-RPM) Bf 109C #00264 (1999->)
- Aero Plast (ex-RPM) Bf 109D #00271 (1999->)
- Airfix Bf 109E #02048-8 (1976) – Renumbered #02048 in 1983, #902048 in 1985, #02048 in 1986, reissued

Notes	
3dp	– 3D Printed (resin)
fg	– Fibreglass
inj	– Injection Moulded Plastic
ltd inj	– Limited-run Injection Moulded Plastic
mtl	– White-metal (including Pewter)
pe	– Photo-etched (brass or steel)
res	– Resin
vac	– Vacuum-formed Plastic
(1999)	– Denotes date the kit was released
(1994->)	– Date denotes start of firm's activities, the exact date of release of this kit is however not known
ex-	– Denotes the tooling originated with another firm, the original tool maker is noted after the '-'

in late 1988 in the 'Aircraft of the Aces Special Edition' series as #02086, reissued in 2000 as #02048, issued as a 'Starter Set' in 2001 #92048, issued as a Gift Set #02048G in 2005, renumbered 2008 #A02048, issued as Gift Set in 2008 #A50088
- Airfix Bf 109E-4 #A01008 (2012) – Also issued as a 'Starter Set' with paint/glue/brush #A55106 at same time, reissued with the Spitfire Mk Ia as a 'Dogfight Double' in 06/2012 (#A50135). Also issued with the Spitfire Mk Ia and P-51D as a boxed set entitled 'Aircraft of the Aces' in association with the IWM (#A50143) – *due reissue with Spitfire Mk Ia and Hurricane Mk I as the 'Battle of Britain Experience' gift set (#A50153 £24.99) in 2013*
- Airfix Bf 109E-4/E-7 #A02048A (2010)
- Airfix Bf 109E-7/E-7 Trop #A02062 (2013)
- Airfix 'El Alamein' #A50148 (2012) – *Included the Bf 109E-4B Trop and Tomahawk IIB*
- Airmodel [res/mtl] Me 109 TL jet project #AM-2075 (mid-1980s) – Reissued, same kit number, in 5/1995
- Airmodel [res] Bf 109 V1 #AM-3003 (mid-1980s)
- Airmodel [res] Bf 109B #AM-3006 (mid-1980s)
- Alanger [ex-ICM] Bf 109E #49027 (20??)
- AMG Bf 109V-7 'Dubendorf 1937' #72413 (2021)
- AMG Bf 109B-1 #72403 (2017)
- AMG Bf 109B-2 'Spanish Air Force Era' #72424 (2020)

Revell #04916

Academy #2133

Academy #2214

AeroPlast #00257

AeroPlast #00264

AeroPlast #90019

AHM #SK-10

Airfix #02048-8

Airfix #02048

Airfix #02086

Airfix #A01008

Airfix #A02048A

Airfix #A01008A

A-Model #7205 1st edition

A-Model #7205 revised box

A-Model #72117

A-Model #7214

AML #72 028

AML AMLA #72 016

Avis #BX72007

Avis #BX72010

Avis #BX72012

Eduard #2136

Eduard #84167

Eduard #84178

Hasegawa #00672

Hasegawa #AP101

Hasegawa #AP9

Hasegawa #JS-107

Heller #101

Heller #234

Heller #236

Heller #80234 (1987)

Heller #80234 (post 1987)

ICM #72131

ICM #72133

ICM #72134

Heller #80236

ICM #72135

ICM #DS7202

JMK #003-72

JMK 72nd #Bf 109E-1

Matchbox #40017

Matchbox #PK-17 later version

- AMG Bf 109C 'Legion Condor' #72407 (2019)
- AMG Bf 109C-2(N) 'Night Fighter' #72420 (2020)
- AMG Bf 109D 'Legion Condor' #72410 (2019)
- AMG Bf 109D 'Poland 1939' #72406 (2019)
- AMG Bf 109D-1 'Swiss Air Force' #72425 (2019)
- AMG Bf 109D-2 'German Air School Service' #72418 (2020)
- AMG Bf 109D-2(N) 'Night Fighter' #72416 (2020)
- AML (ex-Avis) [ltd inj/res/pe] Bf 109V-3 & V-4 in the Legion Condor #AMLA 72 017 (2012)
- AML (ex-Avis) [ltd inj/res/pe] Bf 109B in the Legion Condor #AMLA 72 016 (2010)
- AML [ltd inj] Bf 109D #72 001 (2000)
- AML [ltd inj] Bf 109D #72 008 (1999)
- AML [ltd inj] Bf 109D 'Upgraded' #72 028 (2004)
- A Model (ex-Azis) [ltd inj] Bf 109A #72209 (2010)
- A Model [ltd inj] Bf 109E 'Hans Phillip' #7205 (1999) – Later reissued with new box art and listed just as a Bf 109E
- A Model [ltd inj] Bf 109T #7214 (1999)
- A Model [ltd inj] Bf 109E-3 'Rumanian Aces' #72116 (2004)
- A Model [ltd inj] Bf 109E-3/E-4 #72117 (2004)
- A Model [ltd inj] Bf 109X #72191 (2009)
- Aoda (ex/copy-Academy?) Bf 109E-3 #15006 (1993->)
- Aoda (ex/copy-Academy?) Bf 109E-4/-7 #15007 (1993->)
- Aoda (ex/copy-Academy?) Bf 109E-4/-7 Tropical #15008 (1993->)
- Avis [ltd inj] Bf 109A #BX72007 (2008)
- Avis [ltd inj] Bf 109B-1 #BX72009 (2010)
- Avis [ltd inj] Bf 109D-1 #BX72010 (2009)
- Avis [ltd inj] Bf 109C-3 #BX72011 (2009)
- Avis [ltd inj] Bf 109C-1 #BX72012 (2009)
- AZ Model [ltd inj] Bf 109E-0/V13/V14 #TBA – Due 2021
- AZ Model [ltd inj] Bf 109E-1 'Legion Condor' #AZ7802 (2021)
- AZ Model [ltd inj] Bf 109E-1 'Polish Campaign' #AZ7801 (2021)
- AZ Model [ltd inj] Bf 109E-1 'JG26' #AZ7697 (2021)
- AZ Model [ltd inj] Bf 109E-1 'JG27' #AZ7698 (2021)
- AZ Model [ltd inj] Bf 109E-1 'JG51' #AZ7699 (2021)
- AZ Model [ltd inj] Bf 109E-2/3/V20 #AZ7690 (2021)
- AZ Model [ltd inj] Bf 109E-3 'Battle of Britain'

#AZ7658 (2020)
- AZ Model [ltd inj] Bf 109E-3 'Battle of France' #AZ7661 (2020)
- AZ Model [ltd inj] Bf 109E-3 'Bulgarian Eagles' #AZ7677 (2021)
- AZ Model [ltd inj] Bf 109E-3 'In Swiss Service' #AZ7664 (2020)
- AZ Model [ltd inj] Bf 109E-3 'In Yugoslavian Service' #AZ7688 (2021)
- AZ Model [ltd inj] Bf 109E-3 'Over Spain' #AZ7660 (2020)
- AZ Model [ltd inj] Bf 109E-3 'Sitzrieg 1939' #AZ7665 (2021)
- AZ Model [ltd inj] Bf 109E-3a 'In Romanian Service' #AZ7671 (2021)
- AZ Model [ltd inj] Bf 109E-3/4 'Special Markings Part II' #AZ7689 (2021)
- AZ Model [ltd inj] Bf 109E-3/4/7 'Joy Pack' #AZ7707 (2021) – Just sprues
- AZ Model [ltd inj] Bf 109E-3/7 'Special Markings' #AZ7676 (2021)
- AZ Model [ltd inj] Bf 109E-4 'Aces over the Channel' #AZ7682 (2021)
- AZ Model [ltd inj] Bf 109E-4 'In Slovak Service' #AZ7662 (2020)
- AZ Model [ltd inj] Bf 109E-4/7N 'Night Fighter' #AZ7666 (2021)
- AZ Model [ltd inj] Bf 109E-7/B 'Schlacht Emils' #AZ7659 (2020)
- AZ Model [ltd inj] Bf 109E-7/B JaBo 'ZG1' #AZ7683 (2021)
- AZ Model [ltd inj] Bf 109E-7 Trop 'Over Africa' #AZ7663 (2020)
- Classic Plane Bf 109D 'Luftpolizei #CPM 78 (2000)
- Classic Plane (modified ex-RPM) Hispano-Suiza Bf 109E #CPM 023 (2012)
- Dragon Bf 109E #5050 – Announced for 2010, not released to date
- Eduard (ex-Special Hobby) Bf 109E-1 'Overtrees' #7031X (2021) – Available for a limited period directly from the Eduard website only
- Eduard (ex-Special Hobby) Bf 109E-3 'Overtrees' #7032X (2021) – Available for a limited period directly from the Eduard website only

- Eduard (ex-Special Hobby) Bf 109E-4/7 'Overtrees' #7033X (2021) – Available for a limited period directly from the Eduard website only
- Extraplan [vac] Bf 109T #N/K – Announced in 1992 but never produced
- Face Bf 109T-1/T-2 #N/K (1996)
- Frog 'Penguin' Bf 109 #60P (1939-1941) – Reissued as #060P (1946-1950) – Depicted the Jumo-powered early version
- Frog/Penguin Me 109 #60P (pre-WWII)
- Hasegawa Bf 109E #JS-107 (1973-1977)
- Hasegawa Bf 109E 'Galland' #AP101 (1994)
- Hasegawa Spitfire Mk I & Messerschmitt Bf 109E 'Battle of Britain' (2x kits) #01909 (2010) – Limited edition
- Hasegawa Bf 109E-3 #AP8 (1993)
- Hasegawa Bf 109E-3 'Spanish Air Force' #AP114 (1995)
- Hasegawa Bf 109E-3 'Swiss Air Force' #00672 (2006) – Limited edition
- Hasegawa Bf 109E-4 'Wick' #00263 (2001) – Limited edition
- Hasegawa Bf 109E-4/7 #AP9 (1992)
- Hasegawa Bf 109E-4/7 Trop #AP10 (1993)
- Hasegawa Messerschmitt Bf 109E-7 and Focke-Wulf Fw 190A-5 'IJA' #02014 (2012) – Limited edition
- Hasegawa Bf 109T #00639 (2003) – Limited edition
- Heller Bf 109B-1/C-1 #101 (1978). Renumbered #236 (late 70s) – Renumbered #80236 in 1987 and reissued as this number in 1993. Also issued in 1980s under the Heller-Humbrol label as #HK72004
- Heller Messerschmitt Bf 109E #089 (1975) – Renumbered #234 in the late 1970s and #80234 in 1987. Reissued as a 'Rapid Kit' in 2000 #59772
- HobbyBoss Bf 109E-3 #80253 (2008) – In the 'Easy Model' range
- HobbyBoss Bf 109E-4/7 #80254 (2008) – In the 'Easy Model' range
- HobbyBoss Bf 109E-4/Trop #80261 (2008) – In the 'Easy Model' range
- HR Model [res] Bf 109 V2 #7292 (2002/3)
- HR Model [res] Bf 109 V3 prototype #7293 (2004)
- HR Model [res] Bf 109 V3 'Spanish Civil War' #7294 (2004)
- ICM Bf 109B #72161 – Announced 2002, not released to date

- ICM Bf 109E-3 #72131 (2004)
- ICM Bf 109E-3 #72162 (2007)
- ICM Bf 109E-4 #72163 (2007)
- ICM Bf 109E-4 'Nightfighter' #72134 (2009)
- ICM Bf 109E-7/trop #72133 (2006)
- ICM Bf 109E-7b #72135 (2010)
- ICM Bf 109E-7B/trop #72164 (2007)
- JMK [vac] Bf 109E-1 #A3 (1987->) Later also carried item number #003-72 and revised header-card artwork (both colour and mono versions of the header-card are known)
- JMK [vac] Bf 109E-4 #A6 (1987->)
- K&K (vac) Bf 109E #N/K (1991-1993)
- LF Models [res] Bf 109E-0 #7279 (200?)
- LF Models [res] Bf 109 V13 #7282
- LF Models [res] Bf 109 V14 #7278
- Legion Vacuform [vac] Bf 109B-1/C-1 #N/K (1993-1995)
- Mareska [res] Bf 109B #None (1996-1998)
- Matchbox Bf 109E #PK-17 (1974) – Reissued under Revell's control in 1991 as #40017
- Matchbox Bf 109E – *Issued as part of 'Classic WWII Fighters' boxed set (#PK-1003) in 1986 with the Fw 190, Spitfire Mk IX and Hurricane Mk IIc*
- Mavi (Model Aviation) [vac] Bf 109B-1/B-2 #39 [also #7039] (1993->)
- Mavi (Model Aviation) [vac] Bf 10E-4/E-7 #7031 (1993->)
- Minicraft (ex-Hasegawa) Bf 109E #1107 (1970s-1985)
- Model News Bf 109T-0/T-1/T-2 #72001 (1995)
- MPC (ex-Airfix) Bf 109E #5007 (1965-1985) Also as #1-4006, 2-0104 & 2-5007
- MPM [ltd inj/pe] Bf 109 V1 #72029 (1997)
- MPM [inj/res] Bf 109 V1 'Upgraded kit' #72128 (1999)
- MPM [ltd inj/pe] Bf 109T #72066 (1995)
- MPM [ltd inj/res] Bf 109T 'Upgraded kit' #72132 (2000)
- Nemecek (Miroslav Nemecek) Bf 109T-0/T-1/T-2 #N/K (1996)
- Otaki 1/62nd Bf 109E #OA-19 (mid-1970s-1985)
- Parc Models (ex-ICM) Bf 109E-3 #PM7205 (2009)
- Parc Models (ex-ICM) Bf 109E-4 #PM7206 (2009)
- Planet Models [res] Me 109TL #004 (1996)
- Revell Bf 109E #H-612 (1963) – Reissued in 1967 as #H-682, 1969 as #H-684, 1970 as #H-223, 1972 as

#H-612, 1974 as #H-63, 1976 as #H-663 and 1978-1980 as #H-49 (also marked as #0049). Reissued as a Bf 109E in 1980s as #4149, in 1994 as #04149 and as Bf 109E-4 in 2010 as #04679
- Revell Bf 109E & Tempest V 'Fighting Deuces Series' #H-223 (1970-1972)
- RPM (modified ex-Face) Bf 109B-1 #N/K (1998) – *Modification of the Bf 109T*
- RPM (modified ex-Face) Bf 109E-1 'Hiszpania 38-39' #72008 (1998) – *Modification of the Bf 109T*
- RPM (modified ex-Face) Bf 109E-1 'September 39' #72009 (1998) – *Modification of the Bf 109T*
- RPM (ex-Face) Bf 109T-0 #72005 (1996) – Reissued in 1998 as #72110
- RPM (ex-Face) Bf 109T-2 #72006 (1996) – Reissued in 1998 as #72109
- RS Models [res] Bf 109X #72131 (2002/3)
- RS Models [ltd inj/res/pe] Bf 109X #92051 (2009)
- RS Models [ltd inj/res/pe] Bf 109X #92085 (2010)
- Seminar Bf 109E #014 (1999)
- Special Hobby Bf 109E-1 'J/88 Legion Condor' #SH72459 (2021)
- Special Hobby Bf 109E-1 'Lightly-Armed Emil' #SH72454 (2021)
- Special Hobby Bf 109E-3 #SH72443 (2021)
- Special Hobby Bf 109E-3 'Simple Set' #SS018 (2021) – Just the sprues
- Special Hobby Bf 109E-4 #SH72439 (2020)
- Special Hobby Bf 109E-4 'Night Fighter' #SH72??? – *Due 2022*
- Special Hobby Bf 109E-4/B #SH72??? – *Due 2022*
- Special Hobby Bf 109E-7 #SH72??? – *Due 2022*
- Special Hobby Bf 109E-7 Trop 'Braving Sand and Snow' #SH72462 (2022)
- St Michael Modelmaker (ex-Airfix) World War II Fighter Aircraft #2140-400 (1979) – *Included Spitfire Mk I (#01065), Bf 109E (#02048) and P-51B (#02066) – issued exclusively by St Michaels (Marks & Spencers)*
- Storia dell'Aviazione (ex-Revell) Bf 109E #61 (1973 & 1977-78) – *Issued bagged along with a book on the subject by publishers Fabbri Editori on two occasions on the dates quoted*
- Sword [ltd inj/res] Bf 109D #SW72005 (1999)
- Tamiya Bf 109E-3 #60750 (2000)
- Tamiya Bf 109E-4/7 Trop #60755 (2001)
- Toga Bf 109T #0203 (1995->) – *Probably ex-Face?*

1/46th- 1/50th

All 1/48th unless stated otherwise
- Academy (ex-Hobbycraft) Bf 109D #2178 (2000)
- Academy (ex-Hobbycraft) Bf 109E-3 'Heinz Bär' #12216 (2009)
- Academy (ex-Hobbycraft) Bf 109T-2 #12225 (2010)
- Airfix Bf 109E-1/E-3/E-4 #A05120 (2010)
- Airfix Bf 109E-1/E-3/E-7 Trop #05122 (2010)
- Airfix Bf 109E-3/E-7 'Club Edition' #A82012 (2012)
- Airmodel [vac/inj] Bf 109B/C #AM-4805 (1969-2000)
- Airmodel [res] Bf 109 V1 #AM-3003 (1980s-2000)
- Airmodel [res] Bf 109B #AM-3006 (1980s-2000)
- AMG Bf 109B-2 'Spanish Air Force Era' #48727 (2020)
- AMG Bf 109B-2 'Luftwaffe Service' #72424 (2020)
- AMG Bf 109C-2 'Poland 1939' #48720 (2020)
- AMG Bf 109C-2(N) 'Night Fighter' #48715 (2020)
- AMG Bf 109D 'Legion Condor' #48723 (2018)
- AMG Bf 109D 'Swiss Air Force' #48730 (2019)
- AMG Bf 109D-2 'German Air School Service' #48728 (2020)
- AMG Bf 109D-2(N) 'Night Fighter' #48718 (2020)
- Aurora 1/46th Me 109 #55 (1952-1976) – Later reissued as #55-59, 55A-69, 55-69, 55A-79, 55-79, 55-80, 55-100 and 343-79
- Bandai (ex-Monogram) Bf 109E #8907 (1976)
- Classic Airframes [ltd inj/res] Bf 109A #4123 (2006)
- Classic Airframes [ltd inj/res] Bf 109C/D #4125 (2006)
- Classic Airframes [ltd inj/res] Bf 109D #4134 (2006) – Reissued 2009
- Condor Models International [res] Bf 109 V1 #RC48-001 (late 1990s)
- Cynus [res] Bf 109B #48-1 (1986) – *Made exclusively for them by JN Models*
- Cynus [res] Bf 109E #48-2 (1986) – *Made exclusively for them by JN Models*
- Dragon Bf 109E-4 '*Gruppenkommandeur* Adolf Galland, JG 26 Battle of Britain' #5550 – *Announced for 2010, not released to date*
- Eagle's Talon [res] Bf 109 V1 #ET510 (1985-1988, 1990-2000)
- Eduard [inj/pe/r] Bf 109E 'Royal Class' #R0007 (2012)
- Eduard [inj/pe] Bf 109E-1 'ProfiPACK' #8261 (2012)
- Eduard Bf 109E-1 'Weekend Edition' #84158 (2020) – *Different decals options to #84164*

Matchbox #PK-17   MPM #72128   MPM #72132   Revell #04149   Revell #04679

Revell #4149   Revell #H-612   Revell #H-63   RPM #72005   RPM #72006

RPM #72008   Special Hobby #SH72439   Special Hobby #SH72443   Special Hobby #SH72454   Special Hobby #SH72459

RPM #72009   St Michael #2140-400   Sword #SW72005   Tamiya #60750   Tamiya #60755

Academy #12216   Academy #12225   Academy #2178   Airfix #A05120   Airfix #A82012

Aurora #55A-69

Aurora #55

Classic Airframes #4125

Classic Airframes #4134

Eduard #8261

Eduard #8262

Eduard #8263

Eduard #84164

Eduard #R0007

Eduard #8263

Hasegawa #09624

Hasegawa #09892

Hasegawa #CH24

Hasegawa #J1

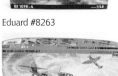

Hasegawa #J2

Hasegawa #J3

Hasegawa #JT112

Hasegawa #JT169

Hasegawa #JT8

Hobby Craft #HC1518

Hobbycraft #HC1545

Hobbycraft #HC1567

Hobbycraft #HC1568

Hobbycraft #HC1569

Hobbycraft #HC1570

- Eduard Bf 109E-1 'Weekend Edition' #84164 (2012)
- Eduard Bf 109E-3 'Overtrees' #8271X (2012) – *Just the sprues in a plain white box only available for a limited period directly from the Eduard website only*
- Eduard [inj/pe] Bf 109E-3 'ProfiPACK' #8262 (2012)
- Eduard Bf 109E-3 'Weekend Edition' #84157 (2019) – *Different decals options to #84165*
- Eduard Bf 109E-3 'Weekend Edition' #84165 (2013)
- Eduard Bf 109E-3 'Overtrees' #8273X (2012) – *Just the sprues in a plain white box only available for a limited period directly from the Eduard website only*
- Eduard [inj/pe] Bf 109E-4 'ProfiPACK' #8263 (2012)
- Eduard Bf 109E-4 'Weekend Edition' #84166 (2013)
- Eduard Bf 109E-4 'Overtrees' #8272X (2012) – *Just the sprues in a plain white box only available for a limited period directly from the Eduard website only*
- Eduard Bf 109E-4 'Balthasar' #BFC070 (2019) – *Limited edition kit only available to members of Eduard's 'Bunny Fighter Club' and sold directly via their website*
- Eduard Bf 109E-7 Trop 'Overtrees' #8274X (2013) – *Just the sprues in a plain white box only available for a limited period directly from the Eduard website only*
- Eduard [inj/pe] Bf 109E-7 Trop 'ProfiPACK' #8264 (2013)
- Falcon [vac] Bf 109B/C #FV009 (1985)
- Falcon [vac] Bf 109E #FV010 (1986)
- Fine Molds (ex-Tamiya) Bf 109E-7 'Japanese Army' #48995 (2020) – *Included figures and equipment plus flexible seat belts*
- Gull Models [vac/mtl] Bf 109B/D #4806 (1982-1989)
- Hasegawa Bf 109E 'Bulgarian Air Force' #JT123 (1996)
- Hasegawa Bf 109E 'Hahn' #09746 (2007) – *Limited edition*
- Hasegawa Bf 109E 'Marseille' #09892 (2010) – *Limited edition*
- Hasegawa Bf 109E 'Galland w/figure' #09879 (2010) – *Limited edition*
- Hasegawa Bf 109E-1 #09369 (2001) – *Limited edition*
- Hasegawa Bf 109E-1 'Sitzkrieg' #09482 (2003) – *Limited edition*
- Hasegawa Bf 109E-3 #U9 (1988) – This was renumbered in 1989 as #J1, revised and reissued in 1994 as #JT8, reissued again under this number in 2001
- Hasegawa Bf 109E-3 'Swiss Air Force' #JT104 (1996)

- Hasegawa Bf 109E-3 'Legion Condor' #JT169 (1998) – *Limited edition*
- Hasegawa Bf 109E-3 'Rumanian Air Force' #09624 (2005)
- Hasegawa Bf 109E-3 'Spanish Civil War' #09601 (2005) – *Limited edition*
- Hasegawa Bf 109E 'Luftwaffe Experten' #JT112 (1995)
- Hasegawa Bf 109E-4 'Battle of Britain' #09823 (2008) – *Limited edition*
- Hasegawa Bf 109E-4/7 #J2 (1988) – Revised (fuselage) and reissued in 1994 as #JT9
- Hasegawa Bf 109E-4/7 Trop #J3 (1988) – Revised and reissued in 1994 as #JT10
- Hasegawa Bf 109E-4/7 'Jabo' #JT161 (1998) – *Limited edition*
- Hasegawa Bf 109E-4/E-7b 'Jabo' #07316 (2012) – *Limited edition*
- Hasegawa Bf 109E-4/7 'Superdetail' #CH24 (1998)
- Hasegawa Bf 109E 'Galland' #J4 (1989) – Revised and reissued in 1994 as #JT11
- Hasegawa Bf 109T #09326 (1999) – *Limited edition*
- Hasegawa Bf 109T-2 'JG77' #09861 (2009) – *Limited edition* – Reissued, same kit number, 2012
- Hobbycraft Bf 109B #HC1566 (1992)
- Hobbycraft Bf 109C #HC1567 (1992)
- Hobbycraft Bf 109D #HC1568 (1992)
- Hobbycraft Bf 109E-1 #HC1564 (1992)
- Hobbycraft Bf 109E-3 #HC1569 (1992)
- Hobbycraft Bf 109E-4 #HC1570 (1992)
- Hobbycraft Bf 109E-4/7 'Russian Front' #HC1545 (1992)
- Hobbycraft Bf 109E-7 'WWII German Tropical Fighter' #HC1565 (1997)
- Jays Model Kits (ex-Tasman) [ltd inj/vac] Bf 109B #JY0202 (2008)
- Jays Model Kits (ex-Tasman) [ltd inj/vac] Bf 109C-1 #JY0209 (2017)
- JN Models [res] Bf 109B #N/K (mid-80s-1990)
- Karo-AS Modellbau [vac] Bf 109B/C #AM-48.05 (1987-1996)
- LF Models [res] Bf 109 V14 #N/K (2001)
- LF Models [res] Bf 109 V21 #4804 (2001)
- LF Models [res] Bf 109X with P&W Hornet engine #4803 (2001)

- Marusan 1/50th Bf 109E #451 (1950s-1970s)
- Milion Plamo 1/50th Bf 109E #1 (early 1960s) – *Mould origin is unconfirmed*
- Modelsvit [ltd inj/pe] Bf 109C-3 4805 (2019)
- Modelsvit [ltd inj/pe] Bf 109D-1 4806 (2019)
- Monogram Bf 109E #PA74-98 (1962) – Reissued as #6800 (1970s) and with the Hurricane as 'Air Combat Series' in 1988 (#6082)
- Monogram Bf 109E #85-0074 (1999) – *Limited edition reissue with original boxart in the 'Monogram Classics' series*
- MPM [ltd inj/pe] Bf 109T-1/T-2 #48023 (1996)
- MPM [inj/res/pe] Bf 109T-1/T-2 'Hi-Tech' #48043 (2000)
- Nichimo (ex-Marusan*) Bf 109E #S-4807 (1970->) – **which was itself a copy of the Monogram kit*
- Plastic Planet Club (ex-Eduard) Bf 109E01 #PPC-003 (2014) – *Limited edition*
- R&D Replicas (ex-Karo-AS) [vac] Bf 109B/C #48.05 (1994-1999)
- Replica [res] Bf 109V #N/K (1987-1989)
- Replica [res] Bf 109E #N/K (1987-1989)
- Replicast Models [res] Bf 109 V1 #4801 (1994->)
- Revell Bf 109E 'Metal Kit' #8900 (1992)
- Revell (ex-Hasegawa) Bf 109E-4/E-7 Trop #04572 (2002)
- RSL (ex-Marusan*) Bf 109E #451 (1960s) – **which was itself a copy of the Monogram kit*
- Scalecraft 1/45th Bf 109E-4 #S-508 (early 70s) – *Brand name used by KIM Toys, reappeared in USA under this brand in 1979*
- Signum (ex-Hobbycraft) Bf 109B-2 #48012 (1998->)
- Signum (ex-Hobbycraft) Bf 109C #48003 (1998->)
- Signum (ex-Hobbycraft) Bf 109D #48008 (1998->)
- Signum (ex-Hobbycraft) Bf 109E-4 #48011 (1998->)
- Signum (ex-Hobbycraft) Bf 109E-4/7 Trop #48001 (1998->)
- Starfix (ex-Heller) 1/56th Bf 109E #125 (1960s-1990s) – *Production halted in late 80s, resumed in early 90s but ceased by mid-1990s*
- Tamiya Bf 109E-3 #61050 (1997)
- Tamiya Bf 109E-3 'Swiss' #25200 (2020) – *Limited edition*
- Tamiya Bf 109E-4/7 Trop #61063 (1999)
- Tasman 'Kiwi Wings' Bf 109B-1 'Pre-WWII' #KW4804 – *Announced never actually released*

- Tasman 'Kiwi Wings' Bf 109B-1 'WWII' #KW4805 – *Announced never actually released*
- Tasman 'Kiwi Wings' Bf 109B-2 #KW4806 – *Announced never actually released*
- Tasman 'Kiwi Wings' Bf 109B-7 #KW4807 – *Announced never actually released*
- Tauro Model Bf 109E #304 – *Initially announced in 1980, then again in 1989 but never released*
- UPC (Universal Powermaster Corp.) (ex-Monogram) Bf 109E #5072 (N/K) – All kit production ceased in the early 1970s
- Vacukit [vac] Bf 109B #4502 (1987-early 90s)
- Ventura [ltd inj] Bf 109B/C #V0302 (1988)
- Ventura [ltd inj] Bf 109B #V0304 (1989) – *Spanish markings*
- Wingsy Kits [ltd inj/pe] Bf 109E-1 #D5-07 (2021)
- Wingsy Kits [ltd inj/pe] Bf 109E-3 #D5-08 (2021)
- Wingsy Kits [ltd inj/pe] Bf 109E- 'Legion Condor' #D5-09 (2021) – *2x kits in box*
- Wingsy Kits [ltd inj/pe] Bf 109E-4 #D5-10 (2021)
- WK Models [res] Bf 109B #N/K (1988-1997)
- WK Models [res] Bf 109 V1 #N/K (1988-1997)

1/32nd

- AMT (ex-Matchbox) Bf 109E #7202 (1978-1982)
- Dragon/Cyber-Hobby Bf 109E-3 #3222 (2012)
- Dragon/Cyber-Hobby Bf 109E-4 #3204 (2010)
- Dragon/Cyber-Hobby Bf 109E-4/B #3225 (2015)
- Dragon/Cyber-Hobby Bf 109E-7/B #3221 – *Announced but never released*
- Dragon/Cyber-Hobby Bf 109E-7 Trop #3223 (2012)
- Eduard [inj/pe/r] Bf 109E 'Over the Balkan Peninsula' #1156 (2011) – *Limited edition*
- Eduard [inj/pe] Bf 109E 'In the Battle of Britain' #31002 – *Announced for 2011, not released to date*
- Eduard Bf 109E 'Legion Condor (without the wings)' Overtrees #3009X (2019) – *Just the sprues in a plain box*

available for a limited period directly from the Eduard website only
- Eduard Bf 109E (without the wings) 'Overtrees' #11107X (2019) – *Just the sprues in a plain box available for a limited period directly from the Eduard website only*
- Eduard Bf 109E-1 'Weekend Edition' #3401 (2010)
- Eduard [inj/pe] Bf 109E-1 'ProfiPACK' #3001 (2009)
- Eduard [inj/pe] Bf 109E-1 'Weekend Edition' #3401 (2011)
- Eduard Bf 109E-1 'Overtrees' #3001X (2019) – *Just the sprues in a plain box available for a limited period directly from the Eduard website only*
- Eduard [inj/pe] Bf 109E-3 'ProfiPACK' #3002 (2009)
- Eduard Bf 109E-3 'Weekend Edition' #3402 (2011)
- Eduard Bf 109E-3 'Overtrees' #3002X (2019) – *Just the sprues in a plain box available for a limited period directly from the Eduard website only*
- Eduard [inj/pe] Bf 109E-4 'ProfiPACK' #3003 (2009)
- Eduard Bf 109E-4 'Weekend Edition' #3403 (2011)
- Eduard Bf 109E-4 'Weekend Edition' #3403 (2010)
- Eduard Bf 109E-4/E-7 'Overtrees' #3003X (2019) – *Just the sprues in a plain box available for a limited period directly from the Eduard website only*
- Eduard [inj/pe] Bf 109E-7 Trop 'ProfiPACK' #3004 (2010)
- Frog (ex-Hasegawa) Bf 109E #F288 (1973-1974)
- Hasegawa Bf 109E #JS-073 (1973-1977) *Also issued by Minicraft/Hasegawa in USA as #073* – Later renumbered #S5, reissued in 1993 as #ST1
- Hasegawa Bf 109E 'Galland' #SP35 (1990)
- Hasegawa Bf 109E-4 'Major E. Wick' #08118 (2000) – *Limited edition*
- Hasegawa Bf 109E-4 Trop 'Jagdgeschwader 27' #08136 (2002) – *Limited edition*
- Hasegawa Messerschmitt Bf 109E-4/7B 'Jabo' #08228 (2012) – *Limited edition*
- Hasegawa Bf 109E-4/7 Trop 'Marseille' #08207 (2010) – *Limited edition*
- Hobby 2000 (ex-Dragon) Bf 109E-3 #32004 (2022)

- Hobby 2000 (ex-Dragon) Bf 109E-4 #32005 (2022)
- Hobby 2000 (ex-Dragon) Bf 109E-7 #32006 (2022)
- Hobbycraft Bf 109A #HC1719 – Announced for 2010, never released
- Hobbycraft Bf 109B #HC1720 – Announced for 2009, never released
- Hobbycraft Bf 109C #HC1721 – Announced for 2009, never released
- Hobbycraft Bf 109D #HC722 – Announced for 2009, never released
- Matchbox Bf 109E #PK-502 (1977) – Reissued in 1979 and 1983, plus under Revell's control in 1991 as #40502
- Minicraft (ex-Hasegawa) Bf 109E #1073 (1970s-1985)
- Scratchbuilders [res] Bf 109B/C/D #N/K (1992-2002)
- Trumpeter Bf 109E-3 #02288 (2010)
- Trumpeter Bf 109E-4 #02289 (2011)
- Trumpeter Bf 109E-4/Trop #02290 (2010)
- Trumpeter Bf 109E-7/Trop #02291 (2010)

1/24th

- Airfix Bf 109E #Patt. No.1202 (1972) – Renumbered #09321-1 (1973) and #12002-9 in 1976, reissued in 1989 and 1993 as #12002, renumbered 2008 #A12002, reissued as Bf 109E-3/E-4 (#A12002A) in 2011 with different decal options and as #A50176 (Bf 109E-4) with paint, glue etc. in 2016. It was reissued once again in 2020 as part of the 'Airfix Classics' series (#A12002V) complete with the original box art.
- Bandai Bf 109E-4 #8509 (1972) – *Also as #4259-1200*
- Heller (ex-Airfix) Bf 109E #80496 (1993)
- MPC (ex-Airfix) Bf 109E #2-3501 (1973) – Reissued as #2-3507 in 1978 and #1-4607 in 1984

1/18th

- HpH Models [res/fg] Bf 109E #18041L (2016)

Jays Model Kits #JY0202

Karo-AS #AM-48 05

Monogram #6082

Monogram #6800

Monogram #PA74

MPM #48043

Nichimo #S-4807

Revell #04572

Tamiya #61050

Tamiya #61063

Wingsy Kits #D5-07

Cyber-Hobby #3222

Eduard #1156

Eduard #3001

Eduard #3002

Eduard #3003

Eduard #3004

Eduard #3401

Eduard #3402

Eduard #3403

Frog #F288

Hasegawa #ST1

Matchbox #40502

Trumpeter #02288

Trumpeter #02289

Trumpeter #02290

Airfix #12002-9

Airfix #12002 larger box

Airfix #12002 smaller box

Airfix #1202

Appendix: II **Bf 109 V1 to E-9** (inc. T-series) **Accessories**

Below is a list of all accessories for static scale construction kits produced to date for the early Bf 109 series. This list is as comprehensive as possible, but if there are amendments or additions, please contact the author via the Valiant Wings Publishing address shown at the front of this title.

Please note that only canopy, wheel and camouflage pattern masks are included in this section, all masks for specific individual aircraft schemes are in the next appendix.

1/72nd

- Aber [br] Bf 109E Armament Set #72-003
- Aires [res/pe] Bf 109E-3/E-4 Cockpit Set #7081 {Tamiya}
- Aires [res/pe] DB 601E/N engine #7104
- Aires [res/pe] DB 601A engine #7107
- Aires [res] Bf 109E Control Surfaces #7129 {Tamiya}
- Aires [res] Bf 109E/F Wheels & Paint Masks #7245
- Aires [res/pe] Bf 109E-3/E-4 Cockpit Set #7292 {Airfix}
- Airkit Enterprises [res] Bf 109B-2 Conversion #AIR038 {Airfix Bf 109E}
- Airkit Enterprises [res] Bf 109T-1/T-2 Conversion #AIR037 {Airfix Bf 109E}
- Airwaves [res/mtl] Bf 109B Nose & Propeller #S.C.7255 – *Also issued as #AES72055*
- Airwaves [pe] Bf 109E/G Cockpit Details etc. #AEC72018
- Airwaves [pe] Bf 109E Detail Set. #AEC72094 {Hasegawa}
- Airwaves [pe] Bf 109E-3 to E-8 Exterior Panels #AEC72137
- AML [res] Bf 109B Interior Set #AMLA7206 {Heller}
- AML [res/pe] Bf 109B Interior Set #AMLA7208 {Heller}
- AML [res] Bf 109E Propeller with tool #AMLA7228 {Airfix & Tamiya} – *Due 2013*
- AML [ma] Bf 109E 'Late' Camouflage Painting Masks #AMLA7308 {Airfix & Tamiya}
- Avia Equipage Auto [res/rb] Bf 109B/C/D Wheel set #72001
- Avia Equipage Auto [res/rb] Bf 109E/F/T Wheel set #72002
- BarracudaCast [res] Messerschmitt Bf 109B/C/D/E Mainwheels #BCR72091
- BarracudaCast [res] Messerschmitt Bf 109E/F Mainwheels with ribbed tyres #BCR72438

- Brengun [pe] Bf 109E-4 Cockpit Detail Set #BRL72044 {Airfix}
- CMK [res] DB601 for Bf 109E #7067 {Tamiya}
- CMK [res] Bf 109E ace A. Galland and mechanic #F72369
- CMK [res] Bf 109E Engine Set #7455 {Special Hobby/Eduard}
- CMK [res/pe] Bf 109E FuG VII Radio Equipment #7458 {Special Hobby/Eduard}
- CMK [res] Bf 109E-1/E-5 Wing Machine-Guns #7460 {Special Hobby/Eduard}
- CMK [res] Bf 109E-3/4/7 Wing Guns #7457 {Special Hobby/Eduard}
- CMK [res] Bf 109E-7 Control Surfaces #7314 {Airfix}
- CMK [res] Bf 109E-7 Trop Engine Set #7313 {Airfix}
- CMK [res/pe] Bf 109E-7 Trop Interior Set #7311 {Airfix}
- Cooper Details [res/pe] Bf 109E Cockpit Detail Set #CD7206 {Hasegawa}
- Dangly Bits [res] Bf 109E Cockpit Interior #None
- Dangly Bits [res] Bf 109E Rudders x3 #None
- DB Production [res/mtl] Bf 109B Nose & Propeller #DB66
- Eduard [pe] Bf 109E Detail Set – Zoom #SS141 {Academy}
- Eduard [pe] Bf 109E Detail Set – Zoom #SS164 {Tamiya}
- Eduard [pe] Bf 109E Detail Set – Zoom #SS173 {Hasegawa}
- Eduard [pe] Bf 109E Detail Set – Zoom #SS453 {Airfix}
- Eduard [pe] Bf 109E-1 Detail Set [Pre-painted] #73-751 {Special Hobby/Eduard}
- Eduard [vma] Bf 109E Canopy & Wheel Masks #XS093 {Tamiya}
- Eduard [vma] Bf 109E Canopy & Wheel Masks #XS126 {Hasegawa}
- Eduard [ma] Bf 109E Canopy & Wheel Masks [Kabuki Tape] #CX021 {Hasegawa}
- Eduard [ma] Bf 109E Canopy & Wheel Masks [Kabuki Tape] #CX331 {Airfix}
- Eduard [pe] Bf 109E Detail Set [Pre-painted/SA] #73-453 {Airfix}
- Eduard [pe] Bf 109E Detail Set – 'Zoom' [Pre-painted/SA] #SS453 {Airfix}
- Eduard [pe] Bf 109E Large Blotch Masks #XS551
- Eduard [pe] Bf 109E Small Blotch Masks #XS553
- Eduard [ma] Bf 109E-3 Canopy & Wheel Masks [Kabuki Tape] #CX020 {Airfix}
- Eduard [pe] Bf 109E-3 Detail Set [Pre-painted]

#73-739 {Special Hobby/Eduard}
- Eduard [ma] Bf 109E-4 Canopy & Wheel Masks [Kabuki Tape] #CX010 {Airfix}
- Eduard [pe] Bf 109E-4 Detail Set #72-101 {Hasegawa}
- Eduard [pe] Bf 109E-4 Detail Set [Pre-painted] #73-736 {Special Hobby/Eduard}
- Eduard [pe] Bf 109E-4 & E-7 Detail Set [Pre-painted] #73-199 {Tamiya}
- Eduard [pe] Bf 109E-7 Detail Set [Pre-painted] #73-478 {Airfix}
- Eduard [pe] Bf 109E-7 Detail Set – 'Zoom' [Pre-painted] #SS478 {Airfix}
- Eduard [pe] Bf 109E/F National Insignia Masks #XS507
- Elf Production [rb] Bf 109E Wheels #7217
- Falcon [wm/vac] Bf 109E Detail Set No.1 #4607
- Falcon [vac] Luftwaffe Fighters Part 1 inc. Bf 109B and Bf 109E canopies {Set No.5 {Heller & Airfix/Matchbox}
- Falcon [wm] Daimler-Benz DB 601A engine #None
- Falcon [vac] Luftwaffe Part 3 inc. Bf 109E canopy #Set No.15 {Hasegawa}
- Falcon [vac] Luftwaffe Part 6 inc. Bf 109B-1 'Early' canopy #Set No.29 {Heller}
- Falcon [vac] Luftwaffe Part 7 inc. Bf 109E-1/E-3 and E-4/E-7 canopies #Set No.42 {Tamiya}
- Fotocut [pe] Bf 109E Details #None
- Hawkeye Designs [res] Bf 109E Cockpit Detail Set #111 {Hasegawa}
- HR Models [pe/res] Bf 109B/C/D Upgrade Set #C72016 {AML, Heller & Sword}
- Kora Models [res/dec] Bf 109E-7/B 'Escudilla Azul' #7241
- Kora Models [res/dec] Bf 109E Strela 'Bulgarian Service I' #72108 {Academy, Airfix, Hasegawa, Heller or Tamiya}
- Kora Models [res/dec] Bf 109E Strela 'Bulgarian Service II' #72109 {Academy, Airfix, Hasegawa, Heller or Tamiya}
- Kora Models [res/dec] Bf 109E Strela 'Bulgarian Service III' #72110 {Academy, Airfix, Hasegawa, Heller or Tamiya}
- Kora Models [res/dec] Bf 109D-1 'Swiss AF' #72119 {Avis, AML or Heller}
- Kora Models [res/dec] Bf 109E-1 Schneekufen Set #CSD7271
- Kora Models [res/dec] Bf 109E-3/b, E-4/B, E-7B with SD2 Butterfly Bombs & Rack #CSD7284
- Kora Models [res/dec] Bf 109E-3/b, E-4/B, E-7B with SD2 Butterfly Bombs & Rack #CSD7285 –

Aires #7129

Aires #7245

Brengun #BRL72044

CMK #7067

CMK #7311

CMK #7313

CMK #7314

CMK #7457

CMK #7458

CMK #7460

CMK #F72369

Cooper Details #CD7221

Eduard #72-101

Eduard #SS164

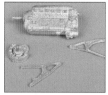
Falcon DB601A engine

Hawkeye Designs #111

Loon Models #LO72209

Master #AM-72-009

Part #S72-054

Part #S72-163

Quick & Easy #Q72098

Quickboost #Q72324

True Details #72464

Quick & Easy #Q72211

Quick & Easy #Q72384

Quick & Easy #Q72389

Quick & Easy #Q72390

Special Hobby #M72009

Special Hobby #M72010

Different decal options to #CSD7284
- Kora Models [res] Bf 109E SD2 Butterfly Bombs & Rack #DS72257
- Loon Models [res] Bf 109B-E Seats without belts #LO72209
- Master Models [br] Bf 109E-3 to E-9 & T Armament Set #AM-72-009
- Modell-Hobby [pe] Bf 109E Instrument Panel #MH0018 {Airfix}
- Moskit [mtl] Bf 109E Exhausts #72-01
- North Star Models [res] Bf 109B/C/E Wheels #NS72005
- Owl [res/dec] Bf 109E-4 Peil G IV 'Spanner Anlage' conversion #OWR72017
- Part [pe] Bf 109B Detail Set #S72-054 {Heller}
- Part [pe] Bf 109E Detail Set #S72-055 {Academy}
- Part [pe] Bf 109E-1 to E-3 Detail Set #S72-147 {Tamiya}
- Part [pe] Bf 109E-4 to E-7 Detail Set #S72-163 {Tamiya}
- Pavla [res] Bf 109 Upgrade Set #7220
- Pavla [res] Bf 109E-3 Canopy #V72003
- Quickboost [res] Bf 109E Control Columns #QB72470 {Academy}
- Quickboost [res] Bf 109E Exhausts #QB72399 {Academy}
- Quickboost [res] Bf 109E Flaps #QB72241 {Tamiya}
- Quickboost [res] Bf 109E Gun Barrels #QB72389 {Academy}
- Quickboost [res] Bf 109E Seat with safety belts #QB72401
- Quickboost [res] Bf 109E Tailwheel (x3) #QB72324 {Tamiya}
- Quick & Easy [res] Bf 109E Wheels #Q72098 {Hasegawa & Tamiya}
- Quick & Easy [res] Bf 109E Exhausts #Q72390 {Special Hobby/Eduard}
- Quick & Easy [res] Bf 109E Propeller & Spinner #Q72389 {Special Hobby/Eduard}
- Quick & Easy [res] Bf 109E Tailwheel with Strengthened Leg #Q72391 {Special Hobby/Eduard}
- Quick & Easy [res] Bf 109E Wheels #Q72384 {Special Hobby/Eduard}

- Quick & Easy [res] Bf 109E-7 Trop Exhausts #Q72211 {Airfix}
- Res-IM [pe] Bf 109E Detail Set [Pre-painted] #PE72036 {Tamiya}
- REXx [mtl] Bf 109E Exhausts #72018
- Rob Taurus [vac] Bf 109B/C Canopy #72033 {Heller}
- Rob Taurus [vac] Bf 109E-3 Canopy #72034 {Tamiya}
- Rob Taurus [vac] Bf 109E-4/E-7 Canopy #72035 {Tamiya}
- SBS Model [res] Bf 109E Exhausts #72038 {Airfix}
- SBS Model [res] Bf 109E Wheel Set #72037
- Squadron [vac] Bf 109B/E Canopies #9106 {Airfix, Heller or Matchbox}
- True Details [res] Bf 109E/C/D/E Wheels #45009 (*later renumbered #72004*)
- True Details [res/pe] Bf 109E Cockpit Detail Set #72464 {Hasegawa}
- Verlinden Productions [res/pe] Bf 109E Upgrade Set #775 {Hasegawa}
- Yahu Models [pe] Bf 109E Instrument Panel #YMA7216 (Airfix)

1/48th

- Aber [br] Bf 109E-3 to G-4 Armament Set #48112
- Aeroclub [wm] Bf 109A/B/C Two-blade Propeller #N/K
- Aires [res/pe] Daimler-Benz DB 601E/N engine #4033
- Aires [res/pe] Bf 109E-3 & E-4 Cockpit Set #4067 {Tamiya}
- Aires [res/pe] Bf 109E-4 Cockpit Set #4090 {Tamiya}
- Aires [res/pe] Bf 109E-3 Cockpit Set #4479 {Academy/Hobbycraft}
- Airwaves [pe] Bf 109B/C/D Detail Set #4839 {Academy/Hobbycraft} – *Also issued as #AC48-39 & AC48039*
- Airwaves [pe] Bf 109E-3 to E-3 Surface Panels #AEC48063
- AML [ma] Bf 109B/C/D Canopy Masks #AMLM4904 {Academy/Hobbycraft}

- AML [ma] Bf 109E-4/E-7 Canopy Masks #AMLM4903 {Tamiya}
- AML [ma] Bf 109E 'Late' Camouflage Painting Masks #AMLM4912 {Eduard & Tamiya}
- AML [res/dec] Bf 109E-4 with PeilG IV Conversion Set #AMLA48055 {Eduard or Tamiya}
- Atol Hobby [pe] Bf 109E Undercarriage Covers #48006 {Eduard}
- Avia Equipage Auto [r/rb] Bf 109B/C/D Wheels #48001
- Avia Equipage Auto [r/rb] Bf 109E/F/T Wheels #48002
- BarracudaCast [res] Bf 109E/F Main Wheels with ribbed tyres #BCR48437
- Brassin [res/pe] 'Big Sin' set comprising wheels (#648058), DB601A/N Engine (#648059), MG17 Mount (#648060) & Cockpit and Radio Compartment (#648074) #SIN64807 {Eduard}
- Brassin [res/pe] Bf 109E Cockpit and Radio Compartment #648074 {Eduard}
- Brassin [res/pe] Bf 109E Cockpit and Radio Compartment #648472 {Eduard}
- Brassin [res/pe] Bf 109E Engine #648474 {Eduard}
- Brassin [res/pe] Bf 109E DB 601A/N Engine #648059 {Eduard}
- Brassin [res/pe] Bf 109E Fuselage Guns #648473 {Eduard}

Notes
If no intended kit is given the item is generic in fitment/use
3dp – 3D Printed
br – Brass
bz – Bronze
conv – Conversion
dec – Decals
ma – Die-cut Self-adhesive Paint Masks [tape]
wm – White-metal (including Pewter)
pe – Photo-etched Brass
res – Resin
vac – Vac-formed Plastic
vma – Die-cut Self-adhesive Paint Masks [vinyl]
{Academy} – Denotes the kit for which the set is intended

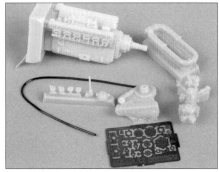

Aires #4033

Aires #4090

Brassin #648059

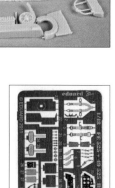

CMK #4059

Eduard #49-525

Brassin 648058

Eduard Space 3DL48055

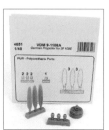

CMK 4051

Hawkeye Designs #303

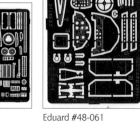

Eduard #48-720   Eduard #48-061

Eduard #FE517   Eduard #FE525

Hi-Tech #004   HI-Tech #009   Hi-Tech #109-505   Jeshs Conversion Factory

- Brassin [res/pe] Bf 109E MG17 Mount #648060 {Eduard}
- Brassin [res] Bf 109E Wheels (inc. tailwheel/yoke) #648058 {Eduard}
- Brassin [res/pe] Bf 109E LööK – Instrument panel & seat belts etc. #644024 {Eduard}
- Cutting Edge Modelsworks [red] Bf 109E Control Surfaces #CEC48249 {Hasegawa}
- Cutting Edge Modelsworks [red] Bf 109E Seat with belts #CEC48399
- Cutting Edge Modelsworks [red] Bf 109E Seat without belts #CEC48397
- Cutting Edge Modelsworks [red] Bf 109E Super Detailed Cockpit #CEC48379 {Hasegawa etc.}
- Cutting Edge Modelsworks [red] Bf 109E Super Detailed Instrument Panel #CEC48413
- CMK [res] VDM9-11081A Propeller for Bf 109E #4051
- CMK [res] Bf 109E Control Surfaces #4057 {Tamiya}
- CMK [res/pe] Bf 109E Engine Detail Set #4058 {Tamiya}
- CMK [res/pe] Bf 109E DB 601A/B Engine #4059 {Tamiya}
- Eduard [pe] Bf 109B/C Detail Set #48-088 {Hobbycraft}
- Eduard [vma] Bf 109B, C & D Canopy & Wheel Masks #XF136
- Eduard [pe/ma] Bf 109C BIG ED – Masks + Interior & Exterior Detail Sets #BIG49254 {Modelsvit}
- Eduard [pe] Bf 109C Detail Sets [Pre-painted] #49-1085 {Modelsvit}
- Eduard [pe] Bf 109C Interior Detail Set – 'Zoom' [Pre-painted] #FE1086 {Modelsvit}
- Eduard [pe] Bf 109C Seat Belts, Steel [Pre-painted] #FE1086 {Modelsvit}
- Eduard [pe] Bf 109C/D Detail Set #48-348 {Hobbycraft/Academy}
- Eduard [pe] Bf 109D Detail Set – 'Zoom' #FE139 {Hobbycraft/Academy}

- Eduard [pe] Bf 109E Access & Scribing Templates #48-419 {Hasegawa}
- Eduard [pe] Bf 109E Access & Scribing Templates #48-445 {Tamiya}
- Eduard [vma] Bf 109E Canopy & Wheels Masks #XF135 {Hasegawa}
- Eduard [ma] Bf 109E Canopy & Wheel Masks [Kabuki Tape] #EX317 {Airfix}
- Eduard [ma] Bf 109E Canopy & Wheel Masks [Kabuki Tape] #EX020 {Hasegawa}
- Eduard [pe] Bf 109E Detail Set [Pre-painted] #49-651 {Eduard 'Weekend Edition'}
- Eduard [pe] Bf 109E Large Mottle Masks #XF561
- Eduard [pe/pa] Bf 109E Seat Belts – Fabric #49-067
- Eduard [pe] Bf 109E Small Mottle Masks #XF563
- Eduard [pe] Bf 109E Tools & Boxes #48-760 {Eduard}
- Eduard [pe] Bf 109E Wheel Well Canvas Covers #48-492 {Hasegawa}
- Eduard [pe] Bf 109E Wheel Well Canvas Covers #48-511{Tamiya}
- Eduard [pe] Bf 109E-1 Detail Set #48-720 {Eduard}
- Eduard [pe] Bf 109E-1 Detail Set – 'zoom' [Pre-painted] #FE1071 {Eduard 'Weekend Edition'}
- Eduard [ma] Bf 109E-3 Canopy & Wheel Masks [Kabuki Tape] #EX019 {Tamiya}
- Eduard [pe] Bf 109E-3 Detail Set #48-061 {Hasegawa}
- Eduard [pe] Bf 109E-3 Detail Set [Pre-painted] #49-205 {Tamiya}
- Eduard [pe] Bf 109E-3 Detail Set [Pre-painted/SA] #49-517 {Airfix}
- Eduard [pe] Bf 109E-3 Detail Set – 'Zoom' #FE205 {Tamiya}
- Eduard {pe] Bf 109E-3 Interior Detail Set – 'Zoom' [Pre-painted/SA] #FE517 {Airfix}
- Eduard [pe] Bf 109E-3 & E-4 Detail Set #48-196 {Tamiya}
- Eduard [pe] Bf 109E-3/E-4 Detail Set #48-774

{Eduard}
- Eduard [pe/ma] Bf 109E-4 BIG ED – Masks + Interior & Exterior Detail Sets #BIG4957 {Airfix}
- Eduard [ma] Bf 109E-4 Canopy & Wheel Masks [Kabuki Tape] #EX117 {Tamiya}
- Eduard [pe] Bf 109E-4 Detail Set #48-082 {Hasegawa}
- Eduard [pe] Bf 109E-4 Detail Set [Pre-painted/SA] #49-525 {Airfix}
- Eduard [pe] Bf 109E-4 Interior Detail Set – 'Zoom' [Pre-painted/SA] #FE525 {Airfix}
- Eduard [pe/3dp] Bf 109E-4 – 'Space' #3DL48049 {Eduard}
- Eduard [pe] Bf 109E-3, E-4 & E-7 Detail Set #48-276 {Tamiya}
- Eduard [pe] Bf 109E-4 & E-7   Detail Set #48-355 {Hasegawa}
- Eduard [pe] Bf 109E-4/E-7 Detail Set #48-780 {Eduard}
- Eduard [vma] Bf 109E-4 to E-7 Canopy & Wheel Masks #XF001 {Tamiya}
- Eduard [ma] Bf 109E-4/E-7 Canopy & Wheel Masks [Kabuki Tape] #EX130 {Tamiya}
- Eduard [pe] Bf 109E-4 to E-7 Detail Set – Zoom #FE101 {Tamiya}
- Eduard [pe] Bf 109E-4/E-7 Detail Set – 'Zoom' #FE220 {Tamiya}
- Eduard [pe] Bf 109E-4/E-7 Detail Set [Pre-painted] #49-2205 {Tamiya}
- Eduard [pe/3dp] Bf 109E-7 – 'Space' #3DL48055 {Eduard}
- Eduard [pe] Bf 109E-7 Trop Detail Set – 'Zoom' [Pre-painted] #FE703 {Eduard 'Weekend Edition'}
- Falcon [vac] Luftwaffe Part 2 inc. Bf 109B/E & E-4 canopies #Set No.16 {Academy/Hobbycraft}
- Falcon [vac] Luftwaffe Part 3 inc. Bf 109E-3 canopies #Set No.35 {Hasegawa & Tamiya}
- Falcon [vac] Luftwaffe Part 4 inc. Bf 109B-1 'Early' canopy #Set No.38 {Academy/Hobbycraft}
- Falcon [vac] Bf 109 Special inc. Bf 109 V3, V13, B/C/D, E-1/E-3, E-4/E/7 canopies #Set No.50

{Academy/Hobbycraft, Hasegawa & Tamiya}
- Fotocut [pe] Bf 109E Details #None
- Hawkeye Designs [res] Bf 109E Detail Set #301
- Hawkeye Designs [res] Bf 109T Conversion #303 {Hasegawa}
- HGW [pe/pa] Bf 109E Seat Belts #148011 {Eduard}
- HGW [pe/pa] Bf 109E Seat Belts #148017 {Airfix, Eduard, Hasegawa & Tamiya}
- Hi-Tech [res] Bf 109E Cockpit & Engine Set #004 {Hasegawa}
- Hi-Tech [res] Bf 109E Detail Set #005 {Tamiya}
- Hi-Tech [res] Bf 109B/C Detail Set #009 {Hobbycraft}
- Hi-Tech [res] Daimler-Benz DB 605A engine [Bf 109E] #505
- Hi-Tech [res] Bf 109E Superdetail Set #109.005 {Hasegawa & Tamiya}
- Hi-Tech [res] Bf 109B/C Superdetail Set #109.009 {Hobbycraft}
- Hi-Tech [res] Daimler-Benz DB 605A engine [Bf 109E] #109-505
- Jesh's Conversion Factory [res] Bf 109E Snow Skid conversion #None {Hasegawa (Bf 109E-4 or 7)}
- JMGT [res/wm/vac] Bf 109C/D Conversion #None {Hasegawa}
- KA Models [res/pe] Bf 109E Detail Parts #48004 {Hasegawa}
- Kelik [3dp] Bf 109E Interior #K3D48009 {Wingsy}
- Kendall Model Company [res] Bf 109E Control Surfaces #48-5006 {Hasegawa}
- Kendall Model Company [res] Bf 109E-3 Update Set #48-4023 {Tamiya}
- Kendall Model Company [res] Bf 109E-4/7 Cockpit Set #48-6019 {Hasegawa}
- Komplekt Zip [res] Bf 109E External Details #48014 {Eduard}
- Master Models [br] Bf 109E-3 to E-9 & T Armament Set #AM48-009 {Hasegawa or Tamiya}
- Medallion Models [res] Bf 109B/C/D Detail Set #MM1 {Hasegawa Bf 109E}
- Medallion Models [res] Bf 109E-1 Conversion #MM2 {Hasegawa}

- Medallion Models [res] Bf 109E/F/early G Wheels #MM3
- Metallic Details [res] Bf 109E Tailwheel Yoke #MDR48102
- MK1 Design[res/pe/br] Bf 109E Detail-up Parts #MA-48004 {Hasegawa}
- Model Technologies [pe] Bf 109E Superset #MT0089 {Hasegawa}
- Montex [vma] Bf 109D Markings and Canopy Masks #MM48136 {Academy #2178}
- Moskit [mtl] Bf 109E Exhausts #48-01
- North Star Models [res] Bf 109B/C/E Wheels 'Metzeler tyres' #NS48018
- North Star Models [res] Bf 109E-1/E-3 Wheels 'Continental tyres' #NS48019
- North Star Models [res] Bf 109E-4/E-7 Wheels 'Continental tyres' #NS48020
- Owl [res/dec] Bf 109E-4 Peil G IV 'Spanner Anlage' conversion #OWR48017
- Part [pe] Bf 109B Detail Set #S48-050 {Hobbycraft}
- Part [pe] Bf 109B, C & D Canopy Frames #S48-055 {Hobbycraft/Academy}
- Part [pe] Bf 109E Detail Set #S48-049 {Hasegawa}
- Part [pe] Bf 109E Canopy Frames #S48-056 {Hobbycraft/Academy}
- Pavla [res] Bf 109D/E Main Wheels #U48-05
- Pavla [res] Bf 109E Update Set (Radiators, gun barrels, wheels & exhausts) #U48-35 {Airfix}
- Pavla [res] Bf 109E Control Surfaces #U48-36 {Airfix}
- Quickboost [res] Bf 109E Corrected Radiators #QB48752 {Eduard}
- Quickboost [res] Bf 109E Exhausts #QB48085 {Tamiya}
- Quickboost [res] Bf 109E Exhausts #QB48942 {Eduard}
- Quickboost [res] Bf 109E Gun Barrels #QB48090 {Tamiya}
- Quickboost [res] Bf 109E Engine (& cowling) #QB48241 {Tamiya}
- Quickboost [res] Bf 109E Exhausts #QB48375 {Airfix}
- Quickboost [res] Bf 109E Air Intake and Cover

Injection #QB48456 {Eduard}
- Quickboost [res] Bf 109E Propeller with tool #QB48473 {Eduard}
- Quickboost [res] Bf 109E Stabilisers #QB48480 {Eduard}
- Quick & Easy [res] Bf 109E Wheels #Q48070 {Hasegawa, Hobbycraft or Tamiya}
- Quick & Easy [res] Bf 109E/F/G/K Control Columns #Q48071 {Hasegawa}
- Quinta Studio [3dp] Bf 109C/D Interior #QD48105 {Modelsvit}
- Quinta Studio [3dp] Bf 109E Control Surfaces #QD48001 {Wingsy Kits}
- Quinta Studio [3dp] Bf 109E Interior #QD48177 {Airfix}
- Quinta Studio [3dp] Bf 109E Interior #QD48097 {Tamiya}
- Quinta Studio [3dp] Bf 109E-1 Interior #QD48176 {Wingsy Kits}
- Quinta Studio [3dp] Bf 109E-1/E-3 Interior #QD48086 {Eduard}
- Quinta Studio [3dp] Bf 109E-3/E-4 Interior #QD48097 {Tamiya}
- Quinta Studio [3dp] Bf 109E-4/E-7 Interior #QD48086 {Eduard}
- Red Fox Studio [3dp] Bf 109C-3 Instrument Panel #RFQS-48006 {Modelsvit}
- Red Fox Studio [3dp] Bf 109E-1 Instrument Panel #RFQS-48003 {EDUARD}
- Red Fox Studio [3dp] Bf 109E-4/7 Instrument Panel #RFQS-48105 {Tamiya}
- Res-IM [ma] Bf 109E-3 Paint Masks #GM48005 {Tamiya}
- ResKit [res] Bf 109E Wheel Set, Weighted #RS48-0339
- REXx [mtl] Bf 109A/B Exhausts #48058 {AMG}
- REXx [mtl] Bf 109C/D Exhausts #48059 {AMG}
- REXx [mtl] Bf 109E Exhausts – Highly Detailed Version #48024
- REXx [mtl] Bf 109E Exhausts #48032
- SBS [res] Bf 109E Seats with Harness #48007
- SBS [res] Bf 109E Seats without Harness #48008
- SBS [res/pe] Bf 109E Cockpit Set #48013 {Hasegawa & Tamiya}

Kendall #48-6019

Master #AM-48-009

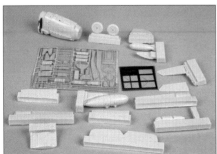

Teknics #TK48034

Kendall #49-4023

Quickboost #Q48473

Quickboost #Q48085

Quickboost #Q48241

Quick and Easy #Q48070

Quick & Easy Q48070

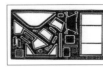

Part #S48-055

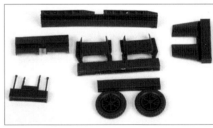

Pavla Models #U48-35

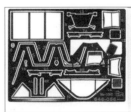

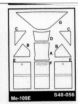

Part #S48-056

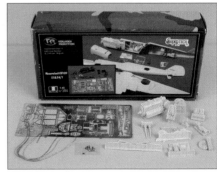

Verlinden #384

- Scale Aircraft Conversions [wm] Bf 109 Landing Gear #48187 {Eduard}
- Scale Aircraft Conversions [wm] Bf 109E-3/4/7 Landing Gear #48224 {TAMIYA}
- Special Mask [ma] Bf 109E-4 Canopy & Wheel Masks #M72009 {Special Hobby/Eduard}
- Special Mask [ma] Bf 109E-1/E-3 Canopy & Wheel Masks #M72010 {Special Hobby/Eduard}
- Squadron [vac] Bf 109B/E canopy #9535 {Hobbycraft}
- Squadron [vac] Bf 109B/E canopy #9235 {Academy/Hobbycraft, Airfix, Hasegawa, Revell and Tamiya}
- Squadron [vac] Bf 109E 'Late' canopy #9236 {Hasegawa & Tamiya}
- Squadron [vac] Bf 109E-3 Canopy #9591 {Hasegawa & Tamiya}
- Squadron [vac] Bf 109E-4 Canopy #9536 {Hobbycraft}
- Squadron [vac] Bf 109E-4 Canopy #9623 {Hasegawa & Tamiya}
- Squadron [vac] Bf 109E-4/E-7 Canopy #9623 {Tamiya}
- Teknics [res/pe] Bf 109E Airframe Update #TK48034 {Hasegawa}
- Teknics [res/pe] Bf 109E Cockpit Superset #TK4825 {Hasegawa}
- True Details [res] Bf 109B thru G-2 Wheels, Radial Tread #46001 (*later renumbered #48003*)
- True Details [res] Bf 109B/E Seats x2 #48410
- True Details [res] Bf 109E-4/E-7 Cockpit [ex-Kendall Model Company] #49005 {Hasgawa}
- Ultracast [res] Bf 109B-E Seats with belts #48022
- Ultracast [res] Bf 109E Propeller with Blunt Spinner #48129 {Tamiya}
- Ultracast [res] Bf 109E Propeller with Pointed Spinner #48130 {Tamiya}
- Ultracast [res] Bf 109E Propeller with Standard Spinner #48128 {Tamiya}
- Verlinden Productions [res/pe] Bf 109E-3, 4 & 7 Superdetail Set #384 {Hasegawa}
- Verlinden Productions [res/pe] Bf 109 Underwing Stores Set #1321

1/32nd

- Aber [br] Bf 109E-3 to E-9 Armament Set #32112
- Aires [res] Bf 109 Wheel Bay #2016 {Hasegawa}
- Aires [res/ma] Bf 109E Wheels & Masks #2090 {Eduard}
- Aires [res/pe] Bf 109E-1 Cockpit Set #2103 {Eduard}
- Aires [res/pe] Bf 109E-4/E-7 Cockpit Set #2104 {Eduard}
- Aires [res/pe] Bf 109E Radio Equipment #2113 {Eduard}
- Alley Cat [res/dec] Bf 109A conversion #AC32008C {Eduard (Bf 109E-1)}
- Alley Cat [res/dec] Bf 109 Spanish Civil War conversion #AC32006C {Eduard (Bf 109E-1 or E-3)}
- Alley Cat [res/dec] Bf 109B Luftwaffe/Spanish conv. #AC32009C {Eduard (Bf 109E-1 or E-3)}
- Alley Cat [res/dec] Bf 109C conversion #AC32004C {Eduard (Bf 109E-1 or E-3)}
- Alley Cat [res/dec] Bf 109D conversion #AC32005C {Eduard (Bf 109E-1 or E-3)}
- Alley Cat [res/dec] Bf 109D Swiss AF conversion #AC32007C {Eduard (Bf 109E-1 or E-3)}
- Alley Cat [res/dec] Bf 109T-2 conversion #AC32001C {Eduard (Bf 109E-1 or E-3)}
- AML [ma] Bf 109E 'Late' Camouflage Painting Masks #AMLM3306 {Eduard & Hasegawa}
- BarracudaCast [res] Bf 109E/F Main Wheels with ribbed tyres #BCR32436
- Brassin [res/pe] Bf 109E BIG SIN (DB 601, wheels & MG17 mounts) #SIN63201 {Eduard}
- Brassin [res/pe] Bf 109E DB 601A/N Engine #632003 {Eduard}
- Brassin [res/pe] Bf 109E Engine #632137 {Eduard}
- Brassin [res/pe] Bf 109E Fuselage Guns #632138 {Eduard}
- Brassin [res/pe] Bf 109E Wheels #632004 {Eduard}
- Brassin [res/pe] Bf 109E SD2 Cluster Bombs & Carrier #632007 {Eduard}
- Brassin [res] Bf 109E MG 17 Mount (inc. ammo boxes) #632009 {Eduard}
- CMK [res] Bf 109E Engine Set #5033 {Eduard}
- Cutting Edge Modelworks [res] Bf 109A Conversions #CEC32134 {Hasegawa Bf 109E}
- Cutting Edge Modelworks [res] Bf 109A/B/C/D Super Detailed Cockpit #CEC32132 {Hasegawa or Matchbox Bf 109E}
- Cutting Edge Modelworks [res] Bf 109B-1 Conversions #CEC32135 {Hasegawa Bf 109E}
- Cutting Edge Modelworks [res] Bf 109B/C/D Super Detailed Cockpit with built-in seat belts #CEC32088
- Cutting Edge Modelworks [res] Bf 109B/C/D Super Detailed Cockpit with separate seat belts #CEC32106
- Cutting Edge Modelworks [res] Bf 109B/C/D Super Detailed Cockpit #CEC32142
- Cutting Edge Modelworks [res] Bf 109C/D Conversions #CEC32136 {Hasegawa Bf 109E}
- Cutting Edge Modelworks [res] Bf 109E Detailed Wheel Wells #CEC32113
- Cutting Edge Modelworks [res] Bf 109E Seat with Pad and Belts #CEC32112
- Cutting Edge Modelworks [res] Bf 109E Seat with Belts but without Pad #CEC32111
- Cutting Edge Modelworks [res] Bf 109E Seat with Pad but without Belts #CEC32108
- Cutting Edge Modelworks [res] Bf 109E Seat without Belts or Pad #CEC32107
- Eagle Parts [res] Bf 109 Oil Cooler #32-24 {Hasegawa}
- Eagle Parts [res] Bf 109E-1 Control Surfaces #32-32 {Hasegawa}
- Eduard [inj/pe] Bf 109E Bomb Set #3005 {Eduard}
- Eduard [ma] Bf 109E Canopy & Wheel Masks [Kabuki Tape] #JX023 {Hasegawa}
- Eduard [vma] Bf 109E Canopy & Wheel Masks #XL014 {Hasegawa}
- Eduard [pe] Bf 109E Detail Set #32-219 {Eduard}
- Eduard [pe] Bf 109E Exterior Detail Set #32-048 {Hasegawa}
- Eduard [pe] Bf 109E-1/E-3 Detail Set [Pre-painted] #32-696 {Eduard 'Weekend Edition'}
- Eduard [pe/ma] Bf 109E-3 BIG ED – Masks + Interior & Exterior Detail Sets #BIG3295 {Trumpeter}
- Eduard [ma] Bf 109E-3 Canopy & Wheel Masks [Kabuki Tape] #JX108 {Trumpeter}
- Eduard [ma] Bf 109E-3 Canopy & Wheel Masks [Kabuki Tape] #JX121 {Eduard 'Weekend Edition'}
- Eduard [pe] Bf 109E-3 Exterior Detail Set #32-251 {Trumpeter}
- Eduard [pe] Bf 109E-3 Exterior Detail Set #32-332 {Dragon/Cyber-Hobby}
- Eduard [pe] Bf 109E-3 Interior Detail Set [Pre-painted/SA] #32-658 {Trumpeter}
- Eduard [pe] Bf 109E-3 Interior Detail Set [Pre-painted] #32-758 {Dragon/Cyber-Hobby}
- Eduard [pe] Bf 109E-3 Interior – Zoom [Pre-painted/SA] #33061 {Trumpeter}
- Eduard [pe] Bf 109E-3 Interior – Zoom [Pre-painted/SA] #33122 {Dragon/Cyber-Hobby}
- Eduard [pe/ma] Bf 109E-4 BIG ED – Masks + Interior & Exterior Detail Sets #BIG3307 {Cyber-Hobby/Dragon}
- Eduard [ma] Bf 109E-4 Canopy & Wheel Masks [Kabuki Tape] #JX124 {Cyber-Hobby/Dragon}
- Eduard [pe] Bf 109E-4 Exterior Detail Set #32-282 {Cyber-Hobby/Dragon}
- Eduard [pe] Bf 109E-4 Interior Detail Set [pre-painted/SA] #32-701 {Cyber-Hobby/Dragon}
- Eduard [pe] Bf 109E-4 Interior – Zoom [Pre-painted/SA] #33089 {Cyber-Hobby/Dragon}
- Eduard [ma] Bf 109E-7 Canopy & Wheel Masks [Kabuki Tape] #JX146 {Trumpeter}
- Eduard [pe] Bf 109E-7 Exterior Detail Set #32-322 {Trumpeter}
- Eduard [pe] Bf 109E-7 Interior Detail Set [Pre-painted/SA] #32-752 {Trumpeter}
- Eduard [pe] Bf 109E-7 Interior – Zoom [Pre-painted/SA] #33114 {Trumpeter}
- Fotocut [pe] Bf 109E Details #None {Hasegawa}
- G-Factor [bz] Bf 109 Undercarriage #32004 {Hasegawa}
- G-Factor [bz] Bf 109E-4 Undercarriage #32026 {Dragon}
- Grand Phoenix [res/pe] Bf 109E Cockpit Detail Set #32004 {Hasegawa}

Aires #2090

Aires #2113

Alley Cat #AC32004C

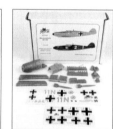

Alley Cat #AC32005C

Brassin #632003

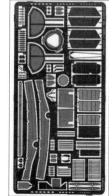

Eduard #32-322

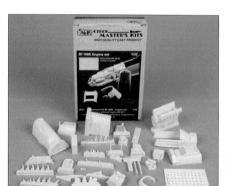

CMK #5033

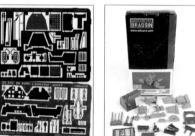

Eduard #32-701

Brassin #632009

Brassin #632004

Quickboost #Q32055

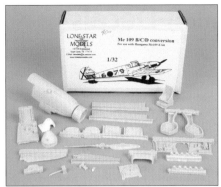

Lone Star Models

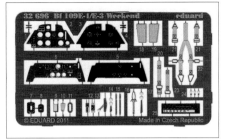

Eduard #32-696

Eduard #32-752

Master #AM-32-005

G-Factor #32026

Quick & Easy #Q32083

Quick and Easy #Q32083

Quickboost #Q32065   Quickboost #Q32133

- HGW [pe/pa] Bf 109E Seat Belts #132001 {Cyber-Hobby, Eduard & Trumpeter}
- HGW [pe] Bf 109E-1 Exterior #132618 {Dragon/ Cyber-Hobby }
- HGW [pe] Bf 109E-1 Interior #132617 {Dragon/ Cyber-Hobby }
- HGW [pe/pa] Luftwaffe Fighters 'Early' Seat Belts #132501
- Horizon Conversions [res] Bf 109B/C Conversion #HDC-3204 {Hasegawa Bf 109E}
- Komplekt Zip [res] Bf 109E External Details #32001 {Eduard}
- Lone Star Models [res] Bf 109B/C Conversion #LSM 30555 {Hasegawa Bf 109E} – *ex-Horizon Conversions*
- Master Models [br] Bf 109E-3 to E-9 & T Armament Set #AM32-005 {Eduard}
- Metallic Details [res] Bf 109E Tail Wheel Yoke #MDR3208
- Montex [vma] Bf 109E-3/E-4 Canopy Masks #SM32039 {Hasegawa}
- Montex [vma] Bf 109E-1 Canopy Masks #SM32096 {Eduard}
- Montex [vma] Bf 109E-4 Canopy Masks #SM32097 {Eduard}
- North Star Models [res] Bf 109B/C /E Wheel Set 'Metzeler tyres' #NS32007
- North Star Models [res] Bf 109E-1/E-3 Wheel Set 'Continental tyres' #NS32008
- North Star Models [res] Bf 109E-4/E-7 Wheel Set 'Continental tyres' #NS32009
- Part [pe] Bf 109B Detail Set #S48-050 {Hobbycraft (Academy)}
- Profimodeller [br] Bf 109E-1 Gun Barrels #32298
- Profimodeller [br] Bf 109E-4/Trop Gun Barrels #32299
- Quickboost [res] Bf 109 Control Levers #QB32018 {Hasegawa}
- Quickboost [res] Bf 109E Exhausts #QB32023 {Hasegawa}
- Quickboost [res] Bf 109E Exhausts #QB32055 {Eduard}
- Quickboost [res] Bf 109E Seat with Safety Belts #QB32133

- Quickboost [res] Bf 109E Ammunition Boxes #QB32065 {Eduard}
- Quick & Easy [res] Bf 109E Wheels #Q32083 {Eduard or Hasegawa}
- Quickboost [res] Bf 109E Seat with safetly belts #QB32133
- Quick & Easy [res] Bf 109E Wheels #Q32083 {Eduard or Hasegawa}
- Quick & Easy [res] Bf 109E/F/G/K Control Columns #Q32084 {Eduard or Hasegawa}
- Quinta Studio [3dp] Bf 109E-1 Interior #QD32047 {Eduard}
- Quinta Studio [3dp] Bf 109E-3 Interior #QD32048 {Eduard}
- Quinta Studio [3dp] Bf 109E-3 Interior #QD32052 {Cyber-Hobby/Dragon}
- Quinta Studio [3dp] Bf 109E-4 Interior #QD32049 {Eduard}
- Quinta Studio [3dp] Bf 109E-4 Interior #QD32053 {Cyber-Hobby/Dragon}
- RB Productions [pe] Bf 109E Radiators #RP-P32033 {Cyber-Hobby/Dragon}
- Roberts Models [res] Bf 109 Wheels #N/K
- ResKit [res] Bf 109E Wheel Set, Weighted #RS32-0339
- REXx [mtl] Bf 109E Exhausts #32001 {Cyber-Hobby/Dragon}
- Scale Aircraft Conversions [wm] Bf 109 Landing Gear #32007 {Hasegawa}
- Scale Aircraft Conversions [wm] Bf 109E Landing Gear #32028 {Eduard}
- Scale Aircraft Conversions [wm] Bf 109 Landing Gear #32053 {Trumpeter}
- Scale Aircraft Conversions [wm] Bf 109 Landing Gear #32055 {Dragon/Cyber-Hobby}
- Squadron [vac] Bf 109E-4 canopy #9409 {Hasegawa}
- True Details [res] Bf 109E Cockpit Set #32452 {Hasgawa}
- Verlinden Productions [res/pe] Bf 109E Superdetail Set #741 {Hasegawa}
- Werner's Wings [res/dec] Bf 109 V13 Record Setter Conv. #32-V13RS {Eduard (Bf 109E-1 or E-3)}
- Werner's Wings [res/dec] Bf 109 V14 Dübendorf

Conversion #32-V14 {Eduard (Bf 109E-1 or E-3)}
- Waldron Model Products [pe] Bf 109E Ammunition Counters #3228 {Hasegawa}
- Wolfpack Design [res/dec] Bf 109T-2 conversion #WPD32009 {Eduard}

1/24th

- Aber [br] MG131 Barrels #24-001 {Airfix & Trumpeter}
- Aber [br] MG17 Barrels #24-002 {Airfix & Trumpeter}
- Airscale [pe] Instrument Bezels inc Bf 109E #24BEZ
- Airscale [dec] Instrument Dial Decals – Bf 109E #24MEA
- Airscale [pe/dec] Bf 109E Instrument Panel Upgrade #24MES
- Airscale [pe] Cockpit Details inc Bf 109E #24DET
- BaracudaCast [res] Bf 109E/F Main Wheels with ribbed tyres #BCR24435
- Eduard [pe] Seat Belts [Pre-painted] #23-003 {Airfix or Trumpeter}
- Eduard [pe] Instrument Bezels [Pre-painted] #23-014 {Airfix or Trumpeter}
- Master Models [br] MG17 Barrels #AM24-002 {Airfix & Trumpeter}
- Master Models [br] MG131 Barrels #AM24-003 {Airfix & Trumpeter}
- Montex [vma] Bf 109E-3/E-4 Canopy Masks #SM24010 {Airfix}
- Scale Aircraft Conversions [wm] Bf 109e Landing Gear #24011 {Airfix}
- Squadron [vac] Bf 109E-1/E-3 Canopy #9802 {Airfix}
- Squadron [vac] Bf 109E-4/E-7 Canopy #9803 {Airfix}
- Waldron Model Products [pe] Bf 109E Ammunition Counters #2428 {Airfix}

1/18th

- Profimodeller [pe] Bf 109E Instrument Panel #18002 {Merit}

Roberts Models #109

SAC #32028

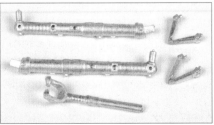

SAC #32055

Master Model #AM24-002

Squadron #9802

Squadron #9803

Appendix III: **Bf 109 V1 to E-9** (inc. T-series) **Decals**

Below is a list of all the decal sheets and masks* produced to date of the early Bf 109s that we could find. This list is as comprehensive as possible, but there are bound to be omissions so if there are amendments or additions, please contact the author via the Valiant Wings Publishing address shown at the front of this title.

For standard canopy/wheel or camouflage pattern masks see Appendix II.

1/144th Scale

LF Models
#C4414 Bf 109E in Romanian Service Part I
E-3, 'Yellow 27', flown by Sit.av I. Dicezore, Gr.7, summer 1941; E-7, 'Yellow 47', floown by Adj.av. C. Lunguiesca, Gr.7, summer 1944; E-3, 'Yellow 64', flown by Adj.av.T. Vinca, Gr.7, Vanatoare, summer 1942

#C4415 Bf 109E in Romanian Service Part II
E-3, 'Yellow 11', flown by A. Serbanescu, Gr.7, Bucharest-Pipera, summer 1942; E-3, 'Yellow 26', flown by Adj.av. S. Greceanu, Gr.7, Escadrille 57, Salz, Bessarabia, September 1941; E-3, 'Yellow 45', flown by Cap.av. G. Iliescu CO of Gr.5, Escadrille 52, Mamaiai, summer 1943

#C44109 Bf 109B Condor Legion
B-1, •6-10, flown by Staffelkapitän Oblt G. Lutzow, Legion Condor, Victoria, Spain, 7th April 1937; B-2, 6•32, flown by ObFw. R. Seiler, Legion Condor, Spain, summer 1937

#C44110 Bf 109E-3a Over Yugoslavia Part 1
E-3a, L-32, 102 Esk, Royal Yugoslavian Air Force, 1940-41; E-3a, L-33, 102 Esk, Royal Yugoslavian Air Force, 1940-41; E-3a, L-42, 2rd Flight School, Royal Yugoslavian Air Force, 1940-41

#C44111 Bf 109E-3a Over Yugoslavia Part 2
E-3a, L-33, 102 Esk, Royal Yugoslavian Air Force, 1940-41; E-3a, L-43, 102 Esk, Royal Yugoslavian Air Force, 1940-41; E-3a, L-53, 2rd Flight School, Royal Yugoslavian Air Force, 1940-41

Print-Scale
#144-014 Bf 109E
'Red 10', 2./J 101, 1939; 'Yellow 14', 6./J 186, 1940; 'Yellow 3', 6./JG 52, 1940; 6•123, 3/J, Spain, 1939; 'Yellow 9', 9./JG 26, 1940; 'Red 1', 2./JG 26, 1940; 'Red 2', 2./JG 26, 1940; 'Black 13', 2./JG77, 1940; S9+6D, 4/b ZG 1, 1942; 'Yellow 47', Romanian Forces, 1942; 'Red 0', JG 26, 1940; 'Blue H', II./JG 1, 1942; 'White 8', 7./ZG 26, 1941; 'Black <<', 1./4G, 1941; 'Black <<', 1./JG 2, 1940

1/72nd Scale

ABT
#3 Bf 109E JG26
Inc. 'Black <-+-' flown by Adolf Galland, KG26; 'Yellow 10' of 9./JG26

#14 Jagdgeschwader 27
Inc. 4x Bf 109Es – *No further details known*

#43 Espana 1936-1939
Inc. Bf 109B-2, 6•56, flown by Hptm. G. Handrick, J88, Legion Condor, Spanish Civil War

#104
Bf 109E, '<<', III./JG2, flown by Hptm Erich Mix, France, May 1940

#138
Bf 109E, 'Black L-12', 6th Fighter Regiment, Royal Yugoslavian Air Force, 1940

AeroMaster
#72-003 Battle of Britain
Inc. Bf 109E-3, E-3b & E-4 – *No further details*

#72-073 Desert War Bf 109s of JG27
Inc. Bf 109E-7/Trop, 'Black <A', I./JG27, flown by Oblt L. Franzisket, Castel Benito, Libya, April 1941; Bf 109E-7/Trop, 'Black <', flown by Oblt L. Franzisket, Libya, October 1941

#72-074 Mediterranean Bf 109s of JG27
Inc. E-4, III./JG27, flown by Hptm. Max Dobislav, Castel Benito, Sicily, May 1941

#SP72-01 Luftwaffe Top Guns
Inc. E-3, W/Nr.3714, flown by Obstlt Heinz Bär, 1./JG51, Pihen, France, September 1940; E-7/N. flown by Obst. Hermann Graf, 9./JG52, Russia, Summer 1941; E-3, flown by Obstlt Hans Philipp, 4./JG54, France, October 1940

Almark
#A14 Bf 109E/F/G of JG 54
Unit badges for I, II, II, IV, 3, 7, 8 & 9./JG54 plus national insignia for Croatian Air Force and Bf 109E/G stencils

#C10 Reichs Defence (Bf 109E-1/Bf 109E-3/ Bf 109E-5)
9./JG 26; 7./JG 53; 6./JG 52; 2./JG 3; 3./JG 2

#C11 Messerschmitt Bf 109E 'Europe'
Oblt G. Schopfel, 9./JG26; Offz Schulte, 7./JGS3; Ofw W. Friedmann; Oblt H. Strupell, 3./JG2; 'Red 2', 3./JG2

APC
#APCR72043 Replacement decals for Matchbox Bf 109E PK-17

Avalon Decals
#7003 Bf 109E Early Emils

Blue Rider
#BR217 Croatian Air Force WWII
Inc. Messerschmitt Bf 109E – *No further details*

#BR220 Slovak Air Force WWII
Inc. Messerschmitt Bf 109E, 12th Fighter Squadron, 1943

#BR221 Kondor Legion
B-1, 6•10; B-2,6•20, flown by Lt Fritz Awe; B-2, 6•29, 2.J/88; B-2, 6•36, flown by Oblt Harro Harder, 1.J/88; B-2, 6•51, flown by Oblt W. Schellmann, 1J/88, December 1937; B-2. 6•23 (5-G-5), Spanish Nationalist Air Force, February 1939; B-2, 6•56, flown by Walter Grabmann, 1J/88; B-2, 6•56, flown by Gotthard Handrick, 1J/88; D, 6•79, flown by Oblt W. Mölders, 3J/88, 1937-38; E-1, 6•99, 3J/88; E-1, 6•109, 3J/88

Cutting Edge
#CED72040 Swiss Bf 109s
D-1, J-307, Training Unit, September 1944-45; D-1, J-310, Fliegerkompanie 15, June 1940; E-3, J-317, Fliegerkompanie 8, 1940-44; E-3, J-318, Fliegerkompanie 9, 1940-44; E-3, J-326, 1939-40; E-3, J-345, Fliegerkompanie 21, 1940-44; E-3, J-346, Fliegerkompanie 15, Thoune, 1940; E-3, J-360, 1940-44; E-3, J-374, Fliegerkompanie 9, flown by Lt Dedompierre; E-3, J-387, Payerne, Spring 1945; E-3, J-399, Altenrhein, 1946-48

Delta Decals
#72-002 Luftwaffe Allies #1 – Bulgarian AF
Inc. E-7, 'White 17', Bulgarian Air Force

#72-003 Foreign Bf 109s
Inc. E-3, 'White 2', Slovakian Air Force

DP Casper
#72006 Forgotten Operations: Operation Merkur, Crete, May 1941
Bf 109E-7, 'Black 1', 5./JG77; Bf 109E-4, 'White 11', II./JG77

#72011 Forgotten Operations: Operation Dynamo, Dunkirk, May-June 1940
Bf 109E-3, 'Black <', I./JG77; Bf 109E-1, 'Red 16', 2./JG26; Bf 109E-4, 'Yellow 6', 3./JG3

EagleCal
EC#50 Major Hans 'Assi' Hahn Part 1
Bf 109E-3, 'Black <', StabI./JG3, Merseburg, Germany 1939; Bf 109E-3, 'White 13', 4./JG2, Northern Germany, Spring 1940; Bf 109E-4, 'White 14', 4./JG2, France, 1940; Bf 109E-4, 'White <<', III./JG2, France, 1940

EC#66 Graf and Grislawski 9./JG52 Part 3
Bf 109E-1, 'Black 17', 2/Erg.JGr, 1940; Bf 109E, 'Yellow 9'

Eagle Strike
#72015 Battle of Britain Emils
E-3, 'Red 7', 6./JG26, early 1940; E-7/Trop, 'Black <A', 1./JG27, Castel Benito, Libya, April 1941; E-3, 'Black <-', JG53, France, August 1940; E-3, 'White 4', 4./JG26, September 1940

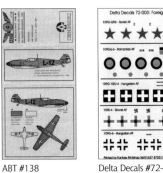

ABT #138

Delta Decals #72-003

Eagle Strike #72015

Lifelike #72-002

Lifelike #72-020   Lifelike #72-021

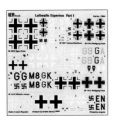

Revi #72004

Revi #72004

Rising Decals #72-012

Rising Decals #72-014

Rising Decals #72-017

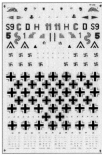

Superscale #72-349

H-Model Decals
#72023 NJG Messerschmitt Bf 109Es
Due 2013, no further details available

#72040 NJG Messerschmitt Bf 109s: German Invasion of Norway
D, N+7, 10.(N)/JG26, 1939; D, N+7, 11.(N)JG2, Vearnes, Norway, 1940; D, N+11, 12.(N)/JG2, Jever, May 1940; D, N+8, 10.(N)/JG77, Oslo, Norway, 1940

Eduard
#D72030 Bf 109E Stencils

Everest Model
#D72001 Bf 109E-1/E-3 Early Emils Part 1

Flying Papa's Decals
#72M-182 Emperor's Emil
E-7 in Imperial Japanese Air Force markings, 1941

Hasegawa Decals
#72004 Bf 109E

HR Models
#HRD7211 Bf 109E in Slovak Service
E, 'hite 1', flown by Capt. O Dumbala, 13 *Staffel* (Slov.) JG 52, Russia, 1941,2-43; E, 'White 6', flown by Sgt J. Reznak, 13 *Staffel* (Slov.) JG 52; e, 'White 10', 13 *Staffel* (Slov.) JG 52, Russia, 1942-43; E-7, Alarm Fighter Flight, Vajnory airfield, 1943-44

Kora
#DEC72.34 Bf 109E-3a Royal Yugoslav Air Force
L-10, 142 Lovacka Eskadrila, Krusedol airfield, April 1941; 'White 11', 6 Vazduhoplovni Lovacki, Zemun airfield, 1940; L-21, 101 Lovacka Eskadrila, Vel Radinci II airfield, 1940; L-80, 101 Lovacka Eskadrila, Vel Radinci II airfield, 1940

#DEC72.41 Bf 109E 7/B Escuadrilla Azul
E-7/B, 'Black M', 15. *Staffel* (Span)/JG27, 1941

#DEC72.92 Bf 109E-3/E-4 Croatian Fighters over Russia
E-3, 'Green 15', 1- Mjesovito Jato Mariupol, Winter 1941-42; E-3, 'Green 17', 4 Zrakoplovna Lovacka Skupina Euratoria, May 1942; E-3, 'Green 2', 4 Zrakoplovna Lovacka Skupina Taganroga, April 1942

#DEC72.93 Bf 109E-4/E-7 Croatian Fighters over Russia
E-4, 'Green 5', 4 Zrakoplovna Lovacka Skupina Euratoria, May 1942; E-7/Trop, 'Green 21', 4 Zrakoplovna Lovacka Skupina Euratoria, May 1942; E-7, 'Green 23', 4 Zrakoplovna Lovacka Skupina Taganroga, April 1942

#DEC72.108 Bulgarian Eagles Part I
E-3, 'White 12', 3 Orliak, Karlovo airfield, Spring 1941; E-7, 'White 19', 3 Orliak, Karlovo airfield, Summer 1942

#DEC72.109 Bulgarian Eagles Part II
E-4a, 'White 4', 3 Orliak, Karlovo airfield, Spring 1942; E-4a, 'White 6', Galata Orliak, Balchik airfield, 1942; E-4a, 'White 7', 3 Orliak, Sarafovo airfield, 1942

#DEC72.110 Bulgarian Eagles Part III
E-4a, 'White 9', 3 Orliak, 682 Jato, Balchik airfield,

1942-43; E-7, 'White 11', 3 Orliak, 672 Jato, Petrovac airfield, 1943; E-7, 'White 17', 3 Orliak, Karlovo airfield, Summer 1942

#DEC72.119 Bf 109D-1 Swiss Air Force
J-302, Fliegerkompanie Fl.Kp.15, Dübendorf airfield, Spring 1941; J-307, Fliegertruppe, Autumn 1944; J-309, Fliegertruppe, January 1939

#DEC72.129 Bf 109D-1 Part II Swiss Air Force
J-303, KDT der Fl.Rgt 4, which crashed at Meiringen, 1948; J-308, Fliegerkompanie 15, Olten AB, May-June 1940; J-310, Fliegerkompanie 15, Olten AB, May-June 1940

#DEC72.130 Bf 109D-1 Part III Swiss Air Force
J-301, Fliegerkompanie 15, early 1940; J-346, Fliegerkompanie 15, Olten AB, Summer 1940; J-387, Fliegerkompanie 15, Olten AB, Summer 1940

#DEC72.131 Bf 109E-3A Emil (Swiss Air Force Part I)
J-301, Fliegerkompanie 15, 1940; J-302, Fliegerkompanie Fl.Kp 15, Dübendorf, Spring 1941; J-303, Fliegerkompanie Fl.Kp 15, Dübendorf, Spring 1941; J-309, Flegertruppe, January 1939

#DEC72.132 Bf 109E-3A Emil (Swiss Air Force Part II)
J-303, KDT der Fl.Rgt 4, which crashed at Meiringen, 1943; J-307, Fliegertruppe, Autumn 1944; J-308, Fliegerkompanie 15, Olten AB, May-June 1940; J-310, Fliegerkompanie 15, Olten AB, May-June 1940

#DEC72.133 Bf 109E-3A Emil (Swiss Air Force Part III)
J-317, Fliegerkompanie 7, Avenches airfield, December 1940; J-334, Fliegerkompanie 7, Avenches airfield, Spring 1941; J-387, Fliegerkompanie 15, Olten airfield, Summer 1940

#DEC72.134 Bf 109E-3A Emil (Swiss Air Force Part IV)
J-360, Fliegerkompanie 8, Avenches airfield, Summer 1940; J-362, Fliegerkompanie 8, Avenches airfield, Summer 1940; J-366, Fliegerkompanie 8, Avenches airfield, Summer 1940

#DEC72.135 Bf 109E-3A Emil (Swiss Air Force Part V)
J-350, Fliegerkompanie 9, Avenches airfield, Spring 1941; J-358, Fliegerkompanie 8, Avenches airfield, Summer 1940; J-359, Fliegerkompanie 8, Avenches airfield, Summer 1940

#DEC72.136 Bf 109E-3A Emil (Swiss Air Force Part VI)
J-320, Fliegerkompanie 9, Avenches airfield, Spring 1945; J-385, Fliegerkompanie 8, Thun airfield, 1945; J-393, Fliegerkompanie 8, Thun airfield, October 1945; J-399, Fliegerkompanie 8, Payerne airfield, 1948;

#DEC72.137 Bf 109E-3A Emil (Swiss Air Force Part VII)
J-320, Fliegerkompanie 9, Avenches airfield, Spring 1945; J-326, Fliegerkompanie 8, Thun airfield, April 1945; J-385, Fliegerkompanie 8, Thun airfield, 1945; J-386, used as a fighter-bomber at Dübendorf airfield, June 1945

#DEC72.138 Bf 109E-3A Emil (Swiss Air Force Part VIII)
J-391, Fliegerkompanie 9, Payerne airfield, March 1947; J-393, Fliegerkompanie 8, Thun airfield, October 1945; J-399, Fliegerkompanie 8, Payerne airfield, 1948

Kuivalainen
#D7202 Luftwaffe Bf 109E over Finland
'Black <', flown by Gunther Scholz, Stab III./JG 5; 'Yellow 7', flown by Horst Carganico, 1./JG 77; 'Black 3', flown by Hermann Segatz, 8./JG 5; 'Red 6', flown by Dieter Widowitz, 5./JG 5; 'White 8', flown by Franz Dörr, 7./JG 5; 'Black 12', flown by Gerhardt Seibt, 4./JG 5 – all based at Petsamo, Finland, in 1941-42

LF Models
#C7207 Bf 109E in Romanian Service
E-3, 'Yellow 27', *Slt.av.* I. Dicezore, Gr.7, Summer 1941; E-7, 'Yellow 47', *Adj.av.* Costa Lungulesca, Gr.7, Summer 1944; E-3, 'Yellow 64', *Adj.av.* Tiberiu Vinca, Gr.7, Vanatoare, Summer 1942

#C7229 Bf 109E in Romanian Service Part II
E-3, 'Yellow 11', Loc.av A. Serbanescu, Gr.7, Bucharest-Pipera, Summer 1942; E-3, 'Yellow 26', *Adj. av.* S. Greceanu, Gr.7, Escadrila 57, Salz, Bessarabia, September 1941; E-3, 'Yellow 45', *Cap.av.* G. Iliescu, Gr.5, Escadrila 52, Mamaiai, Summer 1943

#C7260 Bf 109E-3 over Switzerland – Part I
J-365, Fl.Kp 9, Avenches airfield, 1940; J-347, Fl.Kp 21, Dübendorf airfield, 1940

#C7261 Bf 109E-3 over Switzerland – Part II
J-360, Fl.Kp 8, Avenches airfield, 1940; J-346, Fl.Kp 15, Othen airfield, 1940

#C7262 Bf 109E-3 over Switzerland – Part III
J-346, Fl.Kp 8, Thun airfield, 1944; J-371, Interlaken airfield, 1944

#C72233 Bf 109B Condor Legion
B-1, •6-10, flown by *Staffelkapitän* Oblt G. Lutzow, Legion Condor, Victoria, Spain, 7th April 1937; B-2, 6•32, flown by *ObFw.* R. Seiler, Legion Condor, Spain, summer 1937

Lifelike Decals
#72-002 Bf 109 Part 1
Inc. Bf 109E-1, 'Yellow 5', Hans Troitzsch, 6./JG77, Norway, 1939

#72-019 Bf 109 Part 3
Inc. Bf 109E-1, 'Black 13', 2./JG77, France, 1940

#72-020 Bf 109 Part 4
Inc. Bf 109E-3, 'Black A', JG26, *Oblt* Hasselmann, Audembert, France, Summer 1940

#72-021 Bf 109 Part 5
Inc. Bf 109E-3, 'Black I', III./JG26, flown by *Maj.* E.F. von Berg, Chievres, Belgium, May 1940; Bf 109E-4, flown by Kdr of II./JG26, date and location unknown

Lift Here Decals
#728-LH VVKJ Me 109E and JRV Me 109G
Inc. E-3, No.2511, '11'; E-3, No.2521, 'L-21'

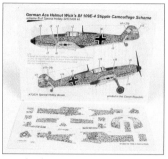

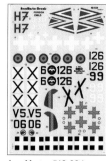

Tally Ho #72012 Third Group #72-005 Xtradecal #X72-118 Special Hobby #K72031 AeroMaster #48-034

#708-LH Royal Yugoslav Aircraft, Part Six
E-3, No.2511, '11'; E-3, No.2521, 'L-21'; E-3, No.2526, 'L-26'; E-3, No.2530, 'L-31'; E-3, No.2532, 'L-33', E-3, 'L-80'; E-3, D-IYWZ

#S-72LH Me 109E
E-3, No.2307, 'L-07'; E-3, No.2310 'L-10'

#M-72LH Messerschmitt Me 109E/G 'War Edition'
E-3a, RYAF, No.2307, 'L-07', April 1941; E-3a, RYAF, No.2310, 'L-10', April 1941

#A-72LH Royal Yugoslav Air Force in April War
Inc. E-3, No.2508, Spring 1940; E-3, No.2551, Summer 1940

Microscale
#72-054
Inc. Bf 109E, *Stab* III./JG 5; Bf 109E-4 flown by Adolph Galland

#72-295 Bf 109B, C & D

Ministry of Small Aircraft Production
#72001 Bf 109E – Poland & France
E-1, 'White 15', I./JG1. August 1940; E-1, 'White 14', JG21; E-1, 'Red 11', IV./JG132, Summer 1939; E-1, 'White 3', JG 132, Franco-German border, September 1939; E-1, 'White 4', 7./JG51, Spring 1940; E-1, 'Yellow 3, 3./JG51, late 1939

#72002 Bf 109E – Battle of Britain
E-4, 'Black <', flown by *Oblt* Franz von Werra, II./JG3, 1940; E-3, 'White 2', flown by Hans Illner, II./JG51; E-4, 'Yellow 1', flown by Gerhardt Schopfel, 9./JG26; E-3, 'White 2', flown by Erich Mummert, 4./JG52; E-3, 'White 13', III./JG54; E-4, ''Yellow M', 6./LG2; E-4, 'Black< |', JG53

#72003 Bf 109E – Russian Campaign
E-7/B, 'S9+CD', III./SKG 210, Central Sector, Autumn 1941; E-7/B, 'White U', flown by Georg Dörffel, 5 Sch.G 1, Stalingrad Front, 1942; E-4, 'Yellow 65', First Fighter Group, Royal Romanian Air Force; E-4, 13(Slovak *Staffel*)/JG52; E-4, 'White 6', unit and location unknown; E-4, 'White 3', III./JG54; E-4/B, 'Black < |', flown by *Lt* Steindl, Leningrad Front, Autumn 1942

Owl
#S7204 Bf 109E-4
'G9+JV', 10/NJG 1, Peil GIV, Germany, 1942

#S72100 Bf 110G-4 & Bf 109D
Inc.
D, N+11, flown by H. Lütje, 12.(N)/JG 2, Köln-Ostheim. Norway, June 1940

Peddinghaus Decals
#EP1771 Me 109E-4
'Black <<', flown by *Hptm*. H. Wick, *Stab* I./JG2, October 1940

#EP1774 Me 109E-4
'Yellow 5', flown by *Oblt* E. G von Kagenreck, 9./JG 27, 1941

#EP1106 Me 109E-3 in Foreign Colours
Swiss AF, J-317, J-318, J-326, J-345, J-360 & J-374

Pieza a Pieza Decals
#PPD72201 Messerschmitt Españoles 'Bipala', 'Tripala','Zacuto' y 'Buchón' Inc.
E-3, 6•119, 1.J/88, Legion Condor, 1939; E-3, 6•111, 3.J/88, flown by *Lt* W. Ursinus, Legion Condor, 1938, E-3, 6•130, 5-G-5 Escuadra Morato, Spanish Nationalist Air Force, September 1939; E-4/B, 15 Spanische *Staffel*, JG27 (1° Esc. Azul), flown by *Maj*. Á. S. Larrazábal, 1941; B-2, 6•36, 1.J/88, flown by *Hptm*. H. Harder, Legion Condor, September 1937; B-2, 6•10, J/88, Legion Condor; D-1, 6•79, 3.J/88, flown by *Hptm*. W. Mölders, Legion Condor, November 1938; B-2, 6•56, flown by *Maj*. G. Handrick, Legion Condor, June 1938; B-2, 6•56, J/88, flown by *Hptm*. W. Grabmann, Legion Condor, November 1938; F-2, 15 Spanische *Staffel*, JG51 (2ª Esc. Azul), 1942; F-2, 23•51, C.4F-145, 23 Regiment, Spanish Air Force, Reus, 1942

Print-Scale
#72-021 Bf 109E Part 1
'Red 10', 2./J 101, 1939; 'Yellow 14', 6./J 186, 1940; 'Yellow 3', 6./JG 52, 1940; 6•123, 3/J, Spain, 1939; 'Blue 8', 7./ZG 26, 1941; 'Black <', 1./4G, 1941; 0./JG 26, 1940; 'S9+6D', 4/B ZG 1, 1942; 'Black H', II./JG 1, 1942; 'Yellow 9', 9./JG 26, 1940; 'Red 1', 2./JG 26, 1940; 'Red 2', 2./JG 26, 1940; 'Black 13', 2./JG77, 1940; 'Black <<', 1./JG 2, 1940; 'Yellow 47', Romanian Forces, 1942

#72-032 Bf 109D
6•56, *Hptm* Walter Grabmann, J88, Spain, 1938; 6•56, *Hptm* Guthard Handrick, J88, Spain, September 1938; 6•79, Werner Mölders, 3./J88, Spain, November 1938; 6•75, *Oblt* Rudolf Goy all Condor Legion, Spain, 1938; JG132 Richthofen, Germany, 1938; 'Yellow 12', 11./JG234, Dusseldorf, 1938; 'White 11', 10N./JG2. Strausberg, Sept. 1939; 'Yellow 1', 3./JG21, Guterfeld, Sept. 1939; 'White 3', 1./JG131, Germany, March 1939; 'Yellow 5', 2./JG 176, Gablingen, Germany, 1939; '6A+MK' Flight School, Zagreb, 1942; 'White 2', 1./ZG2, Poland 1939; 'White 10', 1./JG 1, Germany 1939

RB Productions
#RB-D72012 Romanian Bf 109Es Part 1
E-3, 'Yellow 23', Gr.7, Esc. 57, flown by *Adj.av.* S. Greceanu; E-3, 'Yellow 9, Gr.7, Esc. 57, flown by *Lt. av.* I. Di Cezare, Karpovka, November 1942; E-3, 'Yellow 47', Gr.7, Esc. 58, Nikolaev, November 1942; E-3, 'Yellow 45', Gr.7, Esc. 58, Pipera, 1942; E-3, 'Yellow 48', Gr.7, Esc. 58, Pipera, 1942; E-3, 'Yellow 2', flown by Gr.7 commander *Cmdr.av.* A. Popisteanu; E-7, 'Yellow 63', Gr.7, Esc. 56, Pipera, 1942

#RB-D72013 Romanian Bf 109Es Part 2
E-3, 'Yellow 26' Gr.7, Esc. 57 flown by *Adj.av.* S. Greceanu, September 1941, Saltz-Basarabia, Russia; E-3, 'Yellow 14', Gr.7, Esc. 57, Pipera, 1942; E-3, 'Yellow 39', Gr.7, Esc. 58, Basarabia, 1941; 'Yellow 35', Gr.7, Esc. 58, Pipera, 1942; E-7, 'Yellow 51', Gr.7, Esc. 56, Pipera, 1942; E-7, 'Yellow 64', Gr.7, Esc. 56, flown by *Adj.av.* T. Vinca, Stalingrad, 1942; E-7, 'Yellow 54', Gr.7, Esc. 57, flown by *Adj.av.* S. Greceanu, Pipera, 1942

#RB-D72014 Romanian Bf 109Es Part 3
E-3, 'Yellow 8, Gr.7, Pipera, March 1941; E-3, 'Yellow 24' Gr.7, Pipera, March 1941; E-3, 'Yellow 35', Gr.&, Pipera, March 1941; E-3, 'Yellow 37', Gr.7, Pipera, March 1941

Revi
#72004 Luftwaffe Experten Volume 1
Inc. Bf 109E-1, 'White 2', 7./JG 26, flown by *Lt* Egon Troha, 1939

Rising Decals
#72-012 Foreign Messerschmitts Part 1 (Swiss)
J-311, W/Nr.2159, 1944; J-318, W/Nr.2166, Fl.Kp.9; J-345, W/Nr.2386, Fl.Kp.21, July 1947; J-374, W/Nr.2355, Fl/Kp/9, flown by *Lt* Depompierre; J-371, W/Nr.2352

#72-014 Deutsche über der Wüste
Inc. E-7/Trop, 'S9+CS', III./ZG1, Libya, 1942; E-7/Trop, 'S9+DR', III./ZG1, Libya, 1942

#72-015 Foreign Messerschmitts Part 3 (Spain)
E-3, 6•99, 3.J/88, Spring 1939; 6•109, E-3, 3.J/88, flown by Kurt Sochatzki; E-3, 6•111, 2.J/88, flown by *Lt* Werner Ursinus; E-1, 6•119, 1.J/88, flown by *Oblt* S. Reents

#72-016 Emils over Western Europe & England
E-1, W/Nr.4859, 'Red 9', 2./JG2, Spring 1940; E-4, 'White <-', flown by *Oblt* A. Drehs, *Stab* III./JG54, August 1940; E-1/B, W/Nr.6313, flown by *Uffz*. P. Wacker, 2./JG27, November 1940; E-4, 'Black <', flown by *Lt* E. Schmidt, III./JG53

#72-017 Foreign Messerschmitts Part 2 (Rumania)
E-3, 'Yellow 64', Grupul 7, Stalingrad area, Russia, 1942; E-3, 'Yellow 35', Grupul 7, Kishinev, Russia, 1941; E-3, 'Yellow 9', Grupul 7, Russia, 1941-42

#72-021 Foreign Messerschmitts Part 4 (Slovak)
E-3, 'White 2', Letka 13, Piestany AB, November 1942; E-4, 'White 7', April 1943; E-4, 'White 10', April 1943 on return from Eastern Front where it served with 13./JG2; E-7, Hotovostní stíhací roj (Readiness Unit), Vajnory AB, September 1943

#72-028 Bf 109E over the Balkans
'Black <<', 1.(Jagd)/LG2; 'White 11', III./JG77; 'Yellow 12', 9./JG52; 'Black <<|', *Stab* II./JG54; 'Black <•' *Gruppenstab* II./JG77; 'Black <<', *Stab* III./JG77

#72-041 Under New Management
Inc. Bf 109E-3, W/Nr.1304, ex-1./JG76 in French/RAF colours

#72-044 Foreign Messerschmitts
Bf 109E, 'L-80', 101st eskadrila, 31st vazduchoplavna grupa, Zemud Airfield, September 1940; Bf 109E, 'L-10', 142nd eskadrila, 32nd vazduchoplavna grupa, Kru£edol Airfield, 1941; Bf 109E, 'L-33', 101st eskadrila, 31st vazduchoplavna grupa, Veliki Radinci II Airfield, April 1940; Bf 109E, 'L-31', 101st eskadrila, 31st vazduchoplavna grupa, Veliki Radinci II Airfield, April 1940

Special Hobby
#K72031 Bf 109E-4 Mottle Camouflage for Helmut Wick's 'Yellow 2' in Special Hobby kit #SH72439

Superscale
#72-295 Me 109B, C, Ds
'White 9' 6./JG 132; 6•56, 2.J/88; 'White 2', 1./ZG 2; 'Red 10', JFS/1; 'N+B', 3./ZG26; 'ER+16' of 10(N)./JG26

#72-349 Me 109E
E-7/B, 'S9+CH', 7./SKG 210; E-3, 'Yellow 11', 9./JG545, Channel Front, Summer 1940; E-1, 'Red 1', date and location unknown; E-3, 'Red 5', 1./JG52, France, 1940; E-7/B, 'Black H', 11 *Gruppe* Sch.G 7, Stalingrad, Winter 1942-3; E-3, 'Black <<', JG2

#72-671 Bf 109E Aces (Battle of Britain)
No further details

Tally Ho! (Canada)
#7140 Bf 109B – Legion Condor
B-2, 6•36, flown by *Hptm.* Marro Harder, 1.J/88, September 1937; B-2, 6•38, flown by *Uffz.* Ernst Terry, August 1937; B-2, 6•38, flown by *Uffz.* Ernst Terry, December 1937: D, 6•51, flown by *Hptm.* Wolfgang Schellman, 1.J/88, July 1938; B-1, 6-16, 2.J/88, March 1937; D, 6•56, flown by *Maj.* Gotthard Handrick, *Gruppenkommandeur* J/88, July 1938; D, 6•56, flown by Haptm. Walter Grabmann, *Gruppenkommandeur* J/88, November 1938; D, 6•79, flown by *Hptm.* Werner Mölders, *Staffelkapitan* 3.J/88, November 1938; E-1, 6•123, flown by *Oblt* Hans Schmoller-Haldy, 2.J/88, March 1939

#7218 Spain 1939-1950
Inc. B-2, Spanish Nationalist Air Force, Grupo 5-G-5, Escudrilla Azul ; B-2, Spanish Air Force Ejército del Aire (EdA), Escuela de Caza; E-3, EdA, Grupo 25, Regimento de Caza 13

#72 012 Luftwaffe Nachtjäger Part 1
Inc. D, 'White N+7', flown by Johannes 'Macki' Steinhoff, 10.(N)/JG26, Bonn-Hangelar, 1939

Techmod
#72049 Bf 109E-3
'White 13', *Lt* Walter Blume, 3./JG 26, September 1940; 'Black <', *Lt* Hans Hahn, 1./JG 3, Sept 1939; 'Yellow 1', *Oblt* Josef Priller, 6./JG 51, October 1940

#72052 Bf 109E-4
'White 13', *Oblt* Water Oesau, 3./JG 51, August 1940; 'Black <-', *Oblt* Franz von Werra, *Stab* II./JG 3, August 1940; 'Yellow 2', *Oblt* Helmut Wick, III./JG 2, August 1940; 'Black <<', *Hptm.* Helmut Wick, I./JG 2, October 1940

#72055 Bf 109E Stencil Data
For two aircraft

#72077 Bf 109E-3
'Black >', 1.(J).LG2, Calais, 1941; 'White 1', 1./JG2, 1940; 'III./JG26', *Maj.* Adolf Galland, 1940; 'White 1', 4./JG54, 1940; 'White 13', 1./JG51, Heinz Bär, 1940

#72078 Bf 109E-4
W/Nr.5819, JG 26, *Maj.*Adolph Galland; *Stab.* III/JG 1, Reinhard Heydrich; 'Yellow 1', 9./JG 26, Gerhardt Schopfel; I./JG 3, Hans Von Hahn; *Kommandeur* III./JG 2, Erich Mix

Third Group Decals
#72-005 III Gruppe JG2/52/54/77
E-3, 'Black 10', 7./JG77, April 1941; E-4, 'Yellow 5', flown by *Lt* Waldemar Wübke, 9./JG54, Cherbourg, France, 1941; E-1, 'White 5', 7./JG52, Karabacie, Romania, 1941; E-4, 'Red 4', flown by *Uffz.* Hippel, 8./JG2, France, Summer 1940; E-3, 'Red 6', 8./JG2, France, Winter 1940-41; E-1, 'Red 7', 8./JG52, Hopstädten, Germany, August 1940

#72-008 JG 77 Bf 109E #2
E-3, W/Nr.5057, 'Red <<', flown by *Hptm.* Herbert Ihefelm II.(J)/LG2, France, 1941; E-3, W/Nr.5057, 'Red <<', flown by *Hptm.* Herbert Ihefelm II.(J)/LG2, Kesckemet, Hungary, April 1941; E-1, W/Nr.1276, 'White 5', flown by *Lt* Jakob Arnoldy, 4./JG77, Mandal, France, September 1940; E-4/B, 'Black 1', 2.(J)/LG2, France, November 1940; E-4, 'White 11', flown by *Lt* Heinz Demes, 4./JG77, Westerland/Sylt, Germany, March 1940; E-1, 'Black 12', flown by *Uffz.* Josef Heinzeller, 2.(J)/LG2m September 1939; E-4, 'Black 11', III./JG77, Molaoi, Greece, May 1941

#72-009 Bf 109E-1/3/4
E-4, 'Blue 10', III./JG77, Molaoi, Greece, May 1941; E-3, 'White 13', flown by *Oblt* Helmut Henz, 4./JG77, Poland, September 1939; E-1, 'Red 4', 3.(J)/LG2, Hage, Germany, January 1940; E-4, 'Black 2', 2.(J)/LG2, Radomir, Bulgaria, April 1941; E-1, 'Red 13', flown by *ObFw.* Kurt Ubben, 7./JG77, Trondheim-Vaernes, Norway, July 1940

Topkits Decals
#72-101 Bf 109E Swiss Air Force

Ventura
#V7203 Foreign Messerschmitt Bf 109s
E-1, 6•127, 25 Grupo, 23 Regimiento de Caza, Spanish Air Force, 1952; C, 6•56, J/88 Legion Condor, April 1939

Xtradecal
#X72-118 Battle of Britain 70th Anniversary – Luftwaffe
Inc. E-1, 'Yellow 11', 9./JG 26, *Fw.* Artur Beese, August 1940; E-3, 'Yellow 1', 6./JG 51, *Oblt* Josef (Pips) Priller, *Staffelkapitän*, October 1940; E-4/B, 'Yellow M', 6(Schlact)/LG 2, *Fw.* Erhardt Pankratz, October 1940; E-4, 'White <', 1./JG 27, *Oblt* Gunther Bodo, *Gruppenadjutant*, September 1940; E-4, 'Black 8', 2./JG 52, *Ofw.* Bernhard Lempskemper, August 1940; E-3, 'Yellow 15', 3./JG 52, *Uffz.* Karl Wolff, 3./JG52, France, August 1940

#X72-162 The Battle for Malta – Axis
Inc. E-7, 'White 12', 7/JG26, *Oblt* Joachim Muncheberg

1/48th Scale

AeroMaster
#48-019 Bf 109B-E National Insignia

#48-014 Battle of Britain Bf 109Es Part 1
E-4, 'Yellow 7', 9./JG2, Beaumont-le-Roger, France, September 1940; E-4/B, W/Nr.5901, 'Black 7', 8./JG53, flown by *Oblt* W. Fiel, October 1940; E-4, W/Nr.15188, '<<', *Stab.*/JG1, flown by *Oblt* R. Heydrich, Holland, Summer 1940; E-3, W/Nr.1324, 'Yellow 13', 3./JG53, flown by *Fw.* W. Schulz, September 1940

#48-034 Foreign Emils
E-4, 'Red H7', flown by *Lt* O. P. Csoka, Hungarian Air Force; E-3, 'White 9', Bulgarian Air Force, 1943; E-4, J-371, Swiss Air Force, 1941-42; E-1, '126', 23 Regimento de Casa, 25 Grupo, 1952; E-1, 6•126, Regimento de Casa, 25 Grupo, Spanish Air Force, 1952; E-4, 'Hai Fetito', Royal Rumanian Air Force, 1942; E-4, V5+06, 102nd Fighter Group, Hungarian Air Force

#48-037 Early Warriors
B, 6•51, J/88, Spain; B-2, 6•56, Nationalist Spanish Air Force, Logrono, 1939; D-1, 6•56, J/88, flown by *Hptm.* G. Handrick, Spain, 1938; D-1, 6•56, J/88, flown by *Hptm.* W. Grabmann, Spain, late 1938; C-2, 'N+8', 10(N)./JG26, Jever, Autumn, 1939; C-2, 'GA+MK', Pilot School A/B 123 (Croatian), Agram, Zagreb, March 1942; C-2, 'RF+14', Jagdfliegerschule 1 (JFS 1), Werneuchen, 1940

#48-110 Marauding Emils JG26
E-1'White 1', 1./JG26, March 1940; E-3, 'Red 7', 6./JG26, early 1940; E-1, 'Red 13', 2./JG26, France, early 1940; E-4, 'Red 5', 2./JG26, late 1940; E-3, 'Red 2', 2./JG26, November 1940

#48-127 Desert War Bf 109s of JG27
Inc. Bf 109E-7/Trop, 'Black <A', I./JG27, flown by *Oblt* L. Franzisket, Castel Benito, Libya, April 1941; Bf 109E-7/Trop, 'Black <', I./JG27, flown by *Oblt* L. Franzisket, Libya, October 1941

#48-128 Mediterranean Bf 109s of JG27
Inc. E-4, III./JG27, flown by *Hptm.* Max Dobislav, Castel Benito, Sicily, May 1941

#48-165 Emils over Europe Part I
E-4, 'Yellow 14', 3./JG2, flown by *Lt* F. Fiby, Le Harbe, France, July-August 1940; E-4, 'Green 1', flown by *Hptm.* Wilhelm Balthasar, 7./JG27, 1940; E-4, 'Black 5', flown by *Oblt* Bennermann, 2./JG52, October 1940; E-3, 'White 7', flown by *Lt* Burschgens, 7./JG26, Caffiers, France, August 1940; E-3, 'Black <-', flown by *Oblt* von Crammon, JG53, France, August 1940

#48-165 Emils over Europe Part II
E-3, 'Red 1', *Oblt* Fritz Losigkeit, 2./JG26, September 1940; E-3, 'White 4', *Uffz.* H. Perez, 4./JG26, September 1940; E-4, 'Yellow 5', flown by *Oblt* E. Troha, 9./JG3, October 1940; E-3, 'Black <<', flown by *Hptm.* W. Ewald, I./JG52, Caffiers, France, 1940; E-3, 'Black <<', flown by *Hptm.* H. Knüppel, II./JG26, March 1940

#48-227 Bf 109s of JG53
E-3, 'Yellow 10', flown by *Oblt* H. Bretnütz, 6./JG53, Mannheim-Sandhofen, winter 1939-40; E-1, 'Black <<|', flown by *Oblt* W. Balfanz, *Stab* I./JG53, Kirchberg im Hunsrück airfield, Autumn 1939; E-3, 'Black <', flown by *Oblt* W. Pufahl, Sta II./JG53, Western Reich, May 1940

#48-238 Marauding Emils Part II
E-3, 'Black <-', flown by *Oberst.* Gerd von Massow, JG2, Germany, January 1940; E-4/N, 'White 1', flown by *Hptm.* W. Machold, 7./JG2, France, September 1940; E-3, 'Yellow 1', flown by *Oblt* J. Priller, 6./JG51, October 1940; E-3, 'Red 12', flown by *Fw.* Ernst Arnord, 3./JG27, August 1940; E-3, 'Red 1', flown by *Hptm.* Horst Tietzen, 5./JG51, France, August 1940

#48-248 Marauding Emils Part III
E-3, 'Black <<', flown by Herbert Ihlefeld, I.(J)/JG2, Calais, France, March 1941; E-4, 'Black <<', flown by Wolfgang Lippert, II./JG27, Balkans, April 1941; E-1, 'Red 1', flown by Eduard Neuman, JG26, Germany, 1939; E-7/B, 'S9+RS', 8./ZG1, Russia, Summer 1942

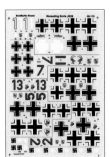

AeroMaster #48-110

AeroMaster #48-128

AeroMaster #48-127

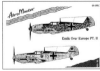

AeroMaster #48-166

AeroMaster #48-227

AeroMaster #48-249

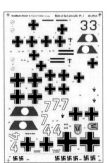

AeroMaster #48-456

AeroMaster #48-457

AeroMaster #48-458

AeroMaster #48-496

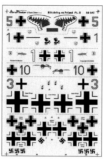
AeroMaster #48-497

AeroMaster #48-685

AML #AMLC8-003

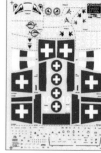
Cutting Edge #CED48040

Cutting Edge #CED48215

Cutting Edge #CED48216

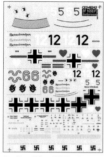
Cutting Edge #CED48243

Cutting Edge #CED48264

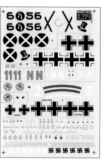
Cutting Edge #CED48265

Eagle Strike #48055

#48-249 Marauding Emils Part IV
E-4, 'Yellow 1', flown by *Oblt* G. Schöptel, 9./JG26, France, August 1940; E-4, 'Black <', flown by *Hptm.* Hans von Hahn, I./JG3, France, 1940; E-4, 'Black <<', flown by Helmut Wick, I./JG2, Belgium, October 1940; E-3, 'White 7', flown by Reinhard Seiler, 1./JG54, Germany, April 1940; E-4, 'White 8', flown by Gefreiter Nittmann, 7./JG27, September 1940

#48-456 Birth of the Luftwaffe Part 1
Inc. B-2, 'Red 3', JG132; D-1, JG 132; C-1, 'White 10' JG130

#48-457 Birth of the Luftwaffe Part 2
Inc. B-2, 'Yellow 12', 6./JG133; D-1, 'Black <<', *Stab* 1./JG233

#48-458 Spanish Civil War Part 1
Inc. B, 6•34, flown by *Oblt* Erich Woitke, 1.J/88; E-1, 6•123, *Oblt* Hans Schmoller-Haldy, 3.J/88; C, 6•56, flown by *Hptm.* Gotthardt Handrick, J/88

#48-459 Spanish Civil War Part 2
Inc. D, 6•79, flown by Werner Mölders, 1.J/88; E-1, 6•119, 1.J/88; B-2, 6•30, based at Leon, J/88

#48-496 Blitzkrieg on Poland Part I
E-1, 'Yellow 14', 6.(J)/*Trägergruppe* 186, Winter 1939/40; E-3, 'Black <o', *Stab* 1./JG53, Weibaden-Erheim, November 1939; E-1, 'Black <', flown by *Obstlt* Carl Schumacher, JG1, December 1939; D-1, 'White 3', 1./JG 131 (1./JG2), flown by *Lt* Hermann Reifferscheidt, March 1939; E-1, 'Red 14', 2./JG3, Zerbst, Winter 1939-40

#48-496 Blitzkrieg on Poland Part II
D-1, 'Yellow 5', 2./JGr 176, Gablingen, August 1939; E-1, 'Red 1', 5./JG77, flown by *Lt* W. Schmidt, Jever, December 1939; E-1, 'White 1', flown by *Oblt* F. Hörnung, 1./JG26, Dortmund, December 1939; E-1, 'Red 10', 2./JGr 101, Fürstenwalde, August 1939; E-3, 'Yellow 3', 3./JG51, Winter 1939-40

#48-514 Blitzkrieg in the West Part I
E-1, 'Black 1', flown by *Oblt* D. Robitzsch, 5.(J)/TR. GR. 186, May 1940; E-1, 'White 12', 4./JG51, Boblingen, April 1940; E-3, 'Red 5', 6./JG26, France, January 1940; E-1, 'Red 8', flown by *Uffz.* Ludwig Beimeir, 2./JG52, France 1940; E-1, 'Yellow 3', 6./JG26, Speyer, March 1940

#48-515 Attack in the West Part 2
Bf 109E, 'Red 16', 2./JG26; Bf 109E, 'Yellow 6', 3./JG3; Bf 109E, 'Black ->', JG26, *Oberlt* Hans Witt, *Geschwader Kommodore*; Bf 109E, 'Red 1', 2./JG27;

Bf 109E, 1./JG20, *Hptm* Trautloft, *Kommandeur*

#48-582 Bf 109E Battle of Britain... Eagle Day Pt.I

#48-583 Bf 109E Battle of Britain... Eagle Day Pt.II

#48-590 Bf 109E Battle of Britain... Eagle Day Pt.III

#48-591 Bf 109E Battle of Britain... Eagle Day Pt.IV
E-1, 'Yellow 11', 9./JG 26, flown by *Fw.* A. Beese; E-3, 'Black 5', 1./JG 52, flown by *Oblt* H. Bennemann; E-3, 'White 2', 4./JG 51, flown by *Ofw.* H. Illner); E-4, 'Black 13', 2./JG 53, flown by *Oblt* H. Tiedmann

#48-643 Bf 109E Battle of Britain Final Throes Part 1
'White 12', JG26; 'Red 7', 2./JG3; 'White 5', 4./JG52' 'Brown 2', 6./JG54

#48-644 Bf 109E Battle of Britain Final Throes Part 2
'Black 7', 8./JG27; 'White 1', 7./JG2, Werner Machold; 'Black <<+', *Gruppenstab* 1./JG26, *Hptm* Rolf Pingel; 'Yellow 5', 9./JG54

#48-645 Bf 109E Battle of Britain Final Throes Part 3
'White G', 2./JG27, *Uffz* Paul Wacker; 'White 9', 1./JG2, Hermann Reifflerscheidt; 'Black 14', JG54; 'Yellow 10', II./JG54

#48-685 Defenders of the Reich 1942-43
Inc. E-3, 'Yellow 25', Jagdfliegerschule 1. Trondheim, Norway, February 1942

#48-707 Kommodore Adolf Galland
Inc. E-3, III./JG26, France, June 1940; E-4, JG26, France, September 1940; E-4/N, W/Nr.5819, JG26, Audembert, France, November 1940

#PAF48-01 Kommodore Adolf Galland
E-3, III./JG26, France, June 1940; E-4, JG26, France, September 1940; E-4/N, W/Nr.5819, JG26, Audembert, France, November 1940

#SP48-01 Luftwaffe Top Guns
Inc. E-3, W/Nr.3714, flown by *Obstlt* Heinz Bär, 1./JG51, Pihen, France, September 1940; E-7/N. flown by *Obst.* Hermann Graf, 9./JG52, Russia, Summer 1941; E-3, flown by *Obstlt* Hans Philipp, 4./JG54, France, October 1940

Almark
#4803 Messerschmitt Bf 109E – Europe
Oblt G. Schopfel, 9./JG26; *Offz* Schulte, 7./JGS3; *Ofw* W. Friedmann; *Oblt* H. Strupell, 3./JG2; 'Red 2', 3./JG3
Also released as #A-3 and #A48-3

AML
#AMLC8 003 Emils in the Spanish Civil War
E-3, 6•119, flown by *Hptm.* S. Reents, *Staffelkapitän* 1 J/88, Spring 1939; 6•123, flown by *Oblt* Hans Schmoller-Haldy, 3./J88, March 1939
Paint masks with decal

#AMLD4829 Bf 109E-7 JG 5 over far north
E-7, W/Nr.1187, 'Red 4', JG5; Bf 109E, 'White 11', 4./JG77

Avalon Decals
#4002 Bf 109E Early Emils

Aviation Usk
#4101 Bf 109E-3A Royal Yugoslav Air Force
L-24, 15.(Kroat)/JG 51, I Fliegerkorps, April 1941

Cockpit Decals
#48/002 Bf 109, Jagdgruppe 88
B-1, 6•7, flown by *Fw.* Norbert Flegel, 2 *Staffel* J/88; B-2, 6•38, flown by Uttz. Ernst Terry; D, 6•56, flown by *Hptm.* Walter Grabmann, *Gruppenkommandeur* J/88, September 1938; D, 6•79, flown by *Oblt* Werner Mölders, 3 *Staffel* J/88; E-1, 6•119, flown by *Hptm.* Siebelt Reents, 1 *Staffel* J/88

Crazy Modeler
#DC-0032 Bf 109E Battle of Britain Eagle Day Pt.IV
No further details available

Cutting Edge
#CED48040 Swiss Bf 109s
D-1, J-307, Training Unit, September 1944-45; D-1, J-310, Fliegerkompanie 15, June 1940; E-3, J-317, Fliegerkompanie 8, 1940-44; E-3, J-318, Fliegerkompanie 9, 1940-44; E-3, J-326, 1939-40; E-3, J-345, Fliegerkompanie 21, 1940-44; E-3, J-346, Fliegerkompanie 15, Thoune, 1940-44; E-3, J-360, 1940-44; E-3, J-374, Fliegerkompanie 9, flown by *Lt* Dedompierre; E-3, J-387, Payerne, Spring 1945; E-3, J-399, Altenrhein, 1946-48

#CED48056 Bf 109E & G Nose Art Special
E-3, flown by *Lt* Terry, 1./JG 51, Krefeld-Uerdingen, 1940; G-4 Trop, 'White 1, 7./JG 53, flown by *Lt* Harder, Sicily, 1943; G-6, 'Red 13', JG 107, Steinamanger, Hungary, 1944; G-6/R6 Trop, 'White 9',

7./JG 53, flown by *Uffz.* Amon, Sciacca, Italy, June 1943

#CED48188 Bf 109E Emils Part 1

#CED48189 Bf 109E Emils Part 2

#CED48191 Bf 109E Emils Part 4

#CED48197 Bf 109E Emils Part 5

#CED48215 Bf 109E – The Augsburg Zoo
E-3, 6•123, flown by *Oblt* Hans Schmoller-Haldy, 3.J/88, March 1939; E-1, 'Yellow 12', JG132, April 1939; E-3, 'Black <-', flown by *Obstlt* Hans-Hugo Witt, JG26, April 1940; E-3, 'White 4', flown by *Uffz.* Horst Perez, 4./JG26, September 1940

#CED48216 Bf 109E/F Desert Eagles
Inc. E-7/Trop, 'White 10', flown by *Fw.* Günther Steinhausen, 1./JG27, Libya, August 1941

#CED48243 Bf 109E/F Operation Barbarossa
Inc. E-4/B, 'Red 5', flown by *Ofw.* Reinhold Schmetzer, 8./JG77, July 1941

#CED48264 Bf 109B/D Early Messerschmitts Part 1
D-1, 6•79, flown by *Hptm.* Werner Mölders, 3.J/88, November 1938; B-2, 6•30, flown by *Uffz.* Wilhelm Staege, 2.J/88, Alar d'el Rey, August 1937; D-1, 'White 3', flown by *Lt* Hermann Reifferscheidt, 1./JG131, March 1939

#CED48265 Bf 109D Early Messerschmitts Part 2
D-1, 6•56, flown by *Hptm.* Gotthard Handrick, J./88, August 1938; D-1, 'White N+7', flown by Johannes 'Macki' Steinhoff, 10.(N)/JG26, Jever, Norway, 1940; D-1, 'Yellow N+11', 12.(M)/JG2, Norway, 1940; D-1, 'White 2', 1./ZG 2, August 1939

#CED48266 Bf 109B/D Early Messerschmitts Part 3
D-1, 'Yellow 5', 2./JGr 176, Gablingen, August 1939; B-1, 6-3, 2.J/88, Herrera de Pisuerga, October 1937; D-1, 'Red 11', 2./JG71, Fürstenfeldbruck, August 1939; D-1, 'Yellow 1', 3./JG21, Gutenfeld, East Prussia, September 1939

EagleCal

EC#50 Major Hans 'Assi' Hahn Part 1
Bf 109E-3, StabI./JG3, Merseburg, Germany 1939; Bf 109E-3, 'White 13', 4./JG2, Northern Germany, Spring 1940; Bf 109E-4, 'White 14', 4./JG2, France, 1940; Bf 109E-4, III./JG2, France, 1940

EC#66 Graf and Grislawski 9./JG52 Part 3
Bf 109E-1, 'Black 17', 2./Erg.JGr, 1940; Bf 109E, 'Yellow 9'

EC#121 Bf 109E-1
'White 13', flown by *Hptm.* HJ. Henz, 4./JG77; 'Red 1', flown by *Oblt* G. Framm, 2./JG27; 'Red 16', flown *Oblt* F. Losigkeit, 2./JG 26; 'Yellow 12'./JG52

EC#122 Bf 109E-1
'Yellow 12', flown by *Fw.* E. Armold, 3./JG 27; 'White 2', flown by *Fw.* P. Boche, 4./JG52; W/Nr.6352, 'Yellow 10', 6./JG54; 'Black 13', 2./JG77

Eagle Strike

#48055 Augsburg's Flyers Part III
Inc. E-4, 'Black <', flown by *Lt* Egon Troba, II./JG3, June 1940; E-7/Trop, 'Black <A', flown by OPblt Ludwig Franzisket, I./JG27, Africa 1941

#48146 Barbarossa 4
Inc. E-4, 'Yellow 3', 11./JG77, June 1941

#48120 Bf 109E of the Balkans Part 1
'Black 10', 9./JG77; 'Black <5', *Stab* II./JG54, Rumania 1941; 'Yellow 0', II./JG77; 'Yellow 8', III./JG52

#48121 Bf 109E of the Balkans Part 2
'Black 1', 5./JG77, Werner Petermann; 'White D', 3./JG77; 'Black L', III./JG77; 'Black <', III./JG77

#48122 Bf 109E of the Balkans Part 3
'White 1', III./JG77; 'Black 10', III./JG77; 'Black 8', 5./JG77; 'Yellow 12', 9./JG52

#48123 Bf 109E of the Balkans Part 4
'Black 12', 8./JG52; 'Black <', III./JG77; 'Black 5', 8./JG77; 'Black <'

#48132 Operation Barbarossa Part 1
Inc. Bf 109E-4/B, 'Red 5', 8./JG77, *Ofw.* Reinhold Schmetzer

#48139 Augsburg Flyers Part 5
Inc. Bf 109E-3, 'Black 4', 11./JG1, Martin Lacha; Bf 109E-7, 'Yellow 1', 9./JG27, *Lt* Von Kageneck, Russia 1941

#48146 Operation Barbarossa Part 4
'Yellow 3', II./JG77; 'Black <', III./JG53, *Hptm* Jurgen Harder; 'White 1', 7./JG77, *Oblt* Wolfdieter Huy

Eduard

#D48011 Bf 109E-4
'Black <<', I./JG28, *Hptm* Rolf Pingel, France 1940; 'Yellow 1', 9./JG3, *Hptm* Egon Troha, France 1940; 'Blue 1', III./JG3, *Hptm* Walter Oesau, France 1940; 'White 13', 7./JG51, *Hptm* Walter Oesau, France 1940; 'Black 5<', II./JG54, Romania 1941

#D48013 Bf 109E Stencils

Everest Model

#D48001 Bf 109E-1/E-3 Early Emils Part 1
Same options as #D72001

Gull Decals
#48D-01 Bf 109E

HGW Models
#248005 Bf 109E inc. stencils

H-Model Decals
#HMD48129 Bf 109B/C/D/E Stencils

HR Models
#HRD4805 Bf 109E in Slovak Service
E, 'hite 1', flown by Capt. O Dumbala, 13 *Staffel* (Slov.) JG 52, Russia, 19412-43; E, 'White 6', flown by Sgt J. Reznak, 13 *Staffel* (Slov.) JG 52, Russia, 1942-43; e, 'White 10', 13 *Staffel* (Slov.) JG 52, Russia, 1942-43; E-7, Alarm Fighter Flight, Vajnory airfield, 1943-44

Iliad Design

#48006 Early Bf 109Es
E-1, 'Yellow 15', 6./JG26, Düsseldorf, August 1939; E-1, 'Red 9', 2./JG20, Brandenburg-Briest, late 1939; E-3, 3./JG1, November 1939; E-3, 'Yellow 3', 3./JG51, late 1939; 'E-1, Red 6', 2./JG3, late Summer 1939.

Jays Model Kits
#JY1202 Bf 109B
6•56, flown by Gotthard Handrick, 2.J/88, Spain, April 1939

Kora
#DEC48.25 Bf 109E-7/B Escuadrilla Azul
E-7/B, 'Black M', 15. *Staffel* (Span)/JG27, 1941

#DEC48.37 Bf 109E-3A Royal Yugoslav Air Force
L-10, 142 Lovacka Eskadrila, Krusedol airfield, April 1941; 'White 11', 6 Vazduhoplovni Lovacki, Zemun airfield, 1940; L-21, 101 Lovacka Eskadrila, Vel Radinci II airfield, 1940; L-80, 101 Lovacka Eskadrila, Vel Radinci II airfield, 1940

#DEC48.53 Bf 109E Strela (Bulgaria)
No details available

#DEC48.69 Bf 109D-1 Part I Swiss Air Force
J-301, Fliegerkompanie 15, 1940; J-302, Fliegerkompanie Fl.Kp 15, Dübendorf, Spring 1941; J-303, Fliegerkompanie Fl.Kp 15, Dübendorf, Spring 1941; J-309, Flegertruppe, January 1939

#DEC48.70 Bf 109D-1 Part II Swiss Air Force
J-303, KDT der Fl.Rgt 4, which crashed at Meiringen, 1943; J-307, Fliegertruppe, Autumn 1944; J-308, Fliegerkompanie 15, Olten AB, May-June 1940; J-310, Fliegerkompanie 15, Olten AB, May-June 1940

#DEC48.71 Bf 109E-3A Emil (Swiss Air Force Part I)
J-315, Fliegerkompanie 6, Thun airfield, Spring 1940; J-317, Fliegerkompanie 6, Thun airfield, Spring 1940; J-353, Fliegerkompanie 21, Dübendorf, Spring 1940

#DEC48.72 Bf 109E-3A Emil (Swiss Air Force Part II)
J-326, Fliegerkompanie 6, Thun airfield, Summer 1940; J-365, Fliegerkompanie 9, Avenches airfield, Summer 1940; J-374, Fliegerkompanie 6, Avenches airfield, Autumn 1941

#DEC48.73 Bf 109E-3A Emil (Swiss Air Force Part III)
J-317, Fliegerkompanie 7, Avenches airfield, December 1940; J-334, Fliegerkompanie 7, Avenches airfield, Spring 1941; J-387, Fliegerkompanie 15, Olten airfield, Summer 1940

#DEC48.74 Bf 109E-3A Emil (Swiss Air Force Part IV)
J-360, Fliegerkompanie 8, Avenches airfield, Summer 1940; J-362, Fliegerkompanie 8, Avenches airfield, Summer 1940; J-366, Fliegerkompanie 8, Avenches airfield, Summer 1940

#DEC48.75 Bf 109E-3A Emil (Swiss Air Force Part V)
J-350, Fliegerkompanie 9, Avenches airfield, Spring 1941; J-358, Fliegerkompanie 8, Avenches airfield, Summer 1940; J-359, Fliegerkompanie 8, Avenches airfield, Summer 1940

Eagle Strike #48120

Eagle Strike #48132

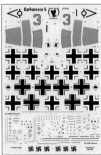
Eagle Strike #48146

Eagle Strike #48146

EagleCals #EC50

Iliad Design #48006

#DEC48.76 Bf 109E-3A Emil (Swiss AF Part VI)
J-320, Fliegerkompanie 9, Avenches airfield, Spring
1945; J-385, Fliegerkompanie 8, Thun airfield, 1945;
J-393, Fliegerkompanie 8, Thun airfield, October 1945;
J-399, Fliegerkompanie 8, Payerne airfield, 1948

Kuivalainen
#D4801 Lu*Fw*affe Bf 109E over Finland
Same options as #D7202

LF Models
#C4807 Bf 109E in Romanian Service Part I
E-3, 'Yellow 27', flown by Sit.av I. Dicezore, Gr.7,
summer 1941; E-7, 'Yellow 47', floown by *Adj.av.* C.
Lunguiesca, Gr.7, summer 1944; E-3, 'Yellow 64', flown
by Adj.av.T. Vinca, Gr.7, Vanatoare, summer 1942

#C4808 Bf 109E in Romanian Service Part II
E-3, 'Yellow 11', flown by A. Serbanescu, Gr.7,
Bucharest-Pipera, summer 1942; E-3, 'Yellow 26',
flown by *Adj.av.* S. Greceanu, Gr.7, Escadrille 57, Salz,
Bessarabia, September 1941; E-3, 'Yellow 45', flown by
Cap.av. G. Iliescu CO of Gr.5, Escadrille 52, Mamaiai,
summer 1943

#C4817 Bf 109E-3 over Swiss Part I
J-365, Fl.Kp. 9, Avenches airfield, 1940; J-347,
Fl.Kp 21, Dübendorf airfield, 1940

#C4818 Bf 109E-3 over Swiss Part II
J-360, Fl.Kp. 8, Avenches airfield, 1940; J-346,
Fl.Kp 15, Othen airfield, 1940

#C4819 Bf 109E-3 over Swiss Part III
J-346, Fl.Kp. 8, Thun airfield, 1944; J-371, Interlaken
airfield, 1944

#C4823 Bf 109E over Swiss Part IV
J-316, Dübendorf airfield, June 1939; J-333, Fl.Kp. 21,
Lt Köpfli, Summer 1939

#C4824 Bf 109 over Swiss Part V
J-301, Fl.Kp. 15, Dübendorf, Spring 1940; J-306,
Dübendorf, Spring 1939

#C48178 Bf 109B Condor Legion
B-1, •6-10, flown by *Staffelkapitän Oblt* G. Lutzow,
Legion Condor, Victoria, Spain, 7th April 1937; B-2,
6•32, flown by *ObFw.* R. Seiler, Legion Condor, Spain,
summer 1937

#C48179 Bf 109E-3a Over Yugoslavia Part 1
E-3a, L-32, 102 Esk, Royal Yugoslavian Air Force,
1940-41; E-3a, L-33, 102 Esk, RYAF, 1940-41; E-3a,
L-42, 2rd Flight School, RYAF, 1940-41

#48180 Bf 109E-3a Over Yugoslavia Part 2
E-3a, L-33, 102 Esk, Royal Yugoslavian Air Force,
1940-41; E-3a, L-43, 102 Esk, RYAF, 1940-41; E-3a,
L-53, 2rd Flight School, RYAF, 1940-41

Lifelike Decals
#48-002 Bf 109 Part 1
Inc. Bf 109E-1, 'Yellow 5', flown by Hans Troitzsch,
6./JG77, Norway, 1939

#48-016 Bf 109 Part 2
Inc. Bf 109E-1, 'Black 13', 2./JG77, France, 1940

#48-017 Bf 109 Part 3
Inc. Bf 109E, 'Black A', flown by *Oblt* Hesselmann.
JG/26. France. 1940

#48-018 Bf 109 Part 4
Inc. Bf 109E-3, 'Black I', flown by *Maj.* E.F. von Berg,
Kdr III./JG26, 1940

#48-033 Bf 109 Part 5
Inc. Bf 109E-3, 'Yellow 3', 6./JG51, flown by *Fw.*
A. Hasse

#48-034 Bf 109 Part 6
Inc. Bf 109E-3, 'Black <', *Stab* I./JG 51, flown by *Lt*
E. Terry

Lift Here Decals
#P-48LH Yugoslav Messerschmitts
Inc. E-3, No.2506 'L-26'; E-3, No.2532 'L-33'

#A-48LH Royal Yugoslav AF In April War, Part I
Inc. E-3, No.2508; E-3, No.2552

Microscale
#48-1195 Bf 109E-1, 6./JG26, II./JG53 & 6./JG52

Ministry of Small Aircraft Production
#4801 Bf 109E – Battles of Poland & Britain
'White 14', JG21; E-1, 'Red 11', IV/JG132, Summer
1939; E-1, 'White 3', JG 132, Franco-German border,
September 1939; E-4, 'Black <', flown by *Oblt* Franz
von Werra, II./JG3, 1940; E-3, W/Nr.3576, 'White 13',
III./JG54; E-4, W/Nr.3726, 'Yellow M', 6./LG2

#4804 Bf 109E – North Africa & Russia
E-4/B, 'S9+DR', 7./SKG 210, El Daba, Autumn 1942;
E-4N/Trop, 'Black <<', flown by Gustav Rodel,
II./JG27, Libya, Summer 1941; E-7/B, 'S9+CD',
III./SKG 210, Central Sector, Russia, Autumn 1941;
E-7/B, 'White U', flown by Georg Dörffel, 5 Sch.G 1,
Stalingrad Front, 1942; E-4, 'Yellow 65', First Fighter
Group, Royal Romanian Air Force

#4807 Bf 109B, C, D
B-2, 'White 9', II./JG 132, Juterborg-Damm, Spring
1937; D-1, 'White 2', 1./JG137, Autumn 1939; D-1,
flown by the operations officer of JG 132, Germany,
1939; 'CL+NR' beleived to be from an aircraft
mechanics' training facility; C-1, 'Red 11', 2./JG71,
Summer 1939; C, 'Black 16', FFS Vienna-Schwechat,
1940

#4816 Legion Condor
Inc. D, 6•51, flown by *Oblt* Wolfgang Schellmann,
1.J/88, July 1938; D, 6•56, flown by Gotthard
Handrick, 2.J/88; E-1, 6•119, flown by *Hptm.* Siebelt
Reents, 1.J/88, Winter 1938-39

#4829 Bf 109E Battle of Britain

Montex
#K48032 Bf 109E-1
'Red 15', flown by Heinz Bretnütz, 2(J)./LG2; 'Yellow
2', 6./JG52, September 1940
*Note – Die-cut self-adhesive marks for main markings plus
waterslide decals for insignia etc. – intended for Hasegawa kit*

#K48033 Bf 109E-3
'Yellow 15', flown by Karl Wolff, 3./JG52, August 1940;
'White 6' of 7.JG26
*Note – Die-cut self-adhesive marks for main markings plus
waterslide decals for insignia etc. – intended for Tamiya kit*

#K48034 Bf 109E-4
'White 12' flown by *Fw.* Heinz Ürlings, 1./JG52,
August 1940; 'Black 8', flown by Ofw. Bernhard
Lampskemper, 2./JG3, August 1940
*Note – Die-cut self-adhesive marks for main markings plus
waterslide decals for insignia etc. – intended for Tamiya kit*

#K48161 Bf 109E-3
J-353, Swiss AF, Dubendorf, 1939/40; J-311, Swiss AF,
1944
*Note – Die-cut self-adhesive marks for main markings plus
waterslide decals for insignia etc. – intended for Tamiya kit*

#K48169 Bf 109E-4
'White 1', flown by *Lt* Wulf-Dieter Widowitz, JG77,
Germany, 1941; 'Red 22', probably from an unknown
training unit
*Note – Die-cut self-adhesive marks for main markings plus
waterslide decals for insignia etc. – intended for Tamiya kit*

Owl
#S4804 Bf 109E-4
'G9+JV', 10/NJG 1, Peil GIV, Germany, 1942

Lifelike #48-016

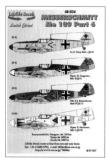
Lifelike #48-034

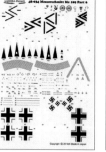
Lifelike #48-034

Montex #K48032

Montex #K48034

Montex #K48161

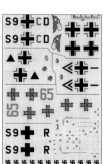
MSAP #4801

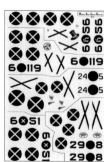
MSAP #4804

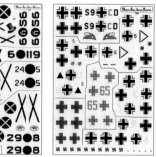
MSAP #4807

MSAP #4816

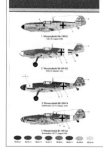
MSAP #7204

Possum Werks

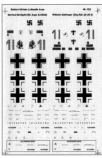
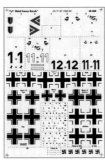
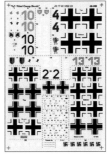
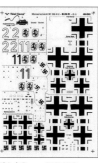

Sky Models #48-027   Superscale #48-703   Third Group #48-008   Third Group #48-009   Third Group #48-043   Ventura #V4803

Peddinghaus Decals
#EP1768 Me 109E-4
'White 1', flown by *Hptm*. W. Balthasar, *Staffelkapitän* 1./JG1, May 1940

#EP1772 Me 109E-4
'Black <<', flown by *Hptm*. H. Wick, *Stab* I./JG2, October 1940

Possum Werks
Johannes 'Macky' Steinhoff
Inc. E-3, 'White 1', 4./JG52, August 1940

Print-Scale
#48-024 Bf 109D Part 1
6•56, J88, Spain, 1938; 6•56, J88, Spain, September 1938; 'White 11', 10N/JG2, Strausberg, Germany, September 1939; 6•79, 3./J88, Spain, November 1938; 'Yellow 5', 2./JG 176, Gablingen, Germany, Autumn 1939; 'White 1', 1./JG 131, Germany, March 1939; 'Yellow 1', 3./JG 21, Gutenfeld, Germany, September 1939

#48-029 Bf 109E Part 1
E-1, 'Red 10', 2./JGr 101, 1939; E-1, 'Yellow 14', 6./J 186, 1939-1940; E-1, Yellow 3', 6./JG 52, 1940; E-3, 9./JG 26, 1940; E-7, 'Black <', 1./JG 2, 1941; E-7/B, 'Blue H', II./SG 1, 1942-1943; E-3, 'Yellow 3', 9./JG 26, 1940; E-4, 'Black <<', I./JG 2, 1940; E-3, 'Red 1', 2./JG 26, 1940; E-3, 'Red 2', 2./JG 26, 1940

#48033 Bf109E Part 2
'Black 13', 2./JG 77, 1940; 'S9+CD', ZG 1, 1941; 'Red 0', 2./SG.1, 1942; 'White 8', 7./JG 26, 1941. 'Yellow 47', Romanian Forces, Russian Front, 1942

Propagteam
#48-002/06 Bf 109E-4/N
'Black <', flown by A. Galland, *Kommodore* JG 26, 1940

#48006 Bf 109D
6•79, flown by *Oblt* W. Mölders, 3J/88, Legion Condor, Spain, 1937-38

#48010 Bf 109
'White <', flown by Reinhard Heyrich, Wangerooge, June 1941

RB Productions
#RB-D48012 Romanian Bf 109Es Part 1
Same options as #RB-D72012

#RB-D48013 Romanian Bf 109Es Part 2
Same options as #RB-D72013

#RB-D48014 Romanian Bf 109Es Part 3
Same options as #RB-D72014

Revi
#48004 Luftwaffe Experten Volume 1
Inc. Bf 109E-1, 'White 2', 7./JG 26, flown by *Lt* Egon Troha, 1939

Rising Decals
#48-012 Unusual Emils
E-7/Trop, 'S9+CS', II./ZG1, Libya, 1942; E-3, J-364, Fl.Kp. 9, Swiss AF, 1940-49; E-7/Trop, 'S9+DR', II./ZG1, Libya, 1942; E-1, 6•119, flown by *Oblt* S. Reents, 1.J/88

#48-014 Under New Management
Inc. Bf 109E-3, W/Nr.1304, ex-1./JG76 in French/RAF colours

Sky Models
#48027 Bf 109
Inc. E-3 'White 3', flown by *Uffz*. L. Froba, 4./JG77, Norway, Oct. 1940; E-4/N, W/Nr.5819, 'Black <-', flown by *Maj*. A. Galland, JG26, Audembert, France, Dec.1940; E-7, 'Black <<', flown by G. Scholz, III./JG5, Petsamo, Finland, 1942; E-4, 'White 1', flown by *Hptm* W. Balthasar, 1./JG1, Monchy-Breton, May 1940; E-4/N, 'Black <-', flown by *Maj*. A. Galland, E.Gr.26, 1941; E-4, 'Yellow 5', flown by *Lt* W. Wübke, 9./JG54, France, 1941; E-4, 'Black <-', flown by *Maj*. H. Wick, JG2, Beaumont, France, Nov. 1940; E, 'White 1', flown by O. Bertram, 1./JG2, Cambrai, May 1940; E-4, 'White 1', flown by *Oblt* W. Machold, 7./JG2, Le Havre, Sept. 1940; E-3, 'Black <-', flown by *Obstlt* C. Schumacher, JG1, Jever, 1940; E-4, 'White 1', flown by *Oblt* H. Philipp, 4./JG54, Hermelingen, Oct. 1940; E, 'Yellow 13', flown by *Fw*. K. Ibben, 6(J)/TrGr.186, Wangerooge, Mar. 1940; E, 'Yellow 5', flown by *Fw*. H, Tritzsch, 6./JG77, Wangerooge, Dec.1939; E, 'Black 1', flown by *Hptm*. H. Tietzen, 5./JG41, Marquise, Aug. 1940; E-4, 'Black <<' flown by *Hptm*. H. Traultoht, 1./JG20, Bonninghardt, Mar. 1940; E-4, 'White 7', 1./JG2, 1940; E-4, 'Black <<', flown by *Maj*. H. Wick, 1./JG2, Mardyck, Belgium, Oct. 1940; E, 'Yellow 10', flown by *Hptm*. H. Bretnutz, II./JG53, France, 1940; E, 'Black <<', flown by *Hptm*. Heinz Bretnutz, II./JG53, France, Autumn 1940; E-1, 'Yellow 12', flown by *Fw*. E. Arnord, 3./JG27, August 1940; E, 'White 4', 6./JG26, 1940; E-7, 'Red E', 2/1/Sch G 1, Russia, 1941; E-4, 'Yellow 1', JG52, 1941

Start
#4803 Luftwaffe in Focus No 3
Inc. Bf 109E-4, 'Yellow 6', 9./JG3, France, 1940

Superscale
#48-460 Bf 109E Aces Part 1
E, 'Red 1', flown by A. Held, 5./JG77, 1940; E, 'Black <|', flown by W. Mölders, 3./JG52, May 1940

#48-461 Bf 109E Aces Part 2 – Battle of Britain

#48-639 Bf 109E-7/7 7./JG26, I./JG27 & III./JG 27

#48-701 Bf 109E-4 Battle of Britain Aces
E-4, 'Black <<', flown by *Hptm*. Helmut Wick, I./JG2; E-4, 'Black <-', flown by *Obstltn* Adolf Galland, JG26

#48-702 Bf 109E-4 Battle of Britain Aces Part 2
E-3, 'White 13', flown by *Uffz*. Heinz Bär, I./JG51; E-3, 'Black <<', flown by *Hptm*. Werner Mölders, III./JG53

#48-703 Bf 109E-4 Battle of Britain Aces Part 3
'Green 1', *Hptm* Wilhelm Balthasar, *Gruppenkommandeur* III./JG3; 'Yellow 1', *Lt* Gerhard Schopfel, *Staffelkapitän* 9./JG 26

#48-828 Bf 109E-3/E-7b
E-3, 'Red 15', 15./JG 52, Russia, 1941; E-7b, S9+CD, III./SKG 210, Russia, 1941

#48-868 Bf 109E-1 I./JG51, 2./JG26 & 6.(J)/TrGr 186

#48-869 Bf 109E-3/E-4
'Black <', JG 1, Carl Schmacher, *Geschwaderkommodore*; 'Black <<', I./JG 3, Hans von Hahn, *Gruppenkommandeur*; 'Black <', I./JG 20, Hannes Trautloft, *Gruppenkommandeur*

#48-1195 Bf 109E-1 Battle of Britain
'Red 1', 6./JG26; 'Yellow 15', II./JG53; 'Yellow 14', 6./JG52

Techmod
#48013 Bf 109E-4
Maj. Adolf Galland, *Kommodore* JG26; 'Yellow 1', *Staffelkapitän Oblt* Gerhardt Schopfel, 9./JG26; *Gruppenkommandeur Hptm*. Hans von Hahn, I./JG3; Grupen-Adjutant *Maj*. Reinhard Heydrich, *Stab*.III/JG1; *Maj*. Erich Mix, *Kommandeur* III./JG2

#48014 Bf 109E-3
'Black <<', *Kommandeur* 1.(J)/LG2; 'White 1', 1./JG2; 'Black <<', *Gruppenkomandeur* III./JG26, flown by Adolf Galland; 'White 1', 4./JG54; 'White 13', 1./JG51

#48080 Bf 109E-3
'White 13', *Lt* Walter Blume, 3./JG 26; 'Black <', *Lt* Hans Hahn, 1./JG 3; 'Yellow 1', *Oblt* Josef Priller, 6./JG 51

#48081 Bf 109E-4
'White 13', 3./JG 51, *Oblt* Walter Oesau, 1940; 'Yellow 2', III./JG2 Richthofen, *Oblt* Helmut Wick, *Staffelkapitän*, Beaumont-le-Roger 1940; 'Black <<', I./JG2 Richthofen, *Hptm* Helmut Wick, *Gruppenkommandeur*, Beaumont-le-Roger 1940; 'Black <', *Stab* II./JG3, *Oblt* Franz von Werra

#48098 Bf 109E Stencil Data
For two aircraft

Third Group Decals
#48-005 Bf 109E-1/3/4 III *Gruppe*, JG2/52/54/77
E-1. White 1', 7./JG 52, Karabacie, Romania, 1941; E-1, 'Red 7', 8./JG 52, Hopstädten, August 1940; 'Yellow 5', 9./JG 54, flown by *Lt* W. Wübke, Cherbourg, France, 1941; E-3, 'Black 10', 7./JG 77, Greece, April 1941; E-3, 'Red 6', 8./JG 2, France, 1940; E-4, 'Red 4', 8./JG 2, flown by *Uffz*. Hippel, France, 1940

#48-008 Bf 109 #2
E-3, W/Nr.5057, 'Red <<', flown by *Hptm*. Herbert Ihefelm II.(J)/LG2, France, 1941; E-3, W/Nr.5057, 'Red <<', flown by *Hptm*. Herbert Ihefelm II.(J)/LG2, Kesckemet, Hungary, April 1941; E-1, W/Nr.1276, 'White 5', flown by *Lt* Jakob Arnoldy, 4./JG77, Mandal, France, September 1940; E-4/B, 'Black 1', 2.(J)/LG2, France, November 1940; E-4, 'White 11', flown by *Lt* Heinz Demes, 4./JG77, Westerland/Sylt, Germany, March 1940; E-1, 'Black 12', flown by *Uffz*. Josef Heinzeller, 2.(J)/LG2m September 1939; E-4, 'Black 11', III./JG77, Molaoi, Greece, May 1941

#48-009 Bf 109 #3
E-4, 'Black 10', III./JG77. Molaoi, Greece, May 1941; E-3, 'White 13', flown by *Oblt* Helmut Menz, 4./JG77, Poland, September 193; E-1, 'Brown 4', 3.(J)/LG2, Hage, Germany, January 1940; E-4, 'Black 2', 2.(J)/LG2, Radomir, Bulgaria, April 1941; E-1, 'Brown 13', flown by *ObFw*. Kurt Ubben, 7./JG77, Trondheim-Vaernes, Norway, July 1940

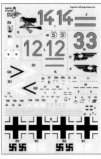

EagelCals #EC120   Eagle Strike #32060   EagleCals #EC121   EagleCals #EC122   Lifelike #32-002   Montex #K32075

#48-043 Bf 109 #12
E-3, 'White 2', flown by *ObFw.* von Hans Illner, 4th *Staffel* JG51, France, August 1940; E-3, 'White 1', flown by Josef Fözö, 4th *Staffel* JG51, France, Summer 1940; E-3, 'Black 1', flown by *Hptm.* Horst Tietzen, 5./*Staffelkapitän* JG51, France, August 1940; E-3, 'Yellow 1', flown by *Oblt* Josef Priller, 6./*Staffelkapitän*, Mardyck, Holland, late 1940

#48-067 Bf 109 #20
E-4, 'White 19', 7 *Staffel*, JG27; E-3, 'Black 1', 8 *Staffelkapitän*, JG27; E-7, 'Brown 18', 8 *Staffel*, JG27; E-4, 'Yellow 1', flown by *Oblt* Erbo Graf von Kageneck, 9 *Staffelkapitän*, JG27

#48-068 Bf 109 #21
E-1, 'Black <<', *Gruppenkommandeur* JG77, September 1939; E-1, 'Red 1', flown by *Hptm.* Hannes Trautloft, 2 *Staffelkapitän*, JG77, September 1939; E-3, 'Black 9', 2 *Staffel* JG77, May 1940; E-4, 'Red 13', 2 *Staffel*, JG77, September 1939

Topkits Decals
#72-101 Bf 109E Swiss Air Force

Ventura
#V4803 Messerschmitt Bf 109s & Me 262s
E-1, 6•127, 25 Grupo, 23 Regimiento de Caza, Spanish Air Force, 1952

#V4877 Rumanian Bf 109E-3
E-3, 'Yellow 37', Grupul 7 Vinatoares, Pipera airfield, April 1941

Victory Productions
Xtradecal
#X48-087 Battle of Britain 70th Anniversary
Inc. Bf 109E-1, 'Yellow 11', 9./JG 26, *Fw.* Artur Beese, Aug 1940; Bf 109E-3, 'Yellow 1', 6./JG 51, *Oblt* Josef (Pips) Priller, *Staffelkapitän*, October 1940; Bf 109E-4/B, 'Yellow M', 6(Schlact)/LG 2, *Fw.* Erhardt Pankratz, October 1940; Bf 109E-3, 'Yellow 15', 3./JG 52, *Uffz.* Karl Wolff, August 1940

1/32nd Scale

AML
#AMLC2 006 Emils in the Spanish Civil War
E-3, 6•119, flown by *Hptm.* S. Reents, *Staffelkapitän* 1 J/88, Spring 1939; 6•123, flown by *Oblt* Hans Schmoller-Haldy, 3./J88, March 1939
Paint masks with decal

Authentic Decals
#32-03 Bf 109E
'Black <<', *Stab* (J)/LG2, 1941; 'RB+1', 7./JG54, France 1940; 'Black 10', III./JG77, *Oblt* Hubert Mulherich, Romania 1941; 'Black 10', 2./JG27, Libya 1941; 'Yellow 6', 9./JG3, France 1940; 'S9+GT', *Uffz.* Werner Ringel, Russia, 1942; 'Black 3' *Hptm.* Herman Segatz, 1./JG5, Finland 1942; 'Yellow 1' *Oblt* Erbo Graf, 9./JG27, 1941; 'G9+AV', IV/NJG1; 'Yellow C', 1./Sch. G1, Russia, 1942

EagleCal
EC#50 Major Hans 'Assi' Hahn Part 1
Bf 109E-3, StabI./JG3, Merseburg, Germany 1939; Bf 109E-3, 'White 13', 4./JG2, Northern Germany, Spring 1940; Bf 109E-4, 'White 14', 4./JG2, France, 1940; Bf 109E-4, III./JG2, France, 1940

EC#66 Graf and Grislawski 9./JG52 Part 3
Bf 109E-1, 'Black 17', 2./Erg.JGr, 1940; Bf 109E, 'Yellow 9'

EC#120 Bf 109E-1 Part 1
'Yellow 14', 6.(J)*Tragergruppe* 186, 1939; 'Yellow 12', 6./JG26, 1940; 'Yellow 3', 6./JG52, 1940; 'Black <', *Stab* 1./JG51, *Lt* Josef `Pips' Priller, 1939

EC#121 Bf 109E-1 Part 2
'White 13', 4./JG77, *Hptm* Helmut Henz, 1941; 'Red 1', 2./JG27, *Oblt* Gert Framm, 1940; 'Red 16', 2./JG26, *Oblt* Fritz Losikeit, 1940; 'Yellow 12', 9./JG52, 1941

EC#122 Bf 109E-1 Part 3
'Yellow 12', 3./JG27, *Fw.* Ernst Arnold, 1940; 'White 2', 4./JG52, *Fw.* Paul Boche, 1940; 'Yellow 10', 6./JG54, 1940; 'Black 13', 2./JG77, 1940

Eagle Strike
#32040 Bf 109E Emil Aces at War
'Black <<+', Wolfgang Lippert, *Kommander* II./JG27, Balkans 1941; 'Yellow 1', 6./JG51, Josef Priller, Belgium 1940; 'White 7', 1./JG54, Reinhard Seiller, Germany 1940

#32001 Battle of Britain Campaign: Bf 109 Part I
E-4, 'Black <', flown by *Hptm.* Hans von Hahn, I./JG3, France, 1940; E-4, 'Red 5', 2./JG26, late 1940; E-4, 'Green 1', flown by *Hptm.* Wilhelm Balthasar, 7./JG27, 1940

#32059 Battle of Britain Luftwaffe Aces Part I
E-1, 'Yellow 8', flown by *Lt* Rudolph rothenfelder, 9./JG 2; E-3, 'Black <o', flown by *Oblt* Werner Pichon-Kalau von Hofe, III./JG51, mid-Summer 1940; E-4, 'Yellow 2', flown by *Oblt* Helmut Wick, 3./JG2

#32060 Battle of Britain Luftwaffe Aces Part II
E-3, 'White 2', flown by *Ofw.* Hans Illner, 4./JG51; E-1, 'Brown 2', 6./JG54, Campagne, France, Autumn 1940; E-7, 'White 7', flown by *Oblt* Werner Machold, 7./JG2, Pas de Calais, France, Winter 1940-41; E-4, 'Black <<', flown by *Hptm.* Rolf Pingel, I./JG26, Audembert, France, November 1940

Eduard
#D32005 Bf 109E Stencils

Euro Decals
#ED-32109 Bf 109E Emils Part 1
E-7/B, S9+RS, 8./ZG1, Russia, summer 1942; E-3, 6•99, Condor Legion, Grupo num.25, 1939; E-3/B, DG200, No.1426 Flight, RAF, 1941; E-3, J-277, Fl.Kp.21, Swiss Air Force; E-4, 'Black 13', 8./JG1, 1941; E-4, 'White 1', Royal Bulgarian Air Force, winter 1944-45; E-4, W/Nr.5244, 'White 10', 13 Sqn, Slovak Air Force, April 1943; E-3, W/Nr.0820, ' White 3', 4./JG77, Norway, October 1940

FCM
#D32-024 Bf 109E/F/G

HAD
#32060 Bf 109A
A, •6-1, VJ/88, December 1935-March 1936; A, •6-1, 2.J/88, March 1937 onwards; V3, W/Nr.760 (ex-D-IOQY), •6-2, VJ/88

HGW Models
#232005 Bf 109E Stencils

#232006 Bf 109E with stencils

Kora
#DEC32.06 Bf 109E Strela (Bulgarian Service)
E-4AA, 'White 6', Galata Orliak, Balchik airfield, 1942; E-7A, 'White 11', 3 Orliak 672 Jato, Petrovac airfield, 1943

#DEC32.15 Bf-109E-3a Yugoslav Air Force
E-3A, L-10, Lovacka Eskadrila, Krusedol airfield, April 1941; E-3A, L-21, 101 Lovacka Eskadrila, Vel Radinci II airfield, 1940; E-3A, 'White 11', 6 Vazdungplovni Lovacki, Zemun airfield, 1940; E-3A, L-80, 101 Lovacka Eskadrila, Zemun airfield, September 1940

#DEC32.18 Bf 109E-3A Emil (Swiss Air Force Part I)
E-3A, J-317, Fliegerkompanie 7, Avenches airfield, September 1940; E-3A, J-326, Fliegerkompanie 6, Avenches airfield, Autumn 1941; E-3A, J-334, Fliegerkompanie 7, Avenches airfield, Spring 1941

#DEC32.19 Bf 109E-3A Emil (Swiss Air Force Part II)
E-3A, J-358, Fliegerkompanie 8, Avenches airfield, Summer 1940; E-3A, J-366, Fliegerkompanie 8, Avenches airfield, Summer 1940; E-3A, J-374, Fliegerkompanie 6, Thun airfield, Summer 1940

#DEC32.20 Bf 109E-3A Emil (Swiss Air Force Part III)
E-3A, J-359, Fliegerkompanie 8, Avenches airfield, Summer 1940; E-3A, J-362, Fliegerkompanie 8, Avenches airfield, Summer 1940; E-3A, J-363, Fliegerkompanie 9, Avenches airfield, Summer 1940

#DEC32.21 Bf 109E-3A Emil (Swiss Air Force Part IV)
E-3A, J-320, Fliegerkompanie 9, Avenches airfield, Spring 1945; E-3A, J-385, Fliegerkompanie 8, Thun airfield, 1945; E-3A, J-393, Fliegerkompanie 8, Thun airfield, October 1945; E-3A, J-399, Fliegerkompanie 8, Payerne airfield, 1948

LF Models
#C3261 Bf 109B Condor Legion
B-1, •6-10, flown by *Staffelkapitän Oblt* G. Lutzow, Legion Condor, Victoria, Spain, 7th April 1937; B-2, 6•32, flown by *ObFw.* R. Seiler, Legion Condor, Spain, summer 1937

#C3265 Bf 109E in Romanian Service Part I
E-3, 'Yellow 27', flown by Sit.av I. Dicezore, Gr.7, summer 1941; E-7, 'Yellow 47', floown by *Adj.av.* C. Lunguiesca, Gr.7, summer 1944; E-3, 'Yellow 64', flown by Adj.av.T. Vinca, Gr.7, Vanatoare, summer 1942

#C3266 Bf 109E in Romanian Service Part II
E-3, 'Yellow 11', flown by A. Serbanescu, Gr.7, Bucharest-Pipera, summer 1942; E-3, 'Yellow 26', flown by *Adj.av.* S. Greceanu, Gr.7, Escadrille 57, Salz, Bessarabia, September 1941; E-3, 'Yellow 45', flown by *Cap.av.* G. Iliescu CO of Gr.5, Escadrille 52, Mamaiai, summer 1943

#C3262 Bf 109E-3a Over Yugoslavia Part 1
E-3a, L-32, 102 Esk, Royal Yugoslavian Air Force, 1940-41; E-3a, L-33, 102 Esk, Royal Yugoslavian Air

Force, 1940-41; E-3a, L-42, 2rd Flight School, Royal Yugoslavian Air Force, 1940-41

#C3263 Bf 109E-3a Over Yugoslavia Part 2
E-3a, L-33, 102 Esk, Royal Yugoslavian Air Force, 1940-41; E-3a, L-43, 102 Esk, Royal Yugoslavian Air Force, 1940-41; E-3a, L-53, 2rd Flight School, Royal Yugoslavian Air Force, 1940-41

Lifelike Decals
#32-002 Bf 109 Part 1
Inc. Bf 109E-1, 'Yellow 5', 6./JG77, flown by *Fw.* Hans Troitzsch, Germany, 1939

Microscale
#32-19 Bf 109E
E, 'Black <<', flown by *Oblt* H. Heydrich, *Stab* III./JG1, Holland; E, 'Yellow 5', 6./JG52, France; E, 'Yellow 10', II./JG51, St Ozer and St Inglevert, France; E, 'Red 2', 4./JG52, France

Montex
#K32067 Bf 109E-3
'Yellow 15', flown by Karl Wolff, 3./JG52, August 1940; 'White 6' of 7./JG26
Note – Die-cut self-adhesive marks for main markings plus waterslide decals for insignia etc. – intended for Hasegawa kit

#K32075 Bf 109E-3
'Black <o', flown by *Hptm.* Dr. Erich Mix, *Stab* I./JG53, Wiesbaden-Erbenheim, November 1939; 'White 5', flown by *Uffz.* Stefan Litjens, 4./JG53, late Autumn 1939
Note – Die-cut self-adhesive marks for main markings plus waterslide decals for insignia etc. – intended for Hasegawa kit

#K32149 Bf 109E-4
'White 12' flown by *Fw.* Heinz Ürlings, 1./JG52, August 1940; 'Black 8', flown by *Ofw.* Bernhard Lampskemper, 2./JG3, August 1940
Note – Die-cut self-adhesive marks for main markings plus waterslide decals for insignia etc. – intended for Eduard kit

#K32145 Bf 109E-1
6•99, Grupo Num 25, Spanish Air Force; 6•88, *Jagdgruppe* J/88, Spain, 1939
Note – Die-cut self-adhesive marks for main markings plus waterslide decals for insignia etc. – intended for Eduard kit

#K32146 Bf 109E-1
'White 2', flown by *Lt* Egon Troha, 7./JG26, Werl, Germany, October 1939; 'White 4', 1./JG20, Branderburg-Briest, September 1939
Note – Die-cut self-adhesive marks for main markings plus waterslide decals for insignia etc. – intended for Eduard kit

#K32147 Bf 109E-1
'White 15', flown by *Gefr.* Josef Bröker, 1./JG53, Rennes, France, August 1940; 'White 9', flown by *Fw.* Herbert Bischoff, 1./JG52, August 1940
Note – Die-cut self-adhesive marks for main markings plus waterslide decals for insignia etc. – intended for Eduard kit

#K32148 Bf 109E-4
'White 1', flown by *Lt* Wulf-Dieter Widowitz, JG77, Germany, 1941; 'Red 22', probably from an unknown training unit
Note – Die-cut self-adhesive marks for main markings plus waterslide decals for insignia etc. – intended for Eduard kit

#K32184 Bf 109E-4/7
'Black 15', Erg.Gr./JG77, Ukrainian Front, Spring 1942; 'Black 7', flown by *Oblt* Walter Fiel, 8./JG53, October 1940
Note – Die-cut self-adhesive marks for main markings plus waterslide decals for insignia etc. – intended for Eduard kit

#K32185 Bf 109E-1/4
'Black 3', 2./JG3, France, late Autumn 1940; 'White 9', flown by *Oblt* Karl Fischer, 7./JG27, September 1940
Note – Die-cut self-adhesive marks for main markings plus waterslide decals for insignia etc. – intended for Eduard kit

Owl
#32010 Bf 109E-4
'G9+JV', 10/NJG 1, Peil GIV, Germany, 1942

Peddinghaus Decals
#321773 Me 109E-4
'Black <<', flown by *Hptm.* H. Wick, *Stab* I./JG2, October 1940

#EP1776 Me 109E-4
Yellow 5', flown by *Oblt* E.G. von Kageneck, 9./JG27, 1941

Print-Scale
#144-014 Bf 109E
'Red 10', 2./J 101, 1939; 'Yellow 14', 6./J 186, 1940; 'Yellow 3', 6./JG 52, 1940; 6•123, 3/J, Spain, 1939; 'Yellow 9', 9./JG 26, 1940; 'Red 1', 2./JG 26, 1940; 'Red 2', 2./JG 26, 1940; 'Black 13', 2./JG77, 1940; S9+6D, 4/B ZG 1, 1942; 'Yellow 47', Romanian Forces, 1942; 'Red 0', JG 26, 1940; 'Blue H', II./JG 1, 1942; 'White 8', 7./ZG 26, 1941; 'Black <<', 1./4G, 1941; 'Black <<', 1./JG 2, 1940

RB Productions
#RB-D32012 Romanian Bf 109Es Part 1
Same options as #RB-D72012

#RB-D32013 Romanian Bf 109Es Part 2
Same options as #RB-D72013

#RB-D32014 Romanian Bf 109Es Part 3
Same options as #RB-D72014

Rising Decals
#RD32004 Unusual Emils Part I
E-7/Trop, 'S9+CS', III./ZG1, Libya, 1942; E-7/Trop, 'S9+DR', III./ZG1, Libya, 1942; E-1, 6•119, 3J/88, Condor Legion, Spain; E-1, 6•119, 1.J/88, flown by *Oblt* S. Reents, Condor Legion, Spain

Start
#3201 Bf 109
Inc. Bf 109E-4, 'Yellow 6', 9./JG3, France, 1940

#3203 Bf 109E/F/G
Inc. Bf 109E-4, 'Yellow 6', 9./JG3, Battle of Britain, France 1940

Superscale
#32-19 Bf 109E

#32-129 Bf 109E Stencils

#320251 Bf 109E-1
'Red 10', 2./JGr102, Fürstenwalde, Germany, August 1939; 'Yellow 2', 6./JG52

#320252 Bf 109E-4
E-4B, 'Black <I', *Stab*.II/JG54, Arad, Rumania, early 1941; 'Black <<', 11./JG27, *Kommandeur Hptm* Wolfgang Lippert, Larissa, Greece, April 1941

Techmod
#32026 Bf 109E-3
'White 13', *Lt* Walter Blume, 3./JG 26, 1940; 'Black <', *Lt* Hans Hahn, 1./JG 3, 1939; 'Yellow 1', *Oblt* Josef Priller, 6./JG 51, Belgium, 1940

#32027 Bf 109E-4
'White 13', 3./JG 51, *Oblt* Walter Oesau, 1940; 'Yellow 2', III./JG2 Richthofen, *Oblt* Helmut Wick *Staffelkapitän*, Beaumont-le-Roger 1940; 'Black <<', I./JG2 Richthofen, *Hptm* Helmut Wick *Gruppenkommandeur*, Beaumont-le-Roger 1940; 'Black <', *Stab* II./JG3, *Oblt* Franz von Werra

#32028 Bf 109E-4
'Black <-', JG 26, *Maj.* Adolf Galland, September 1940; 'Yellow 1', 9./JG 26, *Oblt* Gerhardt Schopfel, August 1940; 'Black <<', 1./JG 3, *Hptm* Hans von Hahn, 1940; 'White <', *Stab* III./JG 1, *Maj.* Reinhard Heydrich, June 1940; *Kommandeur* III./JG 2, *Maj.* Erich Mix, May 1940

1/24th Scale

Eagle Strike
#24002 Messerschmitt Bf 109
E-4, 'Red 4', 9./JG2, Le Havre, France, Summer 1940; E-4, 'Red 5', 2./JG26, late 1940; E-4, flown by *Oblt* Bennermann, 2./JG52, October 1940

Lift Here Decals
#201-LH Big Toys 1
Inc. E-3, No.2530, 'L-31'

Montex
#K24015 Bf 109E-4
'White 12' flown by *Fw.* Heinz Ürlings, 1./JG52, August 1940; 'Black 8', flown by *Ofw.* Bernhard Lampskemper, 2./JG3, August 1940
Note – Die-cut self-adhesive marks for main markings plus waterslide decals for insignia etc. – intended for Airfix kit

#K24042 Bf 109E-3
'Yellow 3', 3./JG51, Winter 1939-40; 'Red 10', 2./JG101, Fürstenwalde, August 1939
Note – Die-cut self-adhesive marks for main markings plus waterslide decals for insignia etc. – intended for Airfix kit

Techmod
#24009 Bf 109E-3
'White 1', 1./JG 2, *Oblt* Otto Bertram, May 1940; 'Black <', 1./JG 3 Udet, *Lt* Hans Hahn, September 1939; 'Yellow 1', 6./JG 51, *Oblt* Josef Priller, Belgium, October 1940

#24010 Bf 109E-4
'White 13', 3./JG 51, *Oblt* Walter Oesau, August 1940; 'Black <', *Oblt* Franz von Werra, *Stab* II./JG 3, August 1940; 'Yellow 1', 9./JG 26, *Staffelkapitän Oblt* Gerhard Schopfel, August 1940

Montex #K32146

Montex #K32148

Montex #K32149

Montex #K32185

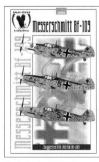

Eagle Strike #24002

Montex #K24015

Appendix IV: **Bibliography**

The list below of Bf 109-related publications is as comprehensive as possible, but there are bound to be omissions so if you have amendments or additions, please contact the author via the Valiant Wings Publishing address shown at the front of this title.

Official Documents
- Bf 109B Handbuch LDv 556/1
- Bf 109B Beschreibung LDv 557
- Bf 109B Schusswaffe LDv 228/1
- Bf 109B Bordfunkanlage LDv 228/1a
- Bf 109B, C und D Bordfunkanlage mit FuG VII D(Luft)T2401/2a
- Bf 109C und D Handbuch LDv 556/2
- Bf 109C1 und D1 Schusswaffe LDv 228/2
- Bf 109C, D, E Bordfunkanlage LDv 228/2a und 3a
- Bf 109D Kurz-Betriebsanleitung L(Luft)T2402/1
- Bf 109E Handbuch LDv 556/3
- Bf 109E Beschreibung von Schusswaffe und Abwur Fwaffe LDv 228/3 und LDv 229/3
- Bf 109E Reparatug-Answeisung D(Luft)T2109/Rep
- GM-1 Anlage Bf 109E-7/Z D(Luft)T2405/12
- 300 Liter Kraftstof-Zusatzanlage Bf 109E-7/E-8 D(Luft)T2405/11
- Bordfunkanlage LDv 228/2a und 3a sowie D(Luft) T2401/2a

Publications
- Aces of the Legion Condor by R. Forsyth, Aircraft of the Aces No.99 (Osprey Publishing 2011 ISBN: 978-1-84908-347-8)
- Aircraft Archive – Fighters of World War Two Volume 1 (Argus Books 1988 ISBN:0-85242-948-7)
- Aircraft from the Battle of Britain, Scale Models Special (Model & Allied Publications Ltd 1982)
- Air Power of the Kingdom of Bulgaria Part IV by F. Ood (Air Sofia 2001)
- The Augsburg Eagle by W. Green (McDonald)
- Aufklärer: Luftwaffe Reconnaissance Aircraft & Units 1935-1945 by D. Wadman, J. Bradley & B. Ketley (Hikoki Publications1997 ISBN: 0-9519899-8-7)
- Bf 109 Storia del Caccia Messerschmitt (Edizioni dell'Ateneo & Bizzarri 1980)
- Bf 109 Aces of North Africa and the Mediterranean by J. Scutts, Aircraft of the Aces No.6 (Osprey Publishing /Reed Consumer Books 1994 ISBN: 1-85532-448-2)
- Bf 109 Aces of Russian Front by J. Weal, Aircraft of the Aces No.76 (Osprey Publishing 2007 ISBN: 978-1-84603-177-9)
- Bf 109 Roumains, Air Mag Hors Série No.1 (Air Magazine 2002)
- Bf 109D/E Aces 1939-41 by J. Weal, Aircraft of the Aces No.11 (Osprey Publishing /Reed Consumer Books 1996 ISBN: 1-85532-487-3)
- Camouflage & Markings Luftwaffe 1939-1945 by M. Reynolds (Argus Books 1992 ISBN: 1-85486-066-6)
- Camouflage & Markings of the Luftwaffe Vol.2 (Kookabura Technical Publications, 1976)
- Camouflage & Markings of the Luftwaffe Vol.3 (Kookabura Technical Publications, 1977)
- Camouflage & Markings of the Luftwaffe Aircraft Vol.1 Day Fighters, Model Art Special No.308 (Model Art Co., Ltd)
- Captured Me 109s by J. Jackiewicz & M. Warwrynski (Atelier Kecav 2007 ISBN: 978-83-924914-0-8)
- Cockpit Profile No.7 – Deutsche Flugzeugcockpits und Instrumentenbretter by P.W. Cohausz (Flugzeug Publiklations GmbH 2003)
- Cockpits – Early WWII by S. Muth, A Peregrine Photo Essay Cockpits No.1 (Peregrine Publishing 2001 ISBN: 1-930432-08-9)
- Colours of the Luftwaffe by S.W. Parry & F.L. Marshall (Clifford Frost Ltd 1987 ISBN: 1-8700666-03-0)
- Condor: The Luftwaffe in Spain 1936-1939 by P. Laureau (Hikoki Publications 2000 ISBN: 0-902109-10-4)
- Die Messerschmitt Me 109 in der Schweizer Flugwaffe – en Stück Zeitgeschichte by G. Hoch (G. Hoch 2000 ISBN 3-905404-10-9)
- Eagles of the Third Reich: Hitler's Luftwaffe by S.W. Mitcham (Airlife Publishing Ltd 1988/Guild Publishing Ltd 1989)
- Fighting Cockpits 1914-2000 by L.F.E. Coombs (Airlife Publishing Ltd 1999 ISBN: 1-85310-915-0)
- German Aircraft of the Second World War by J.R.Smith & A.L. Kay (Putnam, 1972)
- German Night Fighter Aces of World War 2 by J. Scutts, Aircraft of the Aces No.20 (Osprey Publishing 1998 ISBN: 1-85532-696-5)
- German Short-range Reconnaissance Planes 1930-1945 by M. Griehl & J. Dressel (Schiffer 1989 ISBN: 0-88740-190-2)
- Hungarian Air Force by G. Punka(Squadron/Signal Publications 1994 ISBN: 0-89747-349-3)
- Les Messerschmitt Bf 109 Suisses/The Messerschmitt Bf 109 In Swiss Service by P. Osché, Avions Hors Série No.4 (Lela Presse, 1996)
- Les Messerschmitt Yougoslaves by S. Ostric, Avions Hors Série No.26 (Lela Presse 2009)
- Luftfahrt International No. 6 Nov-Dec 1974
- Luftwaffe Aces of WWII, Tank Magazine Special (Delta Publishing 1989)
- Luftwaffe Camouflage & Markings Vol.1, Model Art No.375
- Luftwaffe Colours 1935-1945 by M. Ullmann (Hikoki Publications Ltd 2002/Crécy Publishing Ltd 2008 ISBN: 9-781902-109077)
- Luftwaffe Eagles – The Messerschmitt Fighters – Flypast Special (Key Publishing 1997 ISBN: 0-946219-31-1)
- Luftwaffe Fledglings 1935-1945: Luftwaffe Training Units & their Aircraft by B. Ketley & M. Rolfe (Hikoki Publications 1996 ISBN: 1-9519899-2-8)
- Luftwaffe over Britain: A Pictorial Essay on the German Luftwaffe's Combat Against Britian in World War 2, Combat Pictorial No.1 (Blandford Studio 1977 ISBN: 0-905948-00-9)
- Messerschmitt Bf 109 – Classic WWII Aviation Vol.2 by E. Shacklady (Tempus Publishing 2000 ISBN: 0-7524-2003-8)
- Messerschmitt Bf 109, Famous aircraft and how to model them by R. Cross, G. Scarborough & H.J. Ebert (Patrick Stephens Ltd/Airfix)
- Messerschmitt Bf 109 by A.W. Hall, Warpaint Special No.2 (Hall Park Books 2001)
- Messerschmitt Bf 109, Aircraft & Legend by H. Nowara (Haynes Publishing Group 1989 ISBN: 0-85429-729-4)
- Messerschmitt Bf 109 by H.J. Nowarra (Schiffer ISBN: 0-88740-311-5)
- Messerschmitt Bf 109 by J. Ledwoch & A. Skupiewski, Monografie Lotnicze No.8 (AJ Press, 1992 ISSN: 0867-7867)
- Messerschmitt Bf 109 by J. Ledwoch & A. Skupiewski, Monografie Lotnicze No.8 (AJ Press, 1994 ISBN: 83-86208-02-3) – 2nd edition
- Messerschmitt Bf 109 by J. Scutts, Combat Legend (Airlife Publishing Ltd 2002 ISBN: 1-84037-364-4)

    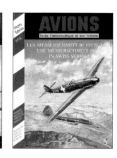 

- Messerschmitt Bf 109 Into the Battle: History, colours and markings of the Messerschmitt 109 from Munich to the Battle of Britain by M. Payne (Air Research Publications 1987 ISBN: 0-904811-10-7)
- Battle of Britain Part II, Topcolors No.16 by M. Góralczyk, M. Lukasik & J. Swiation (Kagero Publishing Sp. z.o.o. 2010 ISBN: 978-83-61220-70-1)
- Fighters over France 1940, Topcolors No.17 by M. Góralczyk, M. Lukasik , A. Sadlo & J. Swiation (Kagero Publishing Sp. z.o.o. 2010 ISBN: 978-83-61220-76-3)
- Messerschmitt Bf 109 – The Operational Record by J. Scutts (Ailife Publishing Ltd 1996 ISBN: 1-85310-557-0)
- Messerschmitt Bf 109 Part 1 In Action No.44 by J.R. Beaman Jr & J.L. Campbell (Squadron/Signal Publications 1980 ISBN: 0-89747-106-7)
- Messerschmitt Bf 109 Part 2 In Action No. 57 by J.R. Beaman Jr (Squadron/Signal Publications 1983 ISBN: 0-89747-138-5)
- Messerschmitt Bf 109 Vol.2 by F.X. Kobel & J.M. Mathmann (Schiffer 1996 ISBN: 0-88740-919-9)
- Messerschmitt Bf 109 Recognition Manual – A guide to variants, weapons & equipment by M Fernadez-Sommerau (Classic Publications 2004)
- Messerschmitt Bf 109 by P. Blackah & M.V. Lowe (Haynes Publishing 2010 ISBN: 978-1-84425-642-6)
- Messerschmitt Bf 109A-E by W. Radinger & W. Schick (Schiffer Publishing 1999 ISBN: 0-7643-0951-X)
- Messerschmitt Bf 109B-1, M-Hobby Special No.8 (M-Hobby 1995)
- Messerschmitt Bf 109B/C/D/E in Luftwaffe & Foreign Service by F.K. Mason, Aircam Aviation Series No.39 Vol.1 (Osprey Publishing Ltd 1973 ISBN: 0-85045-152-3)
- Messerschmitt Bf 109B-E, Famous Airplanes of the World No.11 (Bunrin-do)
- Messerschmitt Bf 109B-E, Model Art Special No.375 (Model Art Co., Ltd 1991)
- Messerschmitt Bf 109C/D in the Polish Campaign 1939 by M. J. Murawski, Air Battles No.13 (Kagero Publishing Sp. z.o.o. 2009 ISBN: 978-83-61220-59-6)
- Messerschmitt Bf 109E by M.C. Windrow, Profile No.40 (Profile Publications 1965)
- Messerschmitt Bf 109E, Aero Detail No.1, Model Graphix Special Edition (Dai-Nippon Kaiga Co., Ltd 1989 ISSN: 18748-4)
- Messerschmitt Bf 109E by Robert Peckowski, Yellow Series No.6102 (Mushroom Model Publications 2001 ISBN: 83-7300-042-9)
- Messerschmitt Bf 109E Vol.I by J. Piewka, Monograph No.37 (Kagero 2008 ISBN: 978-83-60445-42-6)
- Messerschmitt Bf 109E Vol.II by J. Piewka, Monograph No.38 (Kagero 2009)
- Messerschmitt Bf 109E-4 by M. Beckwith & J. Plewka, Topshots No.7 (Kagero 2005 ISBN: 83-89088-74-6)
- Messerschmitt Bf 109E-F, Makettstúdió No.1 (Péta Kladó 1991)
- Messerschmitt Bf 109T Camouflage & Markings

by K. Aakra & A. Kjaeraas, Profiles in Norway Nr.3 (Profiles in Norway 2004 ISBN: 82-92542-02-7)
- Messerschmitt Bf 109T the Luftwaffe's Naval Fighter by M.J. Murawski, Air Battles No.4 (Kagero 2008 ISBN: 978-60445-83-9)
- Messerschmitt Me 109 by The Aeronautical Staff of Aero Publishers Inc., in co-operation with The Air Museum, Aero Series No.1 (Aero Publishers Inc. 1965)
- Messerschmitt Me 109 cz.1, by R. Michulec, Monografie Lotnictze No.42 (AJ-Press 1998 ISBN: 83-86208-65-1)
- Messerschmitt Me 109 cz.2, by R. Michulec, Monografie Lotnictze No.43 (AJ-Press 1998 ISBN: 83-86208-66-X)
- Messerschmitt Me 109 cz.3, by R. Michulec, Monografie Lotnictze No.45 (AJ-Press 2000 ISBN: 83-86208-67-8)
- Messerschmitt Me 109 cz.5, by R. Michulec, Monografie Lotnictze No.49 (AJ-Press 1998 ISBN: 83-7237-009-5)
- Messerschmitt Me 109 cz.6, by R. Michulec, Monografie Lotnictze No.50 (AJ-Press 2000 ISBN: 83-7237-048-6)
- Messerschmitt Me 109 Pt.1, by R. Michulec, Aircraft Monograph No.16 (AJ-Press 2001 ISBN: 83-7237-093-1)

- Messerschmitt Me 109 Pt.2, by R. Michulec, Aircraft Monograph No.17 (AJ-Press 2002 ISBN: 83-7237-098-2)
- Messerschmitt Me 109 Pt.3, by R. Michulec, Aircraft Monograph No.18 (AJ-Press 2002 ISBN: 83-7237-110-5)
- Messerschmitt Me 109 Vol.1 from 1936 to 1942 by A. Elbied & A. Jouineau, PLanes & Pilotd No.1 (Historie & Collections 2001 ISBN: 2-913903-08-8)
- Messerschmitt Me 109 in Swiss Air Force Service by G. Hoch (Schiffer Publishing Ltd 2008 ISBN: 978-0-7643-2924-1)
- Messerschmitt Me 109 Pt.1 by R. Michulec, Aircraft Monograph No.16 (AJ Press 2005 ISBN: 83-7237-93-1)
- Messerschmitt Me 109 Pt.2 by R. Michulec, Aircraft Monograph No.17 (AJ Press 2005 ISBN: 83-7237-098-2)
- Messerschmitt Me 109 Pt.3 by R. Michulec, Aircraft Monograph No.18 (AJ Press 2005 ISBN: 83-7237-110-5)
- Messerschmitt Me 109 Photo Vol.1 by W. Trojca (Model Hobby i Trojca 2001 ISBN: 83-915347-1-5)
- Messerschmitt 109E by P. Cooksley, Aerodata International No. 4 (Visual Art Productions Ltd 1978 ISBN: 0-905469-35-6)
- Messerschmitt 'OnE-O-Nine' Gallery by T.H.

Hitchcock (Monogram Aviation Publications 1973 ISBN: 0-9414144-00-6)
- Me 109 – Messerschmitt Bf 109E, Aeroguide Classics No.2 (Linewrights Ltd 1986 ISBN: 0-946958-18-1)
- Modelling the Messerschmitt Bf 109B/C/D/E by Brett Green, Osprey Modelling (Osprey Publishing Ltd 2006 ISBN: 1-846176-940-1)
- Photo Archive 1 – Luftwaffe Camouflage & Markings 1933-1945 by K.A. Merrick, E.J. Creek & B. Green (Midland Publishing 2007 ISBN: 1-85780-275-6)
- Pilot's Notes for Messerschmitt Bf 109 – Technical Data and Handling Notes, reprint of (Crécy Publishing Ltd 2000)
- Rumanian Air Force: The Prime Decade, 1938-1947 by D. Bernárd (Squadron/Signal Publications 1999 ISBN: 1-89747-402-3)
- Romanian Fighter Colours 1941-1945 by Teodor Liviu Morosanu & Dan Alexandru Melinte (Mushroom Model Publications 2010 ISBN: 978-833-89450-90-6)
- Scale Models Warplane Special (Model & Allied Publications Ltd 1982)
- The Bulgarian Air Force In Action During the Second World War (Air Power of the Kingdom of Bulgaria Part IV) by D. Nedialkov (Air Sofia)
- The Croatian Air Force in the Second World War by T. Likso and D. Canak (Nova 1998 ISBN: 953-97698-0-9)
- The Fighting Me 109 by U. Fest (Arms & Armour Press 1988 ISBN: 0-85368-961-X)
- The Messerschmitt 109 – A Famous German Fighter by H.J. Nowarra (Harleyford Publications Ltd 1963)
- The Messerschmitt Bf 109 by J.F. Craig, Famous Aircraft Series (Arco Publishing Co., Inc. 1968)

Periodicals

- Aircraft Modelworld, Vol.4 No.5 July 1987
- Airfix Magazine, Vol.7 No.3 November 1965
- Fanatique de l'Aviation No.78 (1976)
- Model Airplane International Vol.5 Iss.50 September 2009 & Vol.7 Iss.86, September 2012
- Scale Aircraft Modelling Vol.2 No.12 September 1980, Vol.9 No.12 September 1987, Vol.13 No.11 August 1991 & Vol.14 No.1 October 1991
- Scale Aviation Modeller International Vol.3 Iss.1 January 1997, Vol.5 Iss.6 June 1999 & Vol.16 No.10 October 2010
- Scale Models, Vol.1 No3 December 1969, Vol.3 No.2 February 1972 & Vol.10 No.123 December 1979
- Scale Models International Vol.15 No.178 August 1984
- Sky Model No.7 (October/November 2002)

This images shows an E-series shot down and after salvage, near the Houses of Parliment in London, the wings show high contrast so are most likely RLM 02/71, whilst the fuselage shows some faint mottling that may also be RLM 02. The rudder is yellow, but without being able to see the front of the fuselage you can't say if the cowls were also in this colour and the lack of any tactical number on the fuselage is interesting

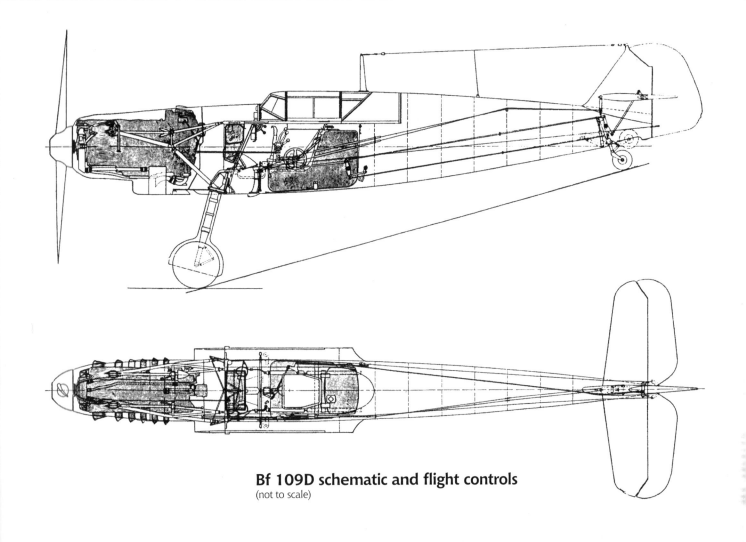

Bf 109D schematic and flight controls
(not to scale)

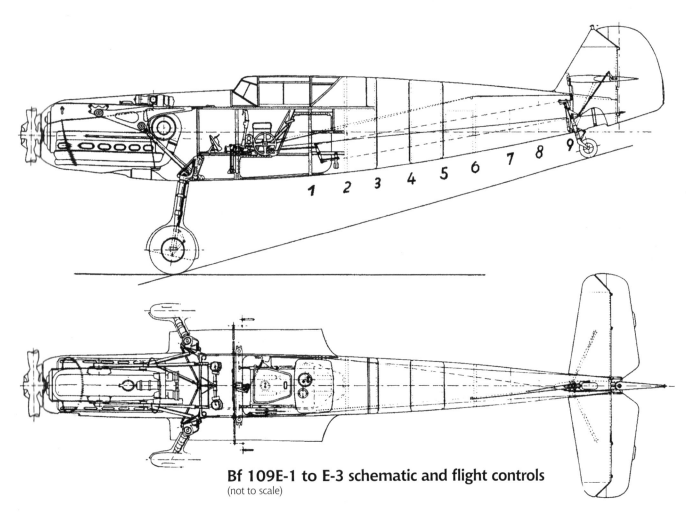

1 2 3 4 5 6 7 8 9

Bf 109E-1 to E-3 schematic and flight controls
(not to scale)

Nose art on a Bf 109E of an unknown unit, Poland 1939

A Bf 109E of 4./JG 53, flown by Lt H. Kroeck, 1939
(© via M. Payne)

The sharksmouth motif of Fl Kp 21

The emblem of 2.JG21 seen on one of their Bf 109D-1s in Germany in 1938

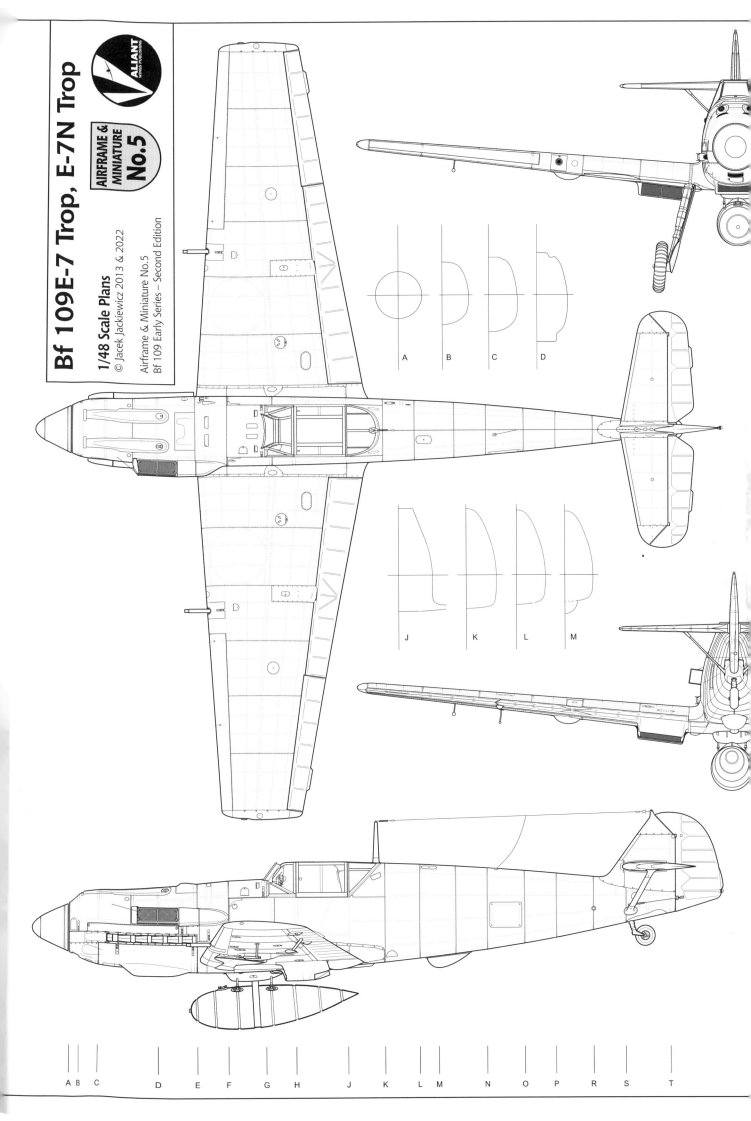

Bf 109E-7 Trop, E-7N Trop

1/48 Scale Plans

© Jacek Jackiewicz 2013 & 2022

Airframe & Miniature No.5
Bf 109 Early Series – Second Edition

AIRFRAME & MINIATURE No.5

A B C D

J K L M

A B C   D   E   F   G   H   J   K   L   M   N   O   P   R   S   T

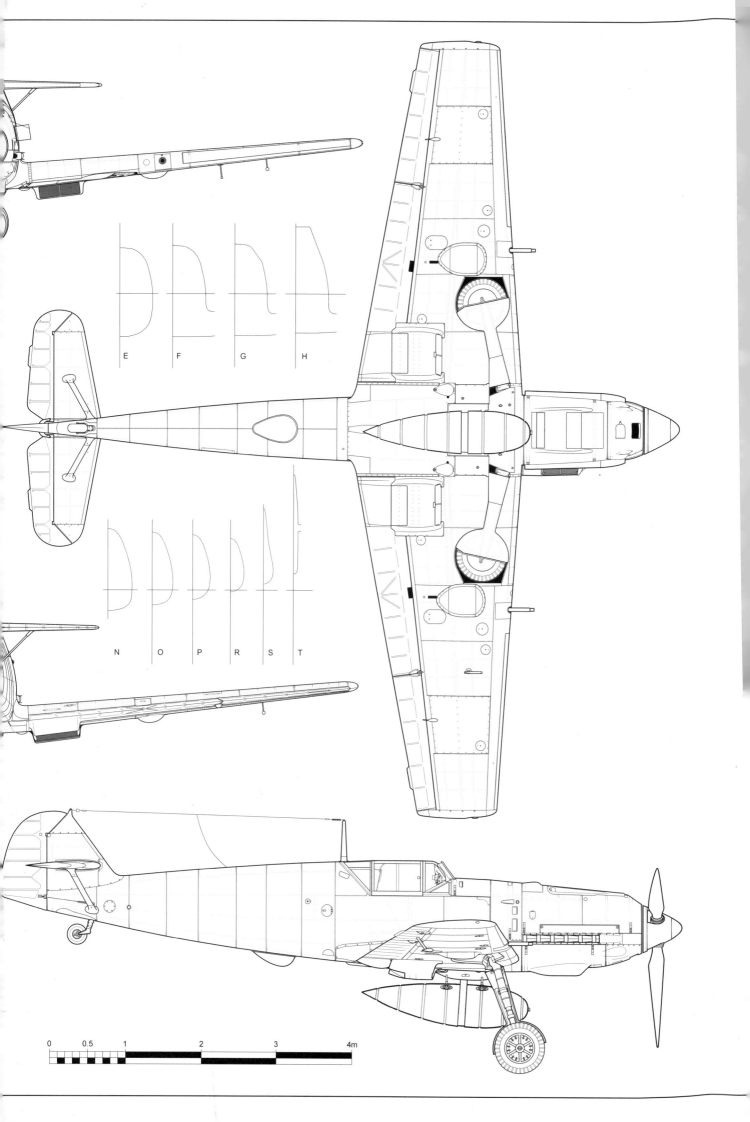

E F G H

N O P R S T

0   0.5   1   2   3   4m